AF544861

Jacques Lipchitz

■

A Life in Sculpture

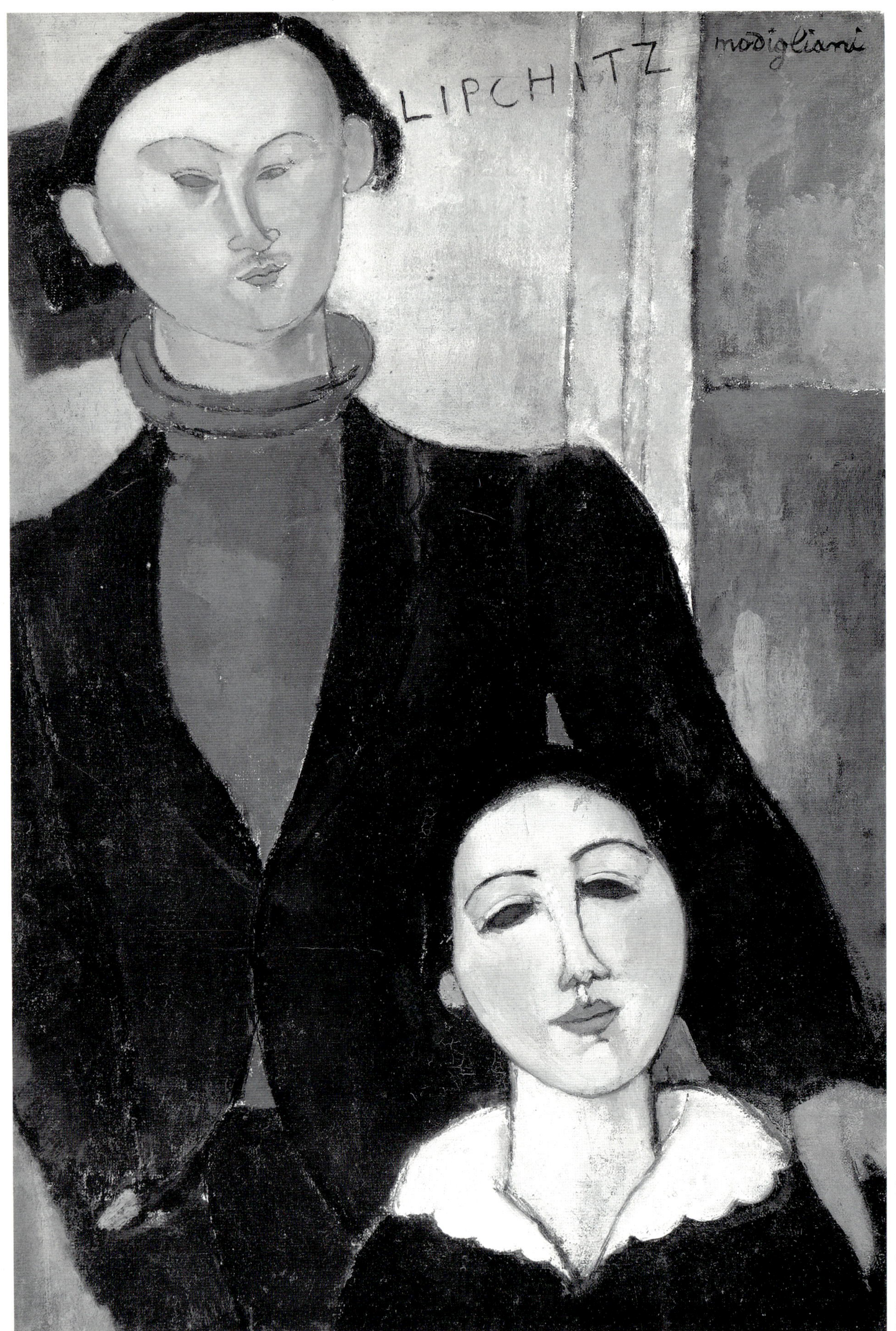
LIPCHITZ
modigliani

Jacques Lipchitz

■

A Life in Sculpture

Alan G. Wilkinson

Art Gallery of Ontario
Musée des beaux-arts de l'Ontario
Toronto, Canada

The Art Gallery of Ontario is generously funded by the Ontario Ministry of Culture and Communications. Additional financial support is received from the Municipality of Metropolitan Toronto – Cultural Affairs Division, Communications Canada and the Canada Council.

Canadian Cataloguing in Publication Data

Wilkinson, Alan G.
Jacques Lipchitz

Exhibition catalogue.
Includes bibliographical references.
ISBN 0-919777-76-7

1. Lipchitz, Jacques, 1891– – Exhibitions. I. Lipchitz, Jacques, 1891– . II. Art Gallery of Ontario. III. Title.

NB553.L55A4 1989 730′.92′4 C89-094857-7

Front Cover:

12
Lipchitz, *Detachable Figure: Seated Musician* 1915
Painted wood
H. 19¾″/50.2 cm
Yulla Lipchitz, New York

Back Cover:

134
Lipchitz, *Sketch for Our Tree of Life* 1971–72
Bronze 6/7
H. 22¼″/56.5 cm
The Estate of Jacques Lipchitz represented by Marlborough International Fine Art AG

Frontispiece

fig. 1
Amadeo Modigliani, *Jacques and Berthe Lipchitz* 1916
Oil on canvas
31¾ x 21¼″/80.7 x 54 cm
Courtesy The Art Institute of Chicago, Helen Birch Bartlett Memorial Collection, 1926.221 © The Art Institute of Chicago 1989.

SPONSORED BY AMERICAN EXPRESS CANADA, INC. AND OLYMPIA & YORK.

Itinerary:

Dates and venues are subject to change.

Art Gallery of Ontario, Toronto
December 15, 1989 to March 11, 1990

Winnipeg Art Gallery, Winnipeg, Manitoba
May 13 to August 12, 1990

The Nelson-Atkins Museum of Art, Kansas City, MO
October 7 to November 25, 1990

The Jewish Museum, New York
January 16 to April 15, 1991

Contents

■

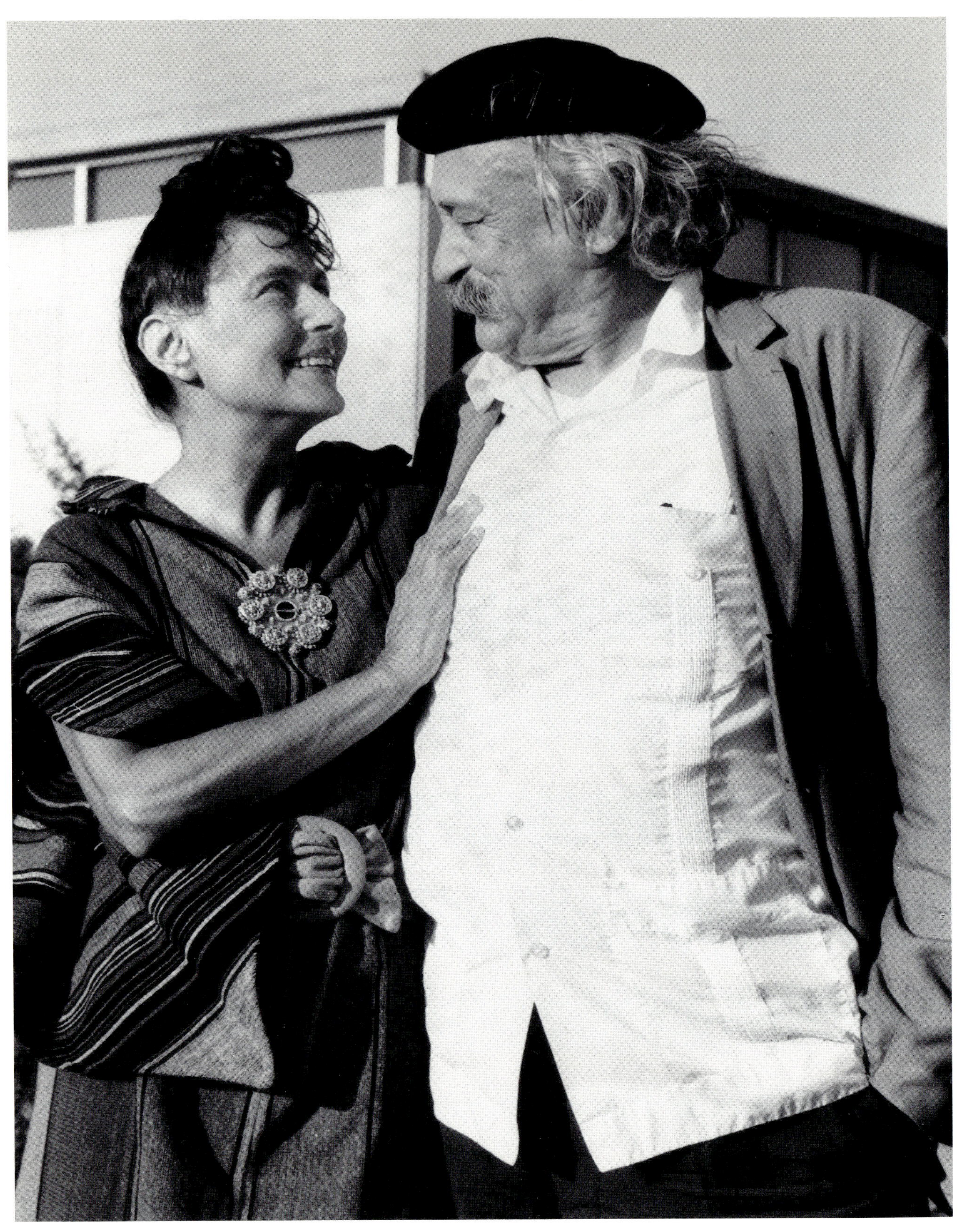

fig. 2
Jacques and Yulla Lipchitz
at The Israel Museum, Jerusalem, 1971.
(Courtesy Yulla Lipchitz)

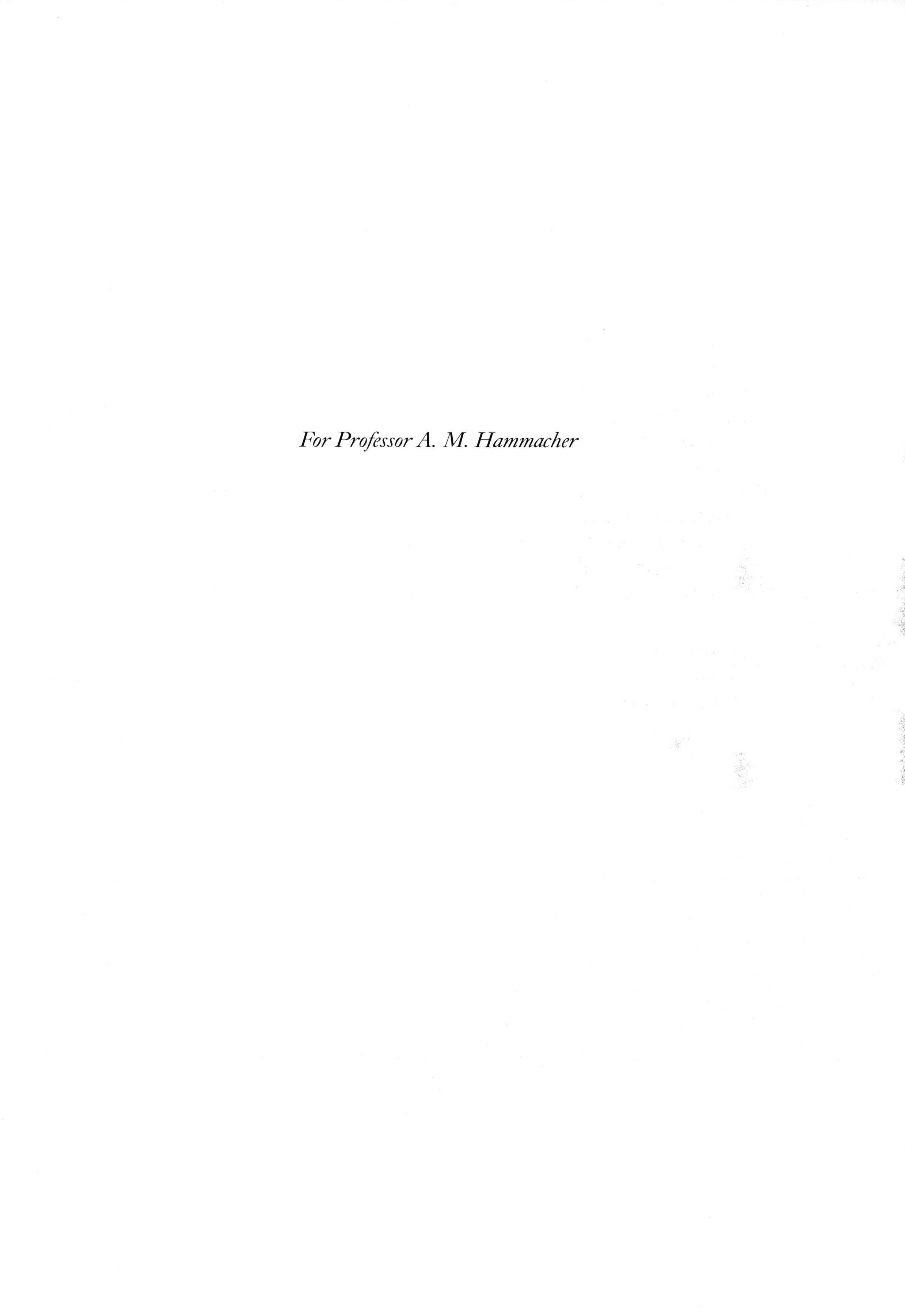

For Professor A. M. Hammacher

Sponsors' Foreword

■

He is the greatest artist who
has embodied, in the sum of his works, the greatest
number of the greatest ideas.

John Ruskin, 1843

IN THE WORK OF JACQUES LIPCHITZ WE DISCOVER A CELEBRATION OF THE INFINITE greatness and courage of the human spirit. Lipchitz, one of the most important sculptors of the twentieth century, extended the limits of the possible in art through his extraordinary imagination and innate talent.

American Express Canada, Inc. and Olympia & York are pleased to join together to support the North American tour of this major exhibition. Canadians and Americans alike may draw inspiration from this magnificent sculpture, which mirrors events in Lipchitz's life – his joys and sorrows, his reactions to the Holocaust, to war, to the history of the Jewish people. We believe it becomes increasingly important in a world where distances are shrinking and boundaries vanishing, through travel and trade, to foster the growth of understanding and tolerance among people.

Morris Perlis
President
AMERICAN EXPRESS CANADA, INC.

Albert Reichmann
President
OLYMPIA & YORK DEVELOPMENTS LTD.

Preface

■

The Art Gallery of Ontario is delighted to have the opportunity to organize the first major exhibition of the work of Jacques Lipchitz since the 1971 show at the Metropolitan Museum of Art, New York. Thirty years ago the Art Gallery of Toronto was one of four Canadian venues for a more modest exhibition of twenty-three bronzes and nine drawings by Lipchitz.

I would like to thank Carol A. Phillips, Director, Winnipeg Art Gallery; Marc Wilson, Director, The Nelson-Atkins Museum of Art, Kansas City, MO; and Joan Rosenbaum, Director, The Jewish Museum, New York, for their interest in this exhibition and participation in the North American tour.

The aim of this exhibition is to present a carefully selected but comprehensive group of Lipchitz's bronzes, carvings and drawings from his long and prolific career, which spanned more than sixty years. The artist's reputation and historical importance as one of the masters of twentieth-century sculpture are still largely based on his great Cubist sculptures, executed between 1915 and 1925, and on the lesser-known but highly innovative "transparents" of the mid-to-late 1920s. Little serious critical attention has been paid to Lipchitz's prodigious creativity during the remaining forty years of his working life. The present neglect of the sculptor's post-Cubist achievements obviously parallels the almost universal disdain for Picasso's late work before the recognition in recent years of its relevance and greatness. In the mid 1920s, Lipchitz abandoned the formal syntax of Cubism and concentrated on a wide range of subjects: the joy and sorrows of his personal life; Biblical and mythological themes; the growing threat of Hitler's Nazi Germany; the Holocaust; and the history of the Jewish people. It is hoped that this exhibition will stimulate an interest in Lipchitz's later work, in its expressiveness, its deeply felt agony, pathos, tragedy and joy. The changing climate of taste in the 1980s that has embraced the late Picasso can surely accommodate the later work of Lipchitz. In the context of the neo-Expressionist, post-modernist developments in Germany and Italy in the late 1970s and 1980s, both Picasso and Lipchitz were ahead of their time.

An exhibition such as this would not have been possible without the generosity of museums and private collectors, to whom we are deeply indebted. We are particularly grateful to The Estate of Jacques Lipchitz represented by Marlborough International Fine Art AG and to Madame Yulla Lipchitz for their full co-operation in the realization of this exhibition.

In closing, I would like to thank Dr. Alan G. Wilkinson, Curator of Twentieth Century Art at the Art Gallery of Ontario, for his initiative in organizing the exhibition and writing this catalogue. And we would especially like to recognize and thank American Express Canada, Inc. and Olympia & York for their generous support as sponsors of this exhibition.

William J. Withrow, Director

Acknowledgements

■

I am indebted to my colleagues at the Art Gallery of Ontario for their support in the organization of this exhibition and the production of this catalogue: William J. Withrow, Director; Dr. Roald Nasgaard, Chief Curator; Dr. David McTavish, former Curator of European Painting and Sculpture; Michael Parke-Taylor, Assistant Curator of Prints and Drawings; Christine Boyanoski, Assistant Curator of Canadian Historical Art; Noni Regan, Head, Art Support, and her Administrative Assistant, Barbara Brownlee; Sandra Lawrence, Chief Conservator; John O'Neill, Conservator; Ralph Ingleton, Practitioner, Conservation Department; Barbara Keyser, on contract in the Conservation Department; Kathleen Harleman, Registrar; Olga Charyshyn, Assistant Registrar; Sandi McKessock, Data Entry Operator; Akira Yoshikawa, Art Storage Co-ordinator; Wilbert Headley, Art Storage Assistant; David Robitaille, Truck Driver; Glenda Milrod, Head, Extension Services; May Wong, Administrative Assistant; Sharon Gaum-Kuchar, Scheduling Officer; Tim Hardacre, Installation Officer; Karen McKenzie, Chief Librarian; Larry Pfaff, Deputy Librarian; Randall Speller, Documentalist; David Wistow, Education Officer; Douglas Todgham, Head, Development; Anne Greaves, Manager, Membership Services; Elizabeth Addison, Head, Marketing and Communications; Jean Keryk, Manager, Marketing; Gail Hutchison, Manager, Public Relations; Alan Terakawa, Head, Publications and Design; Sherri Somerville, Production Co-ordinator; Marilyn Bouma-Pyper, Designer; Terry Hicks, Copy Editor/Proofreader; Kathleen Richards, Freelance Editor; Maia-Mari Sutnik, Co-ordinator, Photographic Services; Faye Van Horne, Assistant, Photographic Services; Carlo Catenazzi, Head Photographer; George Bartosik, Manager, Technical Services; Charles Simpson, Crating Technician; and Erwin Friedel, Carpenter. I owe a special debt of gratitude to my secretary, Debbie Sawatsky, for her help in all aspects of the organization of this exhibition and catalogue.

My interest in Cubism and in the history of modern sculpture dates from my postgraduate studies in London, at the Courtauld Institute of Art, from 1967 to 1974. I was most fortunate to have studied under the distinguished art historians Sir Alan Bowness, Dr. John Golding and Dr. Christopher Green. Their encouragement over the years and their subsequent friendship have meant a great deal to me.

For their encouragement and hospitality at home and on trips abroad, I would like to thank Mrs. Betty Tinsley, Joy Tinsley, Julia Brown, Robert O'Rorke, Charlotte Green, David Fraser Jenkins, Hermione Waterfield, Ayala Zacks Abramov, Martin Weyl, Stephanie Rachum, Franz Plutschow, Mrs. Jane Owen, Deborah Scott, Douglas Walla, Barbara and Murray Frum, Donald L. Matthews, Iain Miller, Paddy Ann and Latham Burns, Peter and Sandy Merry and Henry Smith. I am particularly indebted to Ramsay Derry for his astute editorial advice. I am most grateful to Keith Wagland, architect, who was responsible for the exhibition design. To Joan Mackie I owe a great deal for her tireless help in the research for this catalogue, for her constant enthusiasm and for her indefatigable optimism and encouragement.

This exhibition would not have been possible without the generous co-operation of The Estate of Jacques Lipchitz represented by Marlborough International Fine Art AG. I am deeply grateful to Frank Lloyd and Pierre Levai, Director, Marlborough Gallery Inc., New York, for their support and for agreeing to lend so many sculptures and drawings from The Estate of Jacques Lipchitz. I would like to thank the following members of staff of Marlborough Gallery Inc., New York: Jack Mognaz, Lisa Farrington, Jane Hart, Eileen Dougherty, Sylvia Scarpino and Eva Sternfeld. I would also like to thank His Grace The Duke of Beaufort, Chairman, and Gilbert Lloyd, Director, Marlborough Fine Art (London) Ltd.

During my research for this exhibition, I have had many valuable and enlightening conservations with Yulla Lipchitz about her husband's life and work. She has conveyed to me much of his warmth, energy, vitality and optimism, qualities that I believe are reflected in his sculpture. I am well aware of the invaluable experience of working directly with an artist in researching a catalogue such as this. One man who enjoyed a close friendship and working relationship with Jacques Lipchitz over many years was Prof. A. M. Hammacher, former Director of the Rijksmuseum Kröller-Müller, Otterlo, The Netherlands. He has been most helpful in sharing with me his knowledge of Lipchitz's work and his great affection for the sculptor. I know that Yulla Lipchitz shares my pleasure in dedicating this catalogue to Prof. Hammacher.

A. G. W.

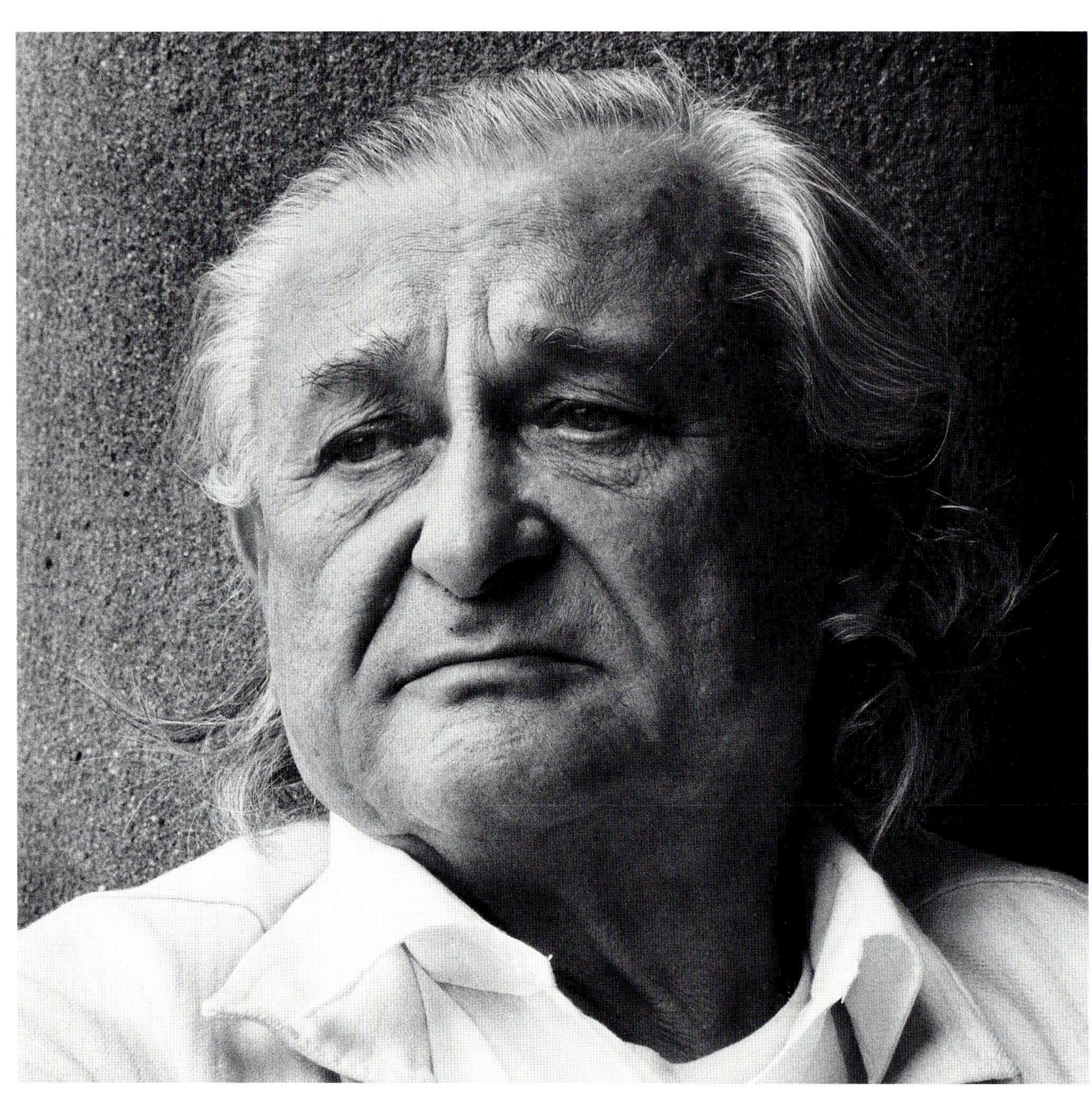

fig. 3
Jacques Lipchitz, 1970.

A Life in Sculpture

■

Lipchitz is a great, sometimes very great, sculptor who presents the critic with a peculiarly difficult problem.[1]

Clement Greenberg, 1954

LIPCHITZ'S REPUTATION AS ONE OF THE MASTERS OF TWENTIETH-CENTURY SCULPTURE is secure. The originality and importance of his contribution to the evolution of early Cubist sculpture in France have never been in doubt or seriously challenged. From 1916, when his works joined those of Picasso, Braque, Léger, Gris and Laurens at the galerie de l'Effort Moderne in Paris, his crucial position in Cubist sculpture was recognized. Seven decades later, Lipchitz was still seen as a member of the elite group of "true" Cubists when his sculpture and that of Laurens were shown in the Tate Gallery's 1983 exhibition *The Essential Cubism 1907–1920*, on an equal footing with the work of Braque, Picasso, Gris and Léger, the most important exponents of pictorial Cubism.

Lipchitz's historical importance as a sculptor is today still largely based on his great Cubist carvings and bronzes of 1915–25, and on the opened-out spatial innovations of the transparents that followed during the next few years. No other twentieth-century sculptor of his stature – not Brancusi, Giacometti or Moore – has been subjected to the injustice of this myopic focus of critical acclaim on the work of a single period of work, in Lipchitz's case a mere fifteen years. Astonishingly little serious critical attention has been given to the prodigious output of sculpture from the remaining forty years of his working life.

The great divide between what is highly esteemed and relevant and what is for the most part neglected and often dismissed as anachronistic is clearly the late 1920s. At that point the purely formal concerns with the syntax of Cubism were superseded by a renewed interest in subject matter as a means of expressing personal emotions and feelings. In retrospect, it is understandable that Lipchitz's later work should present the critic "with a peculiarly difficult problem." The modernist view of art history would by definition find it difficult, if not impossible, to accommodate and come to terms with the expressionist violence, tortured subject matter and seemingly overwrought emotionalism found in many of Lipchitz's sculptures dealing with mythological and Biblical subjects, copulation, rape, strangulation and the horrors of the Nazi death camps. For those attuned to the formalistic, inward-looking leanness of Minimalism, the rhetorical gestures of Lipchitz's so-called Baroque manner must indeed appear undisciplined, self-indulgent and lacking in toughness.

The present state of neglect of Lipchitz's post-Cubist achievements has an obvious parallel in the almost universal disdain for Picasso's late work, prior to the shock of the recognition of its relevance – and indeed of its greatness – ignited by the exhibition *Picasso: The Last Years* at the Solomon R. Guggenheim Museum in 1984 and the *Late*

Picasso show at the Centre Georges Pompidou and the Tate Gallery in 1988. The changing climate of taste in the 1980s that embraced Picasso's work can surely accommodate the later work of Lipchitz. Seen in the context of post-modernist developments in Germany and Italy in the 1970s and 1980s, both Picasso and Lipchitz were ahead of their time. In the 1981 catalogue *A New Spirit in Painting* (Royal Academy of Arts, London), Christos M. Joachimides described the private visions based on individual experience that inform much recent painting:

> The subjective view, the creative imagination, has come back into its own and is evident in a new approach to painting. Artists, no longer satisfied with the deliberately objective view, are beginning to respond to their environment, allowing these reactions to be expressed in the form of images. We are confronted with an art that tells us about their personal relationships and personal worlds. This is a need, of course, that goes far beyond the boundaries of art to permeate all levels of society. It is the need to talk about oneself, to express one's own desires and fears, to react to daily life, indeed to reactivate areas of experience that have long lain dormant.[2]

Lipchitz addressed all these issues in his art from the late 1920s until his death in 1973. Indeed, his work is more autobiographical than that of any sculptor of his generation, reflecting not only the joys, sorrows and obsessions of his personal life, but also his reactions to political events, to war, to the Holocaust and to the past and present history of the Jewish people. In *The Cry (The Couple)* of 1928–29 (no. 54) Lipchitz was trying to come to terms with the deaths of his father and sister. In *David and Goliath* of 1933 (no. 75) he was expressing his outrage at the growing threat of Hitler's Nazi Germany. *Miracle II* of 1948 (no. 95) was made in anticipation of the birth of the state of Israel. His rapturous joy at the birth of his daughter, Lolya, in 1948, when he was fifty-seven, was reflected in the lyrical *Mother and Child* (no. 98), created the following year. *L'Arno Furioso* was made at the time of the disastrous flood in Florence in 1966 (no. 122). At the end of his life Lipchitz was still working on a number of preparatory studies for *Our Tree of Life* (see nos. 133–134), a complex, symbolic exploration of themes from the history of the Jewish people. For more than forty years Lipchitz had reacted with great passion and humanity to an extraordinary range of personal experiences and to some of the momentous events of history as they unfolded. What has long been lacking is an openness, a willingness to look seriously at Lipchitz's later work and to recognize its boldness and its intensity, its spontaneity, its technical innovations and above all its total freedom from rigid stylistic constraints. The late Picasso and the late Lipchitz have much in common, but the latter remains to be discovered.

Chaim Jacob Lipchitz was born on August 22, 1891, in Druskieniki, Lithuania, the first child of Rachel Leah Krinsky and her husband, Abraham, a successful building contractor and a member of a wealthy Jewish banking family. Many years later he recounted the circumstances surrounding his birth:

> When I was born, the small village we lived in was known as a small health resort. People from different cities came there, and one of them was a famous so-called "wonder" rabbi. I was born on a Saturday, and my parents invited this famous rabbi for the next day, Sunday,

to give me a benediction. As I was told, this rabbi did perform the appropriate ceremony, and according to my mother's story, made two statements: one, that I would not become a rabbi, and the second, that he was sure, that he had a premonition, that I should become a 'great person' (meaning a man of fame) among the Israelites. This, I am sure, influenced my mother who continuously and repeatedly expressed the feeling that I was born a chosen one, to accomplish a mission, or to do great things... and during my whole life I could not escape the feeling that I had a special sense of things – that something miraculous guided my life. I could have died a thousand times or abandoned my work if this feeling had not lived in me.[3]

There was little in Lipchitz's liberal Jewish upbringing or in the environment of his childhood to suggest that his mission was to become a great artist. There were no sculptors in the town where he was born. As a youth he had seen plaster molds at school and had assumed that sculpture must be white: "so I painted my clay sketches white and felt that I had become a sculptor."[4] His father, who wanted him to qualify as an architect or an engineer in order to join the family business, had little sympathy or enthusiasm for Lipchitz's ambition to become a sculptor. He faced other obstacles and prejudices, as well. Under the czarist regime, Jews were subjected to certain restrictions. Jewish students were prevented from studying at the St. Petersburg Academy. Travel was also restricted. During his years at high school in Vilna, Lipchitz recalled, "I must have learned about Paris as the center for the study of art, and I developed a passionate desire to go there."[5] His father knew nothing of his plans. With the help of his mother, who gave him some money, and an uncle who helped him cross the border illegally, Lipchitz set off for the French capital. He arrived in Paris in October 1909, at the age of eighteen.

Unlike other foreign artists who were drawn to the artistic centre of Europe – Picasso, Brancusi, Archipenko – Lipchitz had no previous academic training. In 1909–10 he enrolled at the École des Beaux-Arts but soon transferred to the Académie Julian. The curriculum included academic drawing or modelling from life in the mornings, with afternoons free to visit the Louvre and other museums. He made drawings of an anatomical model designed by Jean-Antoine Houdon. There were also classes in stone carving. In the evenings he attended the Académie Colarossi to study drawing, and he also made use of the Académie de la Grande Chaumière, where one would pay by the hour to sketch from the model. Lipchitz's formative training during his first few years in Paris was of a purely academic nature. His early works, such as *Woman and Gazelles* 1911–12 (no. 1) and *Pregnant Woman* 1912 (no. 2), reflect the somewhat idealized naturalistic tradition found in the sculpture of Maillol, Bourdelle and Despiau. In 1911 Lipchitz exhibited with a group of Russian artists at the Galerie Malesherbes, and in the following year at the Salon National des Beaux-Arts and the Salon d'Automne. Rodin apparently praised a portrait by Lipchitz in the Beaux-Arts exhibition in 1912, but Lipchitz resisted the compliment: "at that time I was not prepared for such praise by an artist who seemed to me to represent the older generation from which I was already attempting to escape."[6]

Stylistically there is not the slightest indication in his sculpture of 1911–12 that

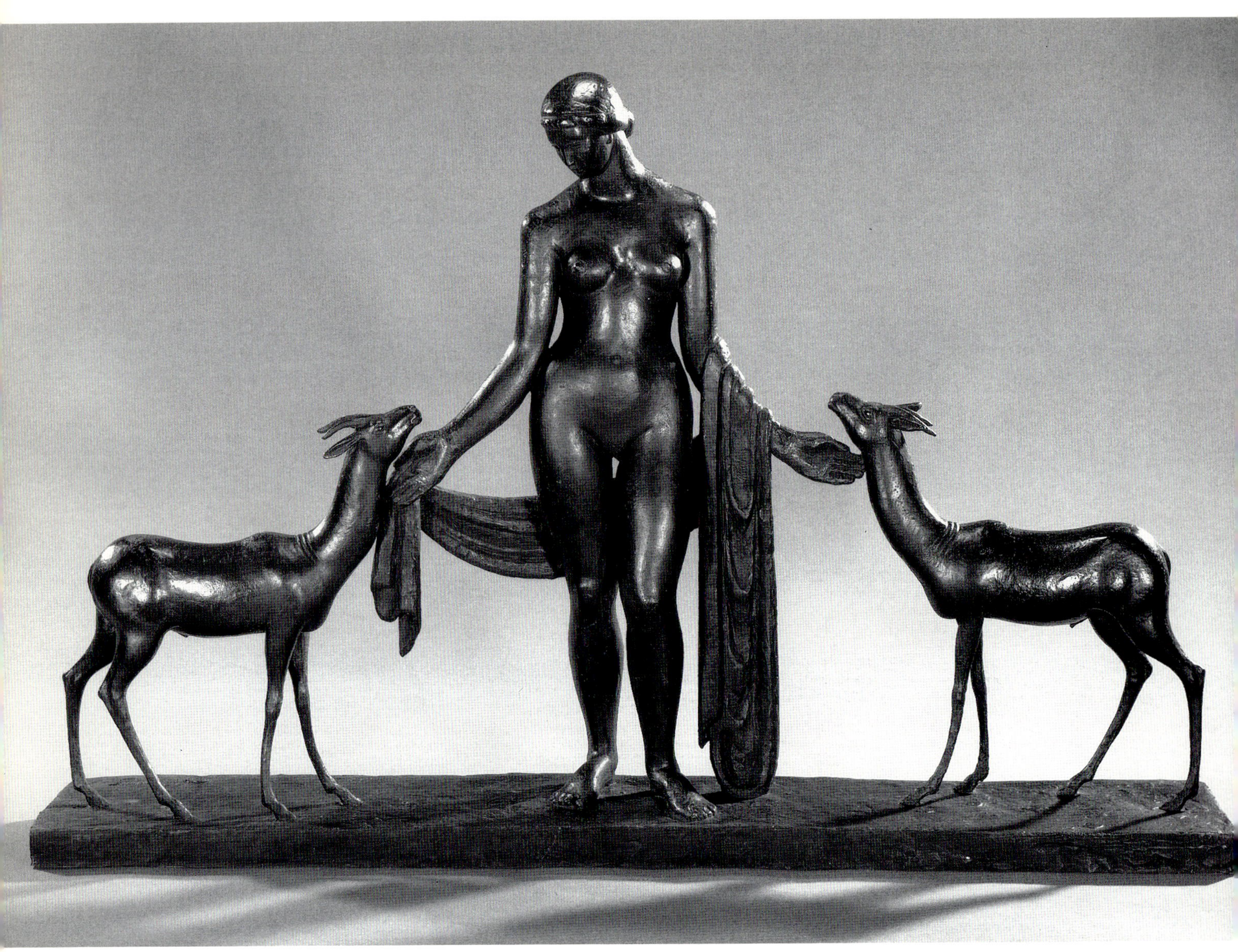

1 *Woman and Gazelles* 1911–12

Lipchitz was aware of contemporary carvings and bronzes by Picasso, Matisse, Brancusi or Modigliani, artists whose work had been reflecting for some years their intense interest in African and Oceanic art. His sculpture was still firmly placed in the classical calm of the Maillolesque tradition. Lipchitz's *Woman and Gazelles* was exhibited at the 1913 Salon d'Automne. In the same exhibition Modigliani showed seven stone heads inspired by Baule masks and Duchamp-Villon his 1911 head of *Baudelaire* and his 1913 bas-relief *The Lovers*.

Lipchitz must have become aware of the work of some of the most important avant-garde artists in 1912. In October, Gleizes, Metzinger, Léger, Gris, Duchamp and Archipenko organized a show entitled *La Section d'Or* at the Galerie de la Boétie. This was the first major exhibition of Cubist works by many of the most advanced artists working in Paris and, as Deborah Stott has pointed out, "was of immense importance for the dissemination of the recent stylistic and theoretical discoveries, and it is very likely that Lipchitz attended."[7] In 1912–13 Lipchitz also saw the work of the Italian Futurists. From February 5–24, 1912, there was an exhibition at Bernheim-Jeune of the Futurist painters Boccioni, Carrà, Russolo and Severini.

Boccioni, in particular, was also developing an intense interest in sculpture, dating from visits to Paris in 1911 and again in the spring of 1912. His *Manifesto of Futurist Sculpture* was published on April 11, 1912. In October of that year he exhibited some sculpture at the Salon d'Automne. From June 20 to July 16, 1913, there was a show of Boccioni's sculpture at the Galerie de la Boétie in Paris. Lipchitz was interested in the sculpture of Boccioni, particularly his *Development of a Bottle in Space* of 1912 (fig. 4), made after he had visited Archipenko and Duchamp-Villon in their studios. The work of the Italian sculptor provided a convincing example of how pictorial Cubist concepts could be successfully translated into three dimensions. Whereas Boccioni's best-known sculpture, *Unique Forms of Continuity in Space* 1913, reflects the Futurists' passion for dynamic movement, the 1912 bronze *Anti-Graceful (The Artist's Mother)* and *Development of a Bottle in Space* are more static. They are basically Cubist-inspired works with Futurist overtones that are ultimately, in their deeply faceted forms, related to Picasso's 1909 bronze *Head of a Woman (Fernande)* (fig. 5).

By 1913–14 Lipchitz was no longer a naive novice on the fringes of the Parisian art world. He was now living in a studio at 54 rue Montparnasse, next door to Brancusi. Lipchitz had developed a close friendship with the Mexican painter Diego Rivera, and it was through Rivera that he met Picasso. Lipchitz indicated that he was still clinging to traditional concepts about the nature of sculpture when Rivera took him to Picasso's studio for the first time, probably in the spring of 1914. Before Picasso arrived, Rivera showed Lipchitz a small painted sculpture, in all probability the painted

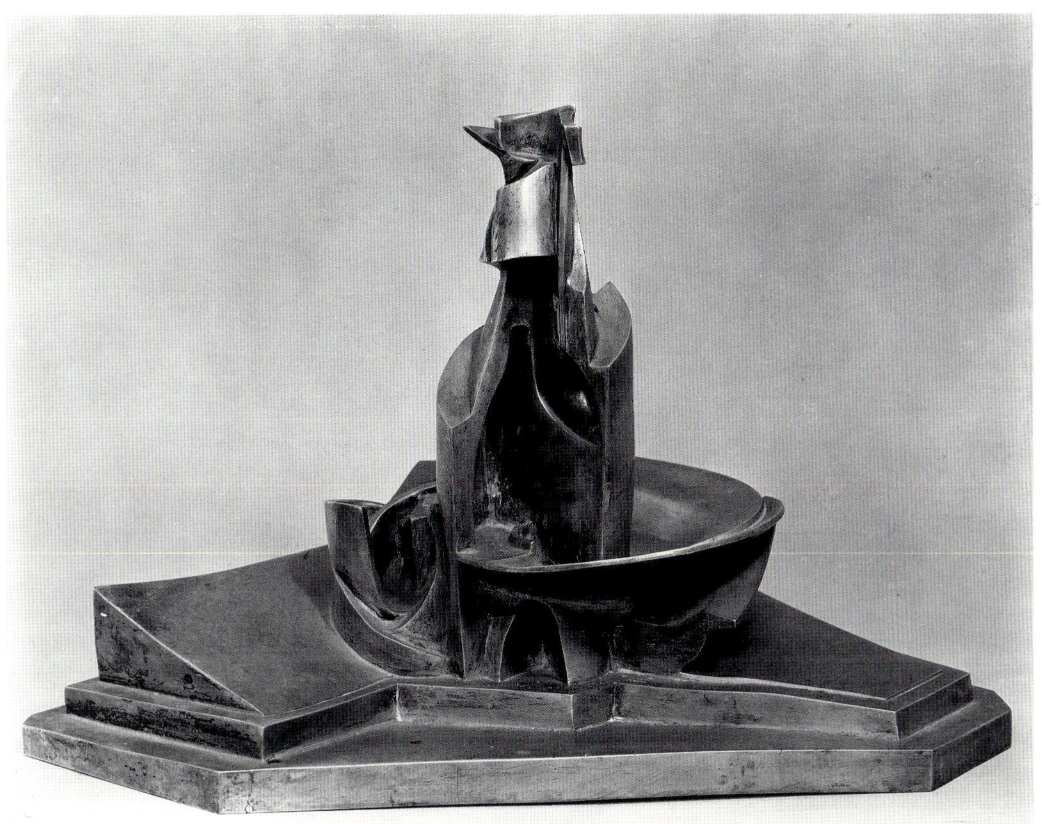

fig. 4 *Umberto Boccioni,* Development of a Bottle in Space, *1912, silvered bronze (cast 1931), 15 x 12⅞ x 23¾"/ 38.1 x 32.7 x 60.3 cm. The Museum of Modern Art, New York, Artistide Maillol Fund.*

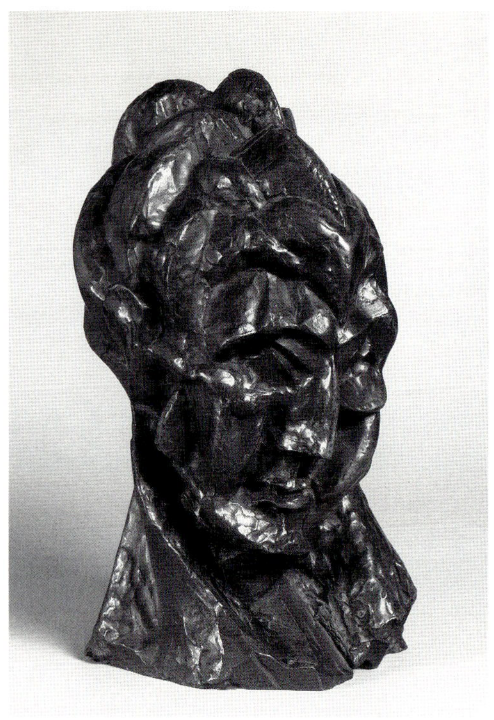

fig. 5
Pablo Picasso, Head of a Woman (Fernande), *1909, bronze, H. 16 1/2"/41.9 cm. Art Gallery of Ontario, Toronto, Purchase, 1949. © Picasso/ VIS-ART Inc. 1989.*

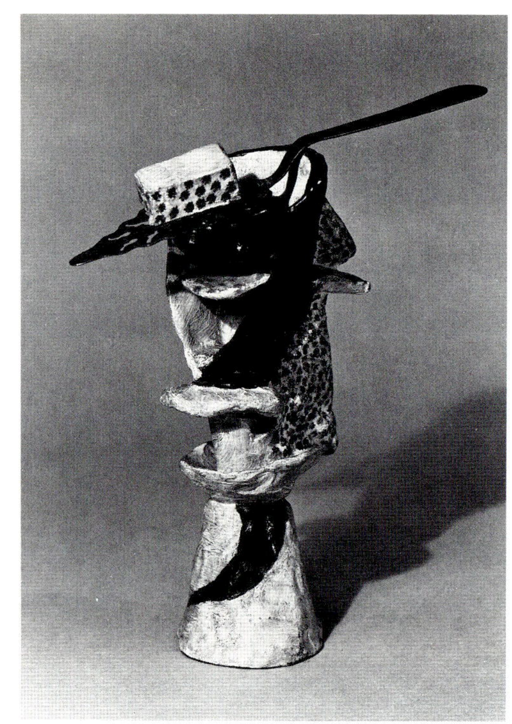

fig. 6
Pablo Picasso, Glass of Absinth, *1914, painted bronze with sugar strainer, 8 1/2 x 6 1/2"/21.6 x 16.4 cm; diameter at base, 2 1/2"/6.4 cm. The Museum of Modern Art, New York. Gift of Mrs. Bertram Smith. © Picasso/VIS-ART Inc. 1989.*

image *Glass of Absinth*, made and cast in the spring of 1914 (fig. 6). Rivera remarked, somewhat condescendingly:

> "And that is a sculpture, by Picasso" as though that was the real thing, not what I was doing. When Picasso came back and I met him, and we came to this piece, I asked him rather naïvely whether he considered it painting or sculpture. Picasso somewhat sarcastically asked if I could tell him what is painting and what is sculpture. I answered that I could not, but that I was sure this piece was not sculpture. Picasso said, "Why? Because it is painted? Look at that Negro mask; it is painted too." And I said, "But look how it is painted; just look at the white, round shapes under the eyes; they are shadows and they are white because the sculpture is black."[8]

When they left, Rivera was angry, assuming that Lipchitz had offended Picasso. Not so. Picasso knocked on Lipchitz's door the following day, and they became friends.

If, as Sir Roland Penrose has written, "Cubism can be described as a movement among painters towards the sculptor's three-dimensional problems,"[9] Cubist sculpture can be described as an effort to work in the opposite direction in order to make tangible the elusive but intensely sculptural forms of Cubist painting. Picasso, the father of Cubist sculpture, had seen the sculptural implications of his Analytic Cubist work three or four years before de la Fresnaye, Archipenko, Boccioni and Lipchitz created their first proto-Cubist sculpture in 1912–13. During his visit to Picasso's studio Lipchitz may well have seen *Head of a Woman (Fernande)*, modelled in the autumn

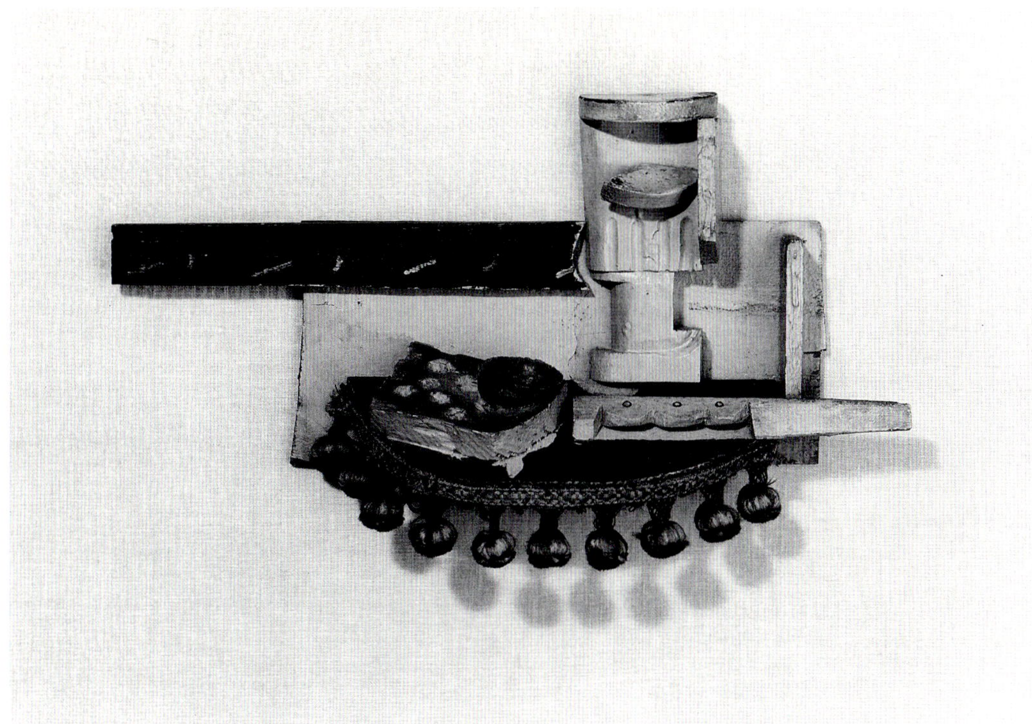

fig. 7
Pablo Picasso, Still Life, *1914, construction: painted wood and upholstery fringe, 10 x 18 x 3⁵⁄₈"/ 254 x 457 x 92 mm. Tate Gallery, London. © Picasso/VIS-ART Inc. 1989.*

of 1909 (fig. 5). It was Picasso's only fully realized early Cubist sculpture, and as such it was a supremely confident and innovative experiment in translating into three dimensions the faceted forms of his Analytic Cubist paintings and drawings of his mistress, Fernande Olivier, made during the summer months of 1909. In his remarks to his friend Julio González about the possibility of transforming his early Cubist paintings directly into sculpture, Picasso could almost be describing the Constructivist method employed by Gabo and Pevsner in their early work or that of Lipchitz when he created his constructed detachable figures in 1915 (nos. 12–13):

> It would have sufficed to cut them up – the colours, after all, being no more than indications of differences in perspective, of planes inclined one way or the other – and then assemble them according to the indications given by the colour, in order to be confronted with a 'sculpture.'[10]

Another sculpture that Lipchitz may have seen on this first or subsequent visits to Picasso's studio was the sheet-metal-and-wire *Guitar* (Museum of Modern Art, New York) made in early 1912, his first sculpture since the 1909 *Head of a Woman (Fernande).* Like the latter, it was a three-dimensional counterpart of his Cubist paintings of the period. In this revolutionary break with the time-honoured techniques of modelling and carving, Picasso had created the first constructed sculpture. Henceforth, sculpture could no longer be defined as something to be carved in stone or wood or modelled in clay or plaster or wax and then cast in bronze. In the spring of 1914 Picasso returned again to constructed sculpture with his series of multimedia reliefs, such as the Tate Gallery's *Still Life*, made of painted wood with upholstery fringe (fig. 7).

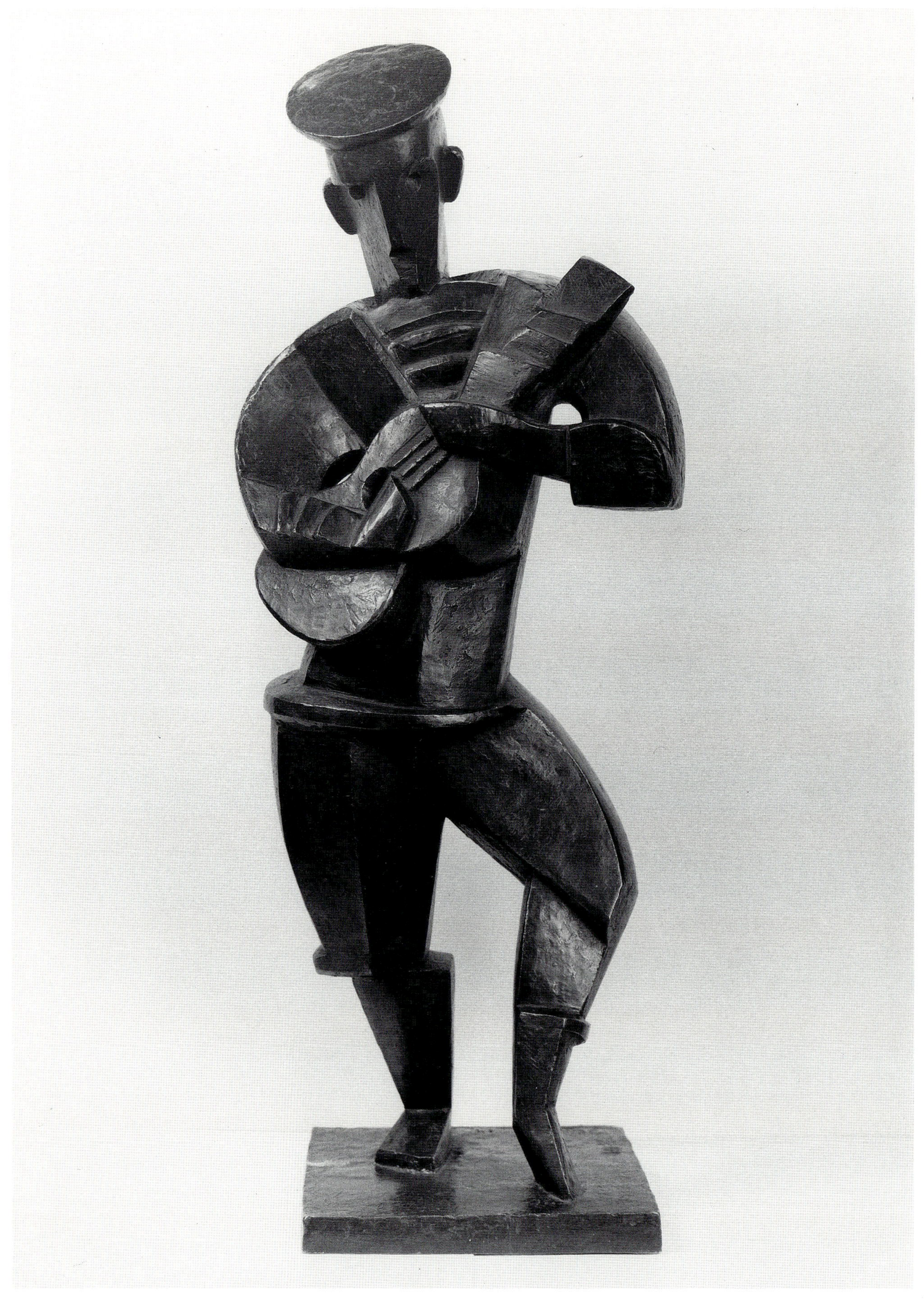

9 *Sailor with Guitar* 1914

It stands to reason that Lipchitz would have been particularly interested in seeing Picasso's sculpture, and it is entirely possible that he saw all or most of the seminal works discussed above, if not on his first visit, then on subsequent visits, as their friendship developed. By 1914 Picasso and Braque had initiated the most important revolutionary concepts of pictorial Cubism: their Analytic and Synthetic paintings and drawings and their collages and papiers collés. But it was Picasso and Picasso alone who created the most radical early masterpieces in the history of Cubist sculpture: his Analytic Cubist bronze *Head of a Woman (Fernande)* of 1909 (the first Cubist sculpture); his sheet-metal *Guitar* of 1912; and his painted wood reliefs of early 1914. Cubist sculpture was, from the outset, inexorably linked to its two-dimensional counterpart. No other style of sculpture in the history of European art had been so completely dependent on the iconographic and formal characteristics of its pictorial equivalent. Now that Lipchitz was familiar with Picasso's three-dimensional interpretations of his own paintings and works on paper, he could go directly to the source, as it were, for inspiration, instead of relying on secondhand interpretations of true Cubism – for example, in the sculpture of Archipenko and Boccioni. By 1914 Lipchitz was beginning to come to terms with the challenge that confronted all Cubist sculptors: how to adapt and translate the elusive spatial ambiguities of pictorial Cubism into a convincing yet independent three-dimensional language.

Although several sculptures of 1913, such as *Woman with Serpent* (no. 4) and *Dancer* (no. 5), reflect Lipchitz's initial, superficial awareness of Cubism, it was not until the summer of 1914, which he spent in Spain, including Majorca, with his friend Rivera, that it began to take hold. Clearly, the 1914 proto-Cubist bronze *Sailor with Guitar* (no. 9) was initially inspired by an actual sailor he had seen dancing around a pretty girl. In describing the sculpture as a final step toward Cubism, Lipchitz succinctly defined the basic distinction between Synthetic and Analytic Cubism: "I was finally building up the figure from its abstract forms, not merely simplifying and geometrizing a realistic figure."[11] For the first time Lipchitz conceived the human figure as a construction, built up of simplified geometric shapes, anatomical equivalents that appear to fit or lock together, like mechanical forms. For example, the legs and torso are linked by a circular disc that is in itself an abstract shape. While the entire figure retains basic human proportions, certain forms, such as the two displaced sections of the right leg, are arranged in a purely arbitrary manner that is structurally interesting but has nothing to do with the observation of nature. The balance has shifted from the demands of naturalism in the direction of purely formal considerations. Separate, abstract Cubist shapes, such as the lower left arm or the lower left leg, assume figurative connotations only when seen in relation to the other forms to which they are joined and to which they relate. Another feature of this seminal work that appears time and time again in Lipchitz's mature Cubist sculpture of 1915–25 is the repetition of similar abstract formal elements and rhythms, such as the three frets of the guitar, which are echoed in the three notches above the right wrist. This not only adds to the overall rhythmic unity of the work but demonstrates the interchangeability of abstract forms, which we read and which become legible according to their position in relation to the rest of the guitar and to the rest of the arm. Lipchitz described two other proto-Cubist works that

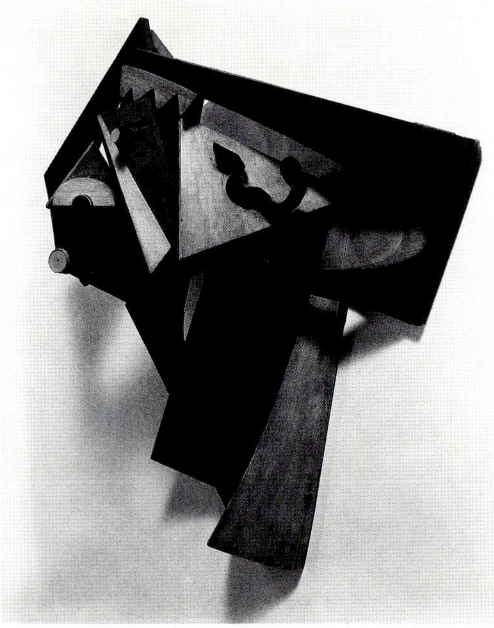

fig. 8
Henri Laurens, Head of a Woman, *1915, wood construction, painted, 20 x 18¼"/ 50.8 x 46.3 cm. The Museum of Modern Art, New York. Van Gogh Purchase Fund.* © *Laurens/VIS-ART Inc. 1989.*

were executed in Spain: "the *Toreador* [no. 7], which is more decorative as a result of his elaborate costume, and the *Girl with Braid* [no. 8] in which the anatomical form is in some ways even more fragmented cubistically than is the case with the *Sailor*."[12] Picasso was not the only source for Lipchitz's early Cubist work. In these two works, the heads are in profile, turned ninety degrees to the right, while the eyes are shown frontally, features that derive from Egyptian relief sculpture.

For lack of documentary evidence, the development of Lipchitz's Cubism and the dating and sequence of individual works cannot be charted with anything like the degree of accuracy with which one can follow, almost month by month, the evolution of Picasso's painting and sculpture. The most reliable source is Lipchitz's own account of his career in *My Life in Sculpture.* While the sculpture made during his visit to Spain in the summer of 1914 are readily identifiable, the exact chronology of his first mature Cubist work of 1915–16 is more difficult to establish.

The 1915 *Bather* (no. 10) was, according to Lipchitz, one of the first sculptures he made after his return to Paris in December 1914. By comparison, the works done in Spain a few months earlier seem merely superficially Cubist in their faceted geometric surfaces. Of his 1915 *Bather*, Lipchitz said: "Here, I would say that the transition to developed Cubism is complete."[13]

Lipchitz described *Bather* (which must first have been made of wood or cardboard) and the ebony-and-oak *Detachable Figure: Dancer* (Cleveland Museum of Art), also of 1915, as among his first attempts at constructed sculpture. It was, he recalled, "an idea then extremely new and very important for the subsequent history of sculpture. They are in some degree like machinery, since I was then interested in the relationship of machine forms to Cubist sculpture."[14] As the entire focus of Lipchitz's sculpture at this time was the human figure, he did not respond, as did Henri Laurens from 1915 (see fig. 8) to Picasso's wood-and-metal reliefs of 1914–15. During the first six months of 1915 Lipchitz continued constructing fully three-dimensional sculptures out of different materials, such as wood, glass and metal. In some of these, he explained, "I carried

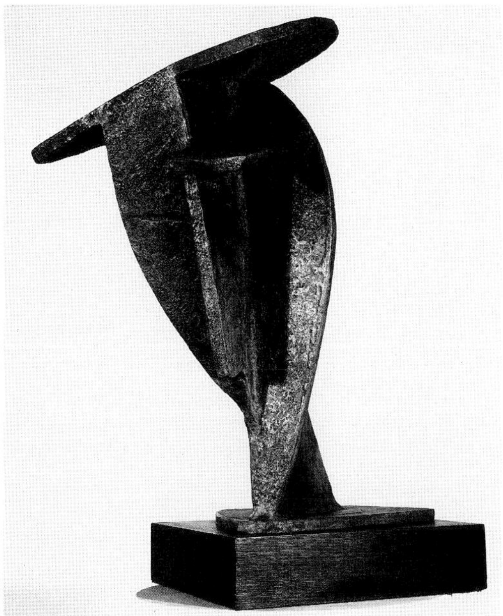

fig. 9
Alexander Archipenko, Head: Construction with Crossing Planes, *1913, bronze, H. 15"/ 38 cm. Perls Galleries, New York.*

my findings all the way to abstraction, but most of these abstract works I have destroyed since I felt that when I had lost the sense of the subject, of its humanity, I had gone too far."[15] Picasso had arrived at a similar point in his paintings done at Cadaquès in the summer of 1910, when he had produced his most abstract and hermetic Analytic Cubist work. As John Golding has pointed out, "Cubism, despite the strong intellectual bias and obvious concern with purely formal pictorial values, was never at any stage an abstract art. In fact the painters themselves and the contemporary writers who were genuinely anxious to understand their work, claimed that Cubism was an art of realism."[16] The 1910–11 paintings of Picasso and Braque did, however, approach the brink of abstraction. The same holds true for Lipchitz's early Cubist sculpture of 1915–16. When in the summer of 1915 he experienced the crisis of abstraction, he did an about-face and resolved the problem by producing *Detachable Figure: Pierrot* (no. 14), constructed in wood and later cast in bronze. The method of construction, the way in which the flat planes slot together, relates to Picasso's 1912 sheet-metal-and-wire *Guitar* (Museum of Modern Art, New York) but may have been directly influenced by Archipenko's 1913 *Head: Construction with Crossing Planes* (fig. 9).

Paradoxically, following the clearly legible figurative detachable sculptures of 1915 (nos. 12–13) Lipchitz embarked on a group of works that he later described as "perhaps my most abstract and architectural in feeling."[17] Several were called simply *Sculpture* (nos. 15 and 16) to emphasize his concern with abstract, formal considerations rather than subject matter. And yet, as Lipchitz pointed out, "A subject or an idea was nevertheless always implicit in even the most abstract works. For instance, in the obelisks [no. 16] there is a subject of a figure set within an architectural frame. In many of my abstract Cubist sculptures, such as [no. 15] and others, the figure or group of figures is suggested by such details as a circular eye-shape."[18] The architectural/figurative bronzes and carvings of 1915–16, such as *Sculpture* and *Seated Figure*, both of 1915 (nos. 16 and 18), and the 1916 *Standing Personage* (no. 20), constitute Lipchitz's most original contribution to the early history of Cubist sculpture. Here he goes far beyond merely

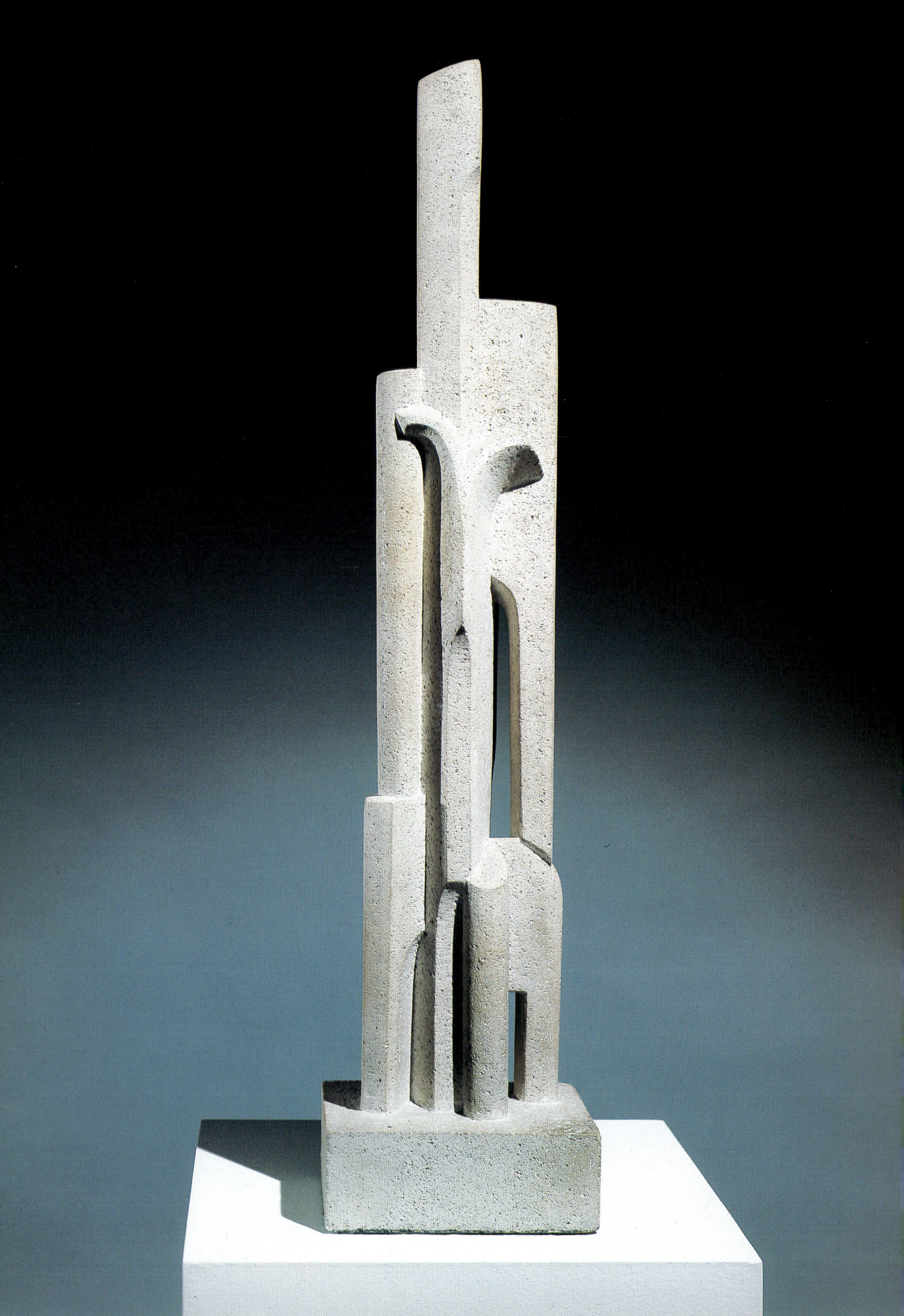

translating images from Cubist painting into three dimensions. Architectural forms become a metaphor for the human figure, or, if anatomical references are dominant, the human figure becomes a metaphor for architecture. For example, Lipchitz later compared the vertical, architectural structure of the 1916 stone *Standing Personage* (no. 20) to "a cluster of skyscraper towers, something like those in Rockefeller Center, New York."[19] He compared the V-shaped curves rising from the sharp vertical in the upper central area to the eyebrows and nose of the 1915 *Head* (no. 17). But they can also be read as shoulder blades from which emerge a long, thin neck and head. Lipchitz's seemingly abstract sculptures of 1915–16, like Braque and Picasso's most hermetic Cubist paintings of 1910–11, challenge the viewer to locate figurative signs or references that serve, however tenuously, to identify the subject matter.

Lipchitz first modelled his sculptures in clay and then had them cast in plaster. Like Rodin, he was by nature a modeller. He explained his working method at the time:

> Many of these abstract architectural sculptures are made in both stone and bronze. Although I have never cared about working directly in stone and, even if I had, was largely prevented from doing so by a recurring bursitis, these works so clearly needed the architectural mass of stone that I began to make them in this way. In the stone sculptures of this period and later I normally worked with a stone cutter, although I always finished them myself.[20]

In 1916 Lipchitz signed a contract with the dealer Léonce Rosenberg, who exhibited the work of the other major Cubist painters and sculptors at his galerie de l'Effort Moderne: Picasso, Braque, Gris, Léger and Laurens. As Lipchitz recalled: "This contract was a tremendous thing for me since for the first time in my career I no longer had to worry about money. Rosenberg paid me three hundred francs a month and all expenses, and I gave him everything I made."[21]

In 1916 Lipchitz met Juan Gris, probably through their dealer, Rosenberg. They soon became close friends, and during the next six years enjoyed an intimate working relationship. Lipchitz has described the stimulating gatherings at his friend's studio:

> This period during the First World War was a very exciting time in Paris, with artists, philosophers, and poets continually discussing and arguing about the work with which they were involved. I remember many sessions at Juan Gris's studio participated in by such people as the mathematician Princet, the poets Reverdy, Jacob, and Huidobro, in which the arguments raged continually...[22]

Although Lipchitz's approach to his art was more intuitive and less intellectual than that of his friend Gris, he was interested, for a brief period, in trying to apply abstract mathematic proportions to his sculpture:

> We were all intrigued by the idea of the golden rule or section, a system that was supposed to have been the basis in the design of Greek classical art and architecture. The golden rule is simply a division of a line or proportion of a geometrical figure such as a triangle or a rectangle in which the smaller dimension is to the greater as the greater is to the whole.

20 *Standing Personage* 1916

> Since I was at the moment working extensively in stone, I would have before me a rectangular block of stone and I would try to divide the block into proportions that seemed the most harmonious. Soon this method of working became irksome to me because it was too mechanical, it was taking away my freedom, so I abandoned it.[23]

Lipchitz and Gris shared a number of fundamental beliefs about the creative process and the distinction between art and nature. For the Spanish painter, art was first and foremost the creation of the mind, of the imagination, with only the most tenuous links with the world of nature as perceived through the senses. As Gris wrote: "Le monde dont je tire les éléments de la réalité n'est pas visuel, mais imaginatif. (The world from which I take elements of reality is not visual, but imaginative.)"[24] According to Deborah Stott, once Lipchitz realized that Cubism meant construction, rather than simplifying existing forms in nature, he changed his approach: "Instead of paring down from nature, he began by imagining some forms, some movements, and then from these made a figure... In other words, rather than reducing from life, he was thinking first about a construction, an abstract idea, and trying to give it life."[25] Lipchitz described his working method in an interview with Paul Dernée in 1920:

> Au premier stade de la création artistique il n'a que des intentions plastiques purs.... Puis vient la découverte du motif qui peut permettre de réaliser ces intentions. Le motif fournit des éléments premiers, des rapports simples de position entre les masses.
>
> (At the first stage of artistic creation there are only pure plastic intentions.... Then comes the discovery of the motif that can permit one to realize these intentions. The motif furnishes the principal elements, simple relations of position between masses.)[26]

Between 1916 and 1922 Lipchitz and Gris shared the same sort of intimate friendship and close working relationship that Picasso and Braque had enjoyed during their collaboration in the creation of Cubism between about 1907 and 1912. What made the close ties between Lipchitz and Gris unique were the ways in which formal and structural ideas were in a sense interchangeable from painting to sculpture and vice versa. For example, in 1917 Lipchitz helped Gris execute his only fully realized sculpture, the painted plaster *Harlequin* in the Philadelphia Museum of Art (fig. 10). In that same year Lipchitz made his first oil painting, entitled *Still Life with Compotier*, which he acknowledged "was certainly inspired by the works of my friend Gris, although it is a simple and somewhat elementary work when compared with his sophistication."[27]

It was in 1918 that the work of Lipchitz first exemplified the clarity and "call to order" that were the dominant traits of the major Cubist painters and sculptors Rosenberg was promoting at the time. Lipchitz's *Seated Man with Guitar* (no. 25), made in early 1918, clearly reflects the large, simplified planes and curved shadows in Gris's 1916 *Woman with a Mandolin (after Corot)* (fig. 11). In the spring of 1918, in order to escape the German shelling of Paris by "Big Bertha," Lipchitz and Berthe Kitrosser, a Bessarabian poet he had met in 1915, joined Gris and his wife, Josette, in the Touraine town of Beaulieu-lès-Loches. As he was not equipped to carry on with his freestanding sculpture, Lipchitz concentrated on drawings and gouaches that were preparatory sketches for a series of bas-reliefs (see no. 150). In these, he said, "perhaps because I was

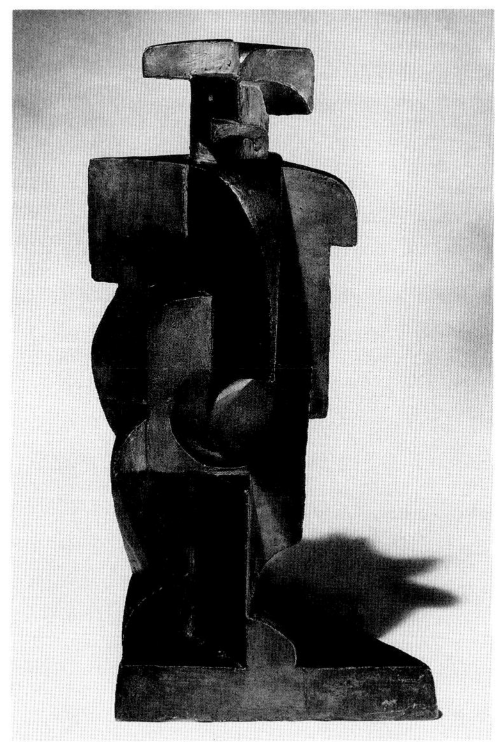

fig. 10
Juan Gris, Harlequin, *1917, plaster, carved and painted, H. 21¼"/60 cm. Philadelphia Museum of Art: A. E. Gallatin Collection.*

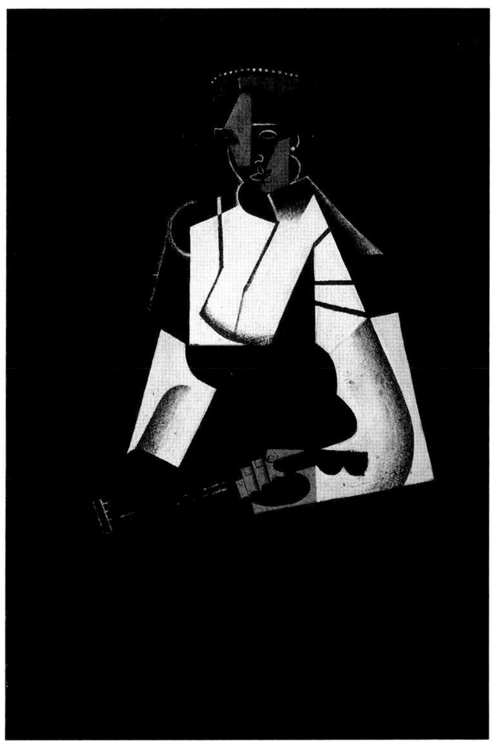

fig. 11
Juan Gris, Woman with a Mandolin (after Corot), *1916, oil on plywood, 36¼ x 23⅔"/92 x 60 cm. Öffentliche Kunstsammlung Basel, Kunstmuseum. Gift of Dr. H. C. Raoul LaRoche.*

thinking them out so completely with colored drawings, I began to experiment with polychrome."[28] In *Bas-Relief I* (no. 26), the painted planes have been graded so that those that project forward farthest are darkest. The paintings of Gris and the bas-reliefs of Lipchitz made during these summer months share a highly sophisticated common vision, as is abundantly clear if one compares Lipchitz's polychromed *Bas-Relief I* with Gris's *Guitar and Fruit Bowl on a Table*, painted in August 1918 (fig. 12). Lipchitz summed up the intuitive way in which influences moved in both directions:

> When I speak of possible influences from a painter like Gris on my sculpture, I am not talking about a one-way street. We were all working so intimately together that we could not help taking motifs from one another. I know as a fact that Gris, to whom I was pretty close, used images that he saw first in my sculptures, so my conscience is clear.[29]

Lipchitz and Berthe returned to Paris in the autumn of 1918. In his work during the next several years, Lipchitz was gradually freeing himself from the purely formal concerns that had informed his work since 1915. For example, he felt his *Still Life* of 1918 (no. 28) had an affinity with the still-life paintings of Chardin, whom he greatly admired. In 1919 he made a charming series of harlequins and Pierrots playing musical instruments (see no. 29 and fig. 13) that again reflected his interest in eighteenth-century French art, particularly the paintings of Watteau. This was clearly a period of transition. Lipchitz's description of his 1920 *Man with Guitar* (no. 31) is indicative of

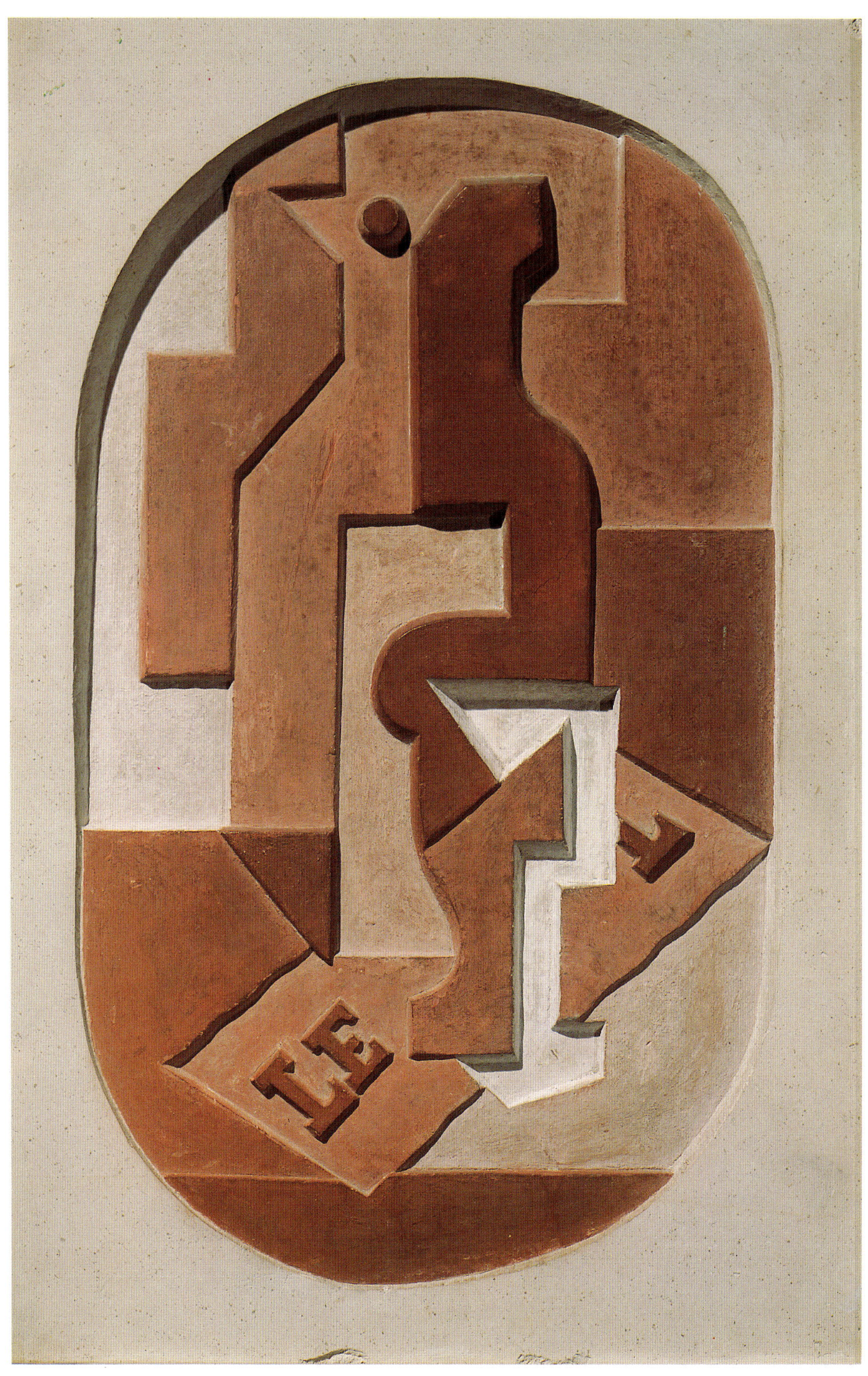
LE

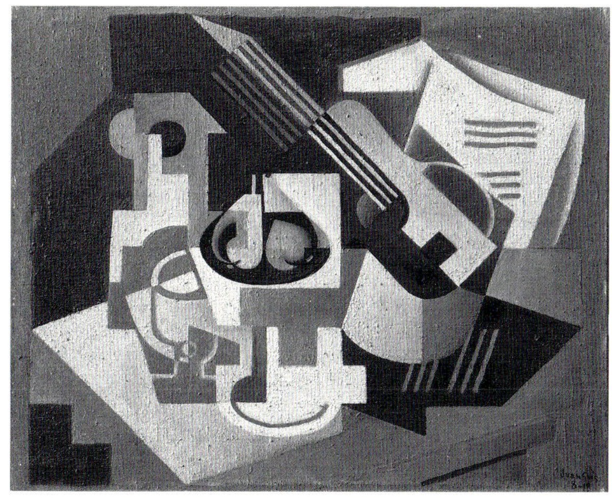

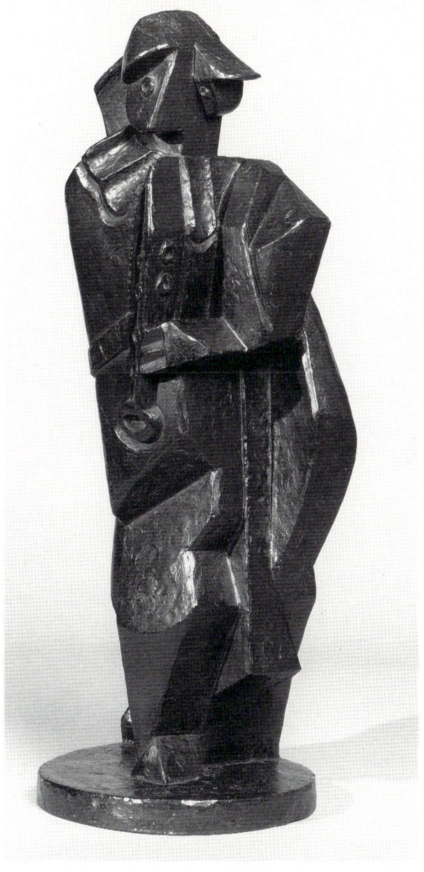

fig. 12
Juan Gris, Guitar and Fruit Bowl on a Table, *1918, oil on canvas, 23⅔ x 28¾"/60 x 73 cm. Öffentliche Kunstsammlung Basel, Kunstmuseum. Gift of Dr. H. C. Raoul LaRoche.*

fig. 13
Lipchitz, Harlequin with Clarinet, *1919, bronze, H. 28¼"/71.8 cm. Private collection.*

several new trends that were to develop in his work of the 1920s:

> *Man with Guitar* is now completely frontalized, composed of massive, integrated blocks... The asymmetrical staring eyes give to the figure a peculiar sense of almost hypnotic power which emphasizes its specific human personality. This is a work that is important to me as an anticipation of the monumental totemistic *Figure* of 1926 to 1930 [no. 51]. Although it is still quite small in dimensions, only about twenty inches, it has a monumental feeling about it that indicates a subconscious desire to work on a much larger scale.[30]

In 1920 Lipchitz had his first one-man exhibition at Léonce Rosenberg's galerie de l'Effort Moderne. That same year, as Lipchitz explained, he had a falling-out with his dealer:

> My reputation was beginning to enlarge, and, as is frequently the case, my dealer was afraid that if I changed my direction the works might be less salable. As a result, we agreed to part in 1920. After a final exhibition at Rosenberg's I was able, through the help of friends, to buy back all my sculptures from him and make casts myself from the plasters.[31]

After the exhibition, Maurice Raynal wrote a book on Lipchitz's work. Waldeman George and other critics took an interest in his sculpture. Although he had lost the financial security that Rosenberg had provided, Lipchitz had gained a new freedom that permitted him to break away from strict Cubist discipline.

26 *Bas-Relief I* 1916

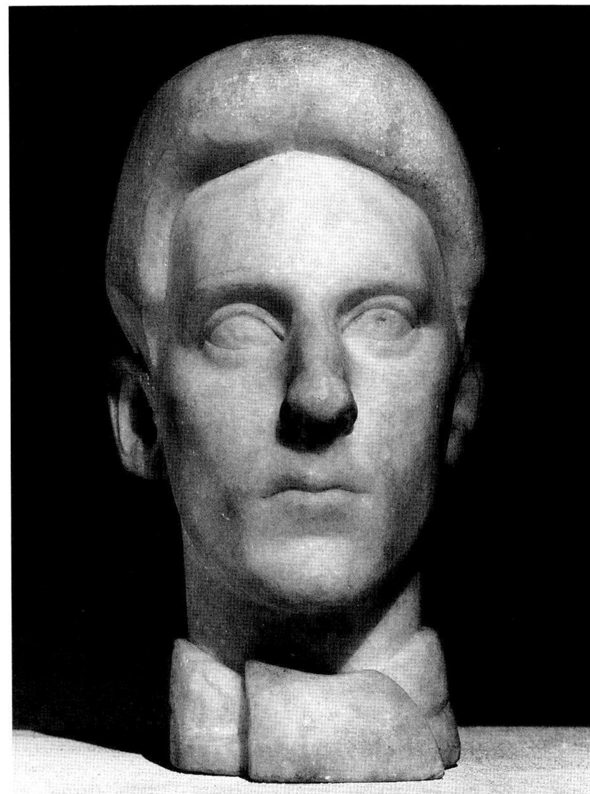

fig. 14
Lipchitz, Portrait of Jean Cocteau, *1920, marble, H. 14"/35.6 cm. Private collection.*

fig. 15
(Right) *Erwin Blumenfeld,* Jacques Lipchitz's Studio, *late 1940s to 1951, silver print,* $10^{1}/_{2}$ *x* $13^{3}/_{8}$*"/ 26.8 x 34.1 cm. Art Gallery of Ontario, Purchase, 1986.*

In 1920 Lipchitz made portraits of the writer Raymond Radiguet and of Jean Cocteau (fig. 14) and Gertrude Stein (no. 32; see fig. 15). As he later pointed out, "there was, after the war, a movement towards realism on the part of many artists in Paris and elsewhere. Picasso had again begun making beautiful, realistic drawings when he was associated with the Russian ballet during the war, and this led him to his second period of classical realism."[32] In 1921 Lipchitz was commissioned to do a portrait head of Gabrielle "Coco" Chanel, the famous couturiere. She also asked Lipchitz to make a pair of andirons for her house to fit in with the rococo Louis XV style of the chimney, which Lipchitz described as "all decorative curves, completely opposed to the geometric Cubist sculpture I had been making. I realized that I must change my entire approach for this commission, and the experiment in curvilinear forms was to have a most profound effect on my sculpture of the next decades."[33] (See no. 33.)

That same year, Coco Chanel also asked Lipchitz to make some designs for garden sculpture, and although, as he explained, "these were not actually carried out in final form, the small clay sketches that I made started a whole chain of events in my career."[34] Up to this point, his Cubist sculptures had been conceived from the outset on a modest scale, between about 24 inches (60.9 cm) and 48 inches (123.0 cm) in height. And it would appear to be correct to say that in all his Cubist work up to this point Lipchitz had used the vertical format. In the two andirons produced for Chanel's fireplace (no. 33), he introduced, probably for the first time, the reclining figure, which was to become an increasingly important motif in his work. Indeed, the reclining figure was also the subject of several of the preliminary maquettes for the garden sculptures: *Reclining Woman* (no. 34) and *Repentant Magdalene* (no. 35), both executed in 1921. The Chanel commission heralded yet another departure for Lipchitz. In the *Repentant*

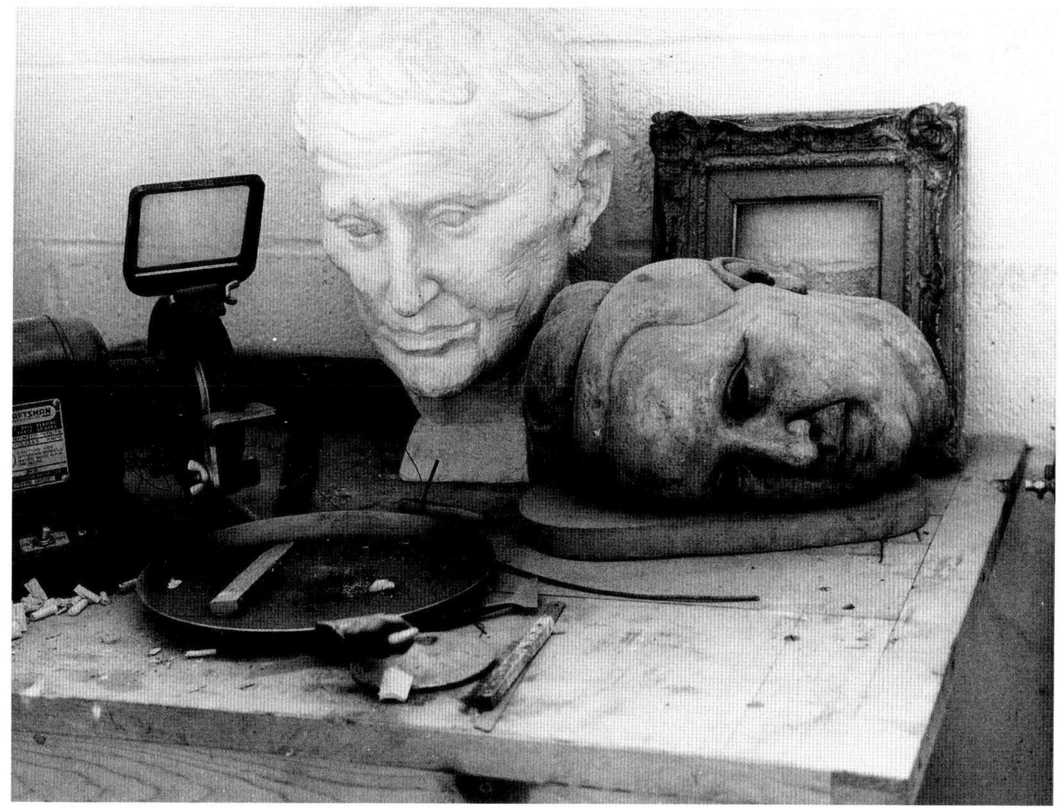

Magdalene he used a Christian subject for the first time. Although in making the sculpture he was not thinking specifically about the Christian theme (there is in the piece a suggestion of a reclining figure reading a book), he subsequently identified with the work his state of mind at this crucial turning point in his career: "There was in my mind some idea of a repentance that I myself felt, conceivably a repentance for my excursion into realistic portraiture."[35]

In late 1922 Lipchitz met the wealthy American collector Dr. Albert C. Barnes, who had asked the dealer Paul Guillaume to arrange a visit to his studio. Barnes, who had previously scorned the Cubists, was greatly impressed by Lipchitz's work. Not only did he acquire eight sculptures, but he also asked Lipchitz if he would design five reliefs for the niches on the facade of the mansion he was building in Merion, Pennsylvania, outside Philadelphia. At first the sculptor declined, because he felt his work would not fit in with the classical style of the building, designed by the French-born architect Paul Phillipe Cret. He finally agreed, however, on condition that he have complete freedom to do anything he wanted. As he later explained:

> The commissions from Barnes were not only useful in themselves. Barnes's reputation as a connoisseur of art helped to promote my sculpture and I was soon selling to other collectors from Philadelphia, New York, and Paris. I thus entered into a period of relative affluence that continued until the Depression of the 1930s.[36]

Lipchitz could now afford to commission Le Corbusier to design a house and studio in Boulogne-sur-Seine, to the west of Paris. He and his wife, Berthe, moved from their Montparnasse studio to the tranquillity of their new residence in early 1925.

In retrospect, the physical move away from the artistic centre of Paris to the rela-

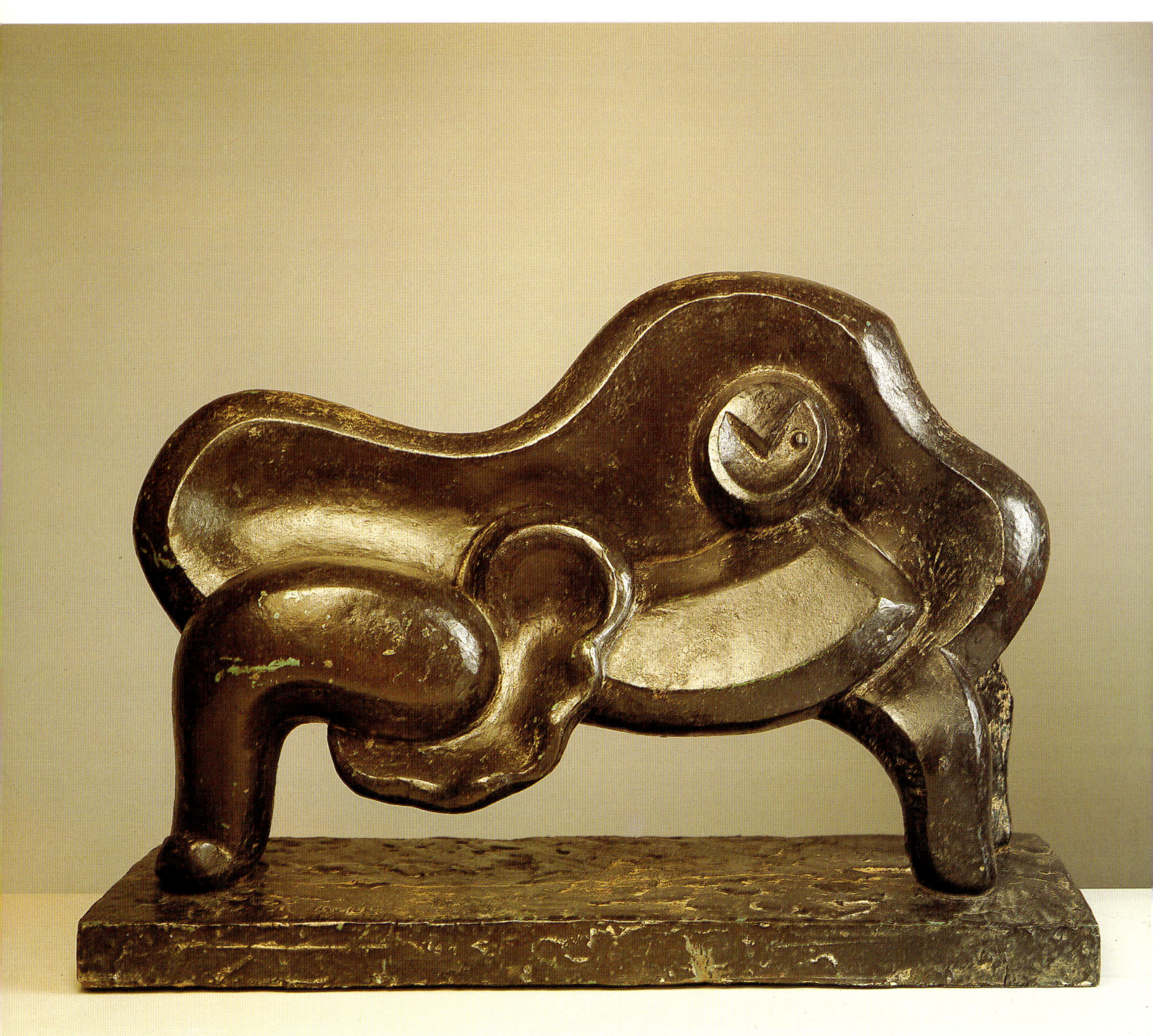

33 *Reclining Woman* 1921

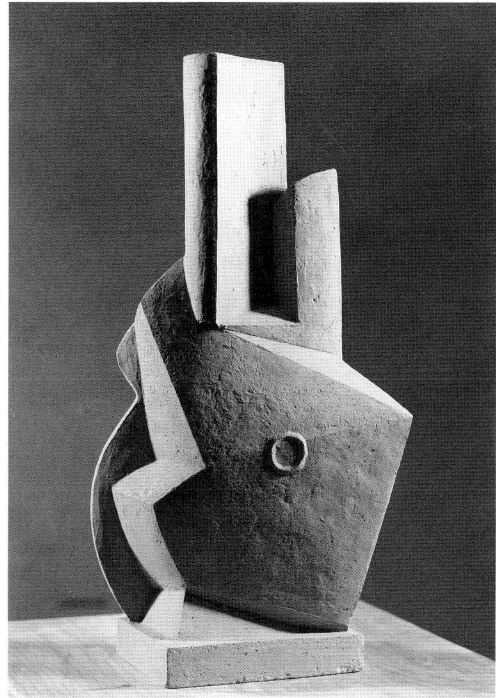

fig. 16
Henri Laurens, Guitar, *1920, terra cotta, H. 14 1/4"/36.2 cm; at base, 4 3/4 x 3 5/8"/10.2 x 9.2 cm. The Museum of Modern Art, New York. Gift of Curt Valentin. © Laurens/VIS-ART Inc. 1989.*

tive seclusion of Boulogne-sur-Seine seems symbolic of Lipchitz's need to break away and distance himself from what he called "the iron rule of syntactical cubist discipline, from all the taboos, regulations, and restrictions we had set up for ourselves, to become a free man."[37] Lipchitz's "essential" Cubist period spanned the decade from 1915, when he executed his first mature Cubist sculptures, until 1925, when he completed work on the large *Bather* (no. 43), which he saw as "my farewell to literal cubism."[38] During these years Lipchitz's work had been more closely allied to the formal elements of Cubist painting than that of any other Cubist sculptor. By comparison, the work of Laurens, the only other "essential" Cubist sculptor, seems more limited in the scope and range of its subject matter. As Christopher Green has pointed out, "Laurens's work between 1916 and 1919 represented above all a deeply personal response to Picasso's initiatives in Cubist sculpture, and especially to the multimedia constructions the Spaniard had begun in 1912 and brought to a first conclusion with pieces like *Violin and Bottle on Table* in 1915 [Musée Picasso, Paris]."[39] In 1919 Laurens abandoned his multimedia constructions and began carving fully three-dimensional works in stone. As Green remarked about Laurens's 1919 stone *Woman with a Guitar* (private collection), "The wit remained: there is a light decorative quality here (in the pleats of the bodice and the waved fall of the hair) which becomes amusing in so heavy a material as stone."[40] In Lipchitz's sculpture of the same year, such as *Harlequin with Clarinet* (no. 29), details like the musical instrument and the right hand are more fully integrated into the overall Cubist structure than are the guitar and hands in the Laurens carving, which appear as isolated features carved in shallow relief on the surface of the stone. While paradoxes and interchangeable forms abound in Lipchitz's sculpture, wit and decorative elements did not become regular features in his work until the mid 1920s.

Unlike Laurens (see fig. 16), Lipchitz focused his attention almost exclusively on the human figure, with the exceptions of the reliefs he made in 1918 and those com-

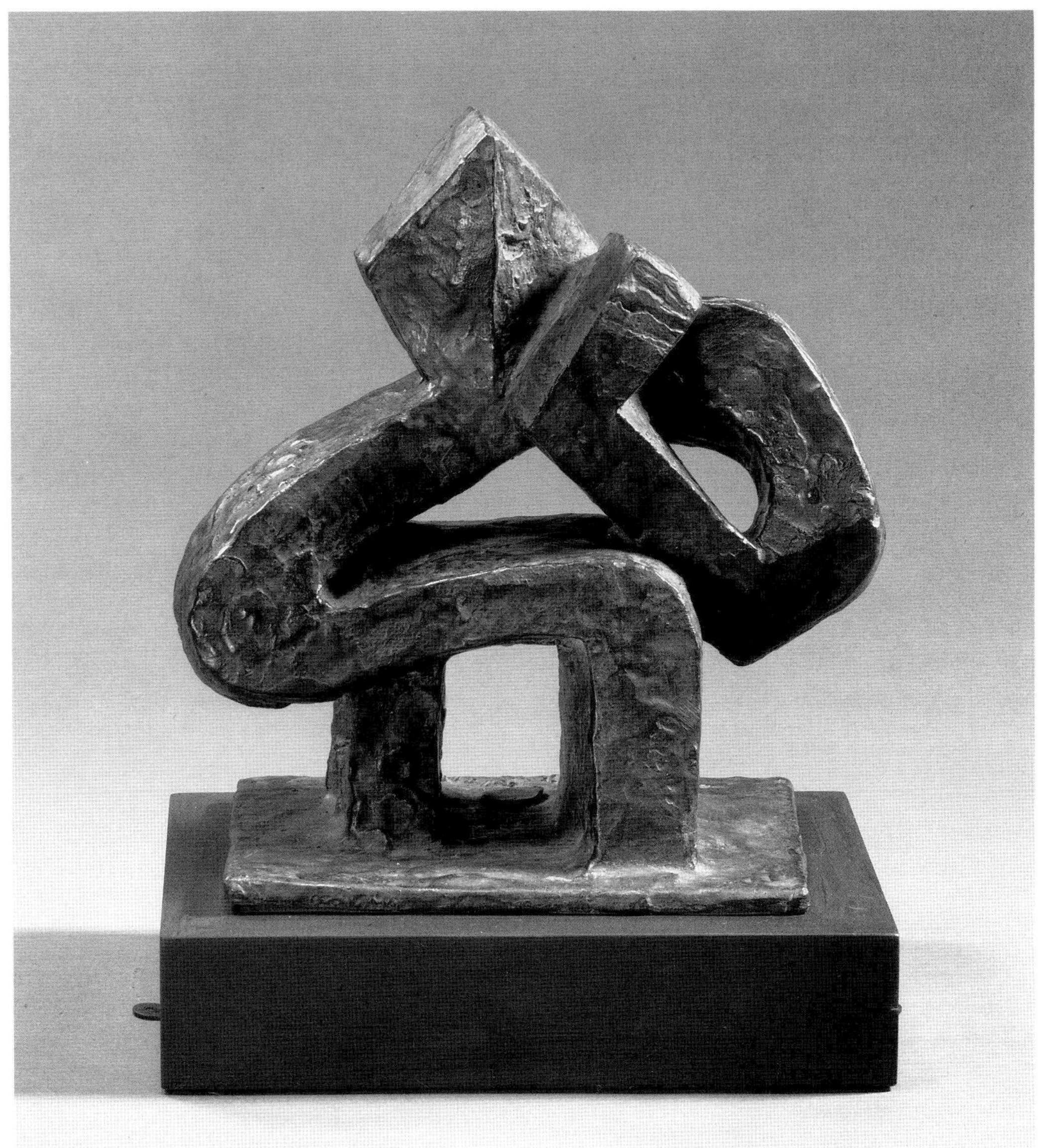

45 *Meditation* 1925

missioned by Dr. Barnes in 1922. The freestanding and relief sculptures he made between 1915 and 1925 present a totally convincing yet independent three-dimensional counterpoint to pictorial Cubism, particularly to the work of Picasso and Gris. The subject matter of Cubist paintings – harlequins, Pierrots, musicians with musical instruments, still lifes comprising simple objects of daily life – was the subject matter of Lipchitz's sculpture. If all visible traces of the Cubist paintings of Picasso, Braque and Gris were to disappear overnight, a comprehensive exhibition of the freestanding sculptures and reliefs Lipchitz executed between 1915 and 1925 would be more revealing than the work of any other Cubist sculptor in helping us to envisage and try to recreate in our minds the subject matter, the range of purely formal elements – the shifting, overlapping planes, the complex faceted forms, the spatial ambiguities and paradoxes – of pictorial Cubism. Lipchitz was the most representative Cubist sculptor of his generation.

Between 1915 and 1925 Lipchitz remained committed to working with the traditional materials of sculpture: clay, plaster, stone and wood. As Christopher Green has pointed out, Lipchitz, unlike Picasso and Laurens, "had never been tempted to entrap surrounding space by means of jagged extrusions from the main body of his pieces." And, Green continued, "It could even be said that such a use of traditional materials [stone and bronze] ultimately enhanced the impact of his sculptural paradoxes, for the instantly grasped density and weight of stone or bronze gives extra force to the reversals of solid and void so straightforwardly declared in a piece like *Seated Man with Guitar*..."[41] (no. 25). In almost all Lipchitz's Cubist sculptures made during the decade under discussion, the traditional monolith mass of the figures remained intact.

The year 1925 marked the most radical change in direction in Lipchitz's work since he had created his first mature Cubist sculptures in 1915. *Meditation* of 1925 (no. 45) introduced two new concepts in terms of subject matter and form that were to become part of Lipchitz's vocabulary for the rest of his working life. He saw the abstract simplification of *Meditation* as growing out of the 1922 *Seated Man* (no. 37), but now, he said, "perhaps because of intervening reflections on the question of personality and mood, of specific subject or identifiable attitude or individual, [it] is much stronger."[42] And equally important, Lipchitz commented, is in terms of form that marks "a most significant departure, the opening up of the spaces to the point where not only are the intervals between the legs and the arm completely interpenetrated, but the torso is actually a void encompassed by the S curve of the solid stone or bronze. Here we can see the first stage in the concept of the transparents, of sculpture as space, as air or spirit rather than as solid mass."[43] In another work of 1925, the small *Man Leaning on Elbows* (no. 44), the concept of transparency is even more pronounced; in this work, as Lipchitz pointed out, "every tradition of solid and void in sculpture is reversed."[44]

Pierrot (no. 47), the first in a series of sculptures that Lipchitz referred to as his "transparents," was made in 1925; it evolved from the opened-out spatial sculptures discussed above. Now that Lipchitz had freed himself from strict Cubist syntax, new ideas often came to him in sudden bursts of inspiration. *Pierrot* was the first of many such revelations. One day, while attending a lecture at the Sorbonne, he became absorbed in his own thoughts, and, as he described the experience many years later, "suddenly I saw how to make something that I had apparently been longing to make for a long time. So I left the lecture and went home. There I built it from cardboard the same evening."[45] The following day he went to the Valsuani foundry and built it up in wax. For the first time he was challenged by the problem of casting thin, delicate forms in bronze.

> The problem was the extreme thinness of the elements and the fact that this kind of casting had not been done before. Little by little we started to be more courageous, and everything came out; it was marvellous. Later, I made things in America, much more difficult, of different materials. I wanted to introduce space and light into sculpture itself and make it quickly, as quickly as my inspiration came and my imagination dictated.[46]

Most of the transparents were made in 1926; two of them, both from that year, are included in this exhibition (nos. 48 and 49). (Most, if not all, the transparents were unique casts, and the whereabouts of many of these bronzes is unfortunately not known. See fig. 17.) *Pierrot Escapes*, made in 1927, was probably the last in the series (no. 52). While the 1921 *Repentant Magdalene* represented Lipchitz's tongue-in-cheek repentance

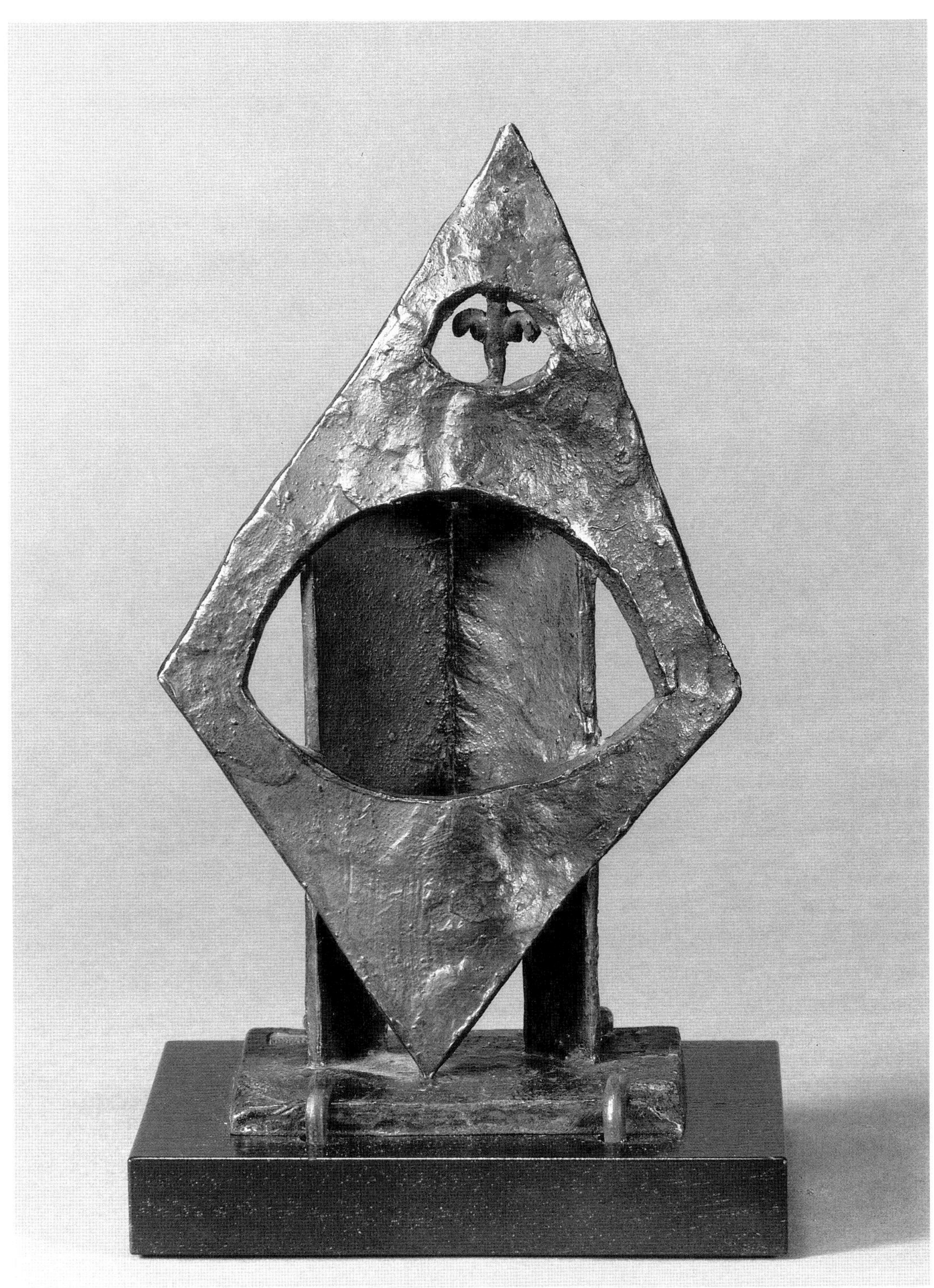

47 *Pierrot* 1925

for having abandoned Cubism and executed a number of realist portraits, *Pierrot Escapes* reflected the sculptor's feeling of liberation "from the more rigid aspects of Cubism and developing a new freedom in my expression."[47] The subject matter was entirely autobiographical, as Lipchitz explained: "The whole idea is extremely personal, a reflection of my excitement in the discovery of the transparents. Pierrot is myself escaping from the iron rule of syntactical cubist discipline...."[48]

Lipchitz has said of the transparents that "among artists, these pieces were extremely successful; Picasso liked them very much and one day spent half an hour studying a

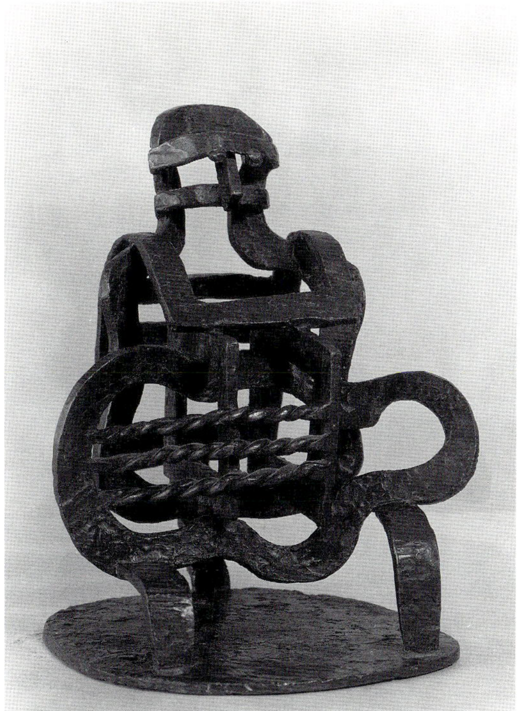

fig. 17
Lipchitz, Man with Guitar,
1926, bronze (unique),
H. 10 1/4"/26.0 cm.
Private collection.

piece at Madame Bucher's gallery."[49] Picasso may also have seen some of the transparents in Lipchitz's studio soon after they were made. One can speculate as to whether some of the transparents Lipchitz made of thin, wriggling and twisting bronze strips, such as the 1927 *Woman with a Guitar* (private collection), may well have influenced Picasso's wire constructions made in late 1928.

Clement Greenberg, without citing individual works, described the originality of Lipchitz's transparents as follows:

> The best works of this period are small, near-abstract bronzes, none more than twenty inches high, whose thin, perforated surfaces and calligraphic straps and cords of metal state the new draftsman's language of modernist sculpture even more clearly in some ways than do Picasso's earlier Cubist constructions. Several of these little bronzes are among the most rightly felt works of sculpture our time can boast of....[50]

The transparents were small, delicate works that proved to be difficult to cast in bronze. Indeed, when Lipchitz asked Spor, a skilled technician at the Valsuani foundry, if it would be possible to cast *Pierrot*, the first transparent (no. 47), "he said that it would not come out. But I said let's try it. So I built it up in wax, a small thing, and we discussed how to cast it and it came out. This gave me courage and I made more complicated things."[51]

But Greenberg, having praised the transparents as "among the most rightly felt works of sculpture our time can boast of," went on to say that they "offer some of the first evidence, if only indirectly, of Lipchitz's arrogant, almost perverse badness of taste or judgment." Why? Because Greenberg believed that "almost every one of them cries out for monumental enlargement, the proof of which is given by the most splendid of all Lipchitz's works: the *Figure* (1926–1930), which is the only large sculpture he has ever done in a manner like that of the small bronzes."[52] But Lipchitz himself did not

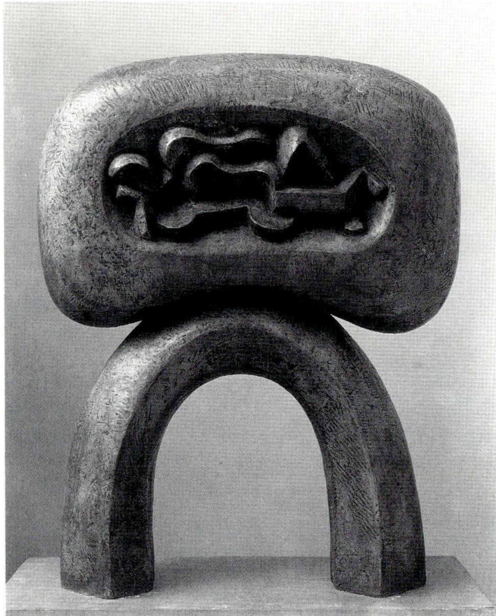

fig. 18
Lipchitz, Ploumanach, *1926, bronze, H. 31"/78.7 cm. Private collection.*

regard *Figure* (no. 51) as one of the transparents. Indeed, it evolved directly from the sketch entitled *Ploumanach* (fig. 18), which was more closely related to the Barnes reliefs than to the transparents. Lipchitz undoubtedly saw the transparents as small, intimate works that were "rightly felt" on the scale in which they were conceived. Greenberg, in accusing Lipchitz of being arrogant and lacking in taste or judgement, seems to have misunderstood the artist's intentions. As the sculptor said of his transparents: "These works have the quality of a sketch, except that they are the final work."[53] In the transparents and in even more complex and intricate works such as the much-later *Freedom* of 1958 (no. 108), Lipchitz was taking the technique of bronze casting "to the limit of the possible," as he called the 1958 series. Lipchitz explained that while engaged on large projects, "I always feel the need to work also on some small experimental pieces in which I am exploring new directions and new ideas."[54] Lipchitz usually modelled directly in clay or worked directly with wax. Indeed, he was without question one of the greatest modellers since Rodin. From his earliest maquettes, such as the 1921 *Repentant Magdalene* (no. 35), to his last small works, such as the 1971 *The Beautiful One* (no. 130), Lipchitz's instinctive ability to handle clay, that most malleable of materials, rarely goes astray. In speaking of his small studies of the mid 1920s, Lipchitz sums up the spontaneous, inspired qualities of his clay sketches:

> I love these little original maquettes. They are so fresh and warm in feeling, not worked out and cooled off. Here I can see my natural capacities. I can sense the periods of struggle and uncertainty and those marvelous moments of lyrical expansion when nothing could go wrong.[55]

The large *Figure* of 1926–30 (no. 51) was the summation of formal elements dating back to 1915. As Lipchitz explained, "it pulled together those different directions of massive, material frontality and of aerial openness in which I had been working during the 1920s. It is also very clearly a subject sculpture, an image with a specific and rather frightening personality."[56] The definitive maquette (no. 50) was enlarged because a

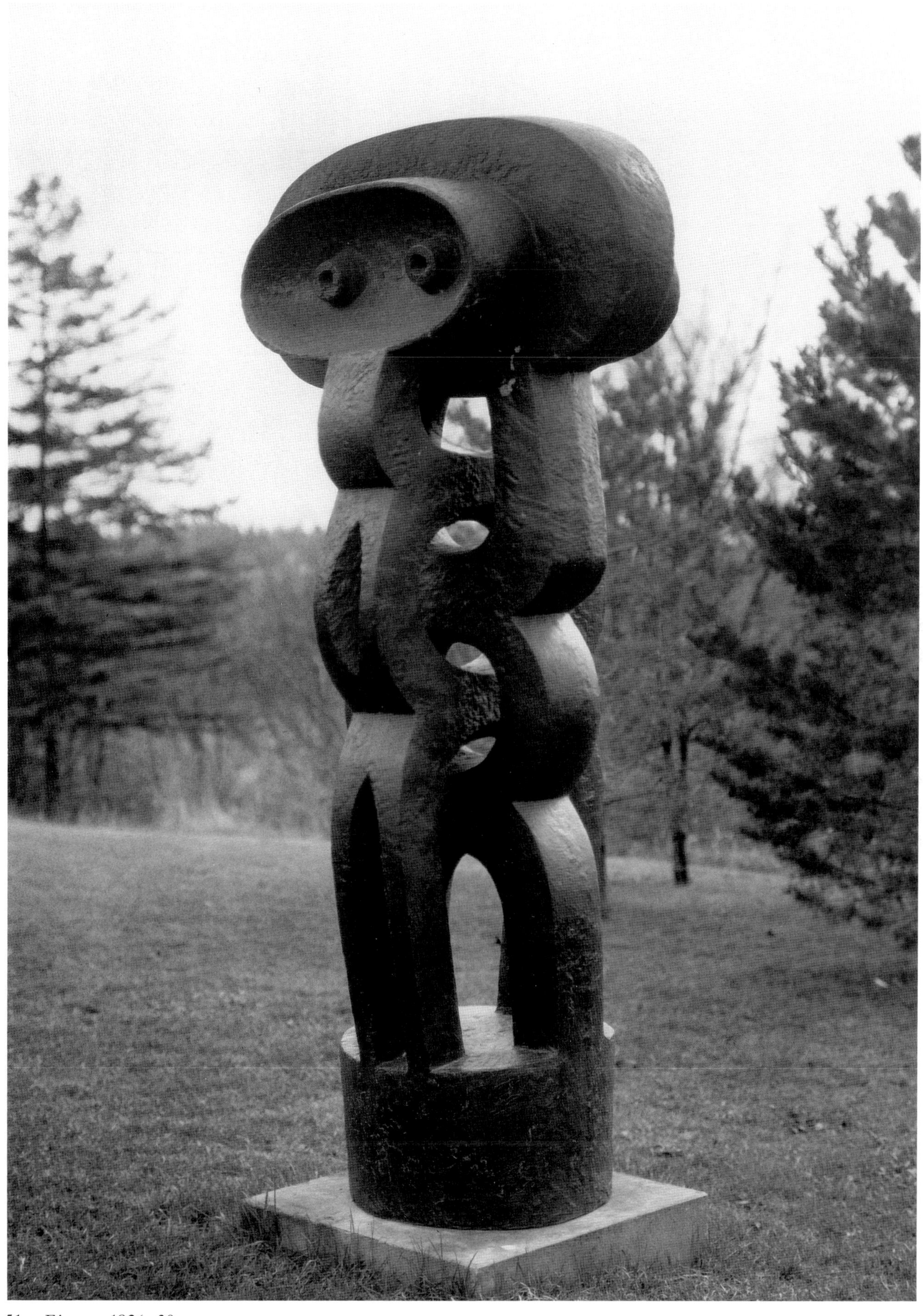

51 *Figure* 1926–30

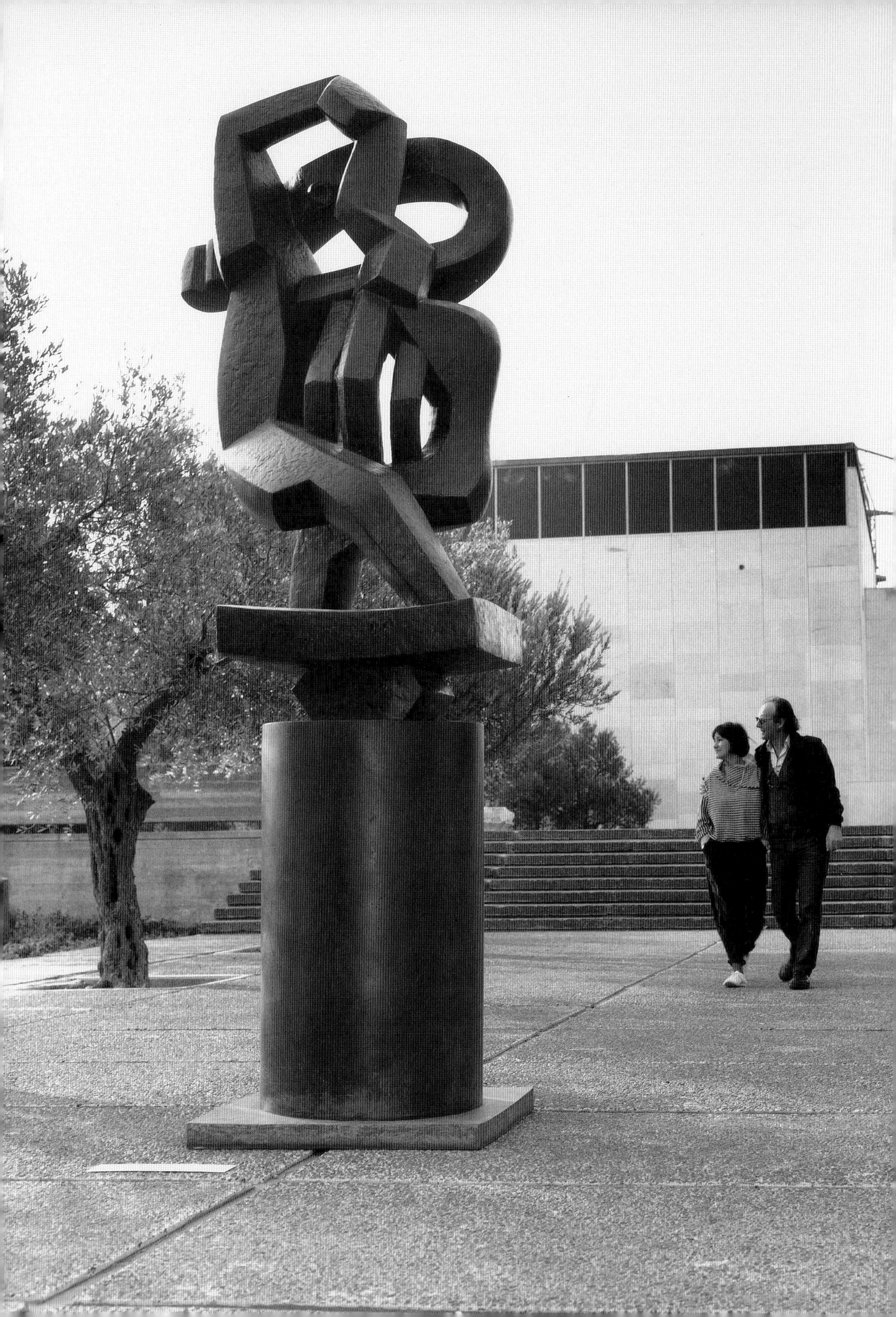

Madame Tachard had seen the terra-cotta sketch and wanted a much larger version of it for the entrance to her house. *Figure* was one of the first large works that evolved from a small sketch that at the time seemed complete as it was. "From this point forward," Lipchitz explained, "I think I began to be concerned more explicitly with this question of monumentality in my sculpture and to look at my maquettes with new eyes."[57]

In 1927 Lipchitz was commissioned by Vicomte Charles de Noailles to create a large sculpture for his estate at Hyères, in the south of France, near Toulon. Lipchitz described the work he created, *Joy of Life (La Joie de Vivre)* (fig. 19), as "a dancing figure with a large guitar, related to and, I think, a result of many things I had done before. It is a culmination of all my findings in Cubism but at the same time an escape from Cubism."[58] Whereas the large *Figure* of 1926–30 was, as was mentioned above, clearly a subject sculpture, with the kind of frightening personality associated with African or Oceanic art, it was in no way autobiographical. The *Joy of Life*, on the other hand, marked a dramatic change in his attitude to his art. When the *Joy of Life* was commissioned, his sister Genia was very ill in hospital, and as Lipchitz explained, "in order to cheer her up, I decided to make something gay."[59] The following year, both Genia and his father died. *The Cry (The Couple)* of 1928–29 (no. 54) was made as a way of trying to deal with the despondency Lichitz felt at the time:

> I was filled with a terrible sorrow and depression, but, since I am not a pessimist by nature, I made this sculpture as a kind of release, a defiance to show that in the midst of tragedy life must continue, that we must live and multiply. In the midst of death there is love and procreation and birth. This is how the sculpture came about, as a hopeful and optimistic reaction to tragedy.[60]

Lipchitz's sculpture of the early 1930s dealt with a variety of subjects: events relating to his personal life; Biblical and mythological themes; new, purely sculptural ideas; and political statements focusing on the growing threat of Hitler's Germany. The 1930 *Chimène*, (no. 58), one of the last of Lipchitz's brilliant series of transparents, reflects a very private and personal reaction or, as Lipchitz described it, "a sublimation of an experience, a sort of poem arising out of a particular emotion. It was inspired by a particular woman, someone who fascinated me for several years."[61] The head and hand captured a particular gesture she made that obsessed the sculptor. It was one of his first "gestural" sculptures on the theme of the head and hand, which Lipchitz continued to explore during the next several years.

The late 1920s and early 1930s were a difficult time for Lipchitz. After the death of his sister and father, he began questioning many things. He asked himself, "For what am I born? For what did I come on this earth?"[62] In late 1929 Lipchitz produced the first *Mother and Child* maquette, followed soon after by the closely related 1930 study *Mother and Child* (no. 62). Lipchitz commented on their personal significance for him: "Both of them involve a cry of anguish that resulted from the tragedy that had befallen me. In the sketches, the mother is wailing for her child, and in the first version of the large sculpture [see no. 64] the child on his mother's shoulders is tearing at her breasts."[63]

fig. 19 Lipchitz, Joy of Life (La Joie de Vivre), *1927, bronze, H. 89¼"/226.7 cm. The Israel Museum, Jerusalem.*

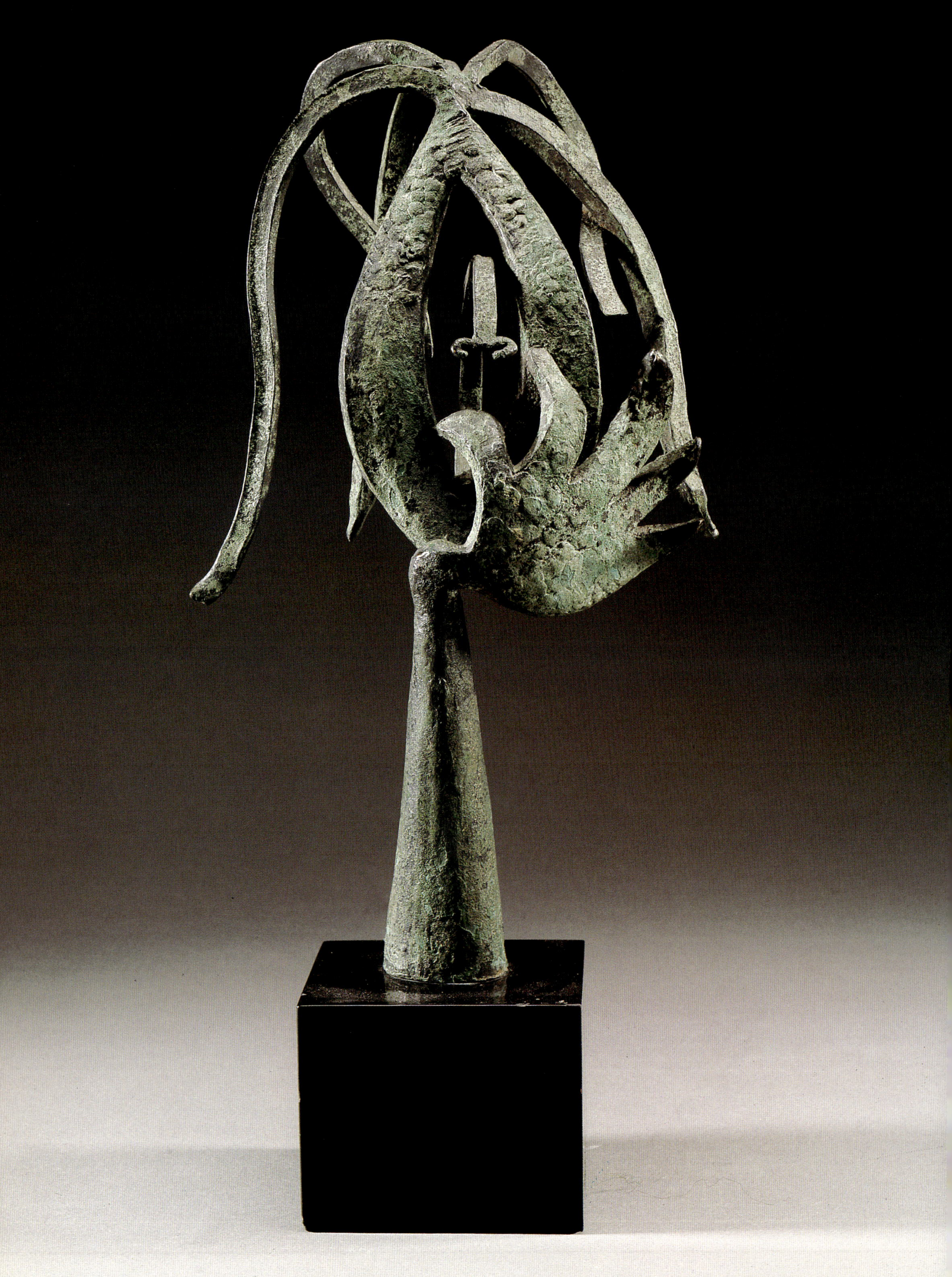

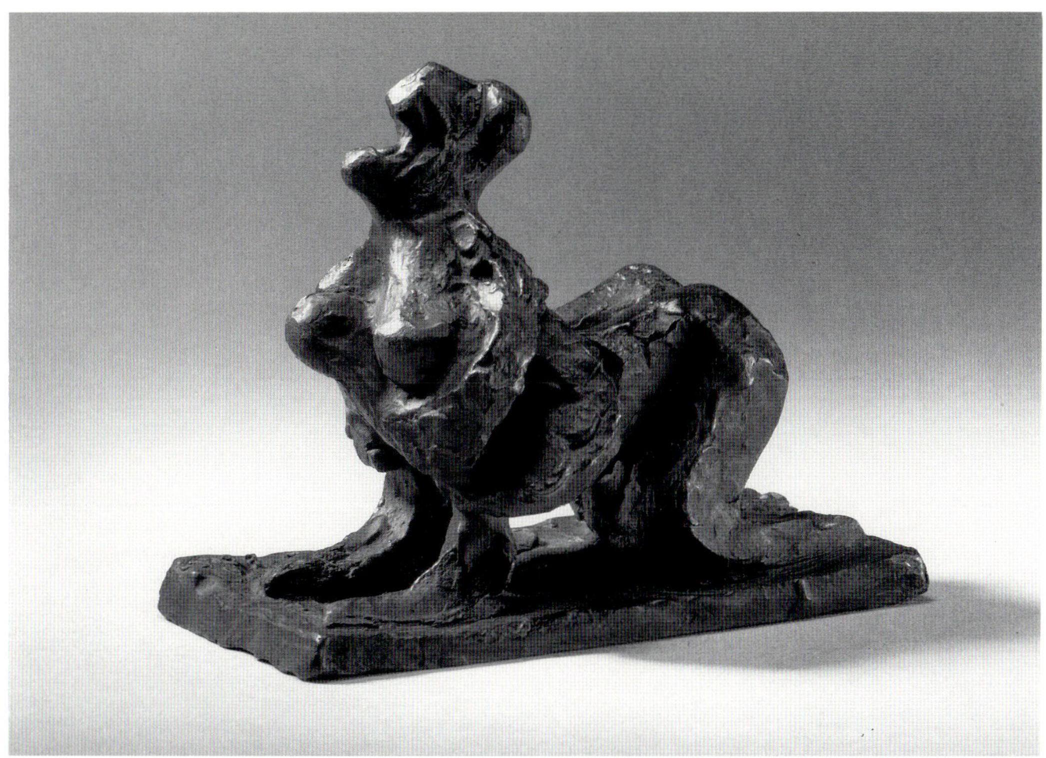

62 *Mother and Child* 1930

In the small *Mother and Child* (no. 62) it is the lack of detail, the lack of realism in the loosely modelled head of the mother and in her large, gaping mouth, that give the tortured, primeval cry its power, expressing a pain that is almost too much to bear. Not even Munch's famous 1893 painting *The Scream* (National Gallery, Oslo) or Rodin's c.1895 bronze *The Cry* (Musée Rodin) approaches the raw intensity of the anguished scream in this extraordinarily powerful little maquette.

In the early 1930s Lipchitz adapted a number of Biblical stories, the first of which, *Return of the Prodigal Son* (no. 61), embodied a personal theme related to his development as an arist. As he explained:

> It had a very personal association to me, the idea of the son who is returning home, the artist who is returning to nature; it is a continuation of the *Pierrot Escapes*, a longing for nature rather than abstraction. In the Biblical story the son returns to his father, but here I have him come back to his mother, Mother Nature.[64]

As so often happened in Lipchitz's work, he began this sculpture with what he called "an intangible feeling,"[64] and only later did he come to associate the subject matter with the Biblical theme. In 1931–32 he became obsessed with Jacob's heroic struggle with the angel, and he produced several maquettes (no. 67) before beginning work in 1932 on the final version of *Jacob Struggling with the Angel* (no. 68). The theme of embracing figures, be they lovers or figures locked in combat, was to be the subject of many sculptures spanning more than forty years, from *The Cry (The Couple)* of 1928–29 (no. 54) to *The Last Embrace* of 1971 (no. 132).

58 *Chimène* 1930

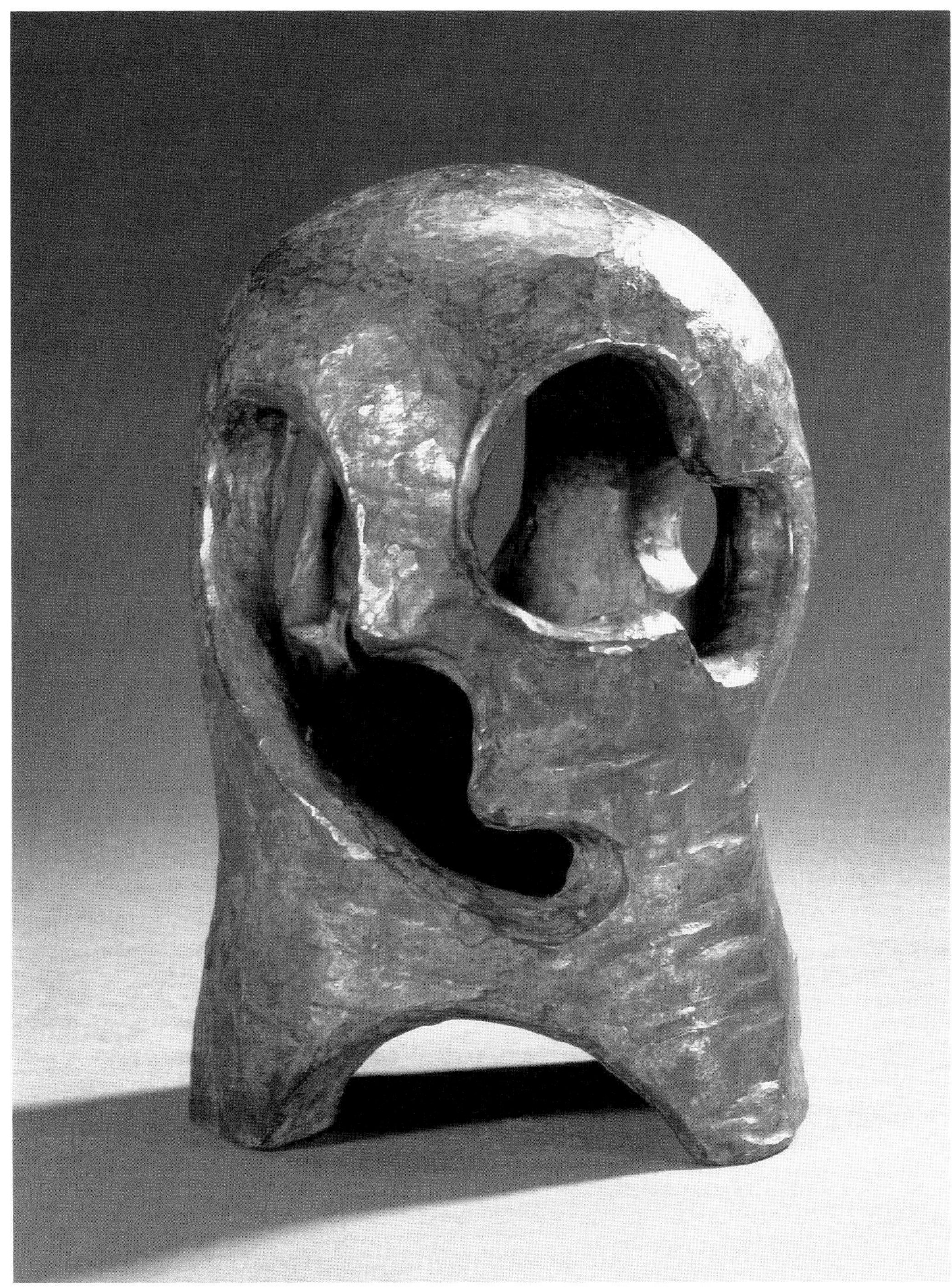

69 *Head* 1932

During the 1930s, Lipchitz's work oscillated between private, purely sculptural obsessions and public statements – what he referred to as "political sculpture."[66] Most of the former were, like Rodin's intimate, experimental innovations, small-scale maquettes that were never intended to be enlarged. With so much critical attention focused on Lipchitz's Cubist period, the formal innovations of his maquettes have not received the acclaim they deserve. The small *Seated Woman* of 1930 (no. 60) has the openness of the transparents while employing the Cubist device, found, for example, in the 1922 *Guitar Player in Chair* (no. 38), in which the figure becomes, as Lipchitz mentioned, "a woman-chair."[67] The gestural sculptures of the head-and-hand motif,

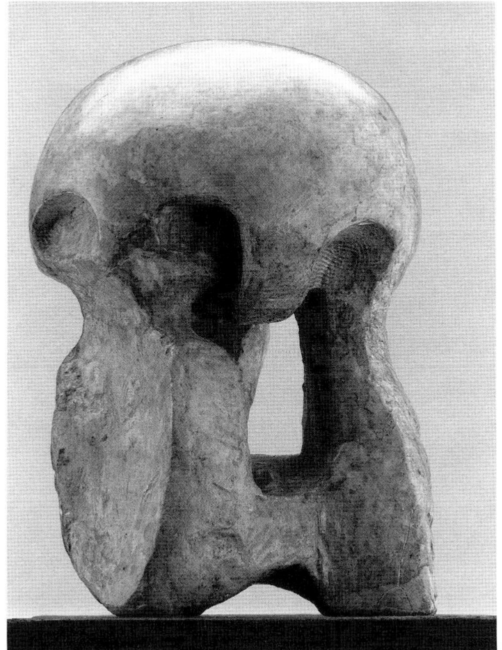

fig. 20
Henry Moore, Maquette for Atom Piece, *1964, original plaster, H. 5⁴/₅"/14.7 cm.*
Art Gallery of Ontario, Toronto. Gift of Henry Moore, 1974.

first realized in the 1930 *Chimène* (no. 58), was the subject of a series of highly original bronzes of 1932–33 (nos. 70–72). The helmet- or skull-like *Head* of 1932 (no. 69) anticipates Moore's far better known 1964 *Maquette for Atom Piece* (fig. 20) by more than thirty years.

In 1933 Lipchitz again turned to a Biblical subject, creating a series of maquettes on the theme of David and Goliath (no. 74) that were, he said, "specifically related to my hatred of fascism and my conviction that the David of freedom would triumph over the Goliath of oppression."[68] Politically, Lipchitz was a remarkably courageous and outspoken artist. He said of his *David and Goliath* (no. 75): "I wished there to be no doubt about my intent so I placed a swastika on the chest of Goliath. The statue cost me considerable difficulty with German agents who in the guise of art critics began to show intense interest in visiting and examining my studio."[69]

In 1935 Lipchitz had his first exhibition in New York, at the Brummer Gallery. Joseph Brummer, a Hungarian, had a passion for sculpture, ancient as well as modern. The following year he brought Alfred Barr, director of the Museum of Modern Art, New York, to meet Lipchitz in Paris. Barr bought or ordered a cast of the large *Figure* of 1926–30 (no. 51). This sculpture, the first work by Lipchitz acquired by the museum, entered the collection in 1937.

Lipchitz continued to create more sculptures of political protest. The 1936 *Scene of Civil War* (no. 79) was, according to the sculptor, inspired by the Spanish Civil War. "[It] shows a woman with a child and a man who is protecting her, shooting. I was desperately disturbed by the Spanish Civil War, which I could sense was a preliminary for a world war."[70]

In 1936 Lipchitz was commissioned by the French government to create a large

75 *David and Goliath* 1933 (p. 34)
79 *Scene of Civil War* 1936 (p. 35)

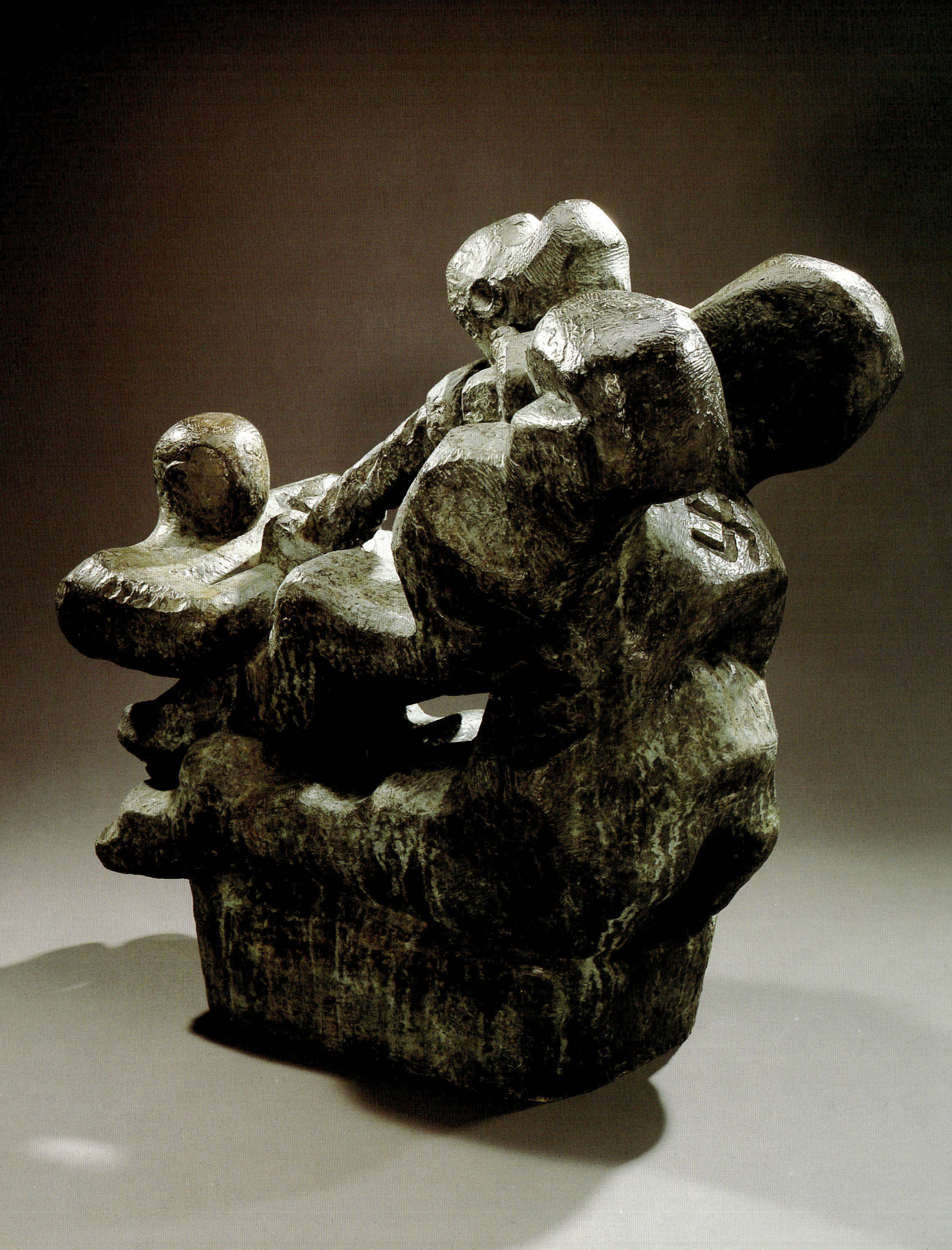

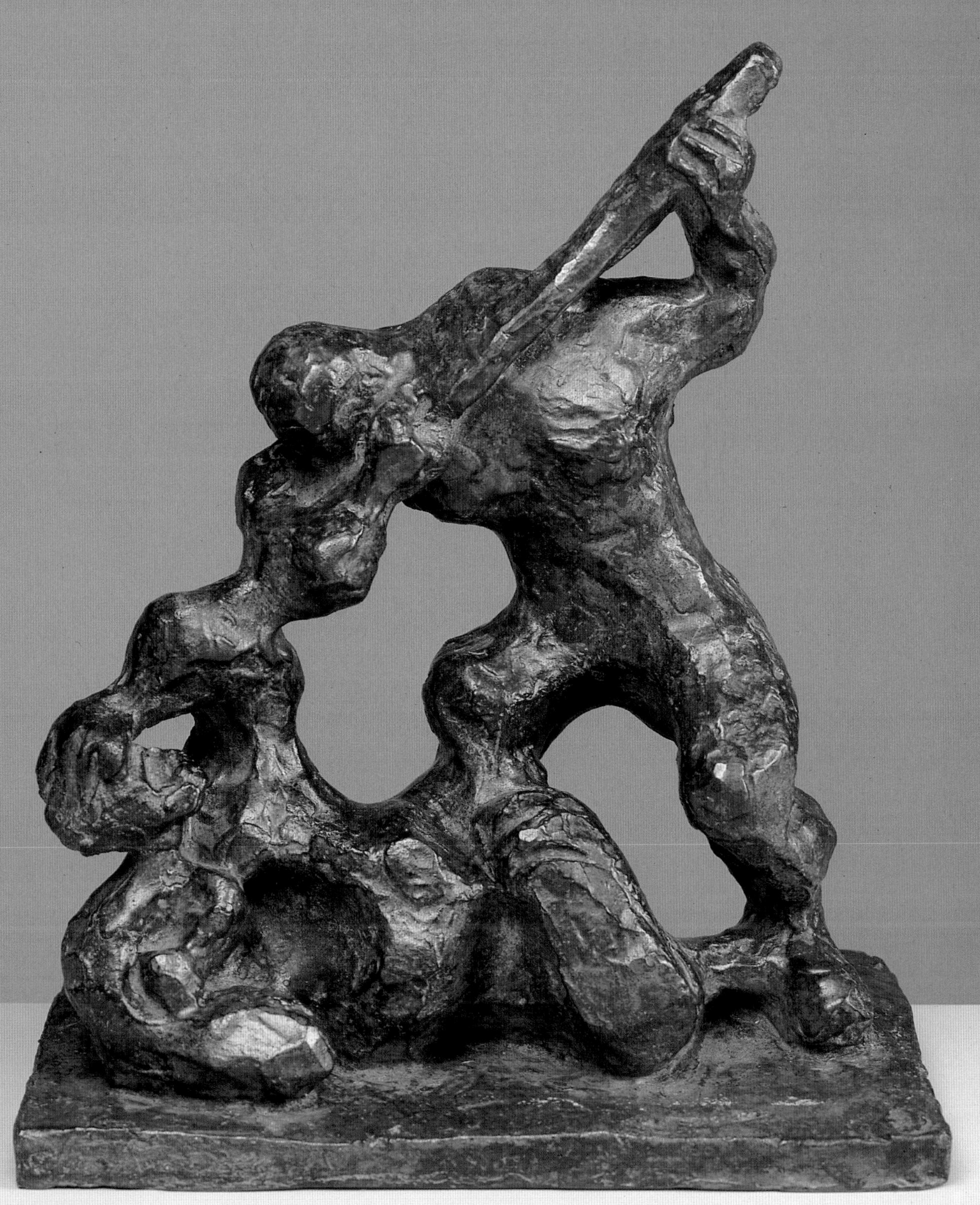

sculpture for the Palais de la Découverte for the 1937 Exposition Internationale in Paris. The myth of Prometheus, the benefactor of mankind and the father of the arts and sciences, had interested Lipchitz for some time and seemed a suitable subject for a pavilion of discovery and invention. As David Fraser Jenkins has pointed out:

> his original idea had been to show him triumphant, having broken his chains, as a personification of human progress. However, the rise to power of the Nazis in 1933 and the events which followed convinced him that "the moment of triumph had not yet sounded: quite the reverse, the moment of death struggle approached."[71]

The first of the two preliminary maquettes, *Study for Prometheus* (no. 77), shows Prometheus holding a flame in one hand while fending off the vulture with the other. Lipchitz then made a larger sketch entitled *Study for Prometheus Strangling the Vulture* (no. 78). Although it shows only the figure of Prometheus, the vulture he is strangling is implied. In the definitive study, and in the nine-metre-high finished plaster, Prometheus, wearing a Phrygian cap (for Lipchitz a symbol of democracy), strangles the vulture with his right hand while fending off with his other hand the claws that are tearing at his vitals. Lipchitz conceived the sculpture as a struggle in which light and education and science were threatened by darkness and ignorance. As Lipchitz remarked: "what I was trying to show was a pattern of human progress that to me involved the democratic ideal. So, in a certain way, this is a political sculpture, propaganda for democracy."[72] The completed plaster was placed some twelve metres above the entrance to the Grand Palais, which housed the Palais de la Découverte. "There were," Lipchitz later recalled, "attacks in newspapers against my *Prometheus*, particularly from reactionary journals."[73] When the exhibition closed, the sculpture was taken down and destroyed.

Between the completion of *Prometheus Strangling the Vulture* and the outbreak of war, Lipchitz made few sculptures. In 1938 he met Gertrude Stein again after a long interval and asked if he might do another portrait of her. In the first portrait of Stein, made in 1920 (no. 32), he depicted her as "a massive, inscrutable Buddha."[74] When they met in 1938 she had lost a great deal of weight and appeared to Lipchitz "like a shriveled old rabbi."[75] In Lipchitz's 1938 bronze *Gertrude Stein* (no. 80), one of his finest portraits, "the massive, self-confident Buddha has become a tired and rather tragic old woman."[76]

In 1938 Lipchitz made three variations on the theme of the rape of Europa (no. 81), which derived from his continuing interest in classical mythology. However, he did not use the subject as a vehicle to symbolize an event in contemporary history or from his own personal life. In this work, Lipchitz said, "the entire theme is tender and erotic love; the bull is caressing Europa with his tongue."[77] In 1941 he again used this myth, but for allegorical purposes, with Europa as a symbol for Europe and the bull as Hitler, whom Europa is stabbing with a dagger (no. 85).

In May of 1940, when Germany invaded France, Lipchitz and Berthe left Paris and fled to the south, where they settled in Toulouse. In 1941, with the assistance of Alfred Barr and the American Rescue Committee, Lipchitz and his wife were able to emigrate to the United States. They travelled by boat via Portugal and arrived in New

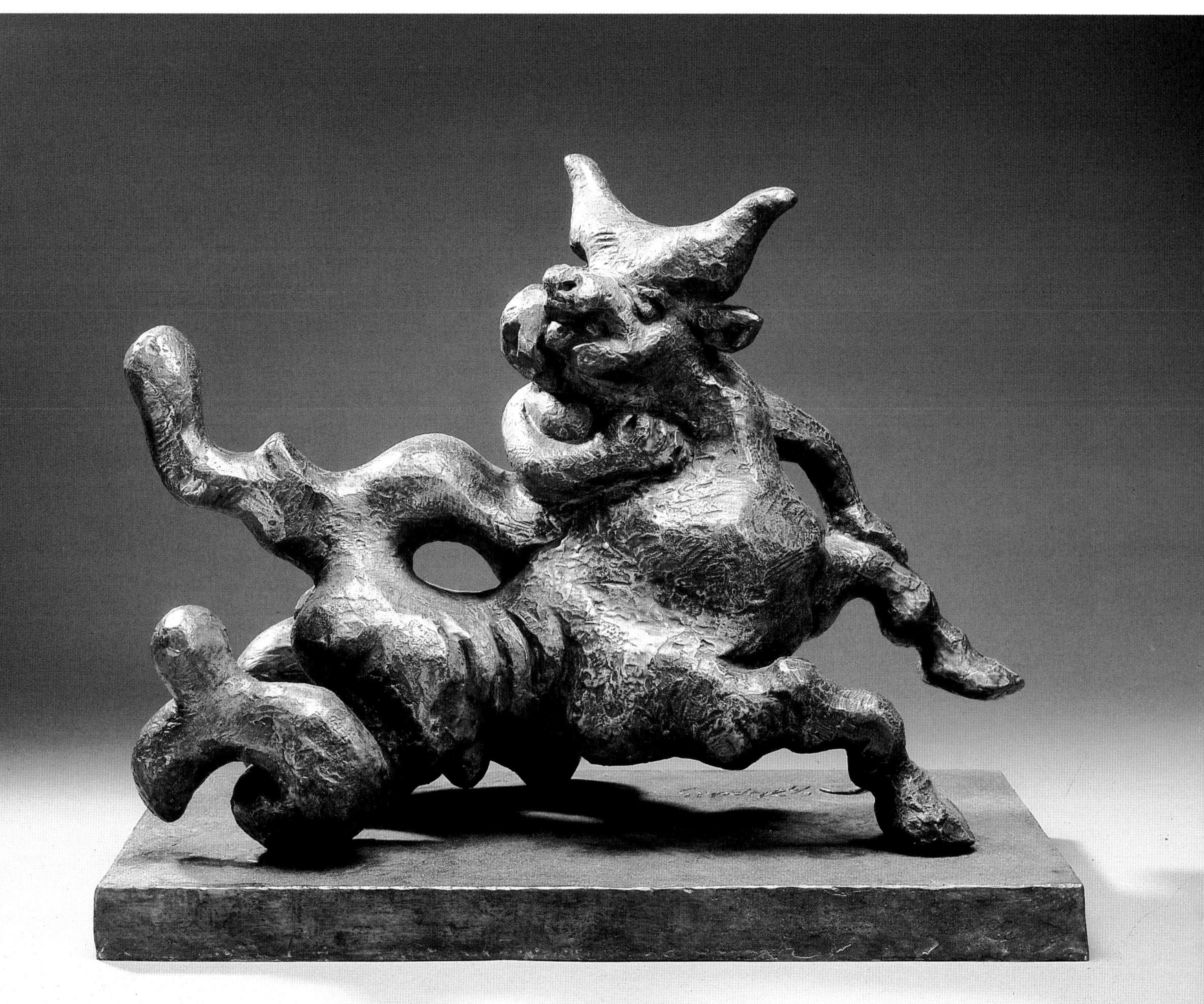

81 *Rape of Europa I* 1938

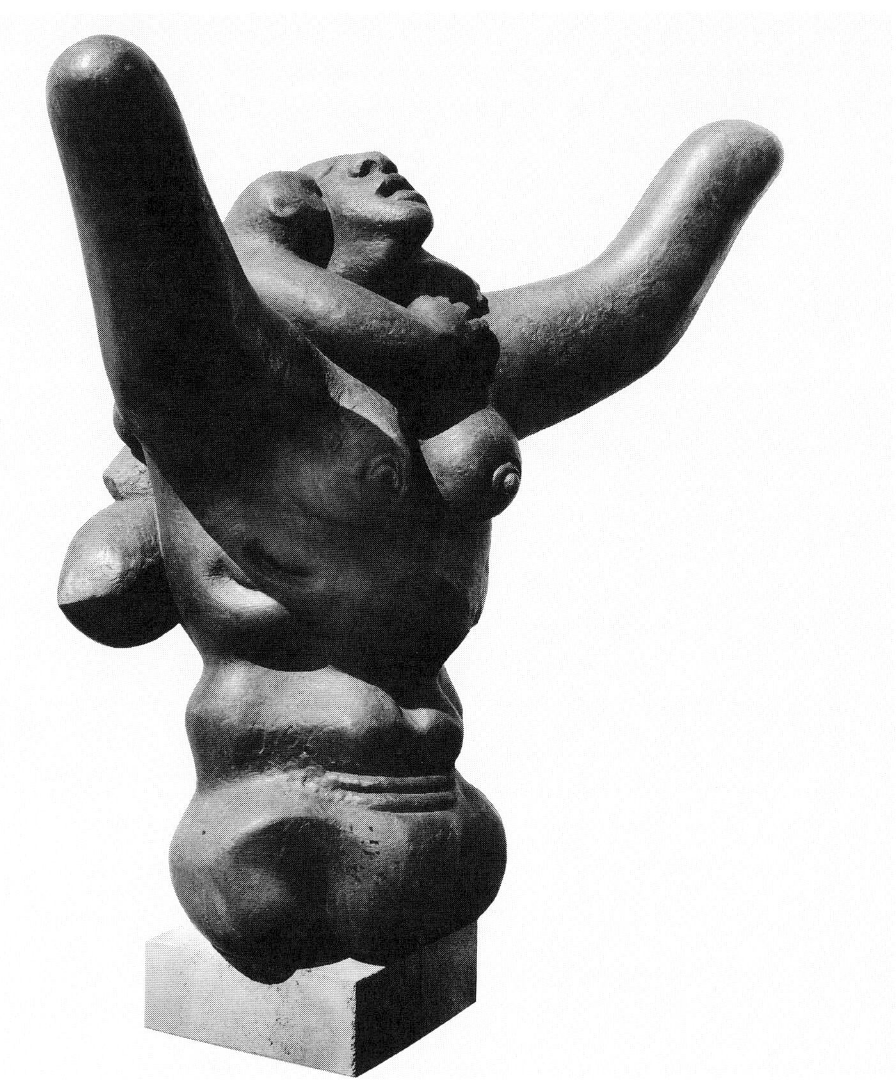

84 *Mother and Child II* 1941–45

York on June 13. They found living accommodation at 42 Washington Square South.

Lipchitz was enormously grateful for the help of the American Rescue Committee, and yet, he said:

> I was frightened about going to the United States, about which I knew very little; and also I had no money or other resources, or even a word of English. It was like starting my life all over again. Despite my concern, curiously enough I also felt a certain exhilaration; I felt young and strong, as though I were just beginning my career once more.[78]

Lipchitz had hoped to be taken on again by Joseph Brummer, who had given him his first one-man exhibition in the United States in 1935, but Brummer was no longer dealing in modern art. Within a few days of arriving in New York, Lipchitz was introduced by Brummer to Curt Valentin. He could not have met a man more sympathetic to the art of sculpture. Lipchitz recalled: "I had only been able to bring with me two plasters and some drawings. Valentin immediately took the drawings and, after a few days, called me and gave me six hundred dollars for those he had sold, taking no commission himself."[79] Lipchitz exhibited at Valentin's Buchholz Gallery at 32 East 57th Street until the dealer's death in 1954.

The first sculptures that Lipchitz made in the United States were, not surprisingly, autobiographical. The 1941 *Arrival*, in which a mother holds aloft a child that has been saved, was a companion piece to *Flight*, made in Toulouse in 1940. Lipchitz associated the 1941 *Return of the Child* (no. 83) with the "feeling of escape from the horror of the fascists to the refuge of the United States."[80] The child is held above the mother's head; this motif, Lipchitz pointed out, went back to his 1914–15 *Mother and Children* (no. 6). As Lipchitz said: "All of my sculpture derives from something in my life, a desire or a dream."[81] He also saw *Return of the Child* as "a symbol of my sculpture that was returning to me."[82] The cast-granite version of *Return of the Child* (Solomon R. Guggenheim Museum, New York) was exhibited in 1945 in the large *European Artists in America* show at the Whitney Museum. In reviewing the exhibition, Clement Greenberg, who was usually critical of the sculptor's larger works, wrote: "Lipchitz's granite *Return of the Child* deserves to be called great...."[83]

Lipchitz, a Jewish refugee now living in New York, continued to express in his sculpture his outrage at the war in Europe. In 1941 he made the *Rape of Europa* (no. 85) in which Europa is fighting against her rapist, Hitler, and trying to kill him. Works such as this, Lipchitz said, "take on a new kind of violence with broken contours and dramatic gestures, perhaps the result of the emotions I felt in relation to the war and the disruption of my entire life."[84]

The 1941–45 *Mother and Child II* (no. 84) originated in a series of drawings Lipchitz had made in Paris in 1939, though he did not begin work on the sculpture until he arrived in the United States. Whereas the 1930 *Mother and Child* (no. 64) evolved from Lipchitz's despair at the death of his sister and father, the 1941–45 sculpture, he said, had to do with the Second World War: "There is despair involved in this sculpture but also, I feel, a kind of hope and optimism and even a form of aggression."[85]

In 1942, when Lipchitz was working at the Modern Art Foundry, he developed an urge to do transparents again, as he had in Paris in the mid 1920s. But, he said, "These were different from the earlier ones in the sense that I had now solved all the technical problems so I could work in an extremely free, lyrical manner."[86] Most of them, such as the extraordinary *Myrah* 1942 (see notes for no. 86) had personal associations for Lipchitz, in that they were inspired by a woman with whom he was in love at the time. *The Prayer* 1943 (no. 88), perhaps the largest sculpture he had made directly in wax, was technically extremely difficult to cast in bronze. The sculpture was Lipchitz's most anguished reaction to the fate of the Jews in Europe. As he explained:

> It was done at the most terrible moment of the war; it was a prayer, a Jewish prayer of expiation... Actually the figure is not a rabbi; it is Everyman, every Jew who has to do this, who is asking for forgiveness... The entire subject is the Jewish people, whom I thought of as the innocent victims in this horrible war... It had something to do with the horror I felt about Auschwitz and the other Nazi concentration camps.[87]

In 1943 Lipchitz began work on an important commission for the new Ministry of Education and Health building in Rio de Janeiro. He returned to the theme of Prometheus strangling the vulture, the subject of the sculpture he had made for the Exposition Internationale in Paris in 1937 (nos. 89 and 90). Due to a misunderstand-

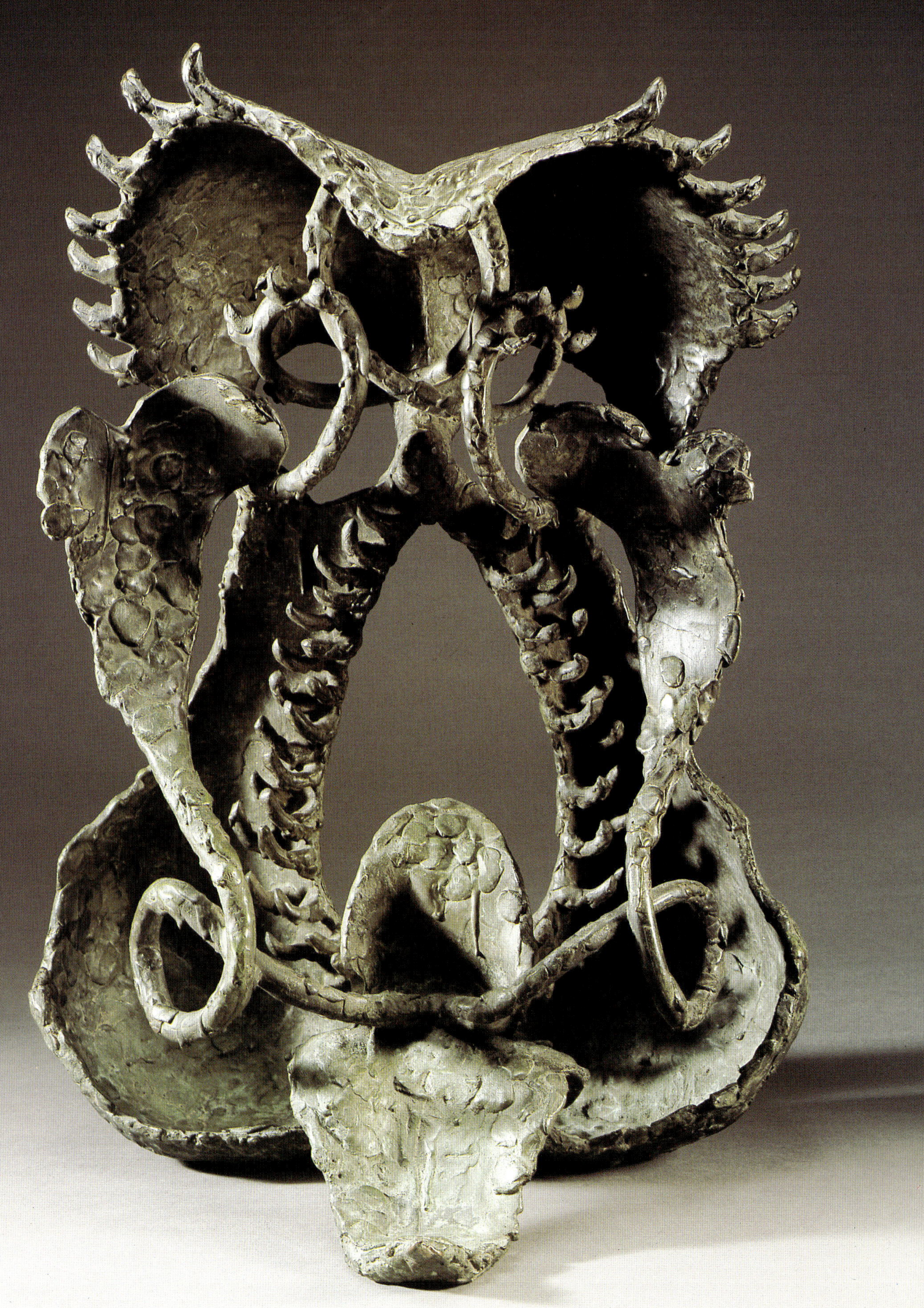

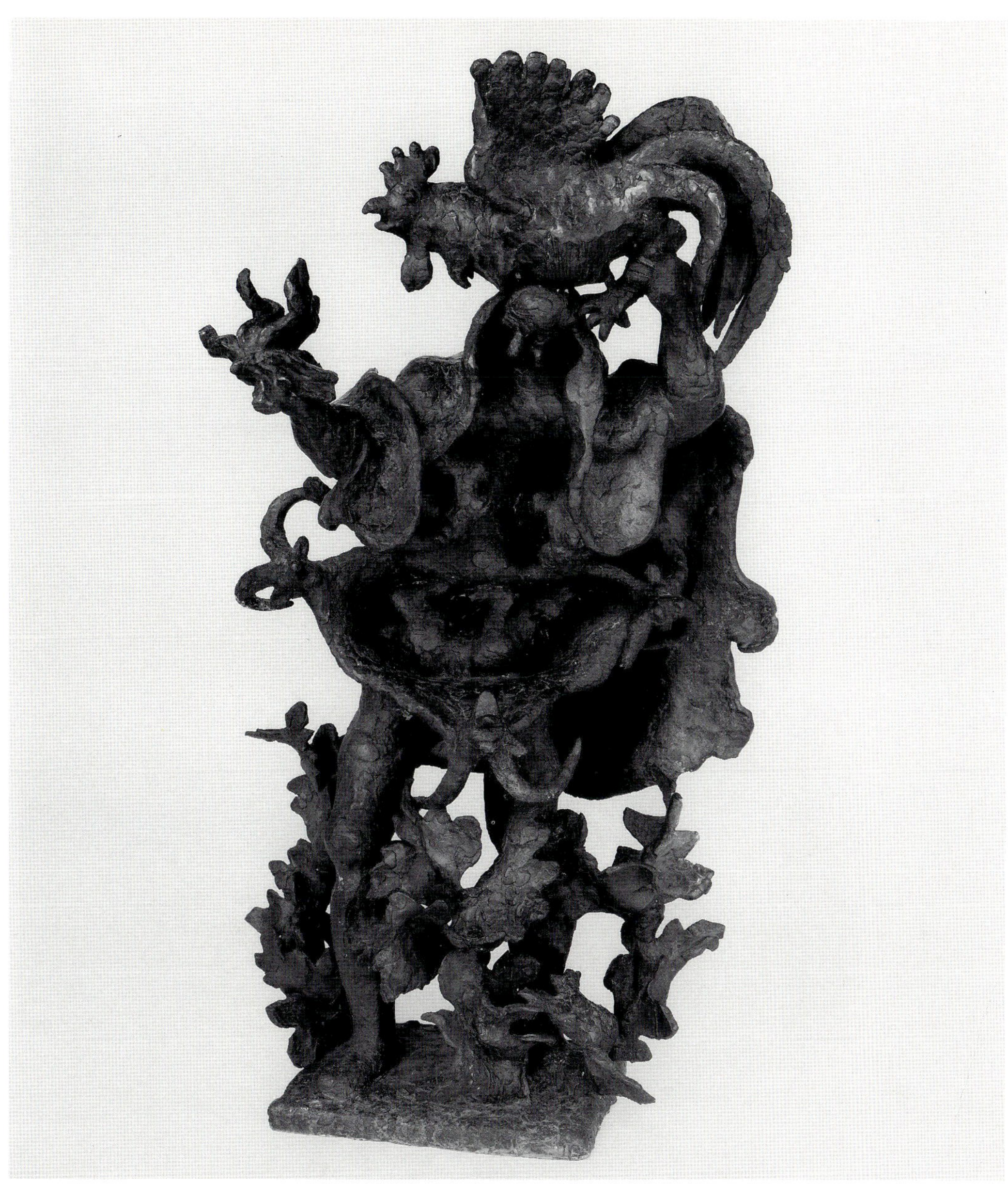

88 *The Prayer* 1943

ing, the model that Lipchitz sent to Brazil, which was about one-third the size of the projected sculpture, was, he explained, "placed on the enormous wall in the reduced scale of the model rather than in the full scale intended."[88] The commission fell through and was never realized. The sculpture was, however, enlarged. There are casts of the 102-inch-high 1944–53 version of *Prometheus Strangling the Vulture* at the Philadelphia Museum of Art and at the Walker Art Center, Minneapolis.

Lipchitz and his wife, Berthe, returned to France in 1946, and he had a large exhibition at the Galerie Maeght. At the opening, Lipchitz was asked if he would consider making a sculpture of the Virgin for the Church of Nôtre-Dame-de-Toute-Grâce at Assy, a village in the French Alps. The work was commissioned by a Father Couturier, who had been a painter before becoming a Dominican monk. Lipchitz described Couturier as an extremely interesting man who "unfortunately died young, but was instrumental in commissioning many modern artists, including Léger, Rouault,

86 *Myrah* 1942

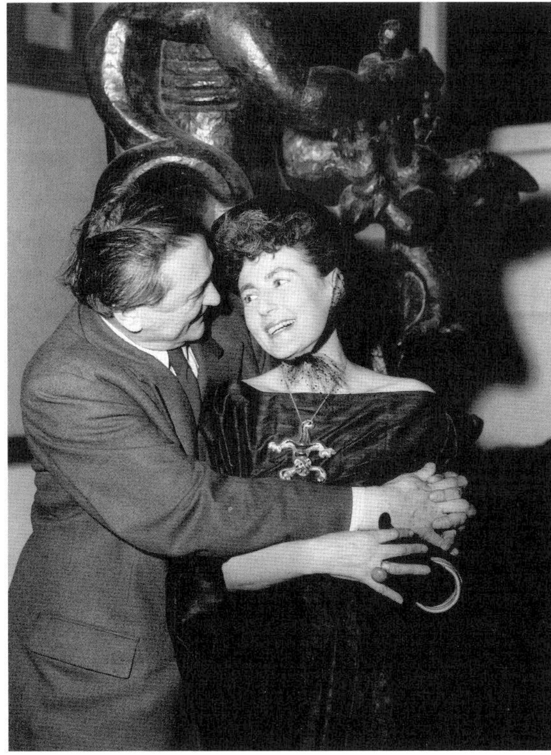

fig. 21
Jacques and Yulla Lipchitz. (Courtesy Yulla Lipchitz)

Bonnard and others to make contemporary religious works for his church."[89] Lipchitz accepted the commission, which he later described as "one of the most important things I have ever done. It has also been, in an emotional sense, one of the pieces with most significance for me."[90]

When Lipchitz was forced to leave France in 1941, he left everything behind and was reconciled to the idea that all his possessions were lost or destroyed. On his return in 1946, as he later explained, "I found that not everything was lost; a great number of things could be retrieved, and so I started to run all over France like a poisoned mouse to recover my possessions – I even bought some of my own things back."[91] He considered settling in France again, but, he said, "I found that the spirit had changed. My old friends had dispersed and I did not like the atmosphere, so I went back to America."[92] Berthe, however, did not like living in the United States, and Lipchitz returned to New York in 1947 without her. They parted on friendly terms.

Lipchitz was not alone for long. In 1944, while he was still working on the ill-fated Prometheus commission, Lipchitz had met Yulla Halberstadt. "She was," Lipchitz recounted, "brought to my studio by the poet and Zionist leader Leif Jaffe. Jaffe had been a friend of my parents, had lived in the same town, and I had met him as a boy. I made a portrait of him and he brought Yulla, who is a sculptor, to look at it. So she came to me as a critic and then became my wife."[93] They were married in 1948 (see fig. 21).

On his return to America Lipchitz settled in Hastings-on-Hudson, north of New York City. His sculpture continued to mirror the fate of the Jewish people and ultimately the birth of the state of Israel. The most important series of sculptures of 1947–48 bore the collective title *Miracle* (see no. 95). In 1947 a shipload of Jewish immigrants sailed from Europe to Palestine, which was then still a British mandate. The Jews were

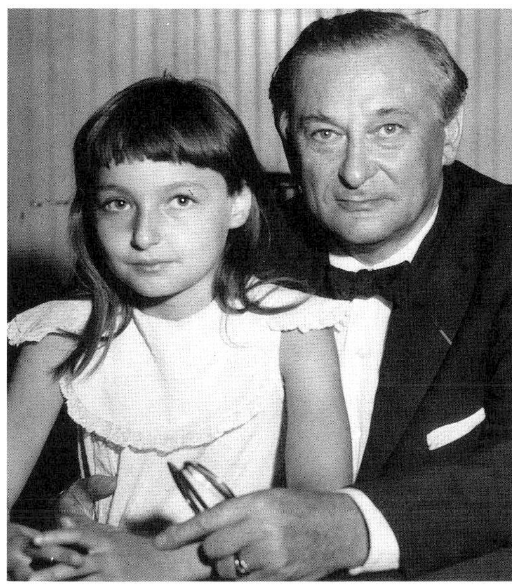

fig. 22
Lipchitz with his daughter, Lolya Rachel. (Courtesy Yulla Lipchitz)

not allowed to disembark, and the *Exodus* was forced to go from port to port. Lipchitz described his reaction as follows:

> It was a terrible event, one that made me sick with anger and despair. There were many prayers and fasts among Jews for the safety of this ship, and I also fasted. It was during my fast that the idea for this sculpture appeared. I was certain that Israel would ultimately become a state, and the sculpture was in effect the birth of this new state of Israel, a candlestick with the Jew praying... *Miracle II* was a prayer of thanksgiving that Israel had officially become a state...[94]

In 1948 and 1949, with the formation of the state of Israel still very much on his mind, Lipchitz turned to the theme of sacrifice (no. 99), of which there were a number of versions. *Hagar I* of 1948 (no. 96) was inspired by Lipchitz's obsession with the mother-and-child theme and by his concerns about the conflict between Israel and the Arabs. "Despite my admiration for and love of Israel," he said, "I feel strongly that the Jews and the Arabs should make peace, that they should live together as brothers, which they were able to do for many centuries."[95] Again Lipchitz has taken his subject from the Bible (Gen. 21) and adapted it in the context of contemporary events.

With the birth of his daughter, Lolya Rachel, in October 1948, Lipchitz's mood of anger and pessimism, which was reflected in *Miracle II* (no. 95) and *Sacrifice* (no. 99), changed dramatically (fig. 22). He later described his feelings at the time:

> It was a fantastic experience at the age of fifty-nine [*sic*] finally to have my own child, particularly a daughter, which is what I wanted, partially because I wanted her to have my mother's name. The result in my sculpture was a series of extremely lyrical works on the theme of the mother and child. These have the curvilinear movement in-the-round of the dancers of the earlier 1940s, but the mood is now much more tender and obviously maternal [see no. 98].[96]

101 *Chisel Piece* 1952 (p. 44)
106 *Here are the Fruits and the Flowers* 1955–56 (p. 45)

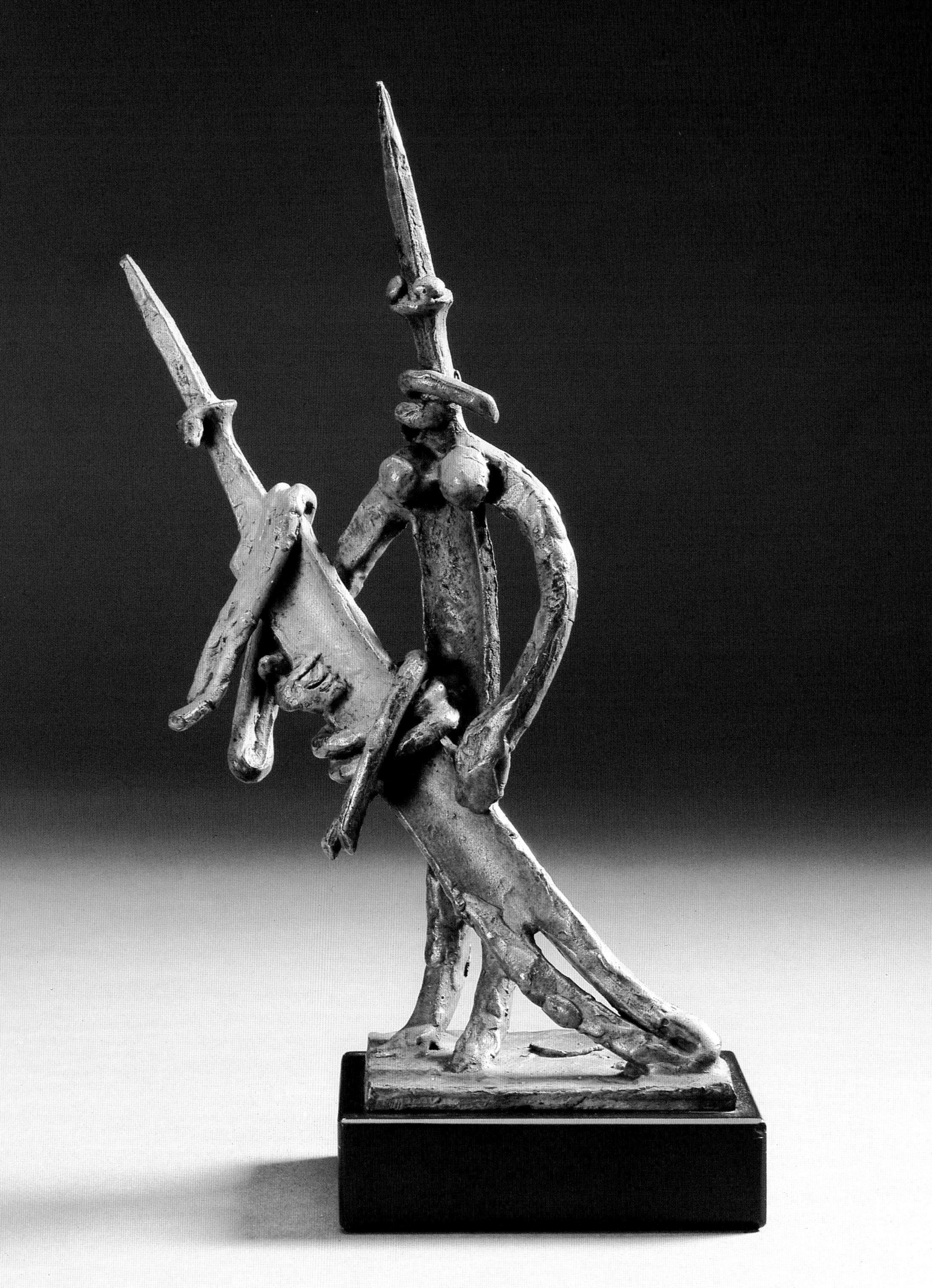

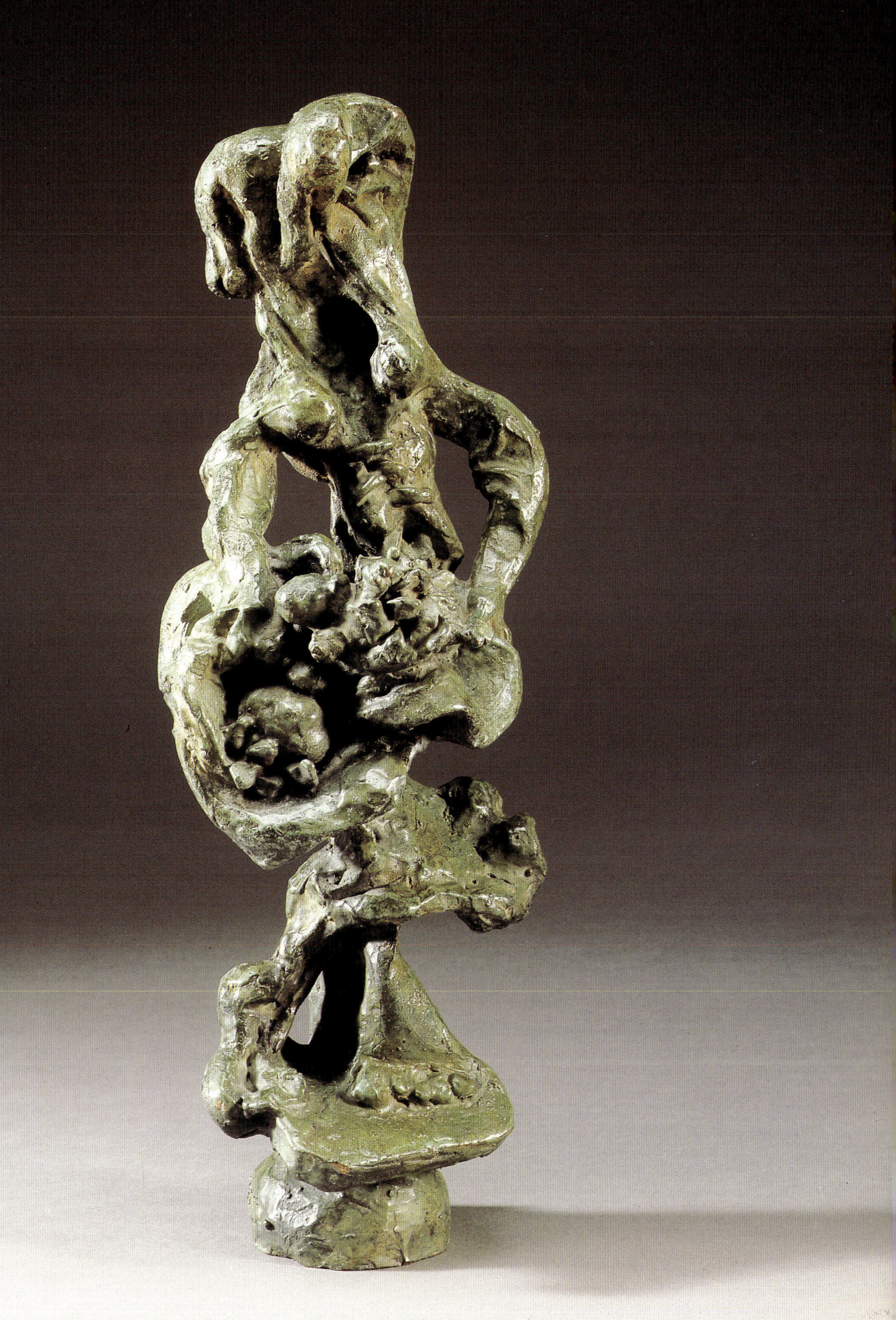

In the early 1950s Lipchitz was beginning to have the opportunity to work on a more monumental scale. In 1950 he received an important commission to create a sculpture for Fairmount Park in Philadelphia. He chose as his theme the spirit of American enterprise. By 1951 Lipchitz was working on two commissions, *Nôtre-Dame de Liesse* (see no. 104), for the church at Assy, France, and the model for the Fairmount Park sculpture (see no. 105). Then, on January 5, 1952, there was a disastrous fire in Lipchitz's 23rd Street studio, which he said was "one of the greatest tragedies of my life."[97] He described the total devastation:

> Almost everything in the studio had burned away, and some parts of plaster that had not burned were demolished. The model of the Virgin had disappeared. The table on which it had been standing had burned and the statue itself had simply melted. The armature for the *Enterprise* was nothing but some bent iron... My pieces from my collection, some of my best African pieces that had not yet been unpacked, were destroyed along with a portfolio of drawings, such things as three Cézannes, a Goya ink drawing, and others by Poussin and Gris. My first reaction was that of horror, as though my entire life, all my children, had been destroyed, but then this changed to a kind of fury, a passionate need to begin working again to recover all the lost years.[98]

Yet again Lipchitz showed his remarkable resilience. He had lost his studio, his sculpture, and his collection. After the fire he had nowhere to work, but the Modern Art Foundry in Long Island City offered him a temporary studio. As he recounted later:

> I did not know how to begin. Here I was sixty-one years old, and I felt empty. So I decided to make a sculpture every day with the wax chisels I had made at the foundry [in 1951], without thinking too much about what I was doing, just working. In twenty-six working days I made twenty-six sculptures, and I was cured of my depression. These little chisel figures [see nos. 100–103] were very spontaneous pieces done rapidly and directly, without much conscious thought. From their almost subconscious spontaneity they could be referred to as "semi-automatics".... I think it is an expression of my ever-growing optimism that these figures, which are light and cheerful and gay, should have emerged so immediately from one of my moments of desperate tragedy.[99]

After the fire, American museums launched a campaign to raise funds to enable Lipchitz to build a new studio at his home in Hastings-on-Hudson. It was designed by Philip L. Goodwin and Martin Lowenfish. Lipchitz moved into the new studio in 1953 and resumed work on the Virgin for the church at Assy and *The Spirit of Enterprise* for Fairmount Park in Philadelphia (see no. 105). In 1954 a major retrospective of Lipchitz's sculpture and drawings was organized by the Museum of Modern of Art, New York; it also travelled to the Walker Art Center, Minneapolis, and the Cleveland Museum of Art. That same year his friend and dealer, Curt Valentin, died. Lipchitz was subsequently represented in New York by Otto Gerson's Fine Arts Associates and then by the Marlborough Gallery Inc., New York.

In 1955, as a reaction to working on his monumental sculptures, Lipchitz began a series he called his semi-automatics. Lipchitz would, he explained, "just splash or squeeze a piece of warm wax in my hands, put it in a basin of water without looking at

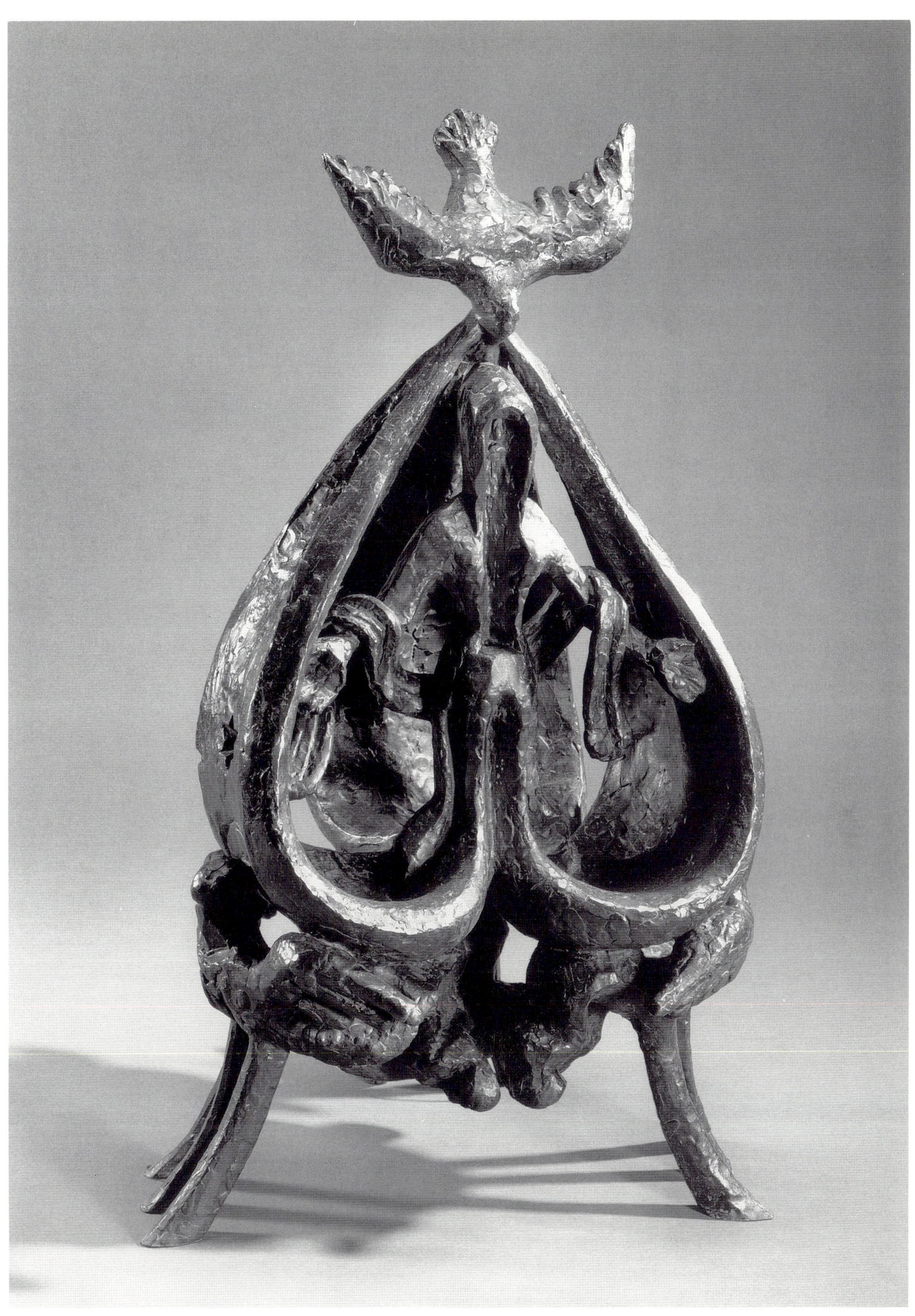

104 *Study for Nôtre-Dame de Liesse* 1953

it, and then let it harden in cold water. When I took it out and examined it, the lump suggested many different images to me. Automatically a particular image would emerge several times and this I would choose to develop and clarify."[100] In the 1955–56 *Here are the Fruits and the Flowers* (no. 106), the overall shape as it emerged from the water obviously suggested the subject, with details such as ribs, toes, fruit and flowers consciously defined later.

For the remainder of Lipchitz's working life he divided his time between large public commissions and the need to work on a fairly regular basis on small, experimental works. For example, in 1958 he was working on several versions of *Between Heaven and Earth* (no. 111) which developed from his *Nôtre Dame de Liesse* (Our Lady of Joy) for the church at Assy. Also in 1958 he worked on a marvellous series of bronzes entitled *To the Limit of the Possible* that grew out of the semi-automatics of 1955–56. Lipchitz explained the new technique:

> After my tentative experiment in 1956 or 1957 of introducing an actual dried-out flower into a semi-automatic, I had the idea of taking real objects which somehow impressed me and incorporating them into wax models for bronze sculpture. The question in my mind was whether it would be possible to cast this combination in bronze.[101]

A work such as *Freedom* of 1958 (no. 108), from the series *To the Limit of the Possible*, challenges one to try to identify the found objects that Lipchitz incorporated into the sculpture. He said he used in the series everything "from driftwood to stuffed birds bought in novelty shops, sculptural mallets, baskets, flowers, and vegetables."[102] In the context of this series Lipchitz mentioned the sixteenth-century Milanese painter Arcimboldo, who painted heads composed of plants and vegetables. In 1971, Lipchitz made a sculpture entitled *Homage to Arcimboldo* (no. 129). It should be noted that Lipchitz was not interested at this time or during his Cubist years (1915–25) in making collages directly out of different materials, as Picasso and Laurens had done. He said of the series *To the Limit of the Possible*: "I wanted to learn how to combine these elements [found objects] into a unity in bronze so that they all became one..."[103]

The series *To the Limit of the Possible* points to several important characteristics of Lipchitz's sculpture and working method that have largely been ignored. Throughout his life he remained constant in his use of bronze and stone, the traditional materials of sculpture. His views on the subject of direct carving (the doctrine of truth to material that Moore and Hepworth believed in passionately in the 1920s and 1930s) and modelling were clearly stated in a 1945 interview with James Johnson Sweeney:

> You asked me, once, what my feelings were on the subject of direct cutting and modelling in sculpture. Let me say that I am, in a manner of speaking, an adversary of direct cutting. For a sculptor today I regard modelling the more adequate technique... Ideas come with an unimaginable rapidity; they are capricious; the artist must catch them and fix them as quickly as possible. And the technique best suited for this is modelling, not the slower method of direct cutting.[104]

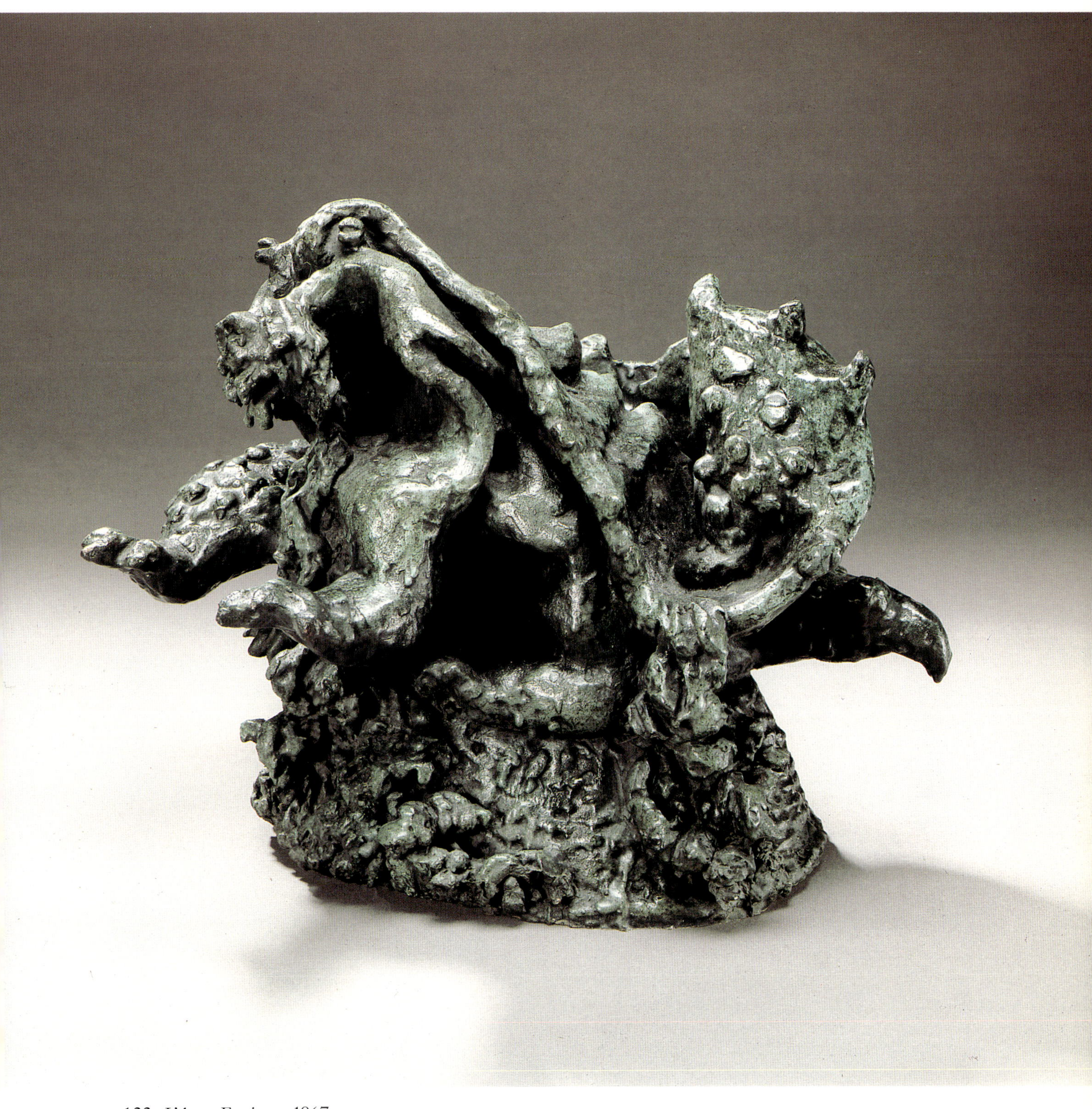

122 *L'Arno Furioso* 1967

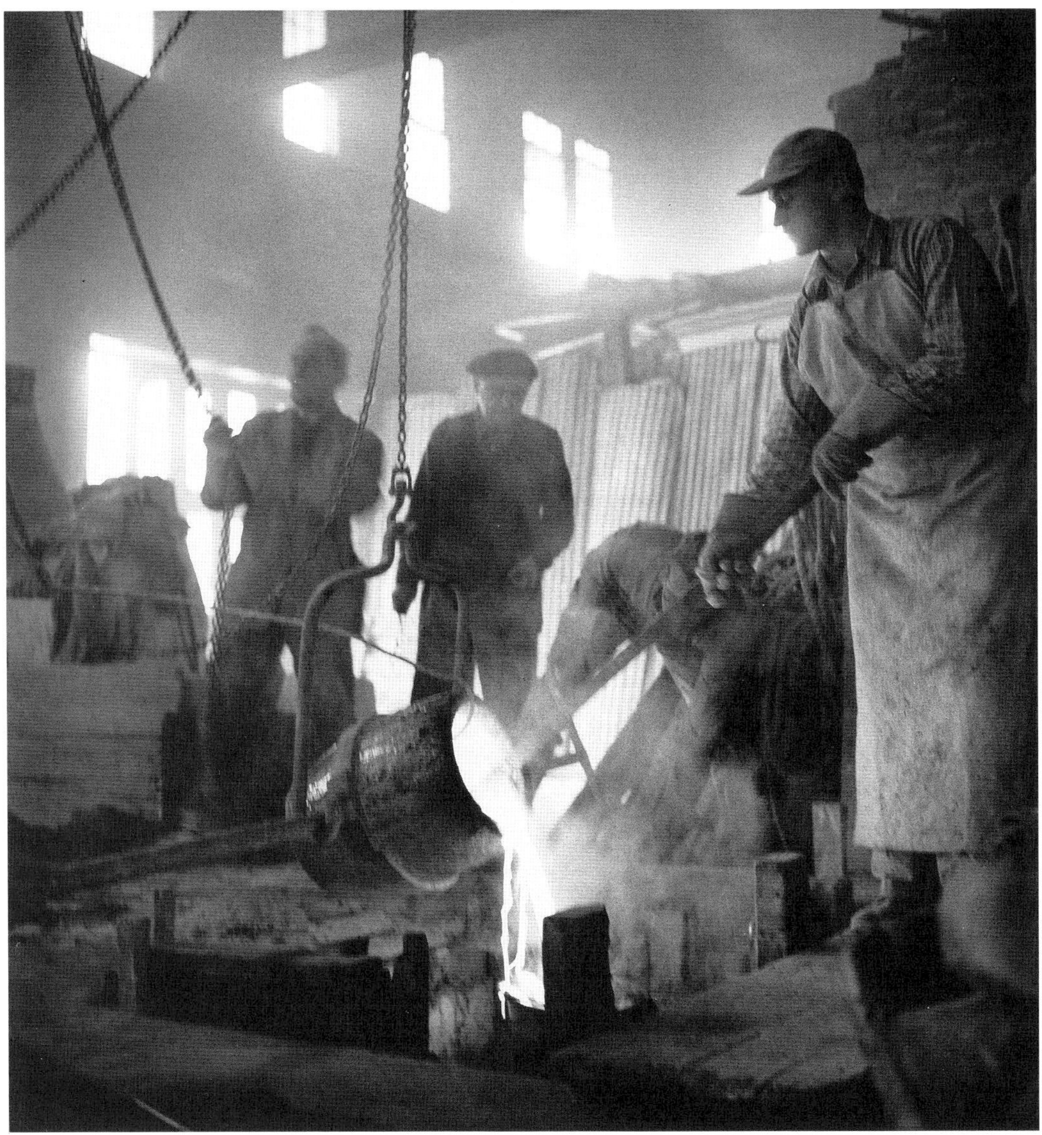

fig. 23 Lipchitz supervising the bronze casting of his sculpture in New York. (Courtesy Yulla Lipchitz)

The point is surely that modelling in clay was the more adequate technique for Lipchitz, as it had been for Rodin. Direct carving in stone or wood was too slow and cumbersome for their explosive imaginations. They both employed professional stone-carvers. And yet Lipchitz had his own belief in truth to materials, and his material was bronze. More than any other sculptor of his generation, with the exception of Brancusi, Lipchitz was deeply involved not only with the initial process of bronze casting but with the finish or patina of his work (see fig. 23). As the significance of his intimate involvement with his bronzes has not been fully appreciated, his comments on the subject are worth quoting in full:

> I have been a bronze worker now for over sixty years, constantly in foundries, since bronze is a material I love, and I think I have seen and myself experimented with almost everything that can be done in bronze. Yet, when I say this, I realize that I am constantly finding new possibilities. My approach to bronze sculpture is at times more poetical than traditionally sculptural. I remember I had the idea almost twenty years ago of seeing whether I could combine certain natural objects, not only twigs and branches but even leaves or

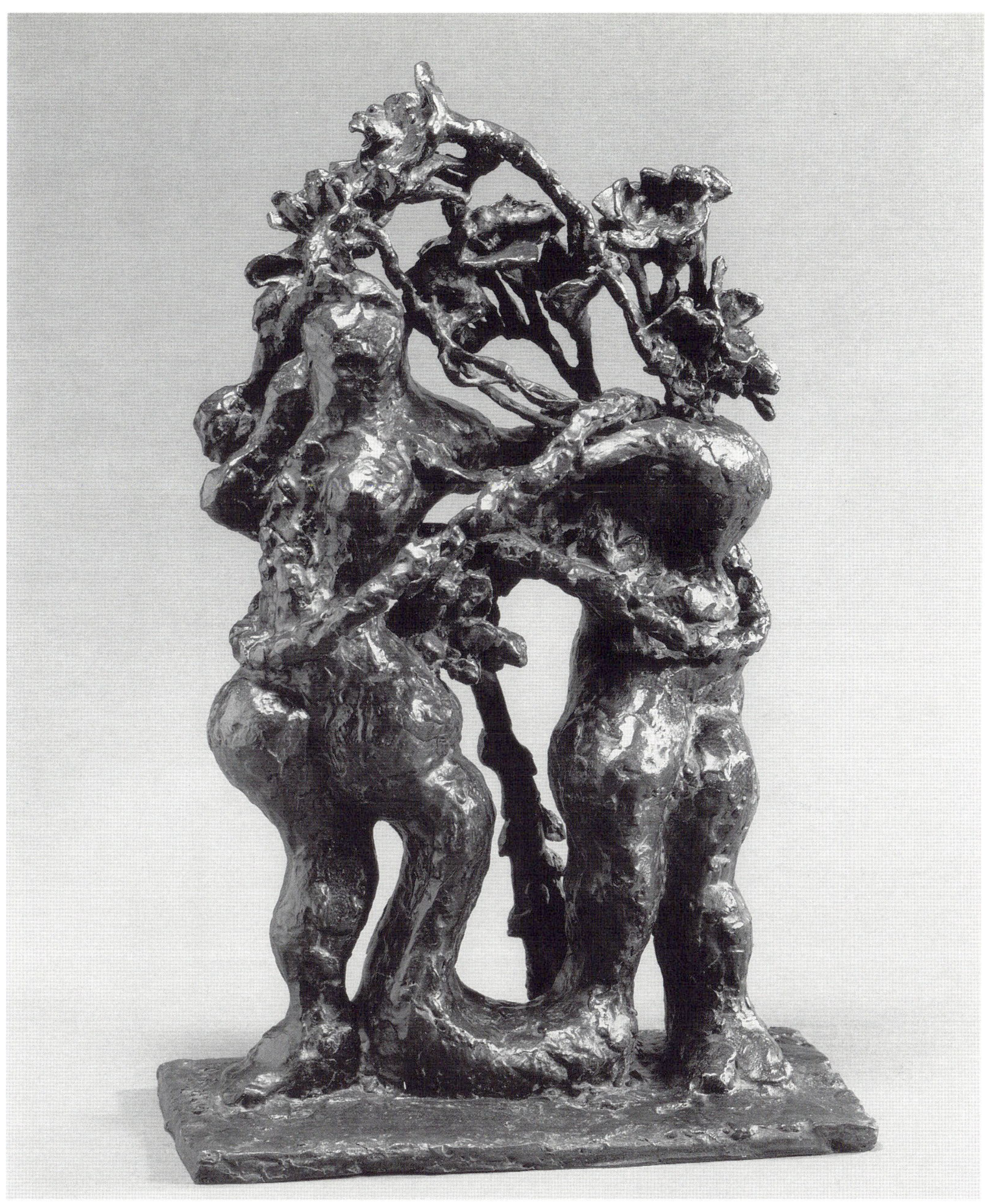

127 *The First Meeting* 1970–71

> flowers... I called this series *To the Limit of the Possible*, meaning the limit of the possibilities of bronze casting. But as I have learned more, these limits have become even further extended. I work both with sand molds and the lost-wax process, but I really prefer the lost-wax because this I can handle and retouch... In many waxes, when I do an edition of seven, I make changes in every one so that each in a sense is unique... I have tried other metals, such as aluminum, but bronze is my first and continuing love because it is so alive, so direct, warm, and fluid. Each piece has my fingerprints all over it.[105]

Lipchitz was the consummate sculptor/craftsman in bronze. His small-scale late works, such as *Freedom* (no. 108), *The Beautiful One* (no. 115) and *The First Meeting* (no. 127), are among the most daring and complex examples of technical virtuosity in the long history of bronze casting.

The late 1950s and the 1960s saw Lipchitz involved with large public commissions and small private sculptures. In 1958 he worked with Philip Johnson on the gateway for the Roofless Church in New Harmony, Indiana (see no. 110 and figs. 25 and 26). Lipchitz visited Italy for the first time in 1962 and began working almost immediately at the Tommasi Foundry in Pietrasanta, near the great marble quarries at Carrara. The first group of bronzes he made was entitled *Images of Italy*; some of them were inspired by Italy, others not. *The Cup of Atonement* (no. 113) was, Lipchitz said, "a personal prayer for forgiveness because I had been unpleasant in some context."[106] *The Tower and Its Shadow* (no. 114) is a strange combination of the leaning tower of Pisa and the draped figure of a woman. Edward F. Fry has summed up the metamorphic, lyric inventiveness of Lipchitz's late work in his description of *The Beautiful One* (no. 115), one of the 1962 *Images of Italy* series:

> Starting with ordinary woven basket handcrafts, he performs a miraculous transformation of his materials into the image of a woman [girl] with fetishistic slit breasts, pigtails, insect-like eyes and nose, and a visage that stares at us with the hollow gaping beauty of an enigma. Such private, lyric works as this, the very casting of which is in itself something of a miraculous accomplishment, should serve to remind us once again of Lipchitz's youthful, endlessly regenerative powers of imagination and expression.[107]

The *Images of Italy* series, although related to the earlier series *To the Limit of the Possible*, is more focused, in that Lipchitz had specific subjects in mind before he began. Before leaving Italy Lipchitz bought a villa in Piere di Camaiore, where he and Yulla subsequently spent their summer months.

In 1963 Lipchitz began work on a commission from the city of Duluth, Minnesota, for a sculpture of the seventeenth-century French explorer Daniel Greysolon, Sieur Duluth (nos. 117–119). In that same year Lipchitz visited Israel for the first time. The visit was, he said, "a very moving experience for me as a Jew. I was fascinated by the old Israel and the contemporary Israel... I feel very emotional about Israel, which has been in a nightmare for two thousand years. But now it is awake."[108] Lipchitz was commissioned in 1967 to do a very large sculpture, *Our Tree of Life* (see nos. 133 and 134), to be placed outside the Hadassah University Hospital on Mount Scopus, Jerusalem's highest peak (see fig. 27). Ever since he had been commissioned in 1947 to make a sculpture of the Virgin for the Catholic church at Assy, Lipchitz had wanted to make something that represented the essence of his Jewish religion. He worked on the ideas that developed into *Our Tree of Life* from the late 1940s until his death in 1973. In 1967 Lipchitz was awarded his last major commission; *Government of the People* (see no. 124) was created for the Municipal Plaza in Philadelphia. From 1967 to 1969 Lipchitz worked on the very large version of *Peace on Earth* (see fig. 24), commissioned for the Music Center in Los Angeles. This sculpture developed from the 1958 bronze *Between Heaven and Earth* (no. 111).

In surveying the long and prolific career of Jacques Lipchitz, one is struck by the depth and range of his emotional reactions to the events of his own life and to the

fig. 24 Lipchitz, Peace on Earth *(plaster for bronze), at Tomassi Pietrasanta Foundry, Italy, late 1960s. The sculptor is seated at right.*

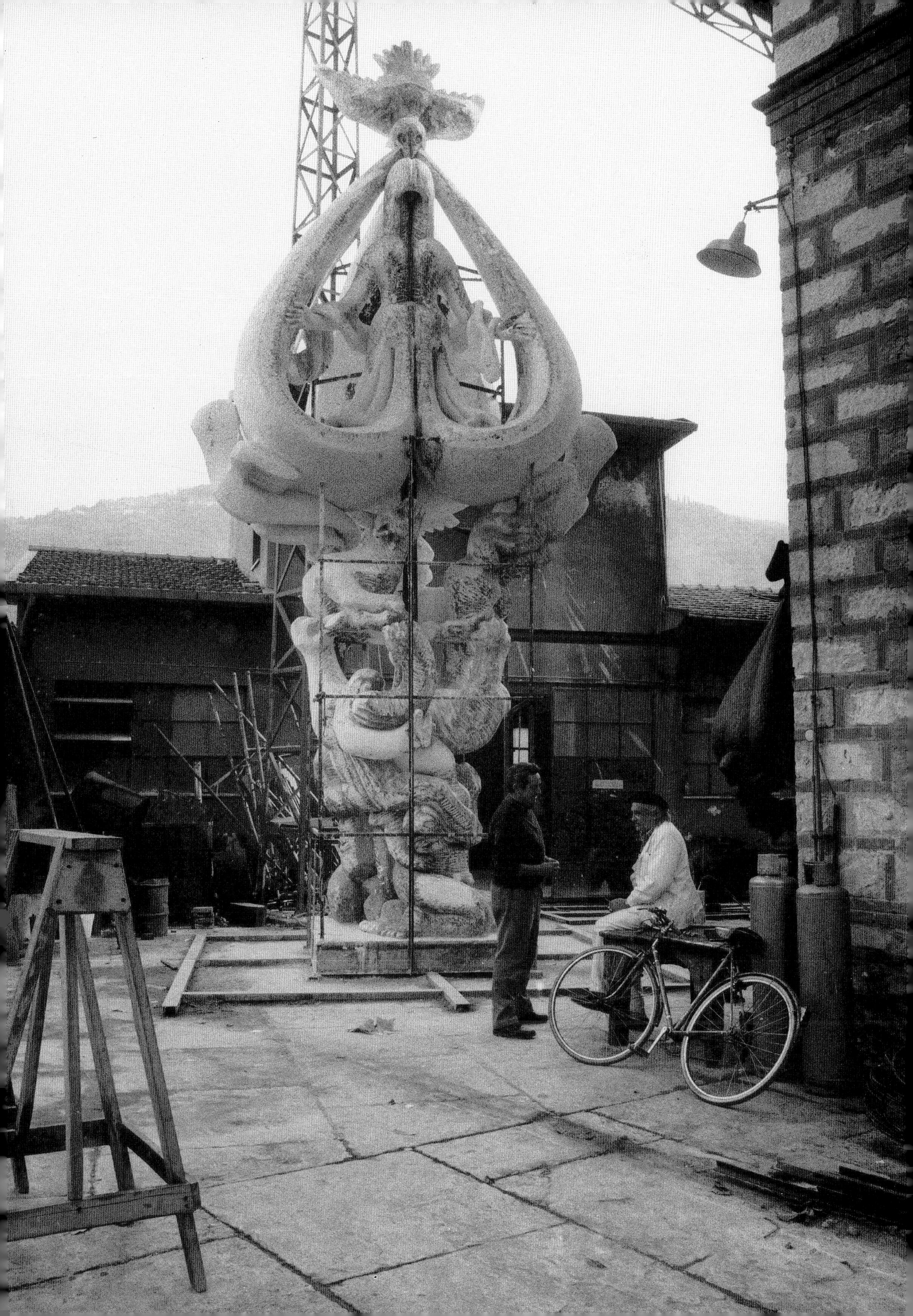

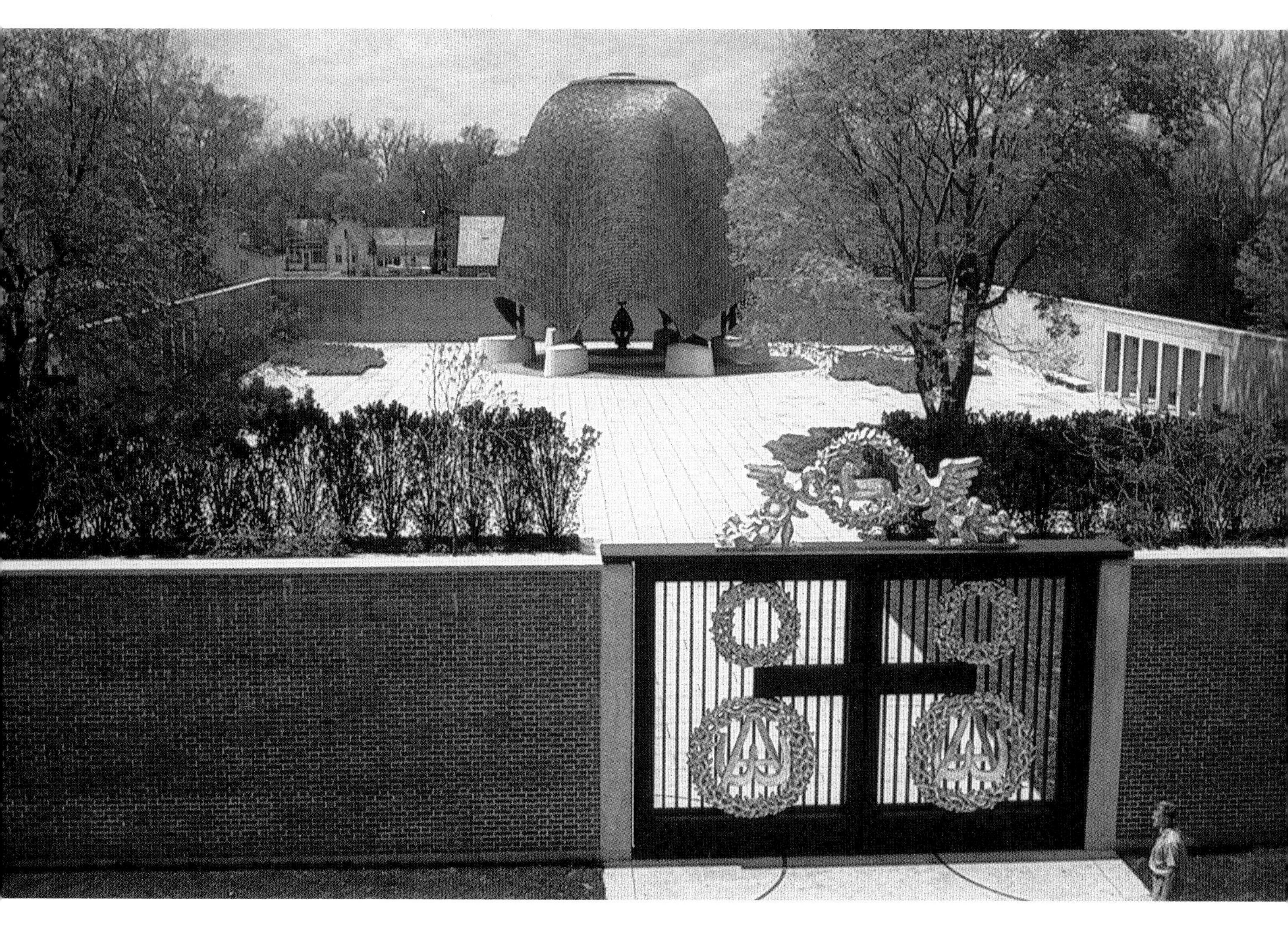

fig. 25
Philip Johnson's Roofless Church, New Harmony, Indiana, which was commissioned for Lipchitz's bronze, Nôtre-Dame de Liesse *(shown above). Lipchitz also designed the ornamental gate in the foreground.*

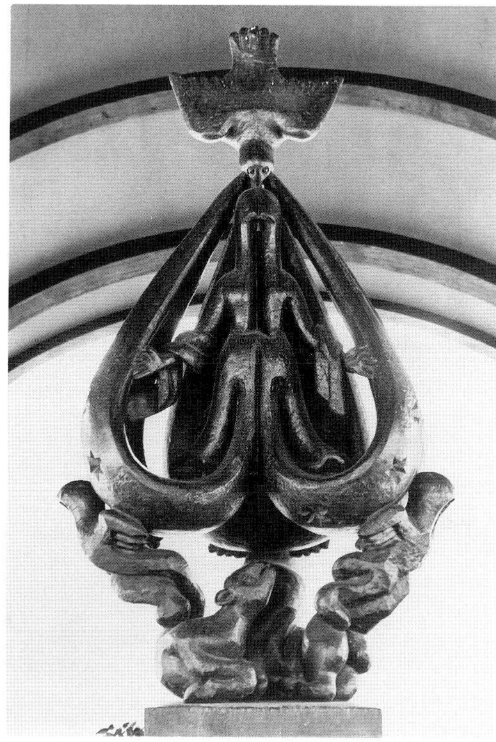

fig. 26
Lipchitz, Nôtre-Dame de Liesse, *1953.*

world around him. For example, after seeing the devastating damage of the flood in Florence in 1966, he recorded his reaction in a series of remarkable small-scale works. The 1967 *L'Arno Furioso* (no. 122) he described as "an animal who is spitting or foaming at the mouth like a dog with rabies. It is very ugly."[109] In *Ponte Vecchio* (no. 123) he translated the bridge into an old woman with a cap and crutches. As Yulla Lipchitz told this author recently, Jacques established a kind of intimate personal relationship with the things he collected. His emotions, she said, were absolutely genuine. Even if a work (*L'Arno Furioso*, for example) was not aesthetically pleasing, it expressed what he felt at the time.

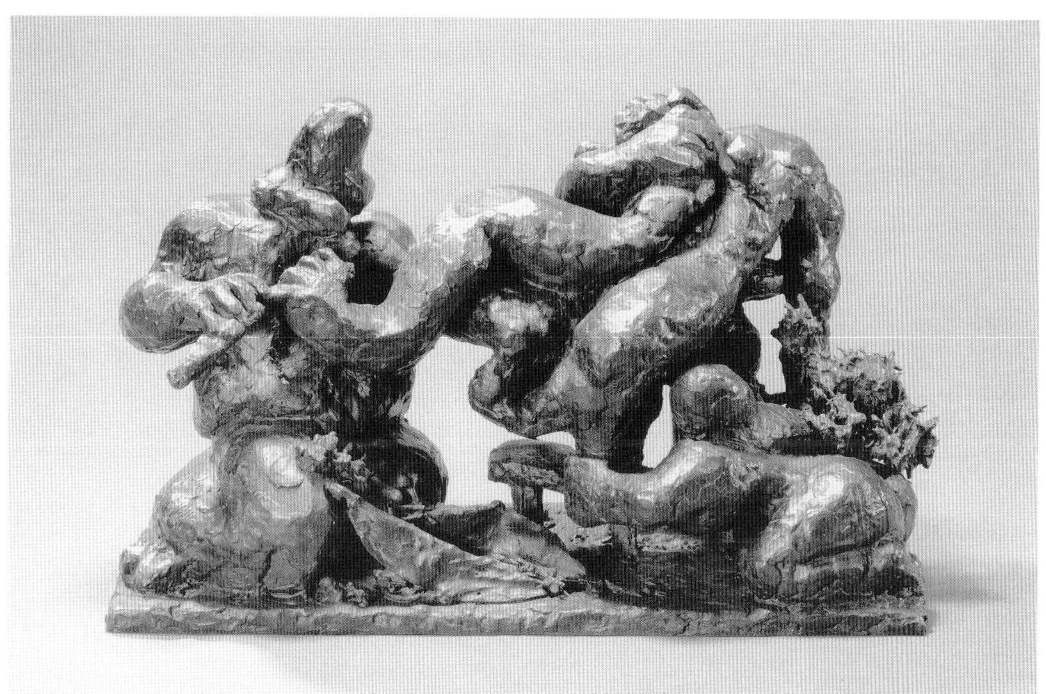

128 *The Death of a Harlequin* 1971

The small, intimate works created during 1970 and 1971, the last years of Lipchitz's working life, reflect somewhat nostalgic interpretations of the work of past artists (*Homage to Dürer* and *Homage to Arcimboldo*, nos. 126 and 129), playful sexuality and an image of feminine beauty (*La danse érotique*, no. 131, and *La Belle*, no. 130). Two of the most moving – and, one can only speculate, the most deeply personal – works are *The Death of a Harlequin* (no. 128) and *The Last Embrace* (no. 132), both made in 1971. The harlequin, the quintessential image of Lipchitz's great Cubist years, is dying. The sculptor proclaimed to the end of his life: "I have always been a Cubist."[110] And now, *The Last Embrace*, the culmination of the theme of so many sculptures over the years: mother and child, lovers, or figures locked in combat. Lipchitz died on the island of Capri on May 26, 1973. On May 29 he was buried in Jerusalem.

Lipchitz, more than any other great sculptor of his generation with the exception of Picasso (Picasso is always the exception), produced a bewildering range of styles and technical innovations. Anyone familiar with modern sculpture will have little trouble identifying the immediately recognizable style of Giacometti, Brancusi, Moore, Hepworth, Arp or Gabo. The same cannot be said of Lipchitz's post-Cubist sculpture, that is to say, that prolific body of work produced between 1925 and 1972. Do *Pierrot Escapes* 1927 (no. 52), *Chimène* 1930 (no. 58), *David and Goliath* 1933 (no. 75), *Myrah* 1942 (no. 86), *Mother and Child* 1949 (no. 98), *The Beautiful One* 1962 (no. 115) and *Homage to Arcimboldo* 1971 (no. 129) appear to be by the same hand? Whereas, for example, Giacometti, Arp and Moore were tenacious in their obsessive focus on producing variations on a limited range of themes or motifs, Lipchitz, like Picasso, was by nature extremely volatile. He worked simultaneously on sculptures that were stylistically and iconographically totally unrelated.

In 1954 Clement Greenberg argued that since breaking away from Cubism Lipchitz "has been unable to develop a principle of inner consistency; none of the different paths he takes seems to lead to the next one..."[111] Thirty-five years later, with Lipchitz's life's work before us, we can see that the richness and extraordinary variety of his images and formal inventions were the result of the sculptor giving free rein to his explosive imagination. If we look closely we discover stylistic and thematic threads running through his work, despite its diversity. Indeed, it was Lipchitz's imagination that provided the inner consistency of his vision.

No one has better expressed the hidden continuity underlying the creative processes of an artist than the poet John Keats. Writing to a friend in 1818, he described the various "shapes" of his own letters. If we substitute the word *sculptures* for *letters*, what an appropriate description we have of the variety of form in Lipchitz's work. Some of his letters, Keats wrote, "are good squares others handsome ovals, and other some orbicular, others spheroid – and why should there not be another species with two rough edges like a Rat-trap?" He goes on to suggest to his friend that "by merely touching the spring delicately and etherially, the rough edges will fly immediately into a proper compactness; and thus you may make a good wholesome loaf, with your own leaven in it, of my fragments."[112]

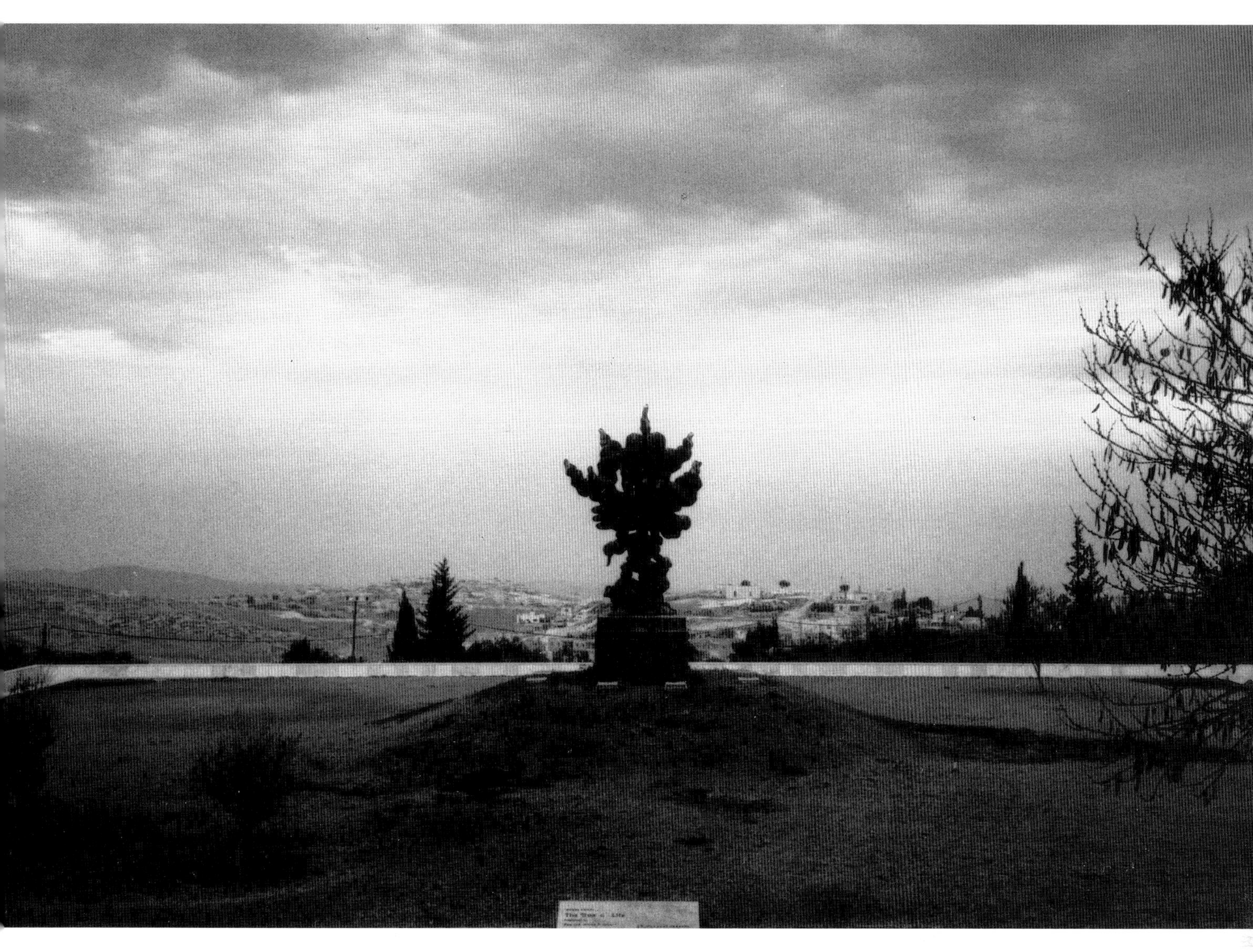

fig. 27
Our Tree of Life, *Mount Scopus, Jerusalem.*

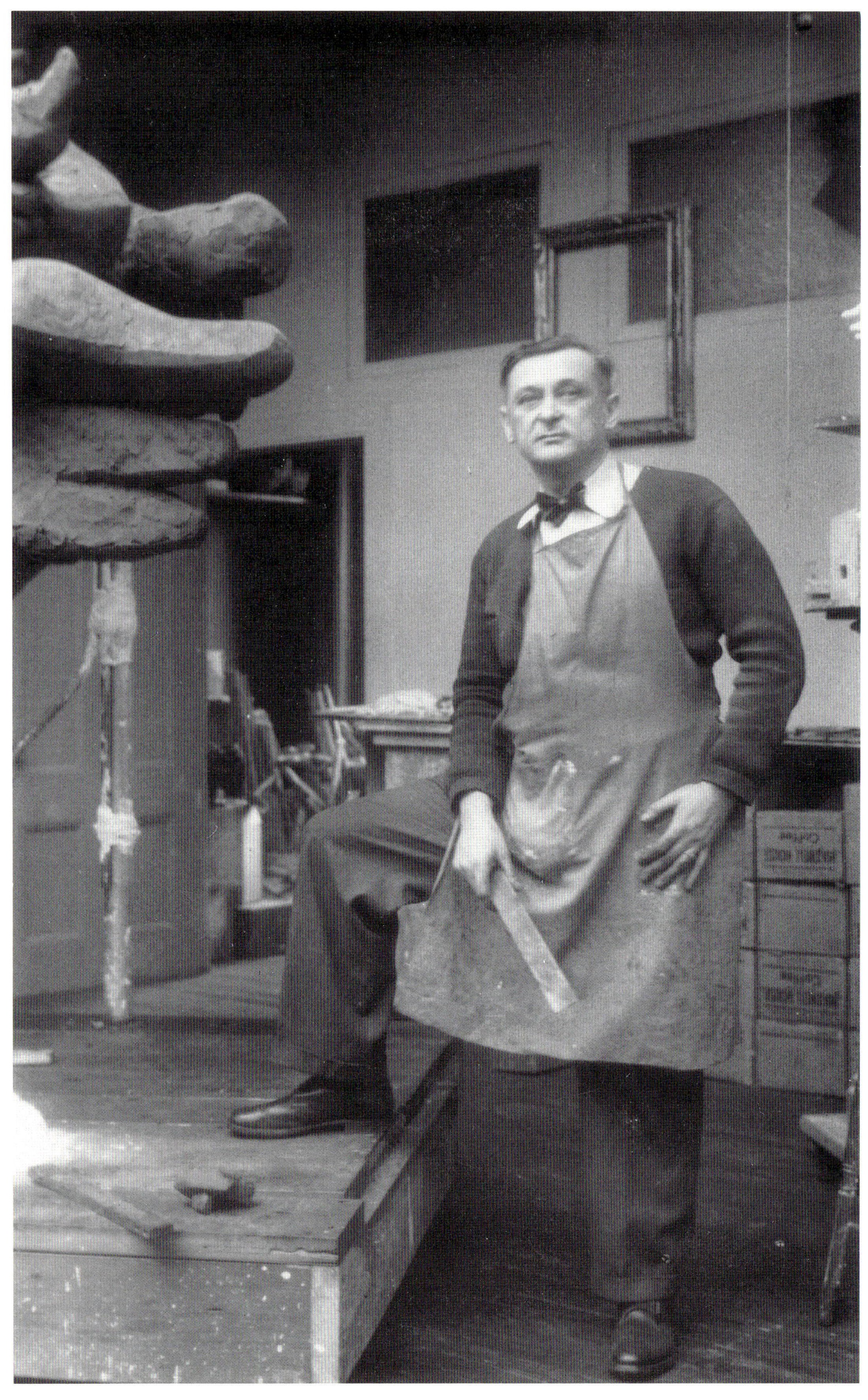

fig. 28
Lipchitz in his studio in Paris.
(Courtesy Yulla Lipchitz)

Catalogue of the Exhibition

■

Sculpture

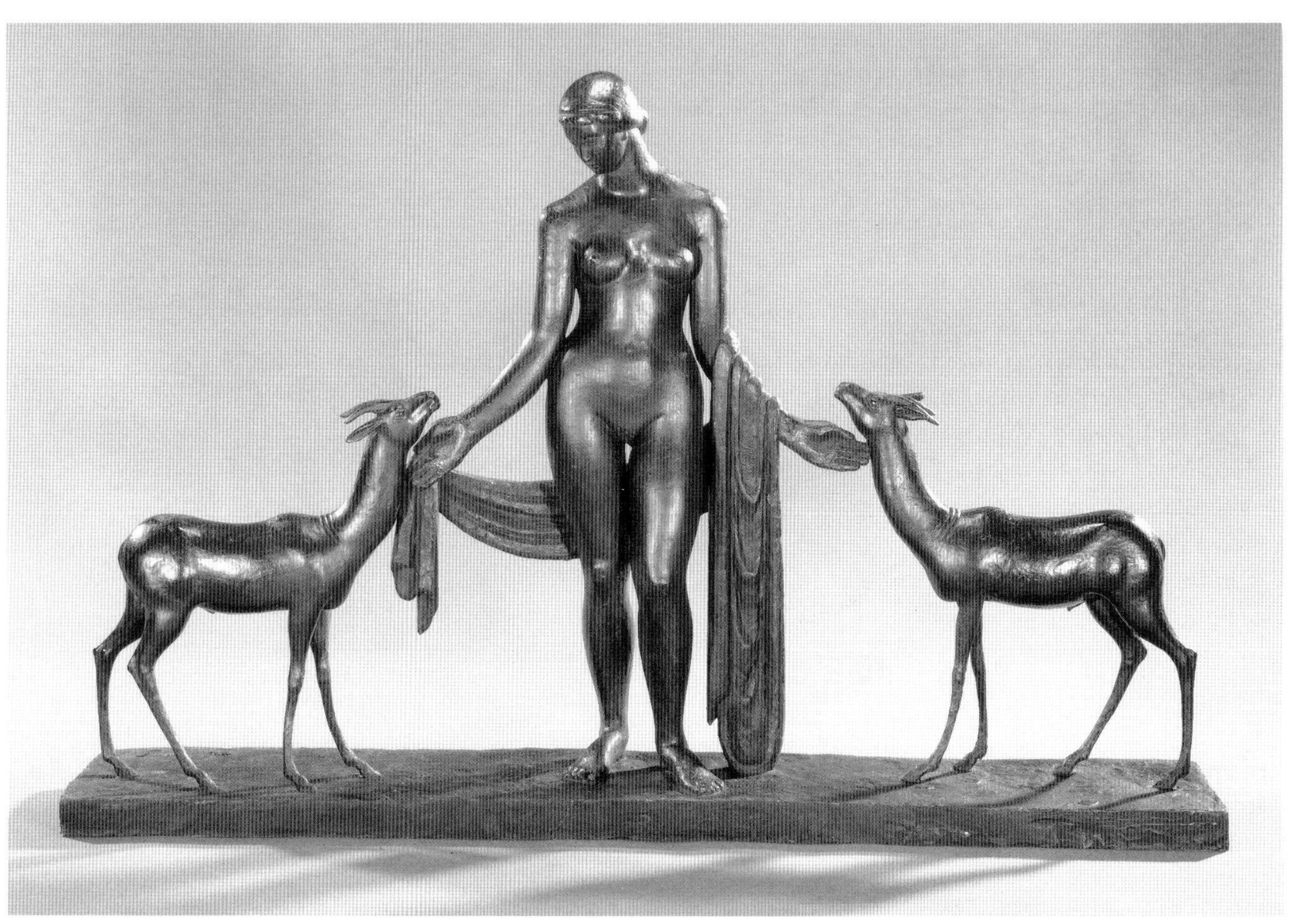

1 *Woman and Gazelles* 1911–12
Bronze 3/7
L. 46½"/118.1 cm
The Estate of Jacques Lipchitz represented by Marlborough International Fine Art AG.

Lipchitz was eighteen when he arrived in Paris in October 1909 from his native Lithuania. Unlike other foreign artists of his generation who settled in the French capital – Picasso, Brancusi, Archipenko and Modigliani – he had little previous academic training. He enrolled at the École des Beaux-Arts, where he studied with Jean-Antoine Injalbert, and then transferred to the Académie Julian, where he worked with Raoul Verlet. His traditional academic instruction included drawing and modelling from life, as well as compositions based on subjects from classical antiquity and from the Bible. It was not until 1913 that his work began, tentatively at first, to reflect the revolutionary discoveries of the Parisian avant-garde.

Woman and Gazelles, Lipchitz's first major sculpture, was made in 1911 or 1912, while he was studying at the Académie Julian. He first made the gazelle after a sketching trip to the Jardin des Plantes, and he subsequently decided to combine it with a female nude, which he modelled at art school. *Woman and Gazelles* met with considerable success when the group was exhibited in plaster at the 1913 Salon d'Automne. The sculpture originally included one gazelle, but Lipchitz decided to balance the composition by adding another.

Lipchitz's work of 1911–12, which includes several portrait heads, has much in common with the continuation of the classical tradition represented in the work of Bourdelle, Dalui, Despiau and, above all, Maillol. Indeed, according to Deborah Stott, "Lipchitz remembered that he was drawn to the balanced, self-contained sculpture of Maillol and works in the Greek galleries of the Louvre...."[1] The figure differs from Maillol's sculpture in the elongation of the arms and the slender body. And yet *Woman and Gazelles*, in the balance and equilibrium of the simplified treatment of the volumes, shares with Maillol's timeless nudes a feeling of classical calm.

2 *Pregnant Woman* 1912
Bronze 1/7
H. 24½″/62.2 cm
The Estate of Jacques Lipchitz represented by Marlborough International Fine Art AG.

Pregnant Woman, LIKE NO. 1 ABOVE, IS FIRMLY ROOTED in the classical/Maillolesque tradition that informed Lipchitz's short-lived academic period (1911–12). Despite the success of *Woman and Gazelles*, Lipchitz felt dissatisfied with the conservative Beaux-arts tradition in which he had been working and became, he said, "more conscious of the new findings in painting that were all around me."[2] This is evidently a reference to the Analytic Cubism of Picasso and Braque, which was soon to change profoundly the development of his sculpture. It was not until 1913, however, that Lipchitz's work reflected his first tentative break from academic conventions.

Pregnant Woman was probably the last major work of his student years. It was done without a model, because, Lipchitz tells us, he couldn't afford one. Could he not have worked from a model in one of the art classes, or was he consciously trying to distance himself from visual confrontation with his subject? Certainly, the disproportionately elongated lower torso and legs suggest a work based on the imagination rather than on the observation of nature. The sculpture, he said, "has to do with the mother-and-child theme, something which – perhaps because of my close attachment to my own mother – has always been of greatest importance to me."[3]

Often, in the formative work of an artist, certain formal characteristics are established that, in retrospect seem prophetic of future trends. Such is the case in *Woman and Gazelles* and *Pregnant Woman*, whose symmetrical poses and frontality are found in many of Lipchitz's later works – for example, the great *Figure* 1926–30 (no. 51). Throughout his life, Lipchitz's oeuvre oscillated between symmetrical compositions on the one hand and a twisting Baroque movement on the other.

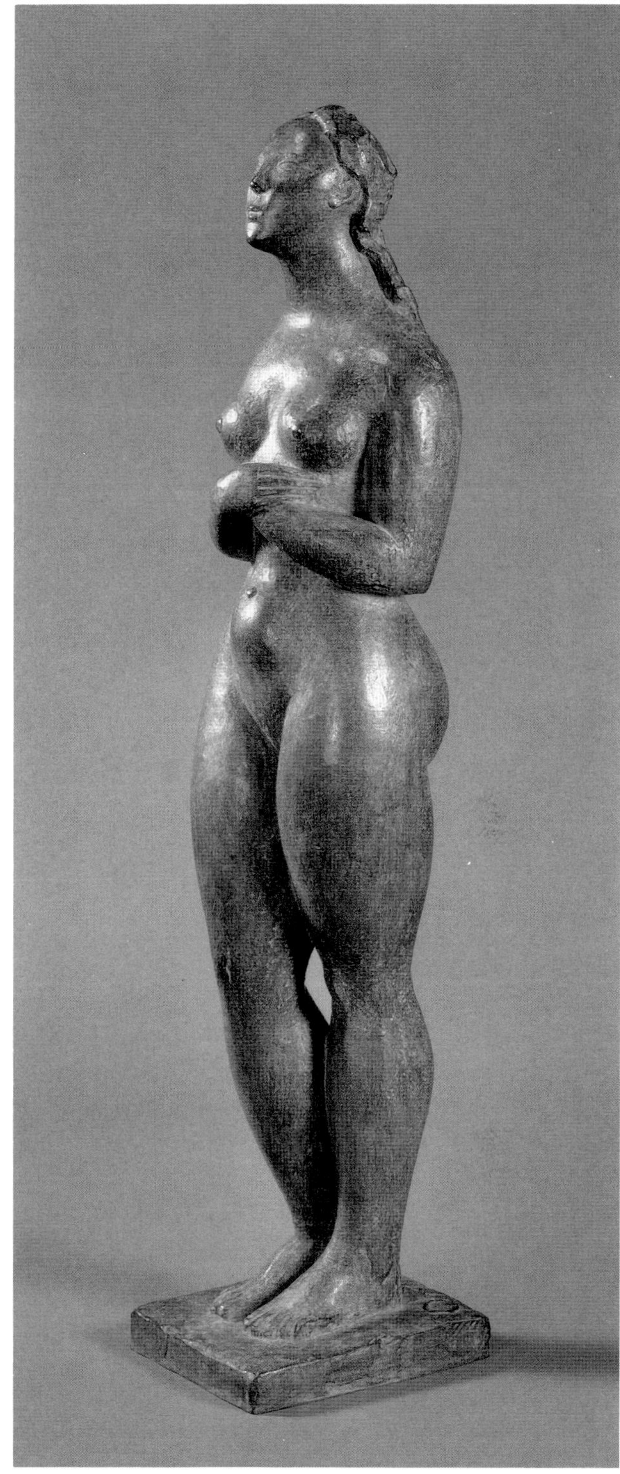

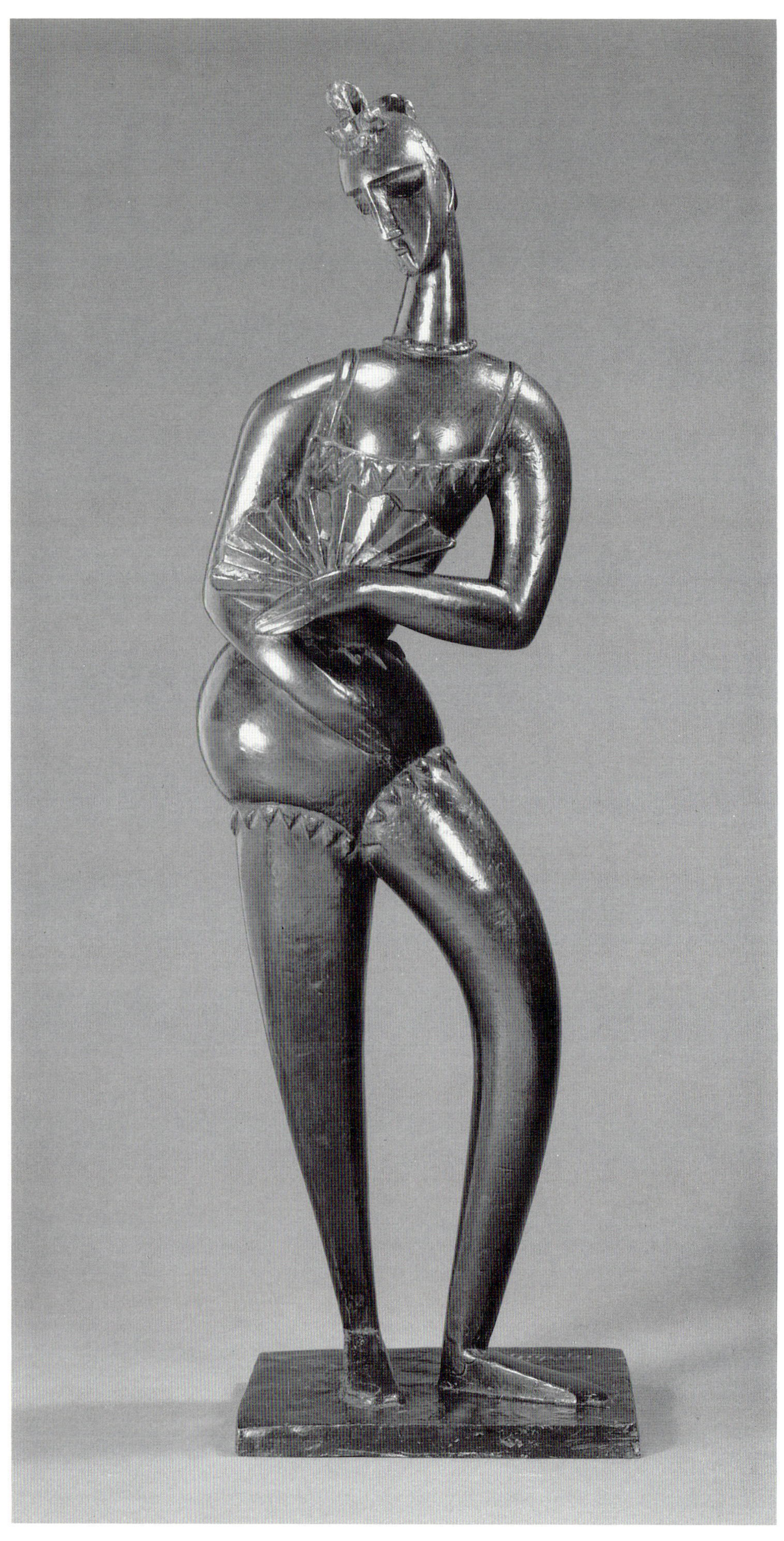

3 *Horsewoman with Fan* 1913
Bronze 7/7
H. 26⅝"/67.6 cm
The Estate of Jacques Lipchitz represented by Marlborough International Fine Art AG.

IN 1913, LIPCHITZ BEGAN A FRIENDSHIP WITH DIEGO Rivera. The Mexican-born artist, who was several years older, was already painting in the Cubist idiom, and he may well have been the initial catalyst for the radical change in the direction of Lipchitz's art during the next several years. Gradually he abandoned working from the observation of nature in favour of creating images from the imagination.

In *Horsewoman with Fan*, the various elements of the body are rendered in a simplified, schematic manner. For example, the head and neck appear to have been made as a separate unit to be fitted on to the shoulders. Similarly, the legs, like those of a mannequin, seem to lock on to the torso. The anecdotal attention to detail of the woman's costume anticipates *The Matador* of 1914 (no. 7). The fan itself was a favourite motif of the Cubist painters.

The subject of this sculpture reflects Lipchitz's interest, shared by a number of his contemporaries, in the Médrano Circus. It is interesting to compare this work with Archipenko's construction *Médrano II (Dancer)*, also of 1913 (fig. 29). It was not until 1915, however, with the brilliant series of detachable figures (nos. 12 and 13) that Lipchitz began to explore constructivist techniques.

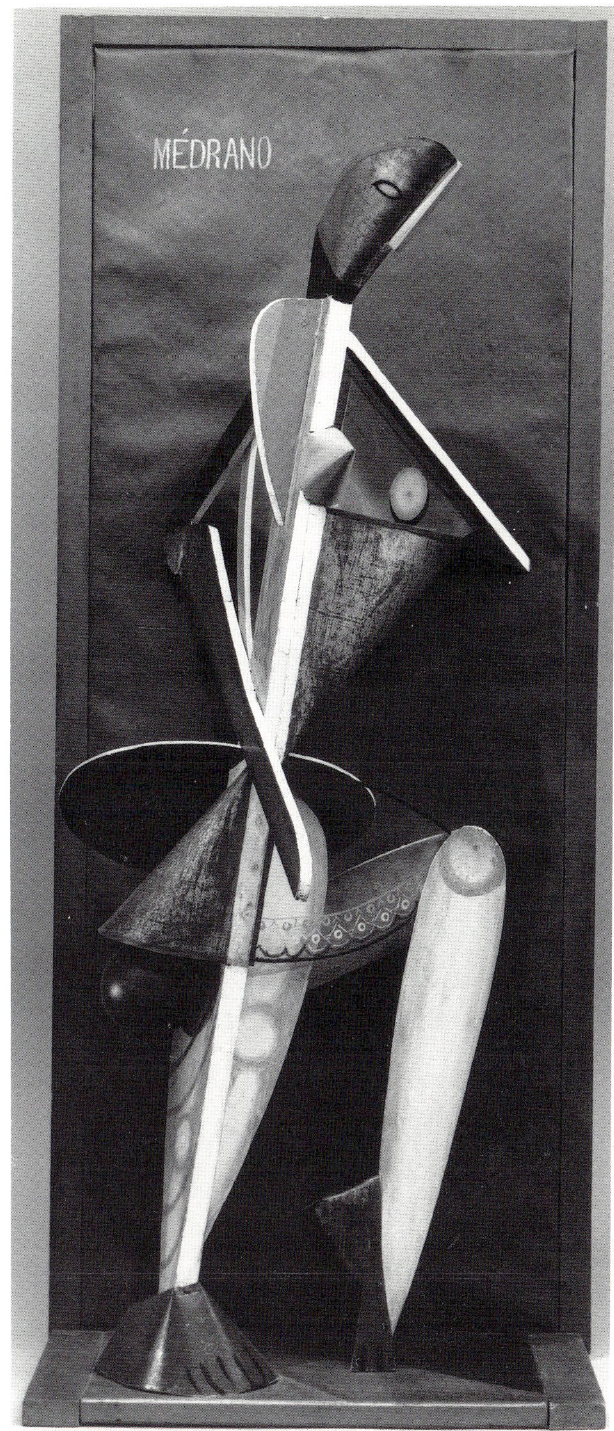

fig. 29 *Alexander Archipenko,* Médrano II (Dancer), *1913, 10¼"/26.*
painted tin, wood, glass, and painted oil cloth, 49⅞ x 20¼ x 12½"/126.6 x 51.5 x 31.7 cm. Solomon R. Guggenheim Museum, New York, 56.1445.

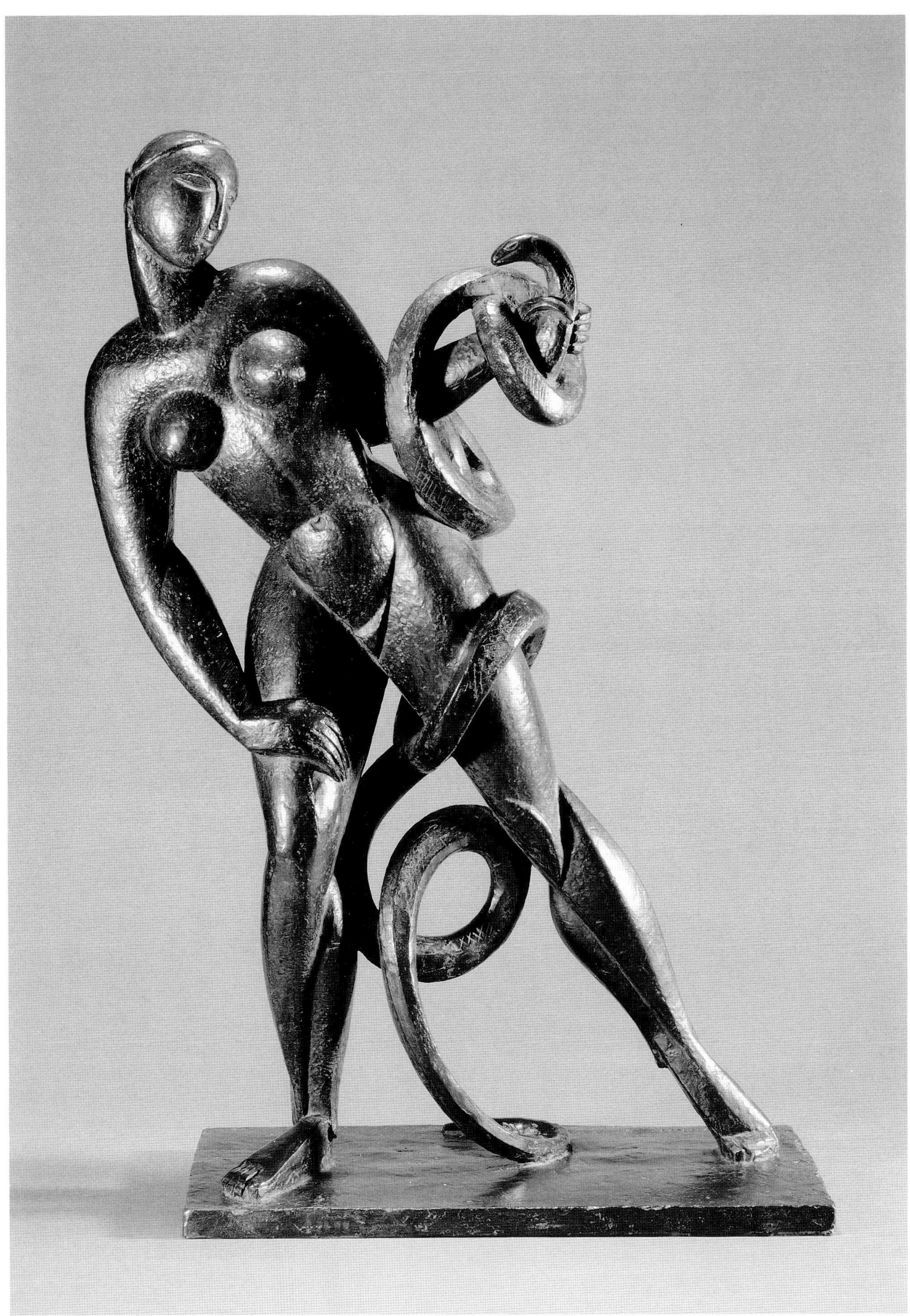

4 *Woman with Serpent* 1913
Bronze 2/7
H. 24″/61.0 cm
The Estate of Jacques Lipchitz represented by Marlborough International Fine Art AG.

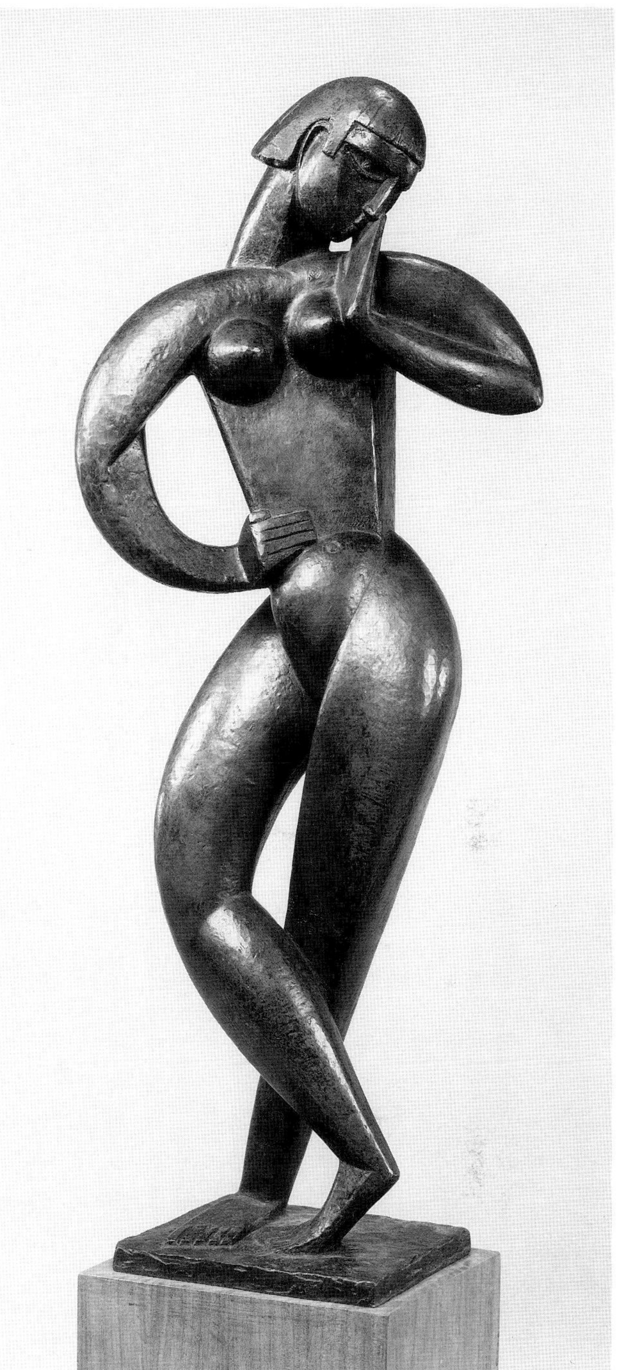

Woman with Serpent REFLECTS LIPCHITZ'S ASSIMILATION of disparate influences ranging from the Hellenistic Laocoön group to the work of his contemporaries Duchamp-Villon and Brancusi. Deborah Stott has described the affinities with specific works of the latter two sculptors as follows:

> The simplified anatomy, in which every part is kept distinct by an emphasis on the junctures of planes, as well as the striding pose, resembles Duchamp-Villon's explorations in sculptural volume in the male and female figure of *Pastorale*, exhibited in 1910. The ovoid neck and head, however, with their flattened and linear features superimposed on a simplified, volumetric head, is reminiscent of Brancusi's 1910 *Sleeping Muse* or the 1912 *Muse*.[4]

Lipchitz himself said of the Laocoön group that it "was probably my first inspiration for the subject."[5] This was the first work that the sculptor described as being in the Baroque manner, and as such, *Woman with Serpent* anticipates his later work. Also prophetic of future developments was his interest, as he said, in the "opening up of the voids; I might almost say that this is my first transparent sculpture."[6]

5 *Dancer* 1913
Bronze
H. 25⅝″/65.09 cm
The Detroit Institute of Arts, Gift of Mr. and Mrs. A. D. Wilkinson.

THE POSE OF *Dancer* RELATES IN A GENERAL WAY TO THAT of *Woman with Serpent* (no. 4). From the waist up, the figure leans to her right. A large void is created between the curved right arm and the body, and the head is shown in profile to the right. Stott has suggested that the contrasting flattened and rounded planes relate to Archipenko's *Blue Nude* of 1913, while "the swinging hip movement and crossed leg stance, on the other hand, recall the pose of Matisse's *Serpentine*."[7] In *Dancer*, the rigid and simplified geometry of the body parts, particularly the conelike breasts and the flat planes of the torso beneath, is even more pronounced than in *Woman with Serpent*. Lipchitz has moved one step farther in the reductive process leading up to his first fully realized Cubist works of 1915.

According to Lipchitz, his friend Diego Rivera introduced him to Picasso in 1913, whereas Rivera maintained that he himself came to know Picasso personally in March 1914.[8] It is difficult to try to sort out the confluence of influences that shaped Lipchitz's sculpture of 1913–14. Just how familiar he was in 1913 with Picasso's work is uncertain, and yet the pose of *Dancer* and the simplified geometry of the figure are remarkably close to Picasso's 1908 *Standing Nude*, in the Rijksmuseum Kröller-Müller, Otterlo, Holland.

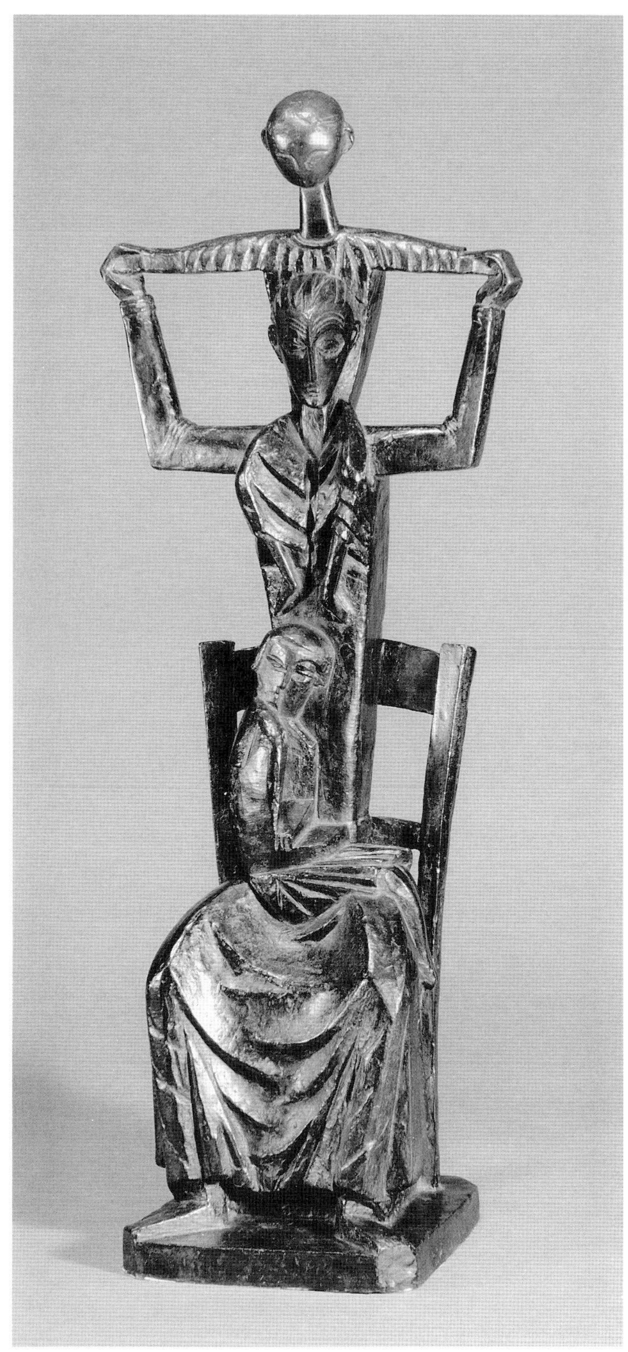

6 *Mother and Children* 1914–15
Bronze 1/7
H. 27¾″/70.5 cm
The Estate of Jacques Lipchitz represented by Marlborough International Fine Art AG.

LIPCHITZ BEGAN WORK ON THIS SCULPTURE BEFORE HIS trip to Spain with Diego Rivera in 1914 and completed it on his return sometime in 1915. In one of his most original early compositions, the mother sits on a chair, with one child sitting sideways on her lap and another on her shoulders.

> Of the works of this period, it is one I particularly like... There is first of all the mother-and-child theme, deriving from my feeling for my own mother – a theme... to which I have returned again and again. There is also the absolute frontality of the group, very different from the circular movement of the *Woman with Serpent* or the *Dancer*. There may be some reflection of my interest in African art in this frontality, but I think that the idea developed unconsciously from some recollection of a Russian Byzantine icon of the Madonna and Child.[9]

This is possible. Influences of African and Byzantine art are difficult to pin down. While Stott has remarked on the similarities between *Mother and Children* and certain Dogon and Luba sculptures,[10] this author has compared Lipchitz's sculpture to the Zulu *Figure of a Man* in the British Museum.[11] These must be seen as affinities rather than direct influences. Contemporary sources, however, are more plausable and specific. The elongated head of the mother and the smooth, rounded head of the child held aloft strongly echo the work of Modigliani and Brancusi respectively.

7 *The Matador* 1914
Bronze
H. 31¾″/80.6 cm
Lent by The Minneapolis Institute of Arts, Gift of Mr. and Mrs. John Cowles.

IN 1914 LIPCHITZ AND HIS FRIEND RIVERA VISITED SPAIN, spending time in Madrid and Majorca. In Madrid Lipchitz was tremendously excited by the work of El Greco and Goya in the Prado.

> I could see at once the relations of El Greco's powerful, expressive, angular paintings to cubism, and I was also deeply impressed by the power of his interpretation of religious subjects... Aside from El Greco and Goya, I was perhaps most moved by Tintoretto, Rubens and Velasquez, by the grandeur and movement of the Baroque.[12]

In Madrid he met the famous bullfighter Joselito, who was later killed. *The Matador* (or *Toreador*) was inspired by him. The sculpture is, in the detailing of the costume, the most elaborately decorative of Lipchitz's early works. The flat, angular planes of the legs are in marked contrast to the more naturalistic sculpture of the previous year.

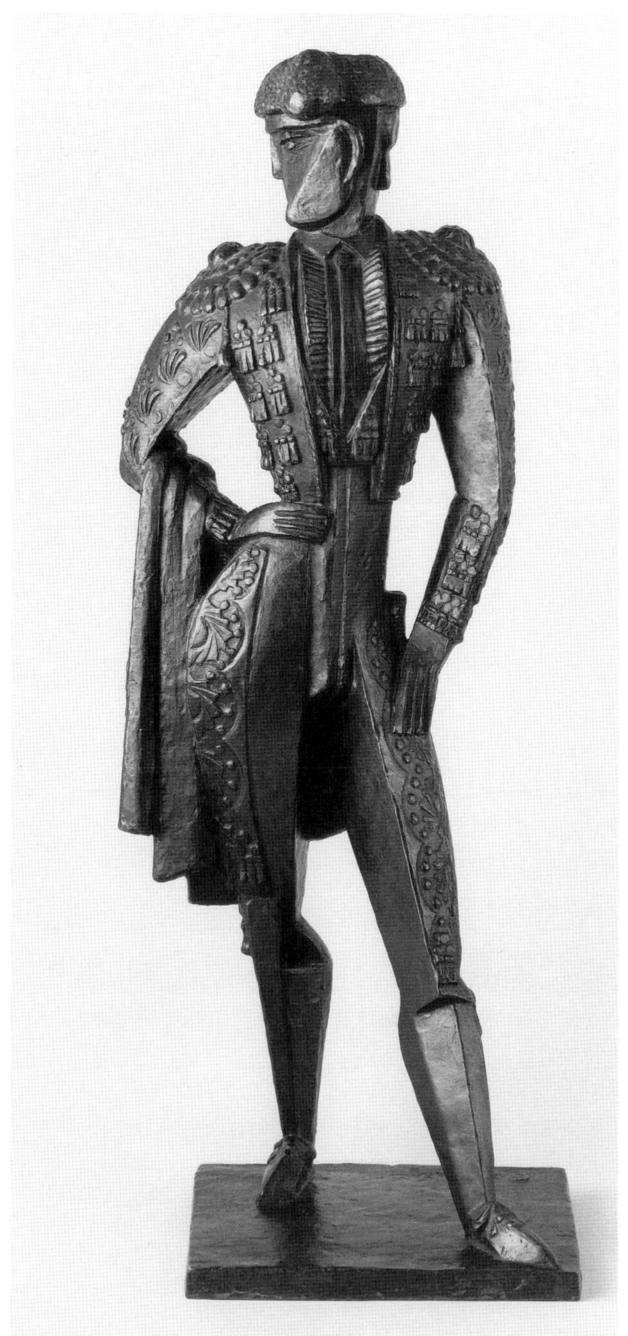

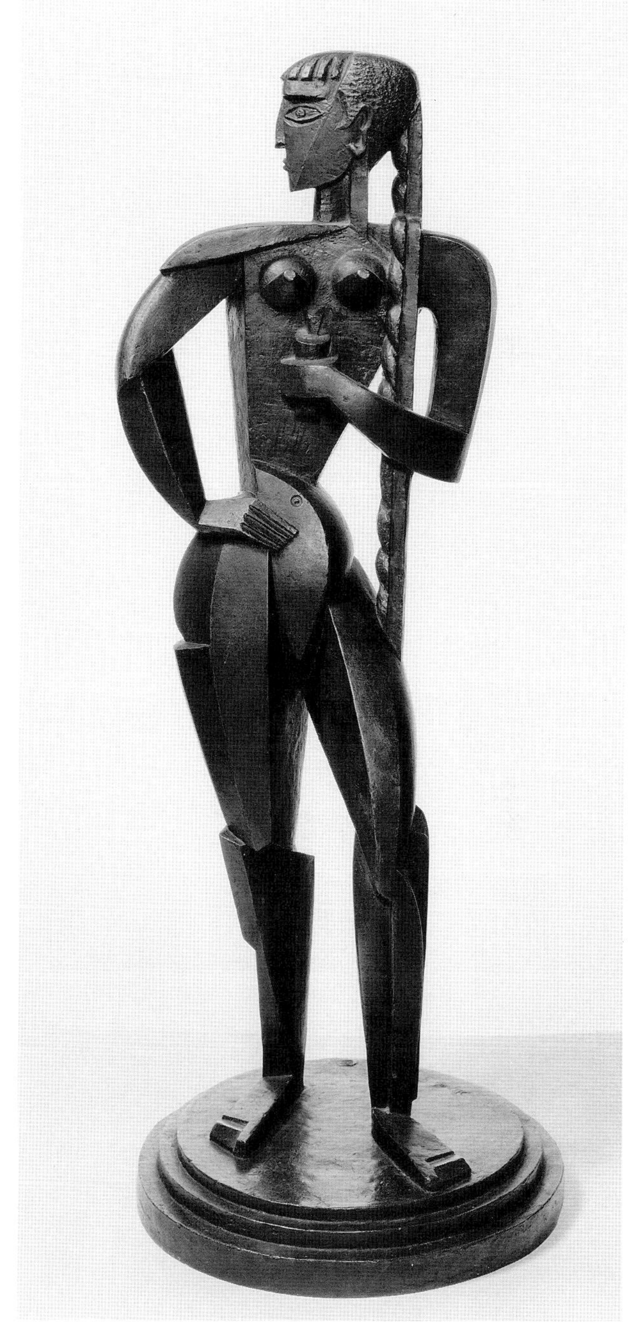

8

8 *Woman with Braid* 1914
Bronze 3/7
H. 32¾″/83.2 cm
Philadelphia Museum of Art, Bequest of Margaretta S. Hinchman.

Woman with Braid IS A PENDANT TO *The Matador* (NO. 7 above). During the summer of 1914, Lipchitz, Rivera, Maria Blanchard and several other artists settled in a fishing village on the island of Majorca. Lipchitz said he was particularly inspired by "a daughter of one of the fishermen who always wore her hair in a long braid with a cloth sewn over half of it, perhaps to protect her clothes from the oil she used in her hair."[13] In the sculpture she holds a bottle of oil in her left hand.

As in *The Matador*, the head is shown in profile to the left with the eye frontalized; these are "Cubist" features Lipchitz attributed to his interest in Egyptian relief sculpture. Even though, as the sculptor has pointed out, the anatomical form of *Woman with Braid* "is in some ways even more fragmented cubistically than in the case with the *Sailor*"[14] (no. 9), he still appears to be working from the acute observation of the model toward geometric, abstract forms.

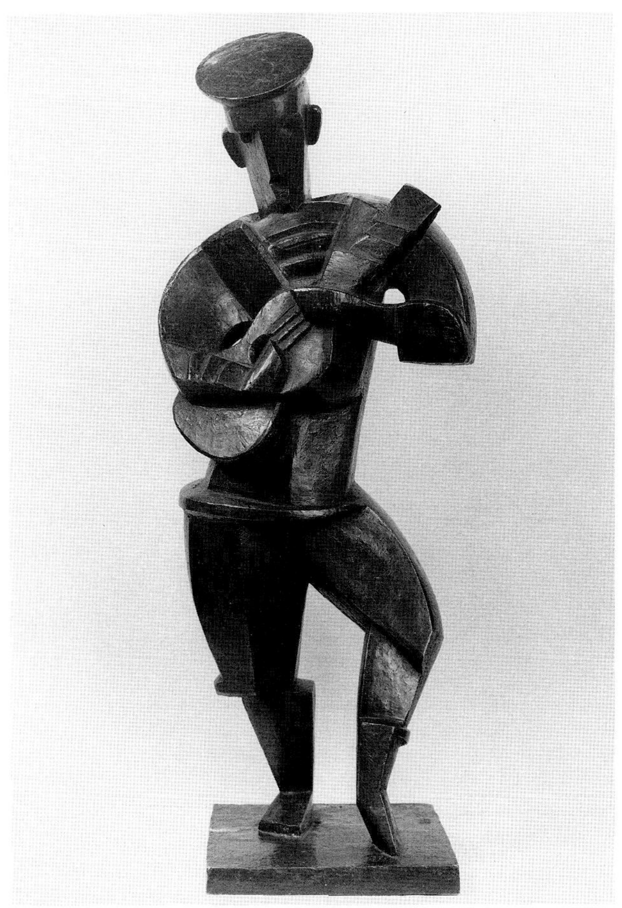

9 *Sailor with Guitar* 1914
Bronze 3/7
H. 30″/76.2 cm
Albright-Knox Art Gallery, Buffalo, NY. Room of Contemporary Art Fund, 1944.

THE SOURCE FOR *Sailor with Guitar*, AS WITH *Woman with Braid*, was an individual Lipchitz had observed in the fishing village where he was staying on the island of Majorca. The sailor had been sent by the government, Lipchitz told Stott, "to observe the local fishermen who were smuggling tobacco. One of the artists had brought a very beautiful model, so they put her near the sailor, and he began dancing around her all the time, playing his guitar instead of watching the fishermen."[15] Lipchitz made a number of drawings of the sailor in situ and made clay and plaster models when he returned to Madrid.

Sailor with Guitar marks a radical departure in Lipchitz's working method, in what he called "the final step toward cubism."[16] While he maintained that the sculpture retained a degree of realism, true to the actual appearance of his subject, Lipchitz also recognized the crucial difference in approach from his previous work: "I was finally building up the figure from its abstract forms, not merely simplifying and geometrizing a realistic figure."[17] Or, as he put it another way: "all the elements of the body derive from different cubist shapes."[18] In a tentative, exploratory manner, Lipchitz was moving in the direction of Synthetic Cubism, in which abstract forms were the point of departure, leading to and ultimately suggesting the subject matter.

Stott has suggested that *Sailor with Guitar* reflects, in a general way, Lipchitz's interest in contemporary sculpture such as Archipenko's *Walking Woman* of 1912 (fig. 33) and Boccioni's 1912 *Development of a Bottle in Space* (fig. 4).[19] The Lipchitz bronze seems even closer to Archipenko's *Médrano II (Dancer)* 1913 (fig. 29), not only in the dancing movement of the figure, but also in the introduction of the flat, disclike form that separates the legs from the rest of the body.

What gives *Sailor with Guitar* its historical importance in the evolution of Cubist sculpture is the shift from a dependence on starting with perceived reality to the freedom of working from the imagination toward the subject matter.

10 *Bather* 1915
Bronze 2/7
H. 33⅝″/85.2 cm
Hirshhorn Museum and Sculpture Garden, Smithsonian Institution. Gift of Joseph H. Hirshhorn, 1966.
(Shown in Toronto only)

Bather WAS ONE OF THE FIRST SCULPTURES LIPCHITZ MADE when he returned to Paris after a lengthy visit to Spain. It may originally have been made in wood or cardboard, as Lipchitz refers to this work as one of his first attempts at constructed sculpture. If in *Sailor with Guitar* Lipchitz was on the threshold of fully understanding how to translate the syntax of pictorial Cubism into three dimensions, in *Bather* the transition was complete. Lipchitz acknowledges this in his discussion of this work:

> Here, I would say that the transition to developed cubism is complete. My ideas were clarified; I knew exactly what I wanted to do. As can be seen, this is an elongated figure with the tilted head enclosed by the upraised arms; folds of abstracted drapery fall down behind the head. The most significant change between the 1915 and 1916 sculptures and the proto-cubist works is that the former are no longer composed around a pivoting axis. Works like the *Sailor with Guitar* [no. 9] or the *Dancer* [no. 5] revolve and create their sense of three-dimensional space by the pivoting of the figure around its axis.[20]

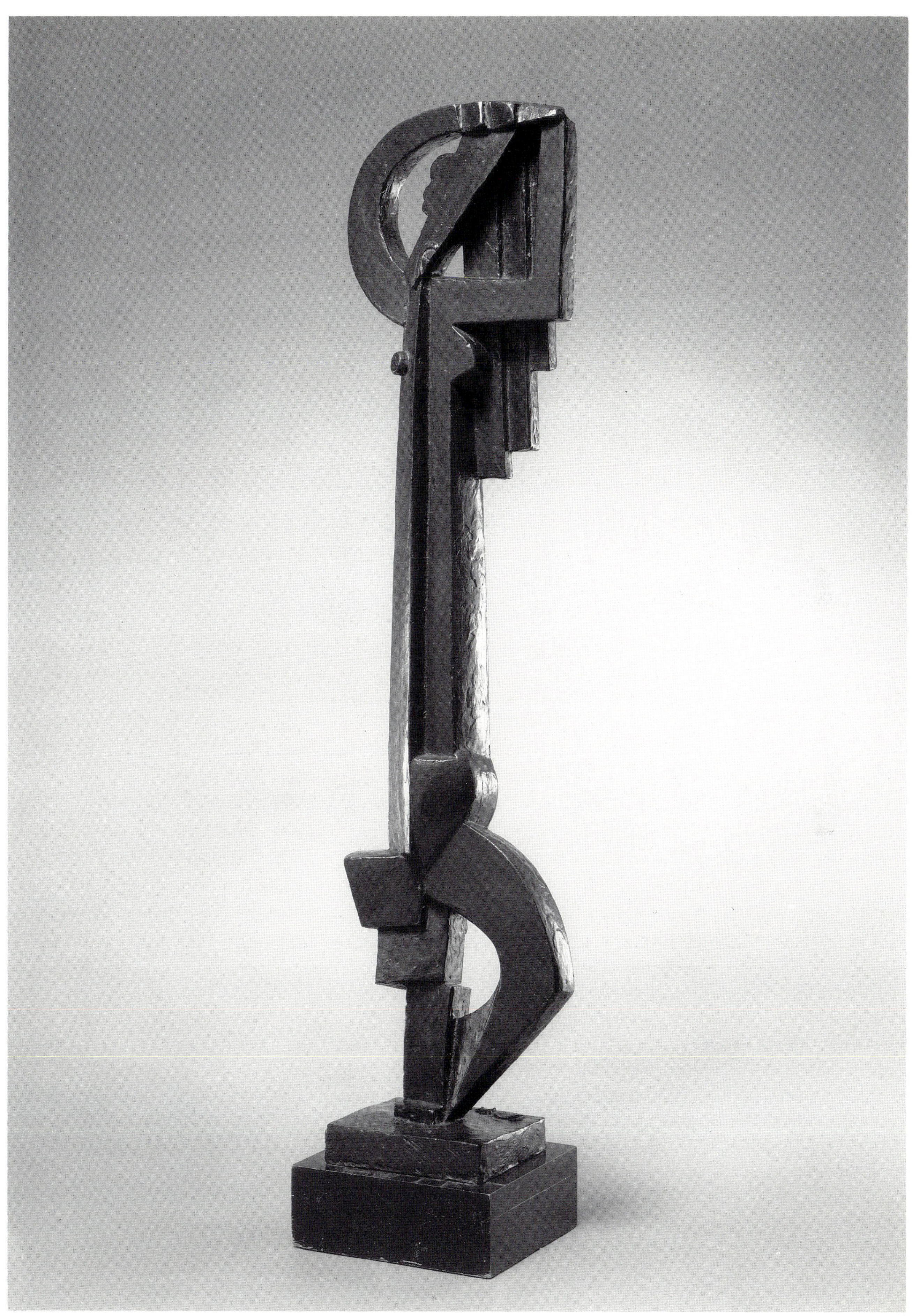

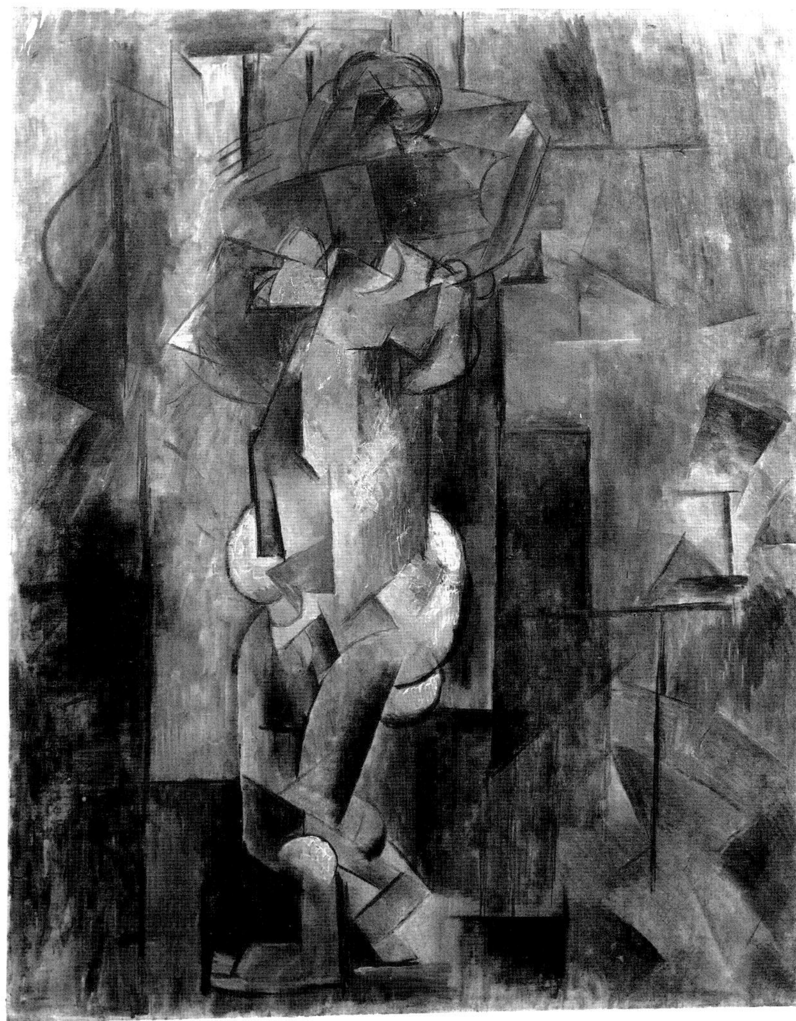

fig. 30
Pablo Picasso, Nude Figure, *1909–10, oil on canvas, 39 x 30¾"/99.1 x 78.1 cm. Albright-Knox Art Gallery, Buffalo, New York, General Purchase Funds, 1954. © Picasso/* VIS-ART *Inc. 1989.*

The disparate sources that have been advanced in connection with *Bather* are indicative of how well Lipchitz assimilated both contemporary and tribal influences. For George Heard Hamilton, "her geometry recalls the angular rigidity of Dogon or Gabun [*sic*] ancestor figures, and her bent leg, which is as stylized as a Bakota figure's, resembles the spread legs of the woman on the right in the *Demoiselles d'Avignon*."[21] Margit Rowell has made a visually convincing comparison between the arms raised around the head in silhouette in Lipchitz's *Bather* and Goncharova's "bathers of 1912 which she often depicted with arms raised to their heads and busts in simultaneous frontal and profile views."[22] Whereas Stott sees the stacking up of vertical elements side by side as relating to Synthetic Cubist paintings, such as Picasso's 1913 *Seated Woman with Guitar* (Pasadena Art Museum),[23] the sculpture seems closer to Picasso's Analytic Cubist work of 1909, such as *Nude Figure* 1909–1910 in the Albright-Knox Art Gallery (fig. 30). Lipchitz himself admits "in the development of my first purely cubist sculptures I was more influenced by the earlier, soberer examples of analytic cubism than by the decorative or rococo cubism to which Picasso and Braque turned after 1914."[24] Indeed, certain features found in Lipchitz's *Bather* – the fitting together of the three blocks forming one leg, the rounded buttock, the flat planes of the torso and the complex knotting together of head, arms and drapery – are remarkably close to the vertical stacking and locking together of similar formal elements in Picasso's *Nude Figure*.

11 *Spanish Servant Girl* 1915
Bronze 7/7
H. 35"/88.9 cm
The Estate of Jacques Lipchitz represented by Marlborough International Fine Art AG.

The subject matter of this work relates to the sculpture done in Spain in 1914, such as *The Matador* (no. 7) and *Woman with Braid* (no. 8). Stylistically, however, it is far more advanced, and like the 1915 *Bather* (no. 10) it clearly belongs among Lipchitz's first mature Cubist works. In all probability this bronze was directly based on the 1915 wood *Detachable Figure: Dancer* in the

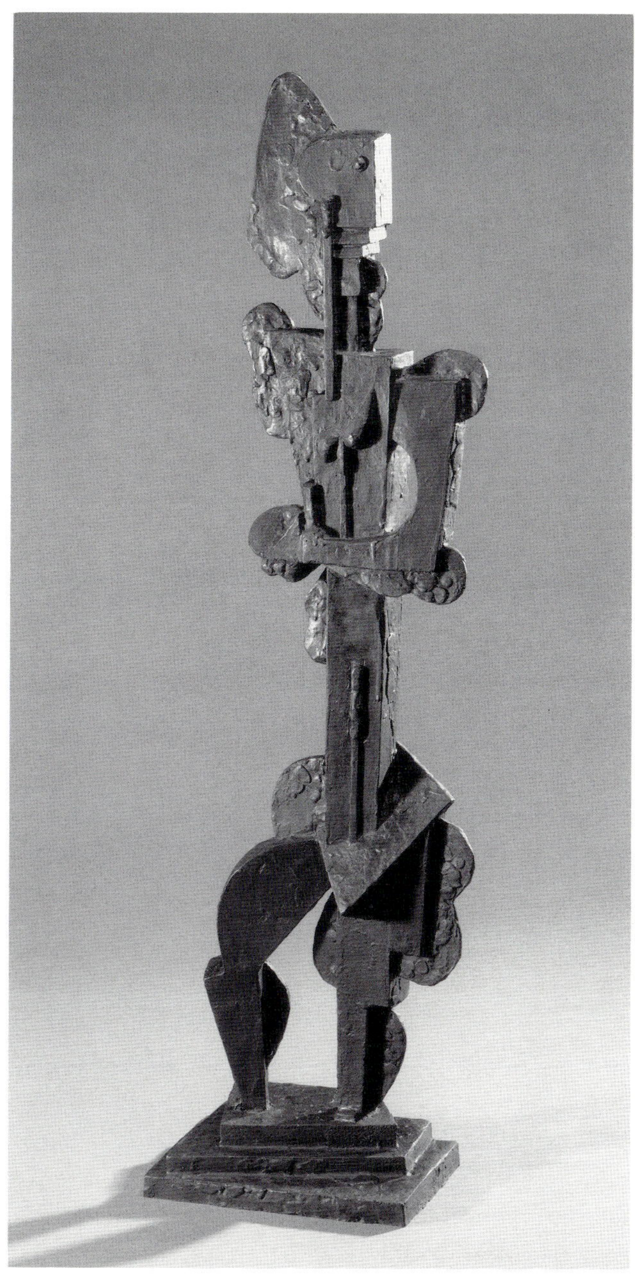

11

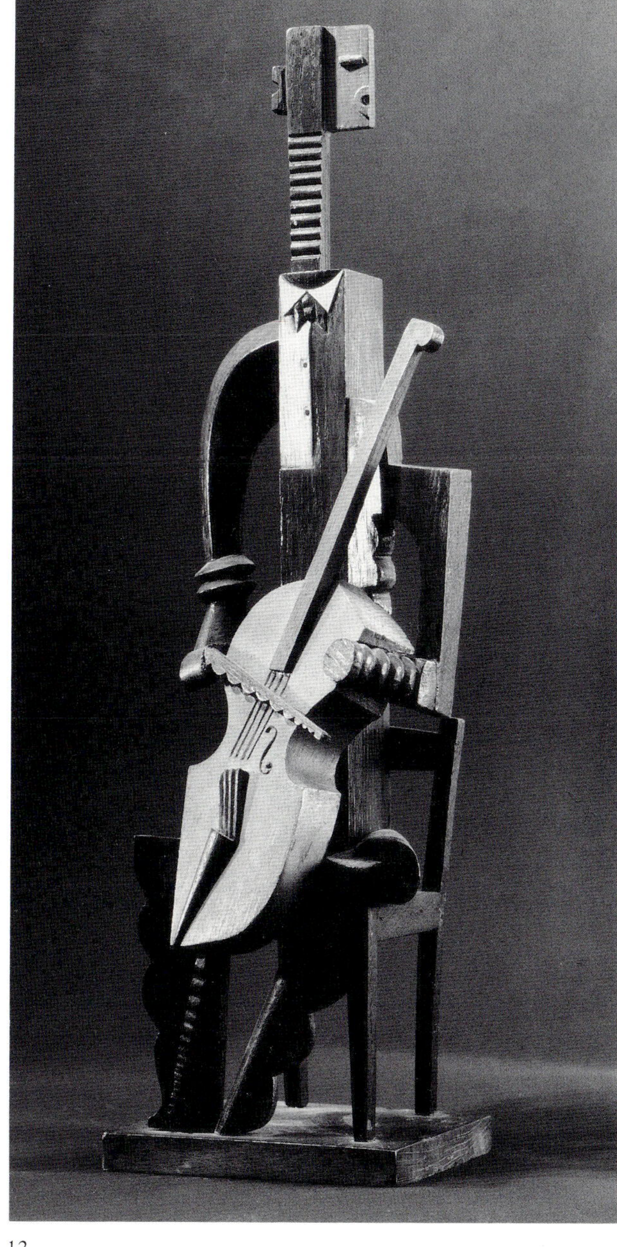

12

collection of Yulla Lipchitz (not in exhibition). It is possible that individual elements of the wood construction (which can be taken apart) were cast in plaster and reassembled and added to; it was from this reconstituted work that the present bronze was cast.

12 *Detachable Figure: Seated Musician* 1915
Painted wood
H. 19¾"/50.2 cm
Yulla Lipchitz, New York.

This is the most legible of Lipchitz's detachable figures of 1915. The frontality of the work, the chair and the rather rigid, elongated cellist recall *Mother and Children* of 1914–15 (no. 6). The long, serrated neck could derive from any number of sources in African tribal art. The right arm and the part of the left arm holding the cello look as if they might have been actual fragments of furniture or molding. The various painted surfaces strongly define the separateness of the individual elements, as, for example, the right profile of the head. Lipchitz has established a counterpoint between those abstract, geometrical forms that, when assembled, create the figure itself and descriptive elements of realism, such as the collar and buttons and the cello itself. This ingenious construction is the most elegant and charming of Lipchitz's early Cubist sculptures.

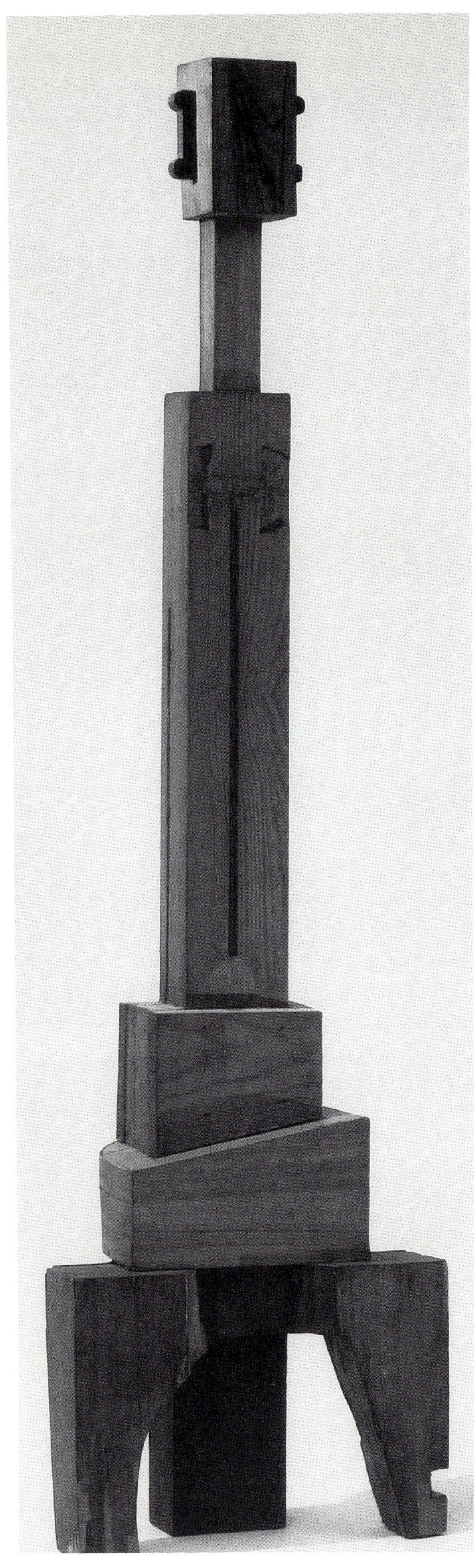

13 *Detachable Figure: Dancer* 1915
Wood
H. 33½"/85.1 cm
Yulla Lipchitz, New York.

This is the most austere and abstract of Lipchitz's detachable figures of 1915. The elongated torso rests on two blocks, which in turn are attached to the short, stumpy legs. Beneath the schematized breasts, a thin incision has been cut down the centre of the torso, ending at the circular navel. The head has no features except for the projecting ears. *Detachable Figure: Dancer* has close affinities with both African art and the work of Picasso. As William Rubin pointed out to this author, the proportions of the Lipchitz sculpture resemble those of the Kambe (Kenya) stele in the Detroit Institute of Art.[25] It is also closely related to Picasso's paintings and watercolours of 1915, such as *Harlequin* in the Museum of Modern Art, New York (fig. 31).

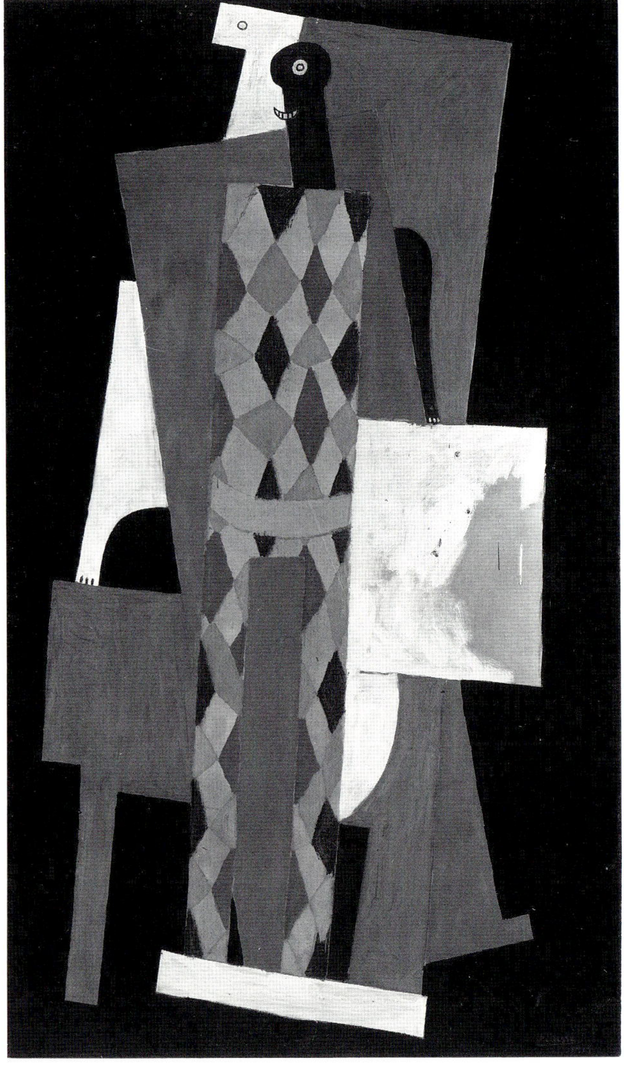

fig. 31 *Pablo Picasso,* Harlequin, *1915, oil on canvas, 6' x 41 3/8"/ 183.5 x 105.1 cm. The Museum of Modern Art. Acquired through the Lillie P. Bliss Bequest. © Picasso/ VIS-ART Inc. 1989.*

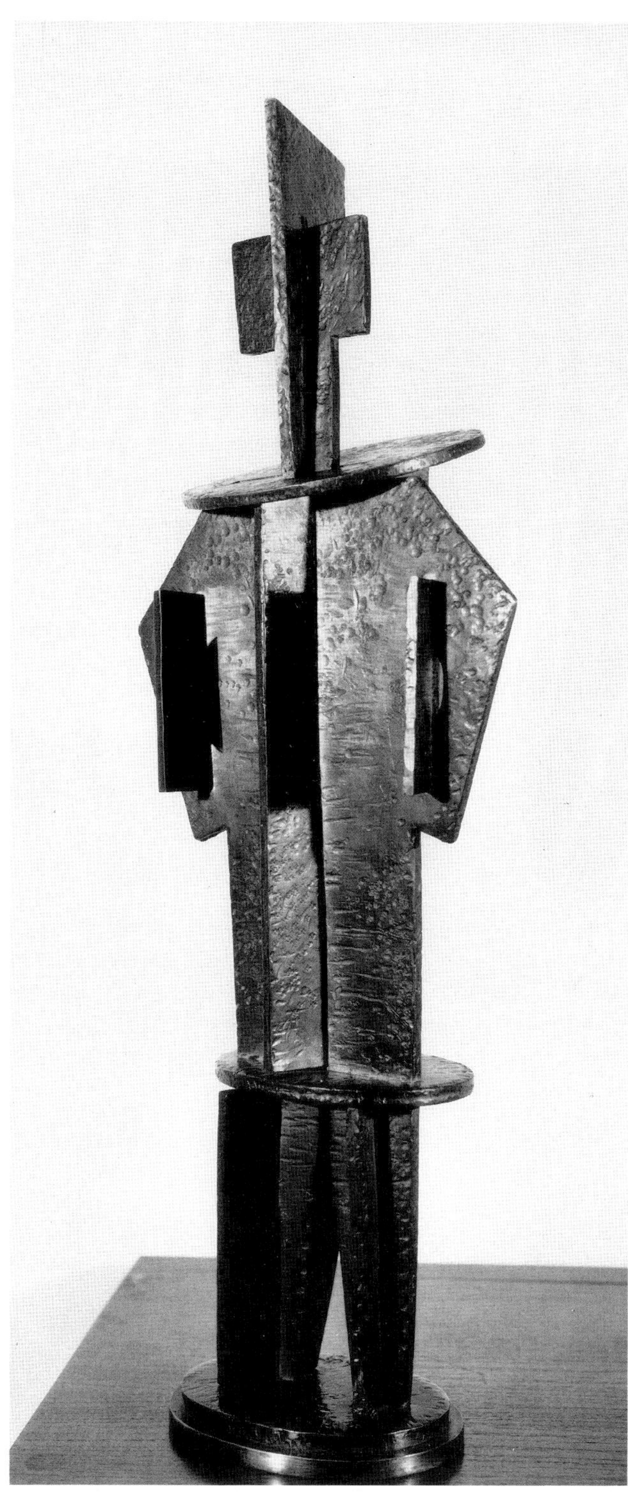

14 *Detachable Figure: Pierrot* 1915
Bronze (unique)
H. 27¼"/69.2 cm
Mrs. Andrea Bollt, New York.

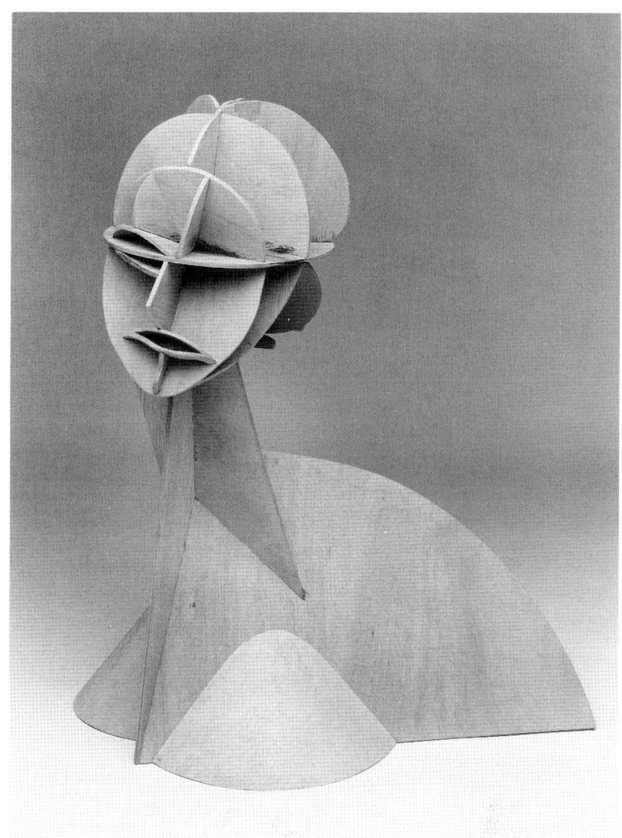

fig. 32 Naum Gabo, Constructed Head No. 1, *1915, triple-layered plywood, H. c.21¼"/54 cm. Collection Miriam Gabo. © Nina and Graham Williams, 1989.*

In a number of the detachable figures he made in the first half of 1915 Lipchitz carried his Cubist constructions, as he said, "all the way to abstraction, but most of these abstract works I have destroyed since I felt that when I had lost the sense of the subject, of its humanity, I had gone too far."[26] (Picasso had faced a similar dilemma with his paintings done at Cadaquès in the summer of 1910, when he produced some of his most hermetic and almost abstract work.) Lipchitz embarked on this detachable figure, made in wood and later worked out in bronze:

> Once I had made this, I felt that again I had found my path and I was able to move forward with certainty and with joy. The figure is a *Pierrot*, even more rigidly vertical and horizontal than the previous ones but now organized, despite its frontality, with a greater sense of three-dimensional depth. The head and body of the figure consist of flat planes placed at right angles to one another in a cruciform shape, tied together by the two horizontal, circular planes. The important new step in this work is the way in which the volume of the figure is created by the voids between the planes.[27]

The detachable – or demountable – figures reflect Lipchitz's short-lived interest in the machine aesthetic that profoundly influenced the work of Léger and Ozenfant. The detachable figures could be taken apart, transported and reconstructed. The way in which the flat planes and circular plates fit together strongly resembles Archipenko's 1913 bronze *Head: Construction with Crossing Planes* (see fig. 9). Gabo, working independently in Germany in 1915, used a similar method of slotting together flat and curved planes of wood in *Constructed Head No. 1* (fig. 32). In Lipchitz's *Detachable Figure*, volume is implied or suggested by the negative space flowing around the abstract flat planes. Lipchitz's detachable figures of 1915 take their place among the early masterpieces of Constructivism, alongside Picasso's metal and wood sculptures of 1912–15, and the early work of Gabo and Archipenko.

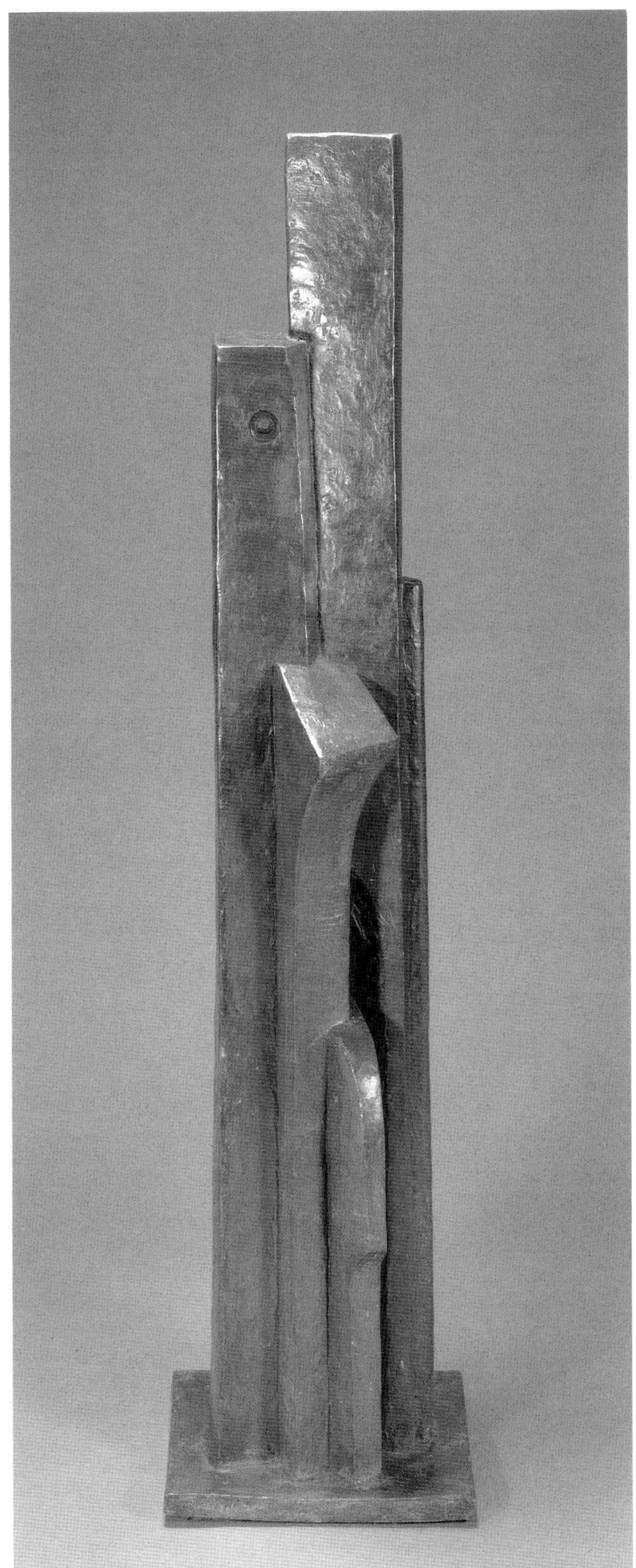

15 *Sculpture* 1915
Lead (unique)
H. 48½″/123.2 cm
The Estate of Jacques Lipchitz represented by Marlborough International Fine Art AG.

THE DETACHABLE FIGURES OF 1915 WERE FOLLOWED BY A series of sculptures that Lipchitz considered to be his most abstract and architectural in feeling. They are among the very few works of his entire career without descriptive titles defining the subject matter.

> These I normally entitled simply *Sculpture* as a result of my preliminary emphasis on the sculptural forms rather than on the subject. Some of them have the feeling of architectural skyscrapers, even though they were made at a time when the skyscraper was scarcely known.[28]

Not even Picasso or Braque took such a radical step in their most abstract and hermetic Analytic Cubist paintings of 1910 and early 1911 as to title individual works simply *Painting*. However abstract Lipchitz's sculpture of 1915–16 may appear, as in the work of Picasso and Braque of 1910–11, there are always clues or signs that suggest the subject matter. For example, in this *Sculpture*, the single circular eye is sufficient to allow us to relate the work, however tenuously, to a standing figure.

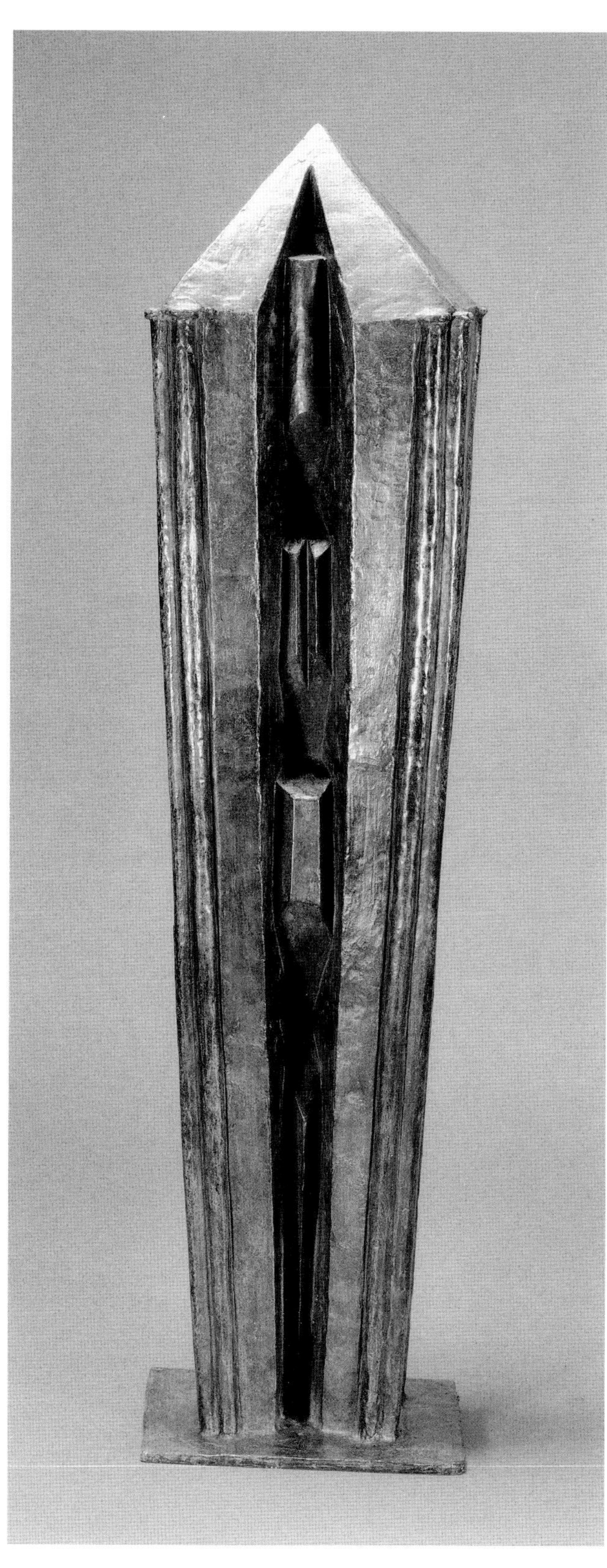

16 *Sculpture* 1915 (1916?)
Bronze 2/7
H. 36″/91.4 cm
The Estate of Jacques Lipchitz represented by Marlborough International Fine Art AG.

THIS WORK MUST SURELY BELONG TO THE GROUP OF architectural, semi-abstract sculptures of 1915 discussed in the notes for no. 15 above, although it has usually been dated 1916. The present sculpture is obviously one of those "related to an Egyptian obelisk"[29] – indeed, it would appear to be the only surviving work of 1915 that fits this description.

While he was working on *Sculpture*, Lipchitz was visited by the novelist Jules Romains, who asked him what he was trying to do with his sculpture. According to Stott, Lipchitz replied: "I would like to make an art as pure as a crystal."[30]

Sculpture is one of Lipchitz's purest and most original early Cubist works. It evokes, at the top at least, finely cut crystal or some precious stone, while the overall form clearly echoes an Egyptian obelisk. The only figurative elements are contained within the incised gash down the centre of the sculpture, suggestive of a thin, Giacometti-like figure, with the female sex clearly indicated in the projecting form just above centre. A similar feature appears in the large *Figure* of 1926–30 (no. 51). In *Sculpture*, Lipchitz has successfully merged an almost monolithic architectural form with figurative references within it. He has indeed produced a work of great clarity, as pure as crystal.

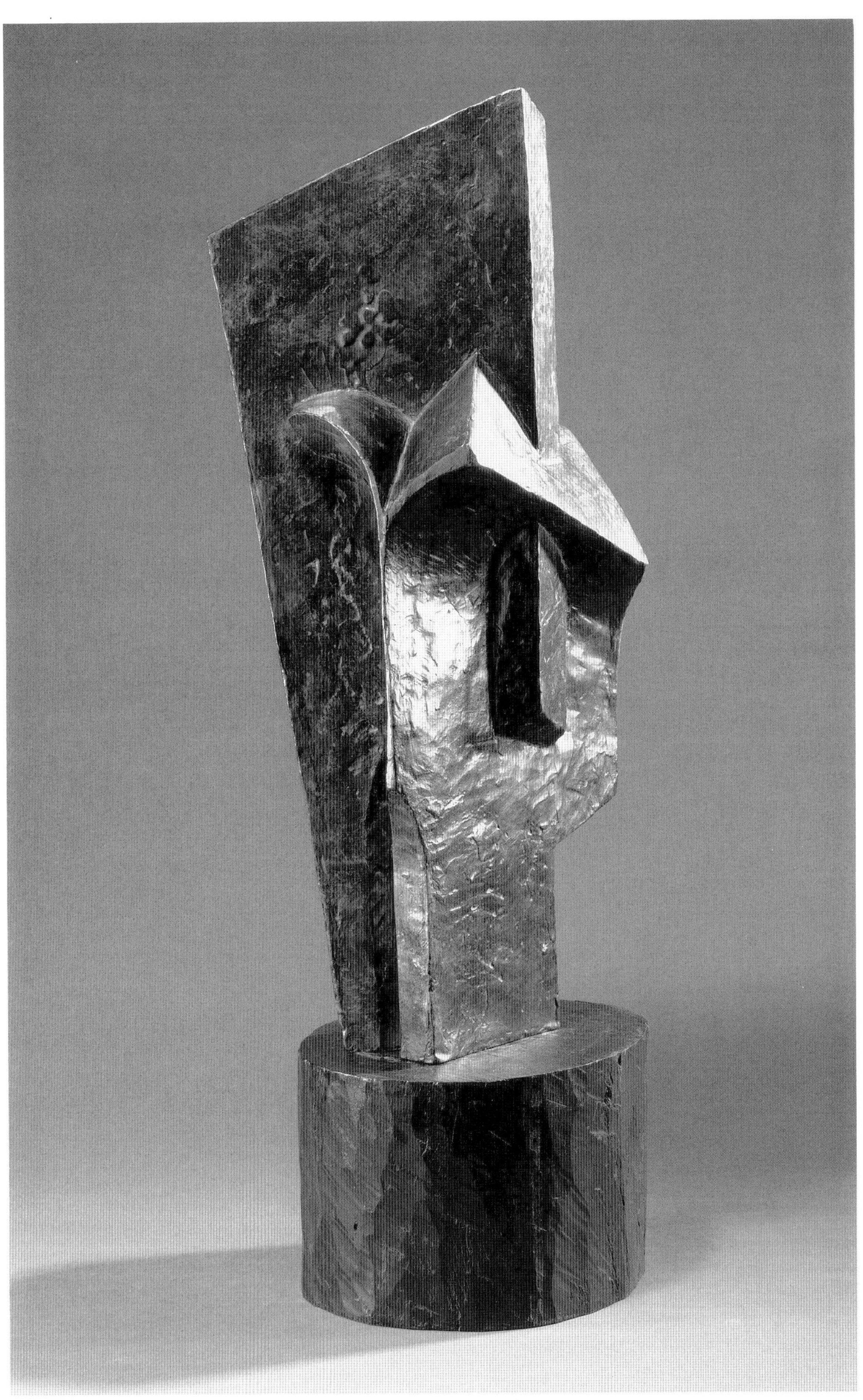

17 *Head* 1915
Bronze 5/7
H. 30½″/77.5 cm
The Estate of Jacques Lipchitz represented by Marlborough International Fine Art AG.

Head HAS SOMETHING OF THE CRYSTALLINE CLARITY OF *Sculpture* (no. 16 above) but is much more legible. *Head*, Lipchitz said, "was made after the moment of my emotional crisis, when I felt that in my exploration of abstract shapes I had lost sight of the human element, the relation to nature that has always been so necessary to me."[31] What is remarkable about this work is the way in which he found his way back to nature, by an ingenious fitting together of abstract planes that strongly evokes a human head. Lipchitz has explained the process:

> It is really a very simple structure, obviously in the same vein as the abstract architectural works that preceded and followed it. There is a large, vertical-rectangular mass that rises up the back of the head and then comes down in front as the forehead and nose. This rectangular plane is bisected almost at right angles by another plane that suggests the face diminishing at the bottom to form the neck and rising in a frontal curve to suggest the protruding line of the eyebrows. There is even an implication of the eyes in the shadows created under this protruding ridge. This is, then, clearly, a human head with even a feeling of monumental dignity. Yet the entire effect is achieved essentially by two interlocking sculptural planes.[32]

Head may well reflect Lipchitz's interest in tribal sculpture. The formal and structural similarities between this work and certain Bakota helmet masks from Gabon are so striking as to suggest that the latter may have been a direct but well-assimilated source of inspiration.[33]

According to Lipchitz's brother, Rubin, *Head* was somehow related (a semi-abstract portrait?) to his friend Grégoire Landau, who had helped the sculptor financially and to whom Lipchitz gave the stone version of the sculpture.

18 *Seated Figure* 1915
Bronze 3/7
H. 34¼″/87.0 cm
The Estate of Jacques Lipchitz represented by Marlborough International Fine Art AG.

THE VERTICAL LAYERING OF CUBES AND CYLINDERS ANTICipates the stepped setbacks of skyscrapers such as the Empire State Building, New York, completed in 1931.

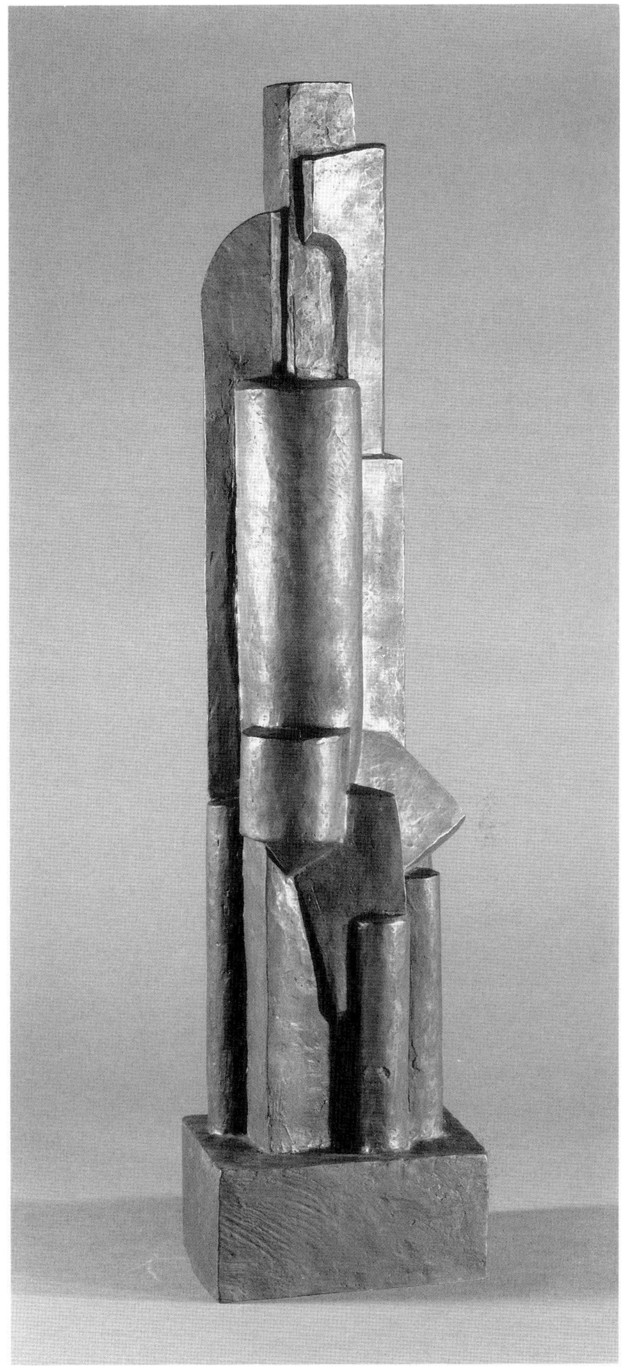

Certain figurative elements, far less legible than in no. 17 above, are integrated into the complex structure. Near the top, one of the planes reads as a long neck, with the head in profile to the left. The only indications that the figure is in fact seated are the angular, tilted planes at right, just below centre, which may represent the bent torso or the seat of the chair supported beneath by two cylindrical legs. *Seated Figure* represents the most hermetic of Lipchitz's early Cubist work, in which it is often difficult to detect any figurative references among the dominant abstract forms.

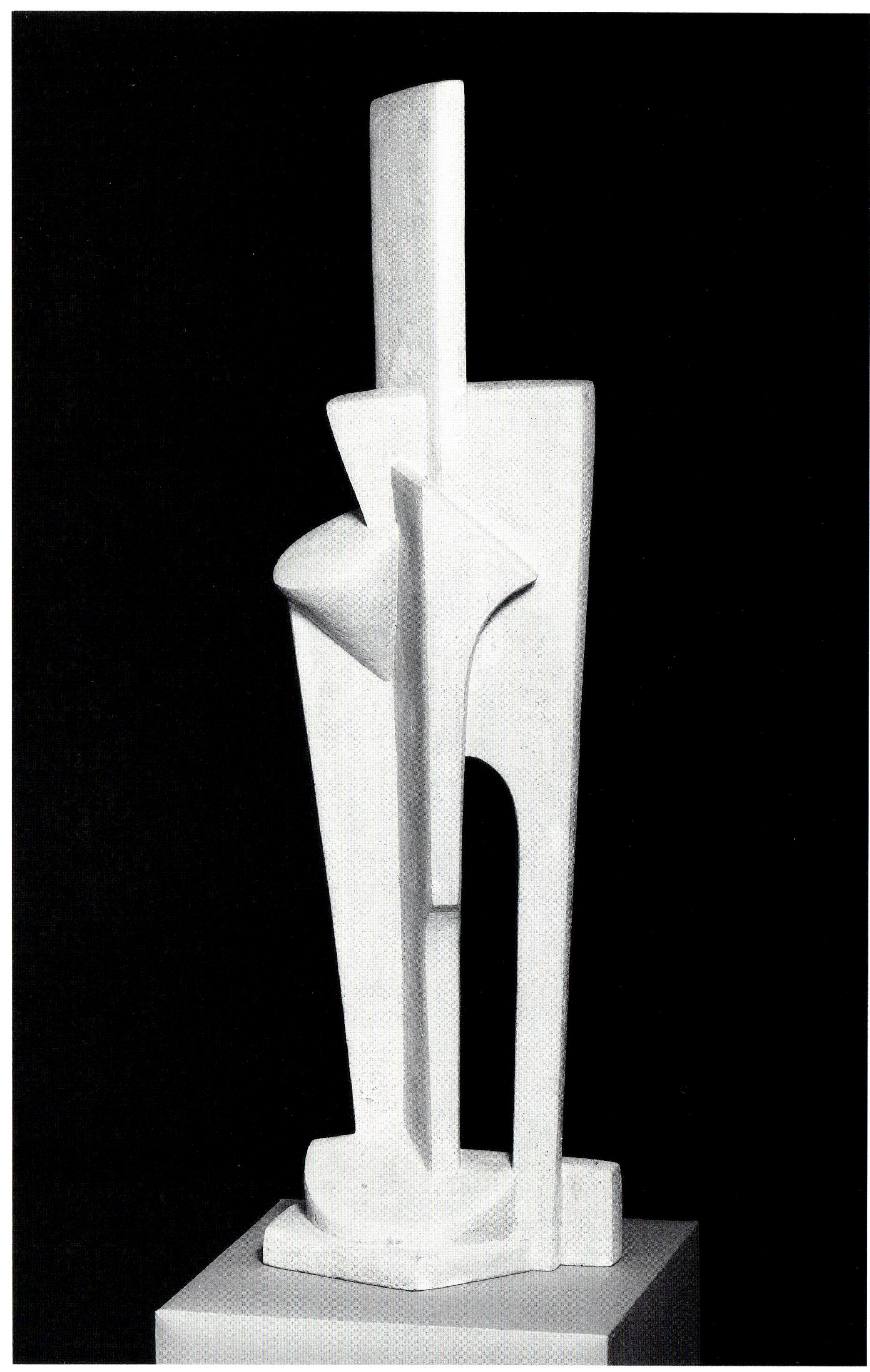

19 *Sculpture* 1915–16 cm
Limestone
H. 38½″/98.0 cm
The Trustees of the Tate Gallery.
(Shown in Toronto only)

David Fraser Jenkins, in the 1986 Tate Gallery catalogue, *The Lipchitz Gift*, has written that Lipchitz's first Cubist stone carvings were executed in 1916: "No more than a few were carved by Lipchitz himself, although he always supervised them, and all were made from original models in clay. These clay models were immediately cast in plaster, the plaster was copied by the carver."[34] In 1916 Lipchitz signed a contract with the dealer Léonce Rosenberg that enabled him to employ a stone carver. Although Lipchitz was by nature a modeller and, unlike Brancusi and Modigliani, never cared for working in stone, he felt that his Cubist work "clearly needed the architectural mass of stone..."[35] *Sculpture* 1915–16 was directly based on a work of 1915 entitled *Half Standing Figure.* Most of Lipchitz's early Cubist work, including this piece, was cast in bronze in an edition of seven at the Modern Art Foundry, New York, between about 1960 and 1970.

Sculpture 1915–16 is almost certainly the work Lipchitz is referring to in the following excerpt from his autobiography, as it is the only sculpture of 1915–16 with a circular section at the base:

> The first of these is a half-standing figure which rises from a circular base that is like the top of a table at which he is sitting. This and the others that followed it were made in clay, then in stone, and later in bronze. All of these, in the construction of interlocking planes, are developments from the earlier demountable figures. In them I was definitely building up and composing the idea of a human figure from abstract sculptural elements of line, plane, and volume; of mass contrasted with void completely realized in three dimensions.[36]

An important new feature is the way in which Lipchitz has cut through and opened out the figure; this was an innovation that had been fully exploited for the first time by Archipenko, in his *Walking Woman* of 1912 (fig. 33). In discussing the small circular hole carved through the 1916 stone *Man with Guitar* (Museum of Modern Art, New York), he said: "The purpose of the hole is simple: I wanted it as an element that would make the spectator conscious that this was a three-dimensional object, that would force him to move around to the other side and realize it from every angle."[37]

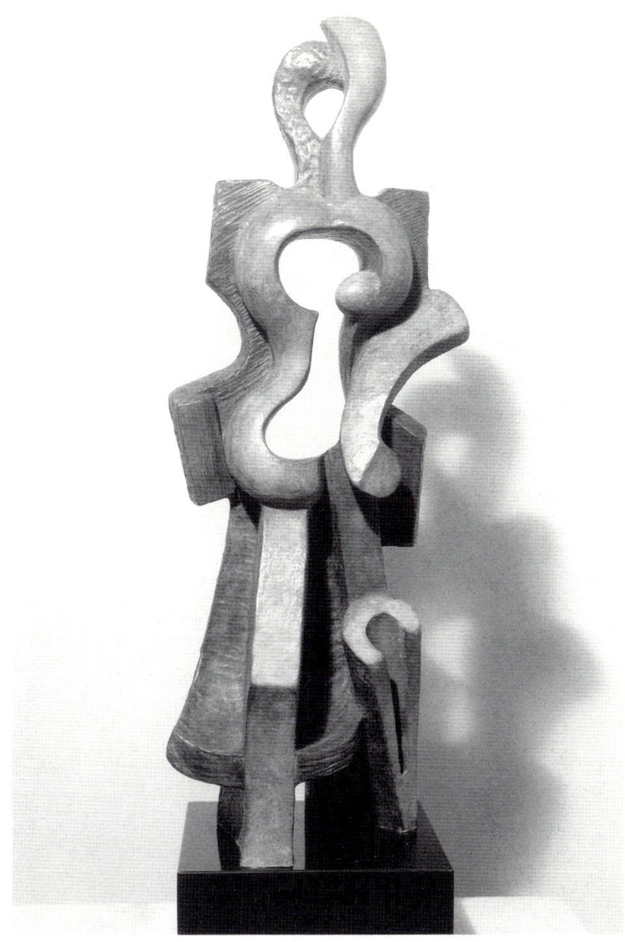

fig. 33 Alexander Archipenko, Walking Woman, *1912, bronze, H. 26½″/67.3 cm. Perls Galleries, New York.*

20 *Standing Personage* 1916
Limestone
H. 42½″/108.0 cm
Solomon R. Guggenheim Museum, New York.

This carving was based on an earlier work of 1915–16 entitled *Standing Figure.* Though the title is slightly different, the subject is identical. An elegant, majestic work, the carving represents the culmination of Lipchitz's architectural Cubism of 1915–16, a point of perfect equilibrium and balance between the human figure and architecture. Lipchitz later explained the architectural and figurative elements:

> It looms up like a cluster of skyscraper towers, something like those in Rockefeller Center, New York. The pointed and curving arches and indentations give it somewhat the feeling of a Gothic tower...While this sculpture is in one sense an architectural construction, it is also clearly a figure or figures. The V-shaped curves rising from the sharp vertical in the upper central area reiterate the eyebrows

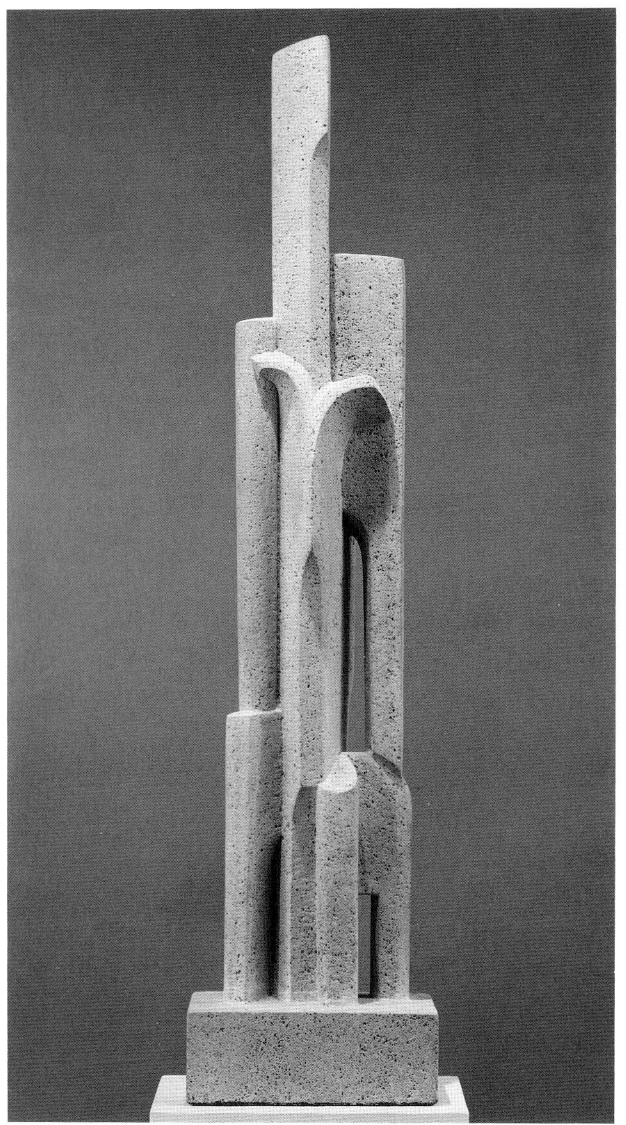

20

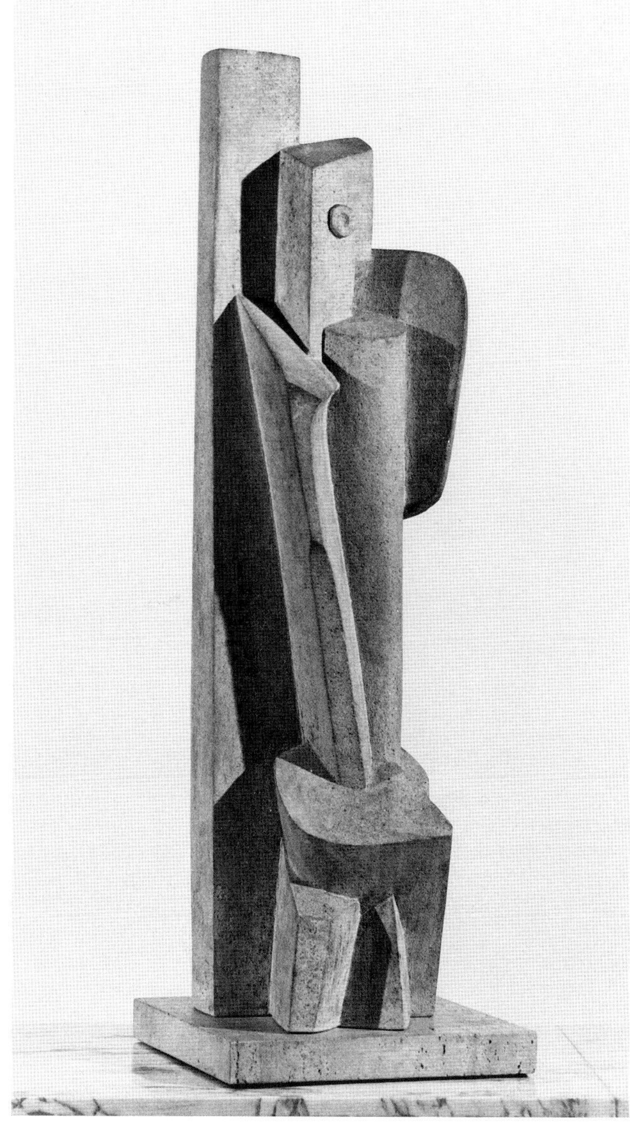

and nose of the slightly earlier head [no. 17], and the angled elements at the bottom can be either the buttresses supporting a Gothic vault or the legs of a seated figure. In this work it can easily be seen how the term "cathedral style" arose.[38]

The complex, often ambiguous interrelationship of Cubist forms lend themselves to various interpretations. The V-shaped curves, for example, can also be read as shoulder blades or breast bones supporting an elongated neck, with the head above the shallow niche, indicating the recess under the chin. The rapidity with which Lipchitz experimented with and fully assimilated the essence of Cubism was remarkable. Within the space of a year, from his proto-Cubist *Sailor with Guitar* of 1914 (no. 9) to *Standing Personage*, Lipchitz had moved beyond the tentative, exploratory gropings of a student attempting to learn a foreign language to become the most representative exponent of mature Cubist sculpture.

21 *Seated Woman* [*Cubist Figure*; *Standing Figure*; *Sculpture*]
1916
Stone (unique)
H. 42¼″/107.3 cm
From the Patsy R. and Raymond D. Nasher collection, Dallas, Texas.

IN CONVERSATION WITH STOTT, LIPCHITZ STATED THAT he began carving the stone himself, instead of having a stone carver do most of the preliminary work for him, as was his usual practice.[39] In that the balance has been tipped away from the severe, vertical, architectural forms that dominate *Standing Personage* (no. 20 above) in favour of more legible figurative forms, it is somewhat surprising that Lipchitz did not call this work *Seated Woman*. He was obviously distancing himself from the more hermetic, abstract work of 1915.

Despite the various titles that have been assigned to

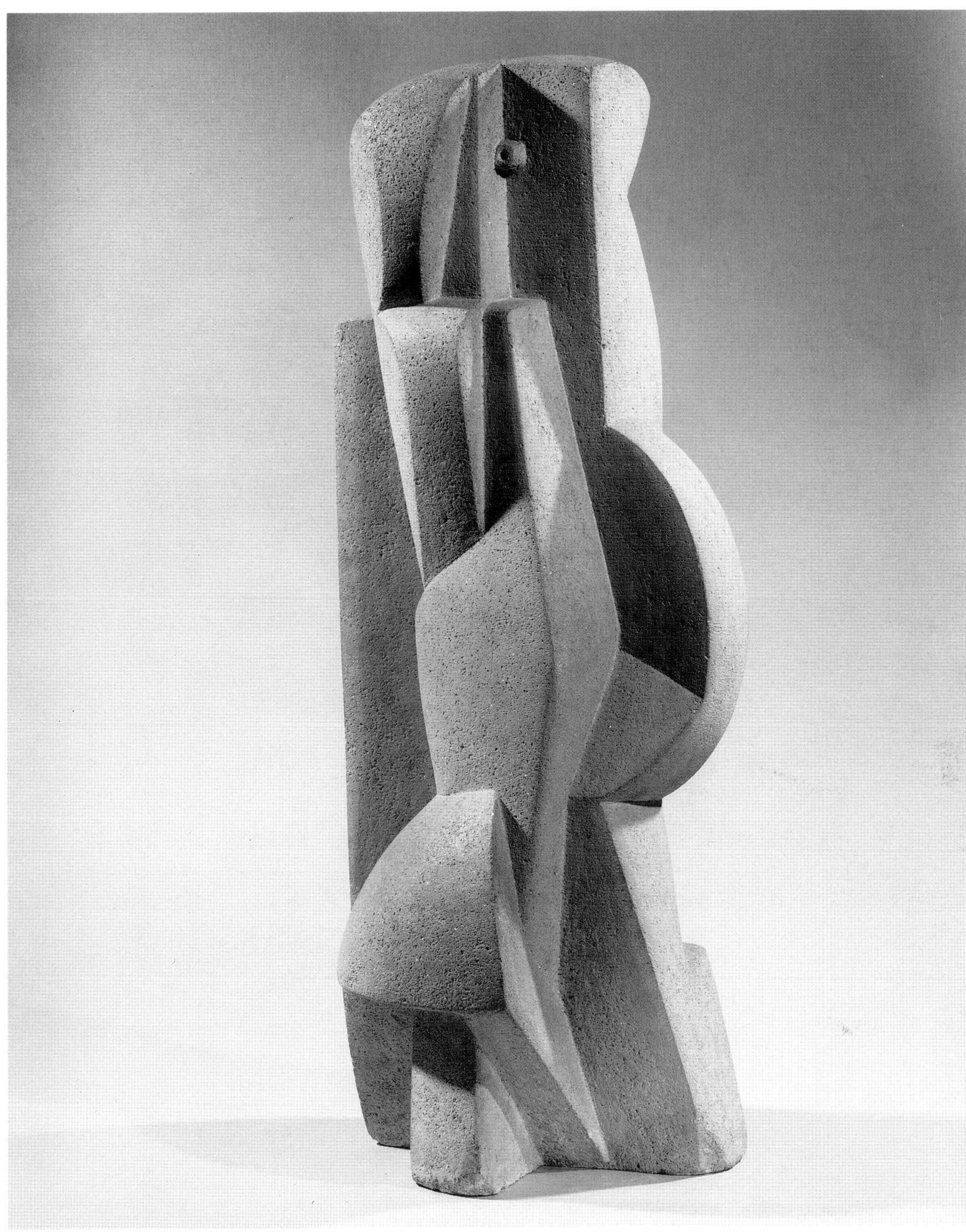

22

this sculpture, Lipchitz described the figure to Stott as a woman seated on a bench or a stone.[40] This is one of the earliest examples in Lipchitz's work in which the figure and the seat become inseparable and are totally integrated. (For a later example, see the 1922 *Guitar Player in Chair* (no. 38).) The head and eyes are clearly legible. When the work is viewed frontally, the flat, sloping plane and the thin form moving diagonally down to the right suggest the bend at the waist of the seated woman and a leg. The work may well be related to Picasso's series of watercolours of seated figures, usually in armchairs, of 1915–16.

22 *Seated Figure* 1917
Limestone
H. 30.3″/77.2 cm
National Gallery of Canada, Ottawa.
(Shown in Toronto only)

During 1916 and 1917 Lipchitz made a series of seated figures and bathers that reflect his struggle to find a balance between abstract and figurative elements in his work. In *Seated Bather* of 1916[41] he abandoned the rigid, vertical, architectural structure of sculptures such as *Standing Personage* (no. 20) in favour of twisting diago-

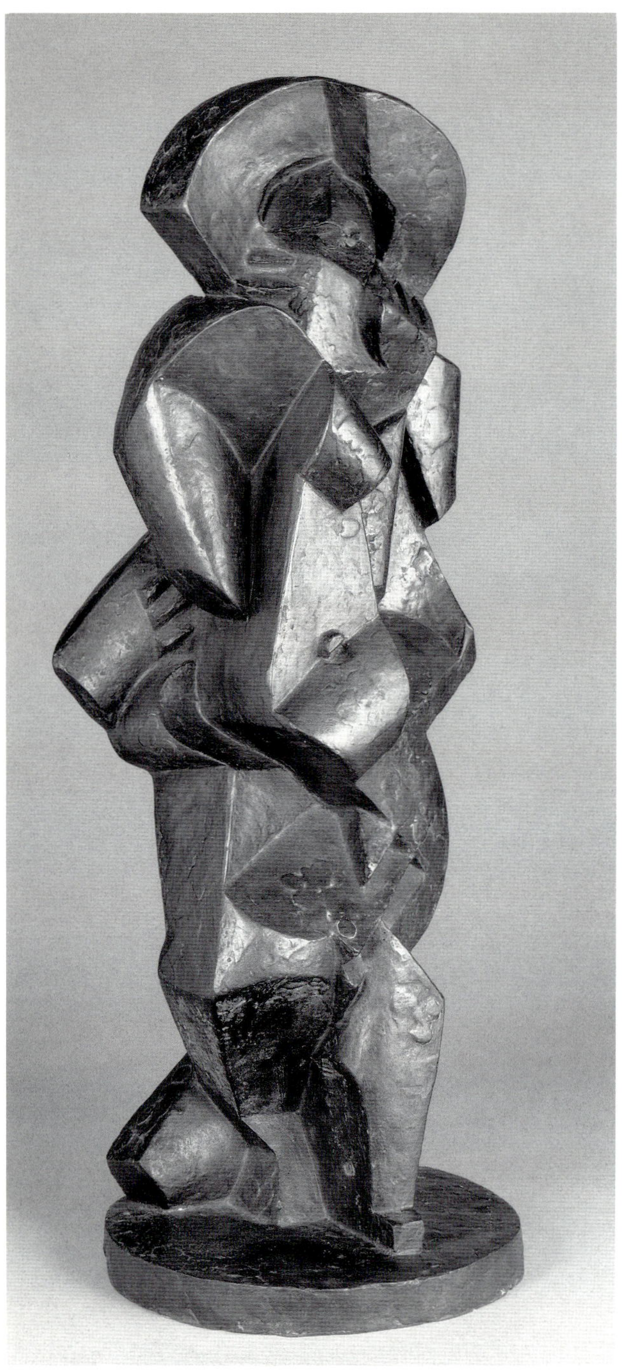

23

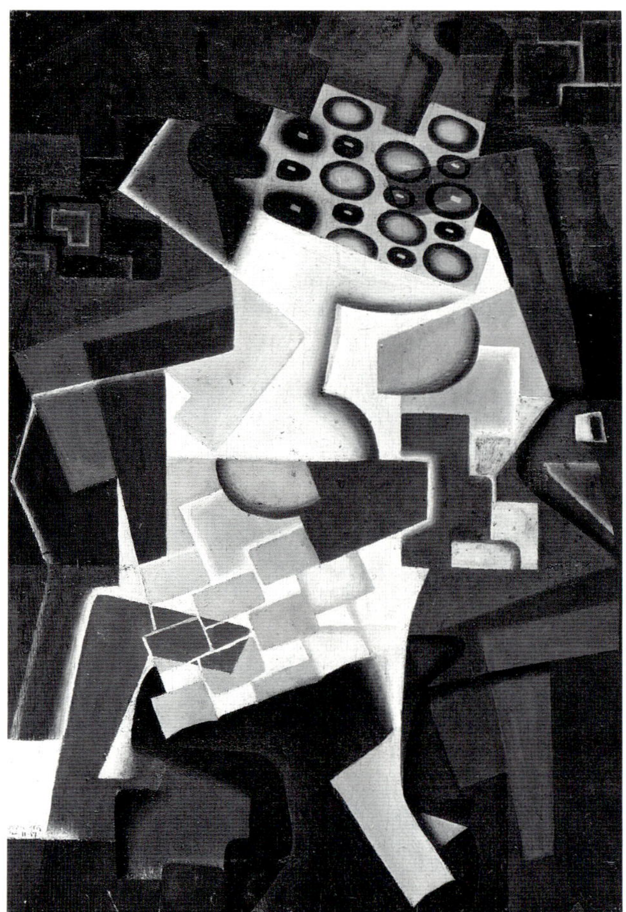

fig. 34 Juan Gris, Fruit Bowl on Checkered Cloth, *1917, oil on wood, 31¾ x 21⅜"/80.6 x 53.4 cm. Solomon R. Guggenheim Museum, New York.*

23 *Bather III* 1917
Bronze 5/7
H. 28¼"/71.8 cm
Art Gallery of Ontario, Gift of Sam and Ayala Zacks, 1970.

nals and curvilinear forms reminiscent of proto-Cubist works such as the 1913 *Dancer* (no. 5) and *Sailor with Guitar* 1914 (no. 9).

The Ottawa carving is related to the 1916 stone *Head*,[42] as well as to *Seated Bather*, mentioned above. As in the 1916 *Head*, Lipchitz said, "I was seeking an extreme simplification of solid, massive forms. Although I think it is a successful piece, I may have felt at that time that it was carried too far in the direction of austere abstraction."[43]

The year 1917 heralded a radical new departure in Lipchitz's working methods, which were closely linked with those of his close friend Juan Gris (see fig. 34). According to Stott:

> Lipchitz said that after his realization that Cubism meant construction rather than simplification or abstraction, he changed his approach. Instead of paring down from nature, he began by imagining some forms, some movements, and then from these made a figure... In other words, rather than reducing from life, he was thinking first about a construction, an abstract idea, and trying to give it life.[44]

In *Bather III* the relative equilibrium and the vertical architectural thrust of his work of the previous two years have been replaced by a tightly integrated network of flat planes and bulging forms, curves and sharp angles, convex and concave surfaces. Christopher Green, in conversation with this author, compared the unstable, jostling diagonals in *Bather III* with Gris's paintings of 1917, such as *Fruit-bowl, Pipe and Newspaper* (Öffentliche Kunstsammlung, Basel, Kunstmuseum). And yet, paradoxically, the complex, interlocking forms seem also related to Picasso's Analytic Cubist work of 1910, such as the *Seated Female Nude* in the Tate Gallery, London.

Individual elements of the human anatomy – the head, arms, and fingers, the navel, the crossed legs – are far more readily identifiable and, despite their origins in abstraction, have been organized in a way that is closer to the basic proportions of the human figure than the forms in his work of the previous two years. Lipchitz's Cubist method, working toward a recognizable subject from imagined, invented forms, is, in the words of Polonius in act II, scene one, of Hamlet: "By indirections find directions art."

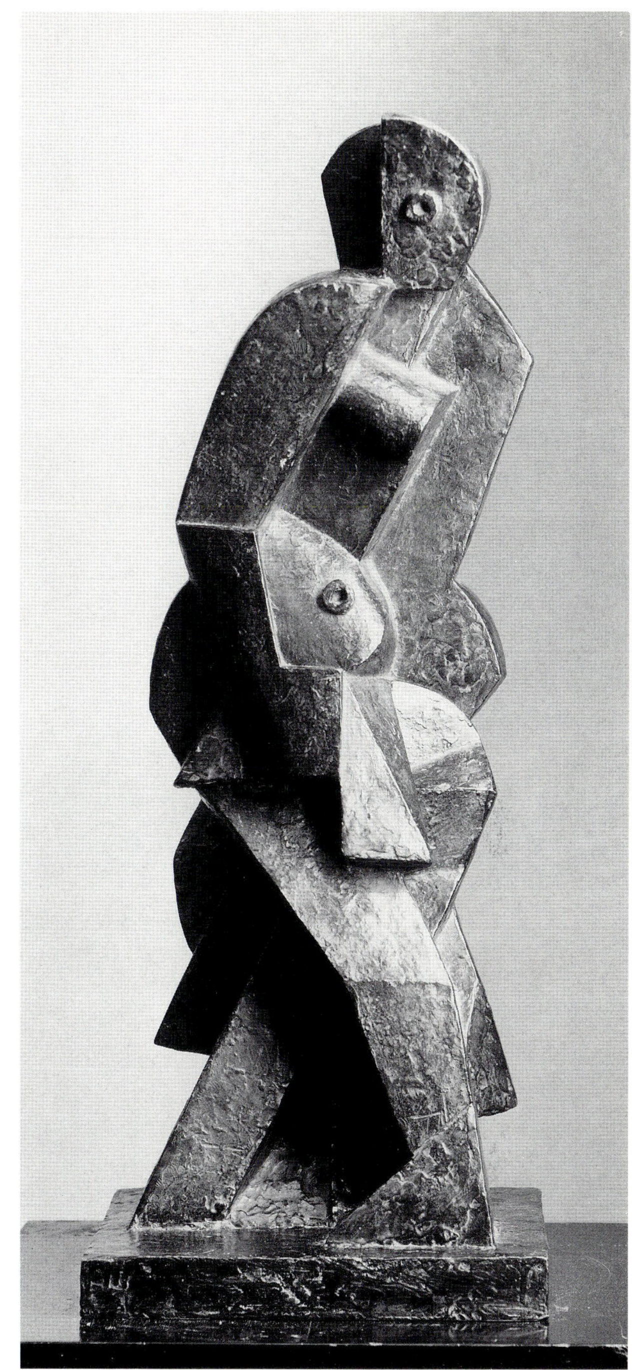

24 *Bather* 1917
Bronze 1/7
H. 34¾"/88.3 cm
The Nelson-Atkins Museum of Art, Kansas City, Missouri (Gift of the Friends of Art).

Bather, LIKE THE TORONTO BRONZE (NO. 23), RETAINS the massive faceted forms that give the appearance of having been hacked out of wood with an axe or a chain saw. Whereas *Bather III* is frontal, as if built outwards from a central vertical line running from the top of the head to the centre of the base, in the Nelson-Atkins's *Bather*, there is, as Lipchitz pointed out, "a sense of twisting movement, of the figure spiraling around its axis."[45] Lipchitz has used a pose very similar to that of the 1913 *Dancer* (no. 5). He saw several of his bathers as reminiscent of this traditional subject in the history of sculpture: "*Bather* [no. 24] is conceived as a bather stepping down to a pool or a river... This is a pose suggestive of certain eighteenth-century bathers by Falconet and other sculptors of the time."[46]

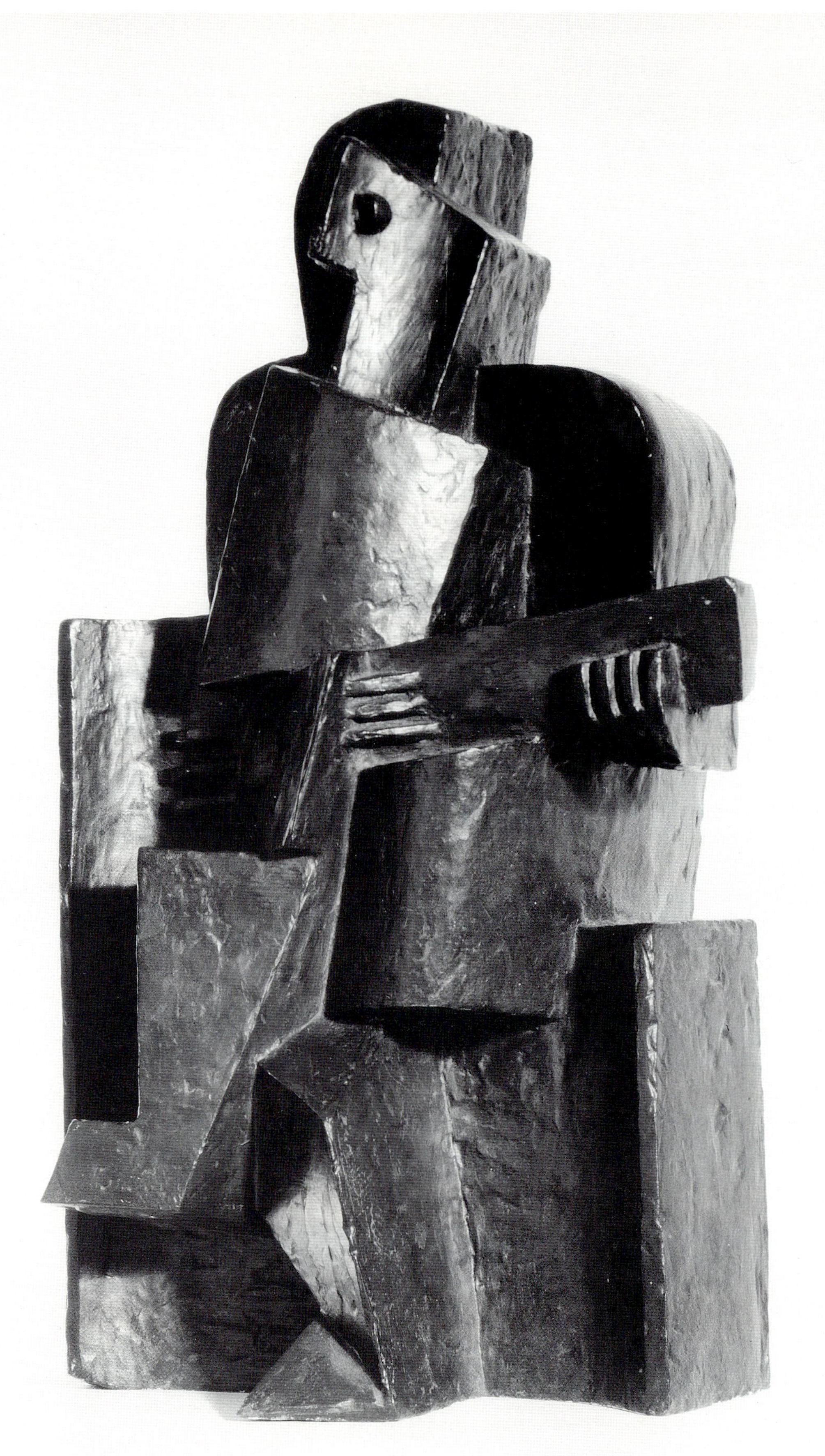

25 *Seated Man with Guitar* 1918
Bronze
H. 30″/76.2 cm
Mr. and Mrs. Alejandro Freites, New York.

THE YEAR 1918 WAS A CRUCIAL YEAR FOR LIPCHITZ, WHO spent the spring and summer months working closely with Gris at Beaulieu-lès-Loches in Touraine (see no. 26). Although *Seated Man with Guitar* was made in early 1918, probably before Lipchitz left Paris, the sculpture is nevertheless closely related to the work of Gris. Indeed, certain details, such as the higher profile of the double head, the curve of the right shoulder and the larger, more simplified, less faceted forms, suggest that Lipchitz's bronze is almost a paraphrase of Gris's *Harlequin with a Guitar*, painted in December 1917.

In discussing his work of early 1918, Lipchitz described his awareness of the effects of negative space as an addition to his vocabulary.

> This was simply a matter of wrapping the solid forms around a void to frame it, in effect using the void rather than the volume of the stone to suggest the form of the head or part of the torso... In this work [no. 25] there is an opposition between the positive volume on the right and the negative volume on the left, a delicate transition from light to shadow in the contrasting curves. Although I had used comparable effects earlier, these now became a significant part of my total vocabulary, one that was to lead to my most open and transparent sculpture of the twenties.[47] (See nos. 47–49).

Seated Man with Guitar also reflects Lipchitz's renewed interest in frontality. Whereas *Bather* 1917 (no. 24) emphasizes what he calls the classical or Renaissance spiral, in *Seated Man with Guitar* "the figure is rather wide and squat, firmly and frontally placed on his chair, with the guitar and the legs at severe right angles, emphasizing the frontal design."[48] Lipchitz saw this as an echo of his early interest in Egyptian, archaic Greek and African art.

26 *Bas-Relief I* 1918
Stone relief, polychrome
22 x 14 x 1¾″/55.7 x 35.7 x 4.4 cm
National Gallery of Art, Washington. Adolph Caspar Miller Fund 1977.29.1.
(Shown in Toronto only)

WHEN THE GERMANS BEGAN SHELLING PARIS IN MID 1918 in the last counteroffensive of the war, Lipchitz and his wife decided to leave and joined Gris in Beaulieu-lès-Loches.

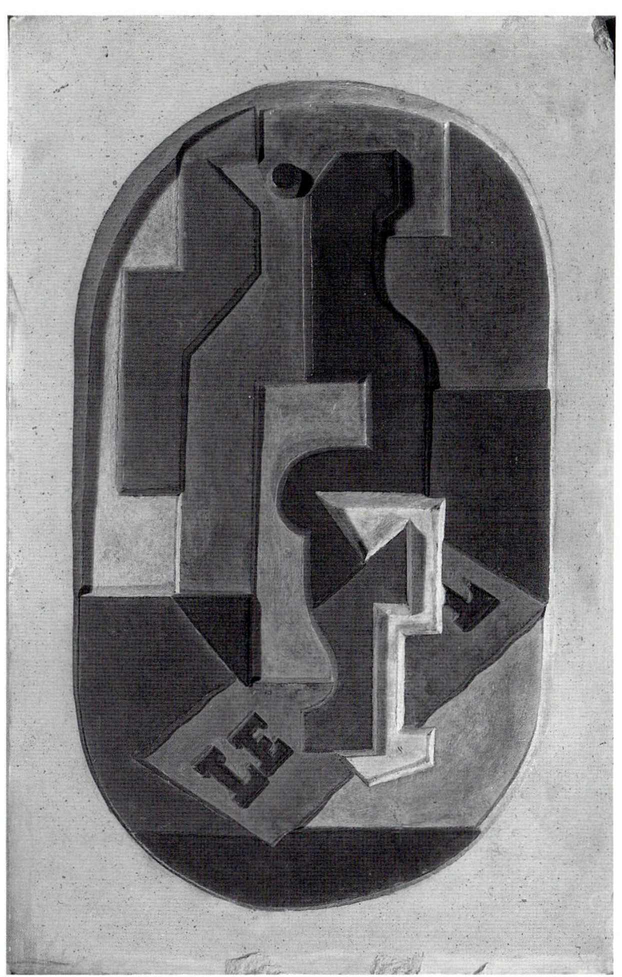

> In Beaulieu, in the spring and summer of 1918, I was not equipped to continue with my free-standing sculpture, so I made drawings and gouaches, preparatory sketches for a series of bas reliefs. In these, perhaps because I was thinking them out so completely with colored drawings, I began to experiment with polychrome.[49]

The Washington carving would appear to be the first of two reliefs that Lipchitz executed at Beaulieu. A second, closely related polychrome stone of 1918 is entitled *Bas-Relief* (it should perhaps be called *Bas Relief II*).[50] Although Lipchitz stated that he was "antagonistic to the use of color on sculpture,"[51] he had painted several of his detachable figures of 1915 (see no. 12). Whereas in fully three-dimensional sculpture colour can, depending on the lighting, distort the volumes and planes, in relief sculpture, which, like painting, hangs on a wall, colour can be more carefully controlled and "can even enhance the sculptural effects one is seeking."[52]

In this work, the clarity of the sharply delineated

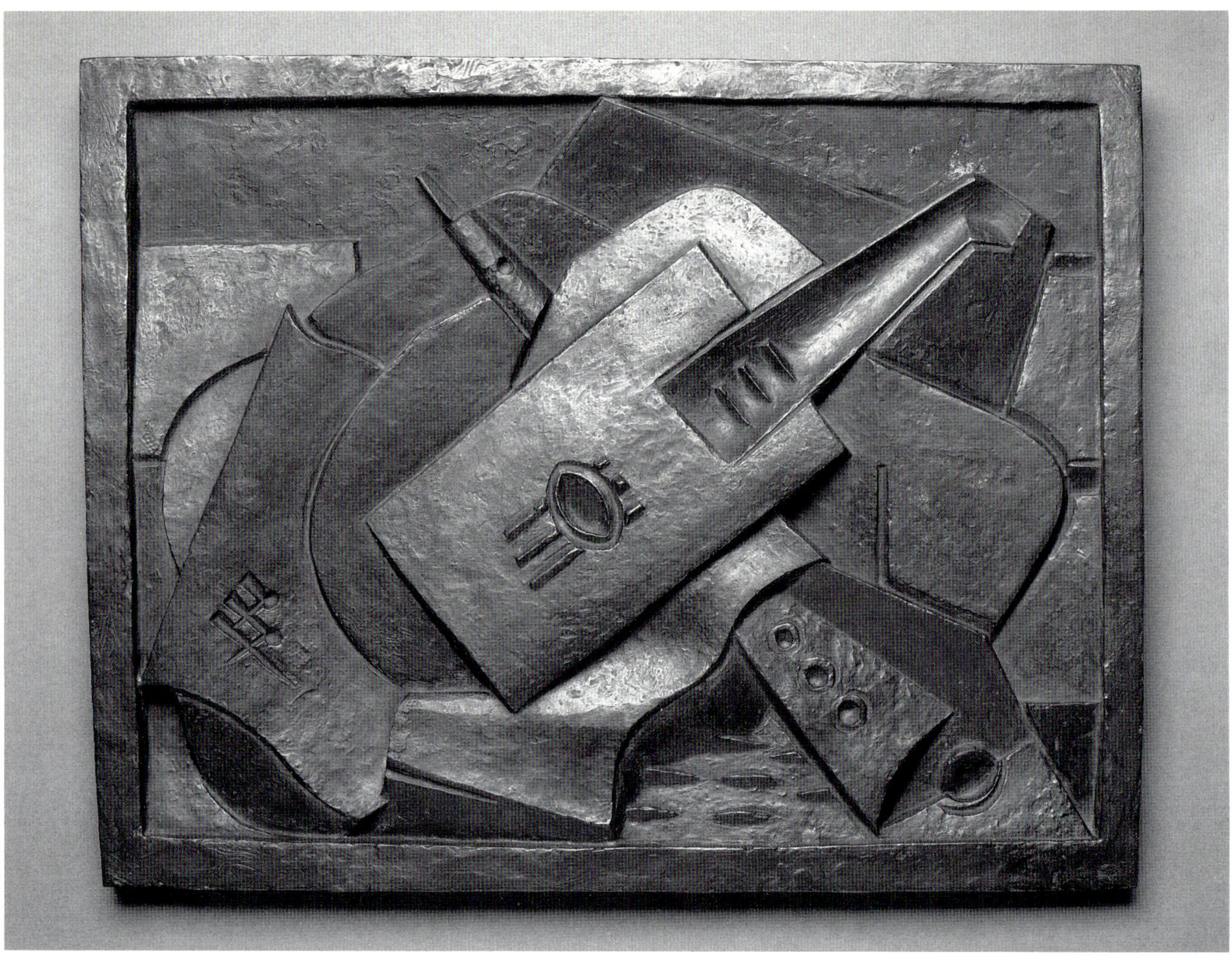

27

forms and the contrast between the darker planes projecting forward and the lighter-coloured planes receding strongly echo Gris's work of the period, such as *Guitar and Fruit Bowl on a Table* of August 1918 (fig. 12). Lipchitz had previously focused all his attention on the human figure, and this was probably his first still-life subject. As Christopher Green has remarked, "the forming of the bottle's head and shoulders is almost exchangable with that of heads and shoulders in earlier figure pieces..."[53]

In 1917, under Lipchitz's supervision, Gris made his only sculpture, the painted plaster *Harlequin*, now in the Philadelphia Museum of Art (fig. 10). In *Bas-Relief I*, an almost two-dimensional work, it was Lipchitz's turn to follow closely the distilled purity of vision of his friend Gris.

27 *Still Life* 1918
Bronze 4/7
22⅛ x 27⅞ x 1⅜"/56.2 x 70.8 x 3.5 cm
The Estate of Jacques Lipchitz represented by Marlborough International Fine Art AG.

The iconography of Lipchitz's Cubist sculptures and reliefs followed closely that of the work of Gris, Picasso and Braque: harlequins and still lifes incorporating everyday objects such as wine bottles, glasses, musical instruments and newspapers. As John Golding has pointed out:

> Cubism, despite the strong intellectual bias and obvious concern with purely formal pictorial values, was never at any stage an abstract art.[54]

In *Still Life*, the formal arrangement of objects is far more straightforward than in *Bas-Relief I*, with its complex spatial ambiguities. Indeed, the main section of the guitar is simply a flat, rectangular surface with an eye-shaped hole, with three rows of strings standing out in low relief. The way in which the concave neck of the guitar slots into the body of the instrument is reminiscent of the detachable constructions of 1915. The curved plane above and attached to the guitar seems to suggest its shadow, or, more likely, that, as in Cubist painting, the side of the object has been brought into the picture plane.

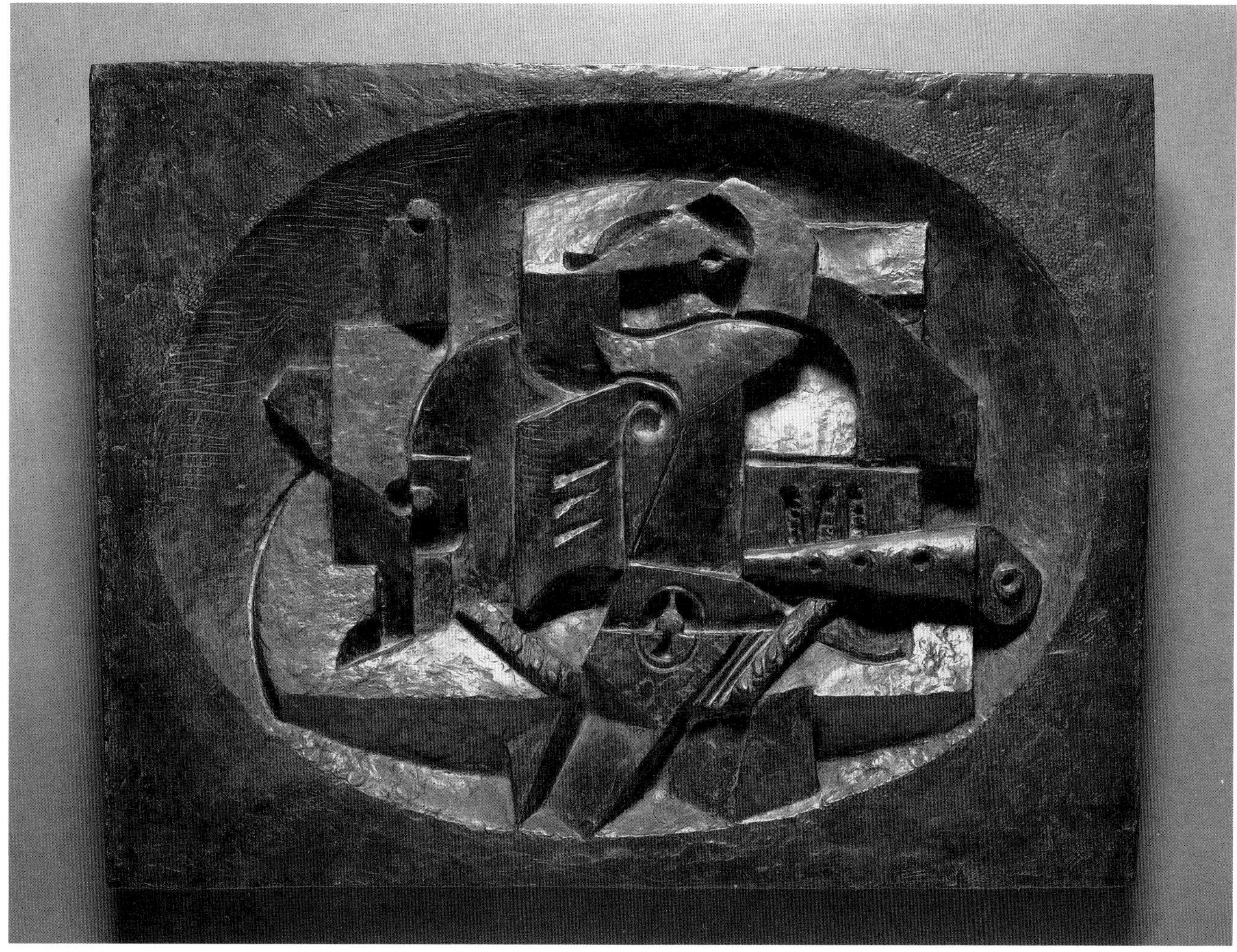

28

The rifle is a most unusual and unexpected addition to the everyday objects that typify the subject matter of almost all Cubist painting and sculpture. The three holes carved into the butt of the rifle may be intended to disguise somewhat this object, by setting up a visual pun between a weapon of war and another musical instrument such as a clarinet (see no. 29). This was the first of Lipchitz's sculptures to reflect the political events around him. This was a trend in his work that was to gather momentum in the early 1930s with Hitler's rise to power.

28 *Still Life* 1918
Bronze 3/7
21½ x 26¾ x 2⅝"/54.5 x 68.0 x 6.7 cm
The Estate of Jacques Lipchitz represented by
Marlborough International Fine Art AG.

THIS WORK, WHICH HAS ALSO BEEN REFERRED TO AS *Still Life with Musical Instruments*, was, like no. 27 above, executed after Lipchitz returned to Paris from Beaulieu in the autumn of 1918. Having abandoned the use of colour, which defined the projected planes and recessed areas in his Beaulieu reliefs, Lipchitz altered his approach to relief sculpture.

> In this I have organized the objects within a rather deeply cut oval which gives them a strong sense of projection from the ground. I am using here, within the oval frame, many clearly curvilinear shapes, curving lines reiterating the oval, spheres and a funnel shape contrasting with rectangles and diagonal projections. The increased use of curvilinear shapes anticipates the direction of my sculpture during the next few years.[55]

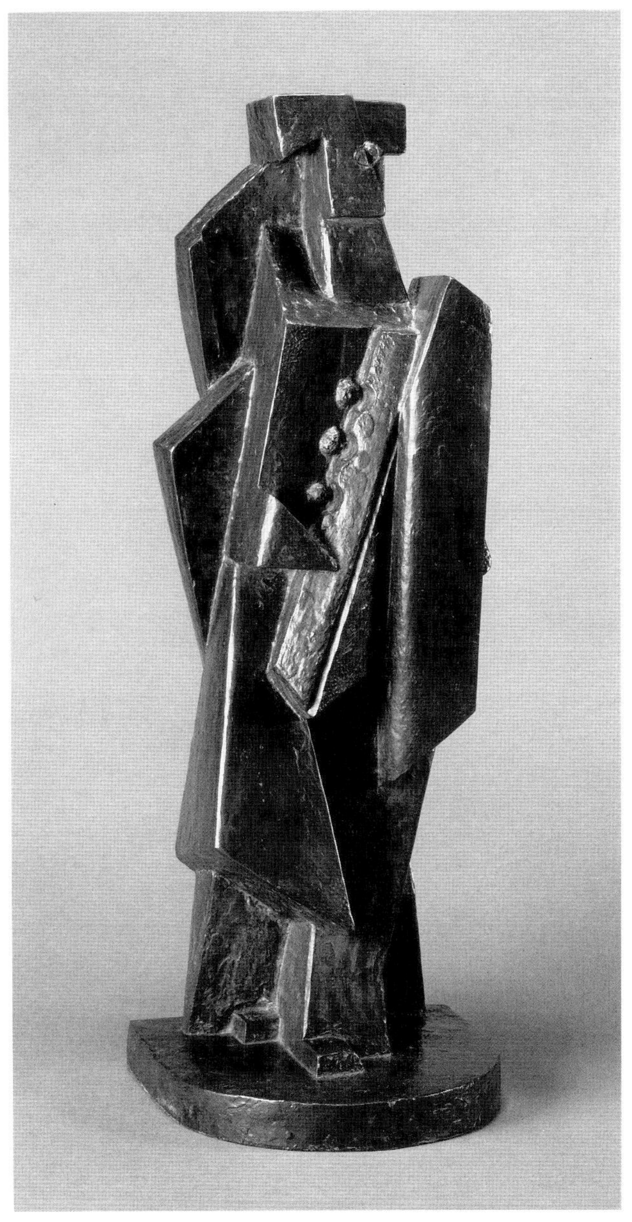

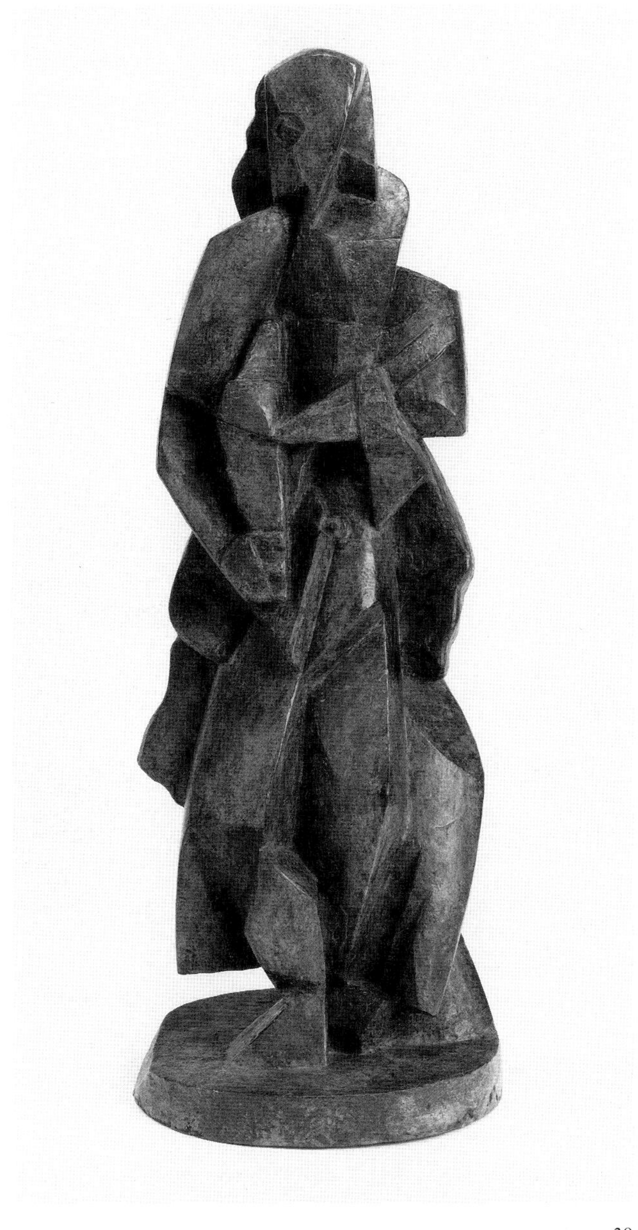

30

29 *Harlequin with Clarinet* 1919
Bronze, edition of 7
H. 28¾"/73.0 cm
The Estate of Jacques Lipchitz represented by Marlborough International Fine Art AG.

In 1919 Lipchitz abandoned relief sculpture and returned to fully three-dimensional work. The charming series of harlequins and Pierrots playing the clarinet or the accordion reflected his interest in eighteenth-century painting, and particularly the work of Watteau:

> The Pierrots and harlequins were part of our general vocabulary, characters taken from the commedia del l'arte, particularly popular in the eighteenth century... Generally, this [1919–20] was a transitional period in which I was playing variations on a number of familiar themes, more or less conscious that I needed to find a new direction, a new stimulus.[56]

The pose of *Harlequin with Clarinet*, with one foot in front of the other, recalls *Bather III* of 1917 (no. 23), while the flatter, less busily faceted forms are closer to *Seated Man with Guitar* of 1918 (no. 25). The break with Lipchitz's previous work is in the treatment of the head (see also fig. 13), which, as in the harlequin paintings of Picasso and Gris of 1918–19, conveys something of the real, masklike appearance of the subject. The cubelike rather than the faceted shape of the head also strongly echoes Gris's only sculpture, the 1917 painted plaster *Harlequin* (see fig. 10).

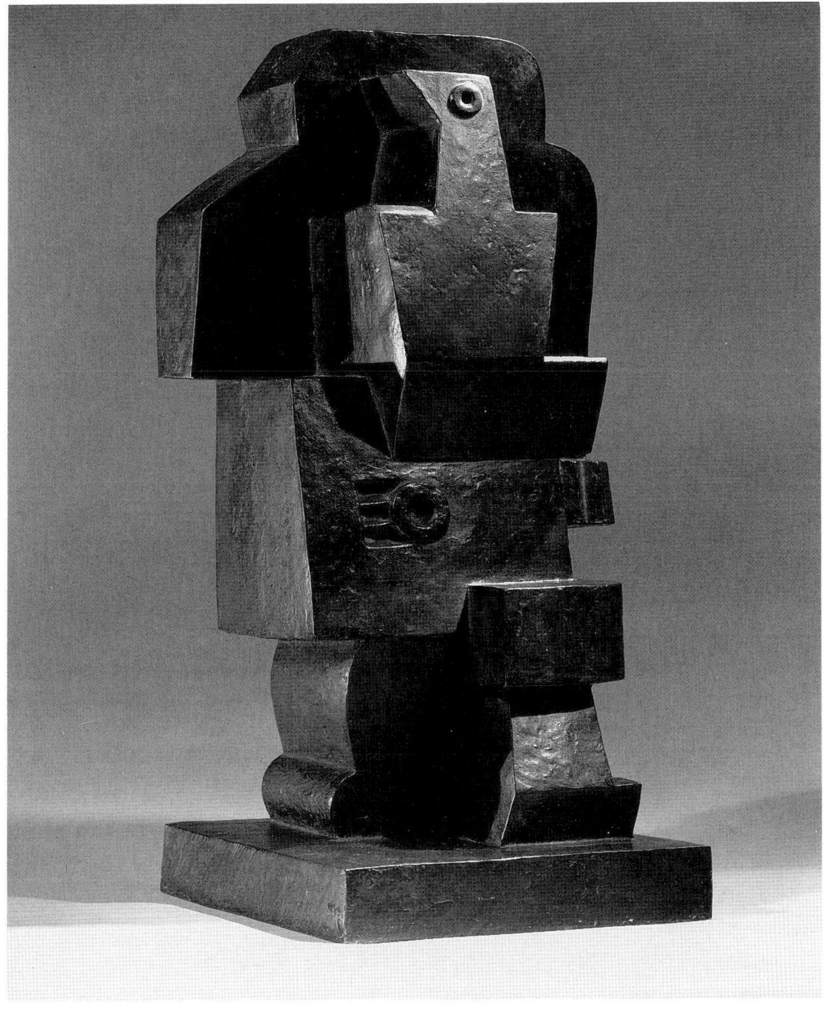

31

30 *Draped Woman* 1919
Bronze 3/7
H. 36¾″/93.3 cm
San Francisco Museum of Modern Art, Gift of Mr. and Mrs. Wellington S. Henderson

This is one of the first sculptures by Lipchitz that seems to echo, however faintly, the freestanding work of Henri Laurens. Three features or details in particular, which do not appear in Lipchitz's previous work, suggest the subtle influence of his French colleague. The first is the juxtaposition of the straight line of the head, turned in profile to the left, and the wavy outline of the hair (as opposed to a single curve). The second is the similar wavy line of the form above the right hand, and the third is the form of the right hand itself, which is almost identical to the right hand in Laurens's 1919 stone *Woman with Guitar* (private collection).[57] In turn, Braque's bronze *Standing Figure* of 1920,[58] his first attempt at working in three dimensions, appears, in its decorative character, to have affinities with the sculpture of both Laurens and Lipchitz.

31 *Man with Guitar* 1920
Bronze
H. 20⅝″/52.4 cm
The Montreal Museum of Fine Arts Collection, purchase, Horsley and Annie Townsend Bequest.

The early 1920s was a period of restlessness as Lipchitz felt the need to find a new direction, a new stimulus. He saw *Man with Guitar* as one of the most successful of those transitional works in which he was continuing with variations on his earlier Cubist subjects:

> This should be compared with the *Seated Man with Guitar* of 1918 [no. 25]...the work that prophesied a movement toward a kind of massive frontality. The later *Man with Guitar* is now completely frontalized, composed of massive, integrated blocks. I even eliminated the shaft of the guitar, squaring off the body and integrating it completely with the torso of the figure. The asymmetrical staring eyes give to the figure a peculiar sense of almost hypnotic power which emphasizes its specific human personality. This is a work that is important to me as an anticipation of the monumental totemistic *Figure* of 1926 to 1930 [no. 51].[59]

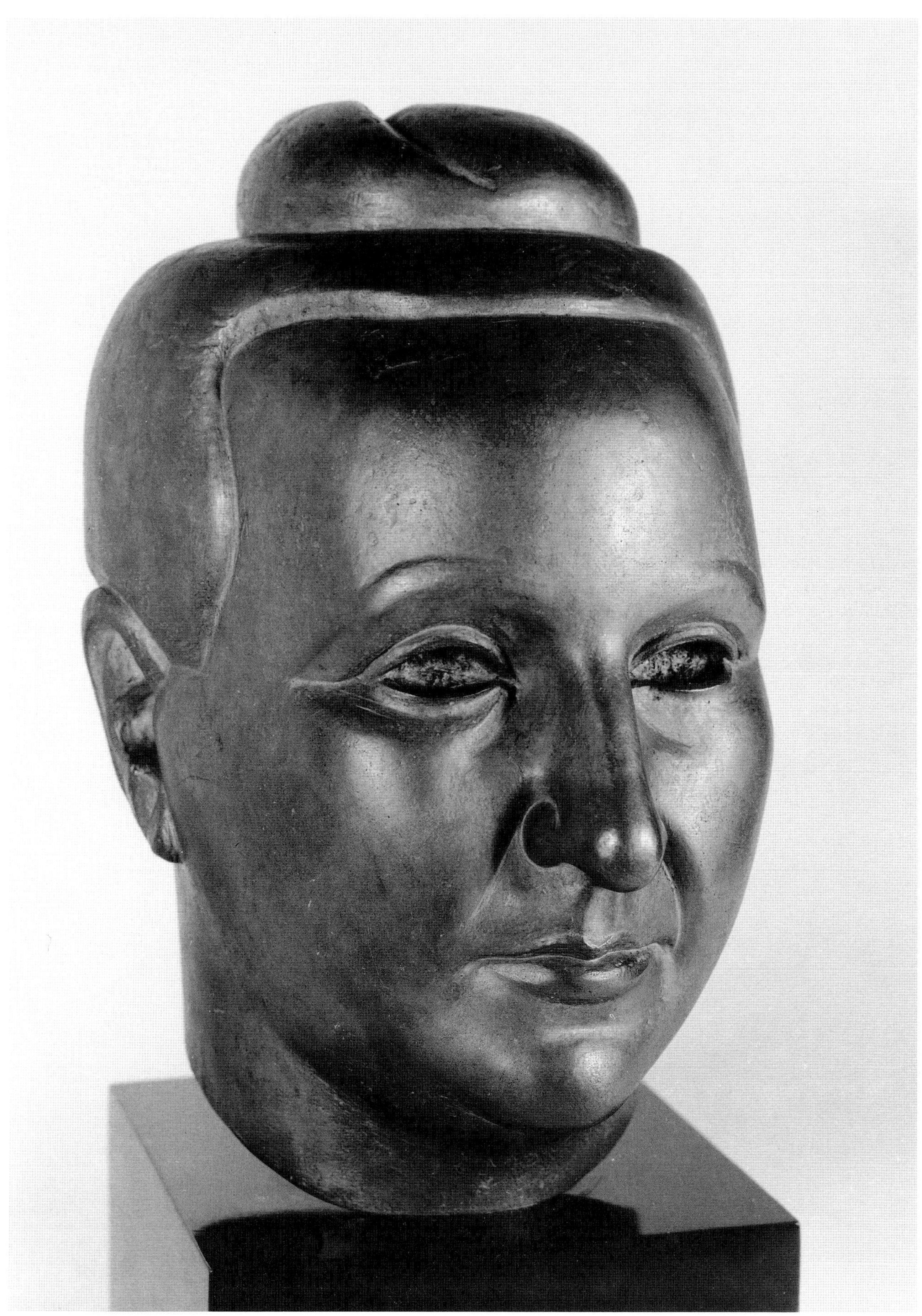

32 *Gertrude Stein* 1920
Bronze
H. 13⅞/34.1 cm
The Baltimore Museum of Art: The Cone Collection, formed by Dr. Claribel Cone and Miss Etta Cone of Baltimore, Maryland (BMA 1950.396).

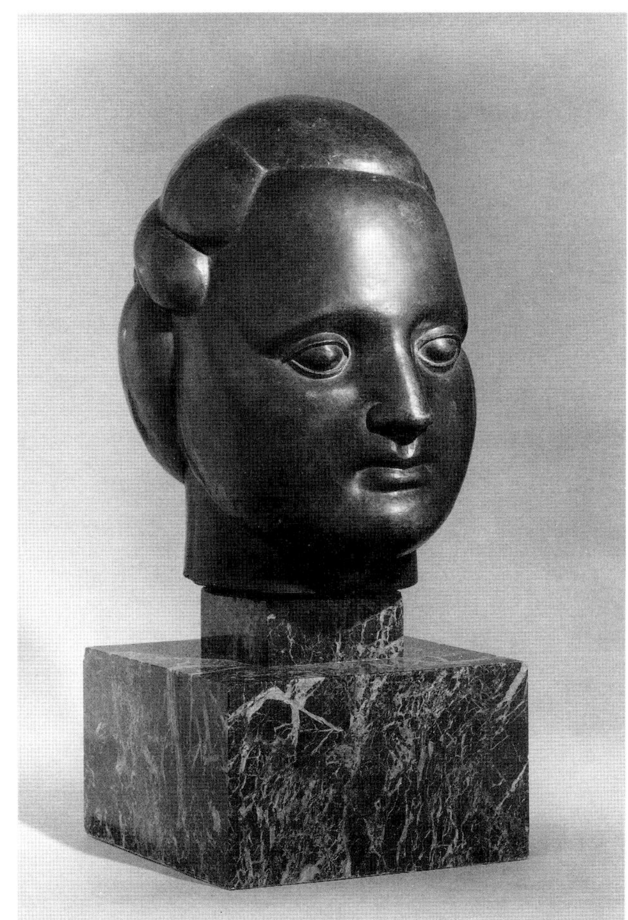

fig. 35 Henri Matisse, Grosse tête, *1927, bronze, H. 12.6"/ 32.1 cm. National Gallery of Canada, Ottawa. © Succession H. Matisse/ARS N.Y. 1989.*

IN 1920 LIPCHITZ MADE A SERIES OF PORTRAITS, AMONG them studies of the young writer Raymond Radiguet and of Jean Cocteau and Gertrude Stein. "There was," Lipchitz remarked, "after the war, a movement toward realism on the part of many artists in Paris and elsewhere. Picasso had again begun making beautiful, realistic drawings when he was associated with the Russian ballet..."[60] These include studies of dancers made during a visit to London in the summer of 1919, as well as portrait drawings of Massine and Diaghilev.

Before the war, Lipchitz had frequented the Stein's well-known apartment in the rue de Fleurus. In 1920, when he met Gertrude Stein again on a Parisian street, he asked her if he could do her portrait, no doubt hoping this wealthy collector would purchase it. In *The Autobiography of Alice B. Toklas*, the encounter is described as follows:

> Gertrude Stein had known Lipschitz [*sic*] very slightly at one time but this incident made them friends and soon he asked her to pose. He had just finished a bust of Jean Cocteau and he wanted to do her. She never minds posing, she likes the calm of it and although she does not like sculpture and told Lipschitz so, she began to pose. I remember it was a very hot spring and Lipschitz's studio was appalling [*sic*] hot and they spent hours there...
>
> And then they talked about art and Gertrude Stein rather liked her portrait and they were very good friends and the sittings were over.[61]

Lipchitz made at least two portraits of Stein in 1920. In the first study (of which there is a bronze cast in the Centre Georges Pompidou, Musée National d'Art Moderne) he included the eyes and pupils, whereas in this sculpture, he explained, "I hollowed out the eyes deeply but did not indicate the pupils, so that they give an impression of shadowed introspection which emphasized the characterization I was making."[62]

Here Lipchitz has represented his famous subject as "a massive, inscrutable Buddha."[63] The smooth, stretched volumes are the antithesis of the varying degrees of planes and faceted forms that had dominated his work since the proto-Cubist sculpture of 1913. This remarkable study of Gertrude Stein, perhaps Lipchitz's greatest portrait, anticipates to a remarkable degree Matisse's 1927 bronze *Grosse tête* in the National Gallery of Canada (fig. 35). In 1938 Lipchitz made two more portrait heads of Stein, very different in character (see no. 80).

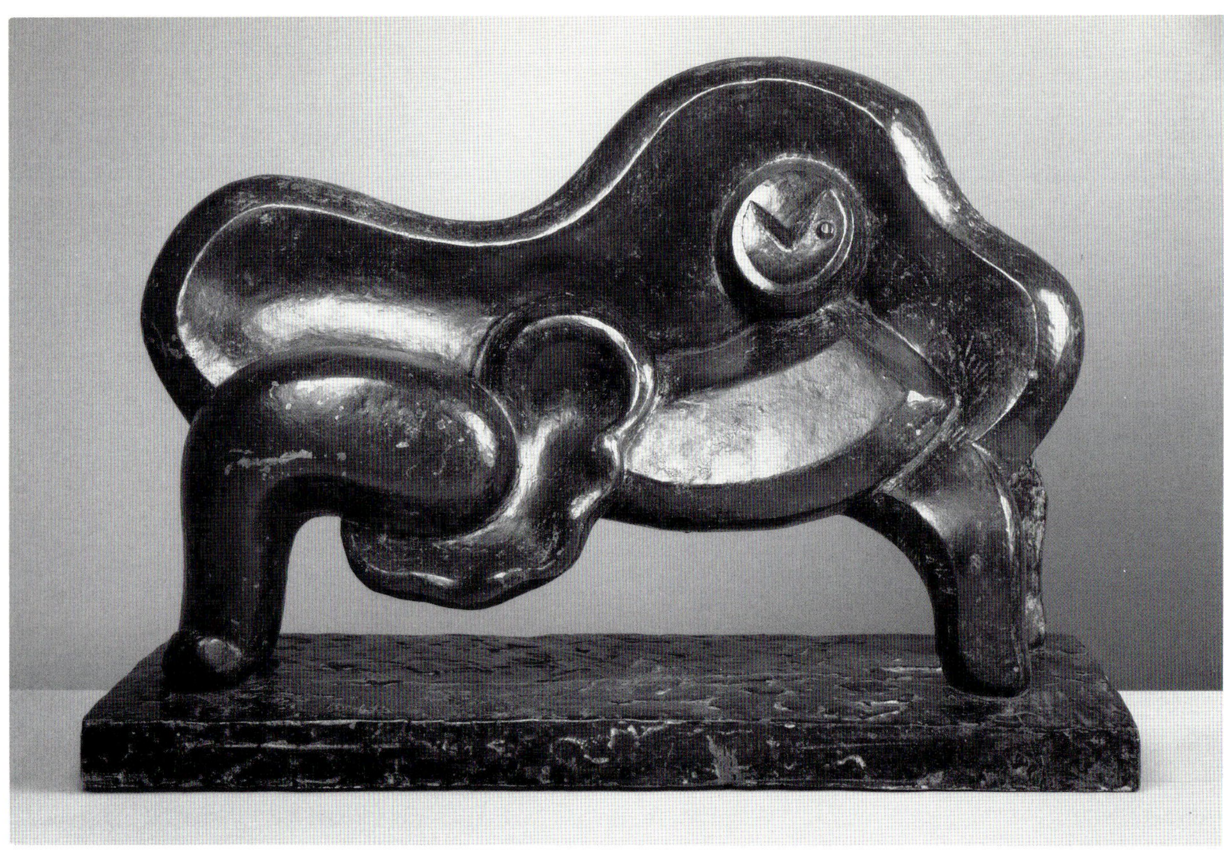

33 *Reclining Woman* 1921
Bronze, edition of 7
L. 19¾″/50.2 cm
The Estate of Jacques Lipchitz represented by Marlborough International Fine Art AG.

Several critical events in the early 1920s were instrumental in setting Lipchitz free, as it were, from the uncompromising, severe Cubist style that had informed his work from 1915 to 1920. As we have seen, he was anxious to try new ideas, but his dealer, Léonce Rosenberg, felt that if he changed direction his work might be less saleable. As a result of this confrontation, they agreed to part after his successful exhibition in early 1920 at Rosenberg's galerie de l'Effort Moderne. With the help of friends, he was able to buy back all his sculpture from the dealer.

In 1921 Lipchitz received an important commission to do a portrait of Coco Chanel, the famous couturiere. The portrait itself was less significant than the ensuing works that she asked Lipchitz to make for her house and garden. The first of these was a pair of andirons that she wanted for her rococo Louis XV-style fireplace and chimney, "all decorative curves, completely opposed to the geometric cubist sculpture I had been making. I realized that I must change my entire approach for this commission, and the experiment in curvilinear forms was to have a most profound effect on my sculpture for the next decades."[64]

In *Reclining Woman*, one of the two andirons, the constraints of the rigorous geometrical style of his Cubist work of the previous five years gives way to fluent, curvilinear rhythms that evoke the sensuousness of the subject and something of the opulent setting for which it was made. Also, the reclining figure was a new subject for Lipchitz. In his proto-Cubist and Cubist sculpture he had concentrated exclusively on a vertical format. As in his early works, the figure, a reclining woman, and its surroundings, the sofa, fuse and become inseparable. The small circular head nestles in the concave form of the sofa. The outline of the main horizontal form of the sculpture suggests at once the soft, curving lines of a reclining woman and the shape of the piece of furniture on which she rests. Lipchitz even introduces a note of slightly risqué, even risky, humour in the earlike shape, which, fittingly, opens out at the top of the large bent (human) leg on the left of the sculpture. Lipchitz told Stott that at the time Chanel was the mistress of an English duke or earl and "he wanted to show in a humorous fashion how she made her living. So he made a woman reclining on a sofa with her skirt up."[65]

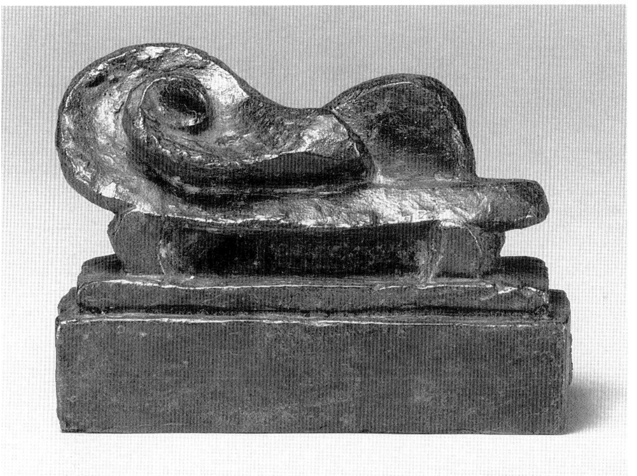

34 *Reclining Woman* 1921
Bronze 2/7
L. 4″/10.2 cm
The Estate of Jacques Lipchitz represented by Marlborough International Fine Art AG.

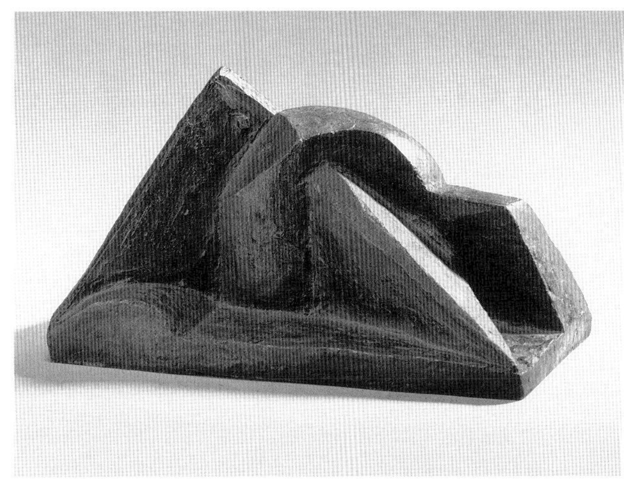

35 *Repentant Magdalene* 1921
Bronze 2/7
H. 3¼″/8.3 cm
The Estate of Jacques Lipchitz represented by Marlborough International Fine Art AG.

Lipchitz's association with Coco Chanel was unquestionably one of the turning points in his career. He was, for the first time, creating sculptures for a specific environment or setting. The rococo style of her fireplace led, in no. 33 above, to the first sensuous, curvilinear Cubist sculptures of the 1920s. As Christopher Green remarked about this new spirit of compromise and accommodation, "To begin with at least, Lipchitz softened his Cubism quite simply to make it more pleasantly decorative."[66]

Coco Chanel also requested that Lipchitz make some designs for garden sculptures, and although the project was never completed he created a series of preliminary studies in the form of very small maquettes. The importance of this sudden change in direction in Lipchitz's working method cannot be overemphasized. For the rest of his working life, preparatory sketches in clay were an integral part of the creative process, a spontaneous way of generating ideas for sculpture.

Among the studies for garden sculptures was a vertical, diamond-shaped column, surmounted by a figure group, that anticipates *Study for Figure* of 1926 (no. 50). He also made this small *Reclining Woman*, which was suggested by the figures on the two andirons. The work, he said, "marked the beginning of this theme in my sculpture as well, perhaps, as in the sculpture of many others during the next decades."[67] This was perhaps an oblique allusion to the dominant theme in the work of Henry Moore.

In two other preparatory maquettes for garden reliefs, Lipchitz abandoned the newly formulated organic, curvilinear style and returned to the severe geometry found in such purely Cubist works as the 1920 *Man with Guitar* (no. 31). In *Seated Woman in Armchair* of 1921, a pendant to no. 35, the figure consists of two simplified, abstracted blocks that are integrated into the curved back of the chair. Here, Lipchitz introduces, for the first time in his work, a Christian subject. He describes below the rather baffling subject of this sculpture, the reclining Magdalene reading a book:

> This is simplified to an asymmetrical pyramid intersected by a curving mass. I gave it the title *Repentant Magdalene* later, although there is to me the suggestion of a reclining figure reading a book. This is perhaps significant as one of my very first uses of a Christian subject, although in making it I was not thinking particularly about the Christian theme. There was in my mind some idea of a repentance that I myself felt, conceivably a repentance for my excursion into realistic portraiture.[68]

It was not until 1926–27 that, as is openly manifest in the title of the transparent *Pierrot Escapes* (no. 52), that Lipchitz felt completely free from the rigid discipline of Cubism.

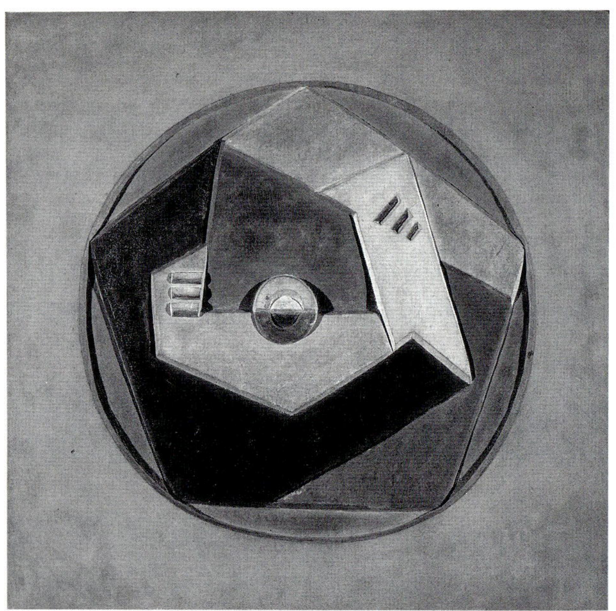

36 *Bas Relief II* 1921
Polychrome relief (unique)
23¾ x 23¾ x 3¾"/60.3 x 60.3 x 9.5 cm
The Estate of Jacques Lipchitz represented by Marlborough International Fine Art AG.

If Lipchitz felt he had betrayed the principles of Cubism with his realistic portraits, such as *Gertrude Stein* 1920 (no. 32), he was firmly back on track with *Bas Relief II*. The objects themselves are inseparable from the entire interlocking structure of the composition contained within the circle. The round hole of the guitar is the central focal point, with the strings indicated by three rectangular shapes in low relief. The arm of the guitar, with the sharp point at the top, looks as if it had been folded up in order to fit into the constricted space within the circle. Rarely did Lipchitz distance himself to this extent from his subject or come so close, in the interplay of these sharply defined forms, to the brink of pure abstraction.

37 *Seated Man* 1922
Brittany granite (unique)
H. 20½"/52.0 cm
Virginia Museum of Fine Arts, General Endowment Fund.

The simplified, blocklike forms of *Seated Man* recall *Seated Man with Guitar* of 1918 (no. 25) and *Man with Guitar* of 1920 (no. 31). Lipchitz thought of this work as a new departure, with the entire form "solidly cubic in a

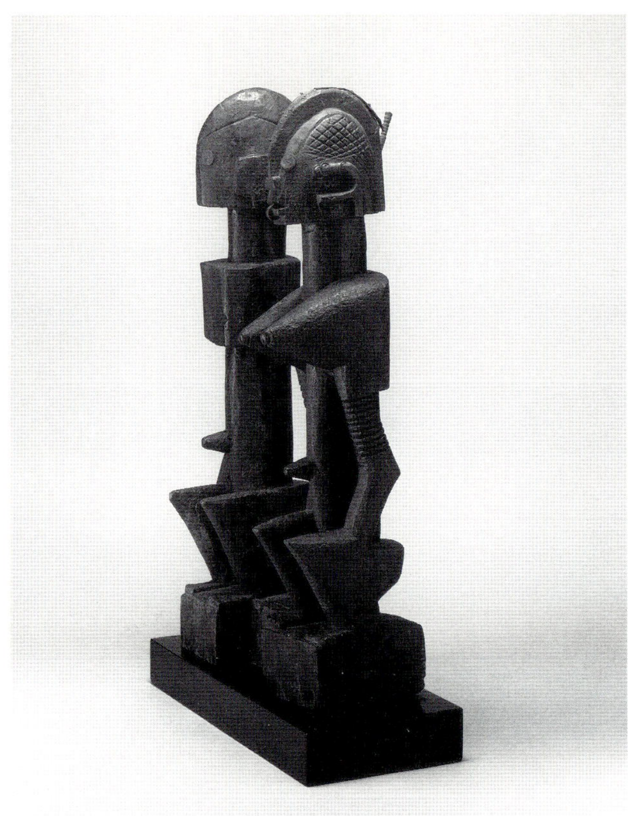

fig. 36 Primeval Couple, *Dogon/Mali, wood and iron, H. 22¾"/57.8 cm. Barbara and Murray Frum Collection, Toronto.*

literal sense rather than traditionally cubist, with the figure frontalized diagonally on the square base, the vertical masses pulled together by the curving, enclosing arms."[69] Here Lipchitz has successfully fused the austere geometry of his work of 1915–17 with the curvilinear lines of the 1921 *Reclining Woman* (no. 33). In the lower half of the figure, the splayed feet and legs and the way in which the arms and hand meet suggest a single figure. While it could be argued that the double heads are a feature borrowed from Synthetic Cubist painting, the sheer physical presence of the heads, locked together, facing in different directions, gives the strong impression or illusion of double figures, or, as Stott wrote, "a highly organized portrait of Siamese twins."[70] In other words, two-dimensional Cubist conventions, such as showing frontal and profile views of a single head, have a very different visual impact when translated into solid, sculptural forms.

Certain of Lipchitz's sculptures of the 1920s reflect well-assimilated affinities with tribal art. It is interesting to compare, as William Rubin has done in some detail, *Seated Man* with the Dogon/Mali *Primeval Couple* in the collection of Barbara and Murray Frum (fig. 36).[71]

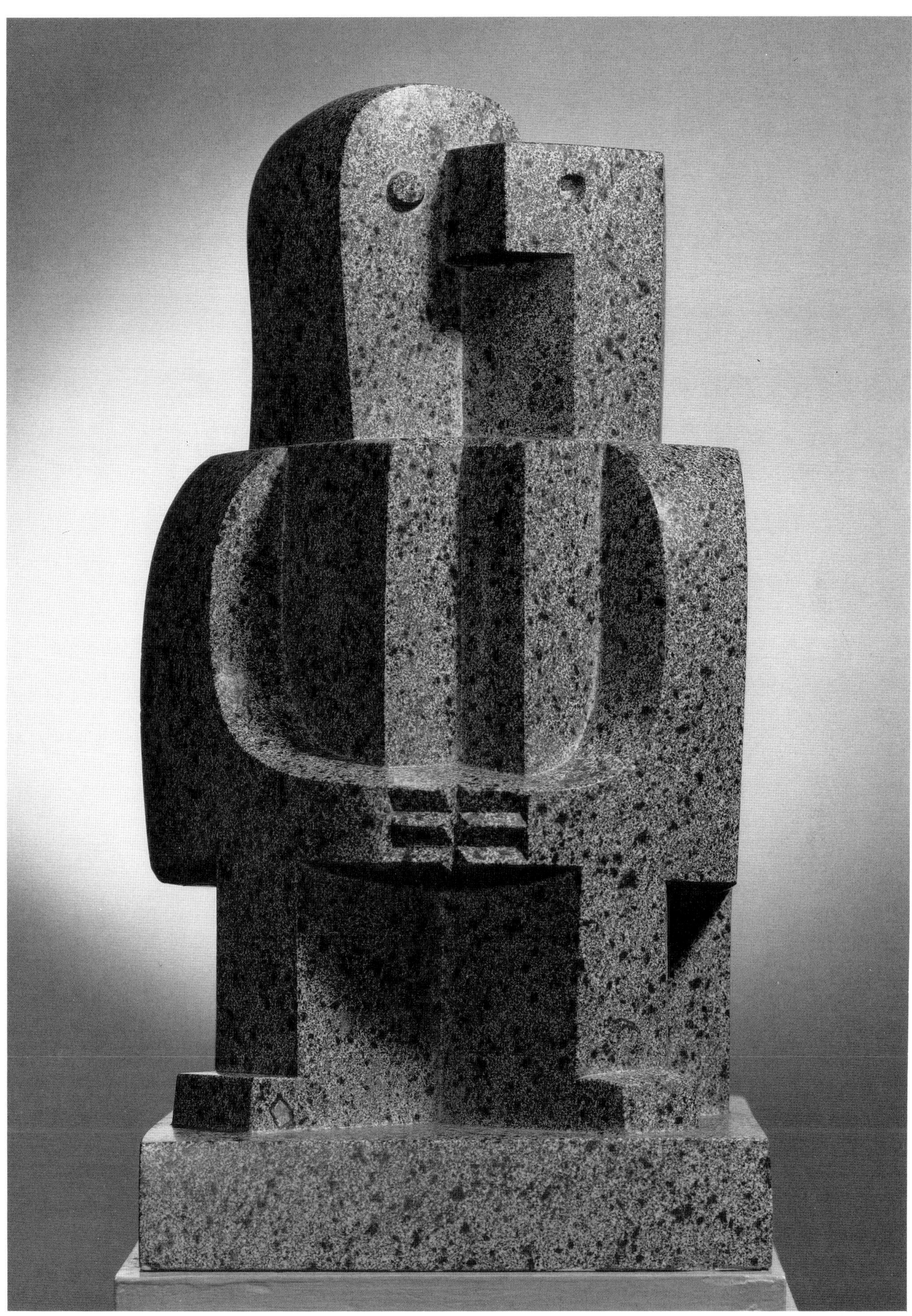

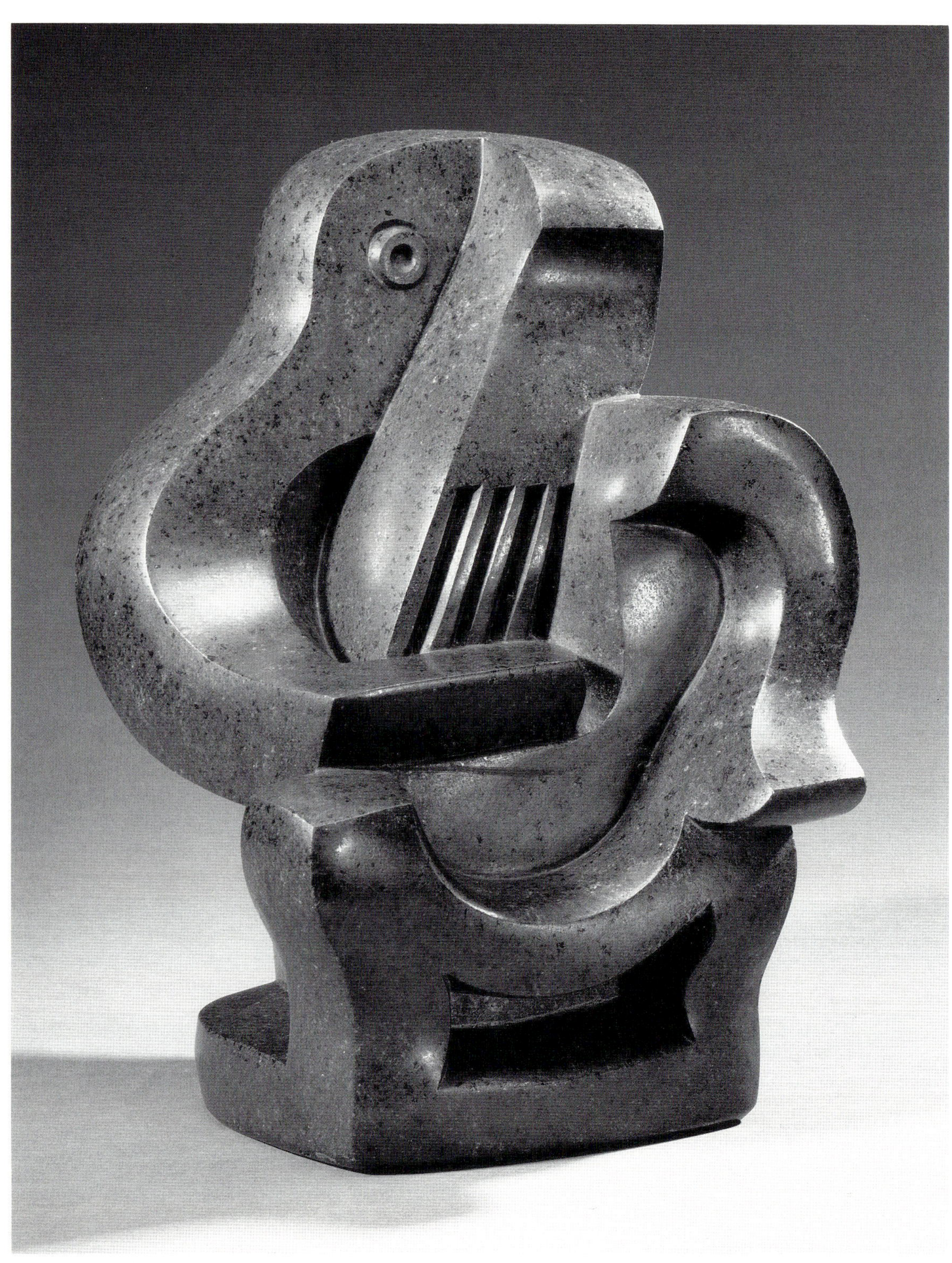

38 *Guitar Player in Chair* 1922
Basalt (unique)
H. 15½″/39.4 cm
The Estate of Jacques Lipchitz represented by Marlborough International Fine Art AG.

WHILE *Guitar Player in Chair* HAS THE SAME SQUAT MASSIVENESS as its more traditionally Cubist cousin, *Seated Man* of 1922 (no. 37), its gently flowing, curvilinear forms are closely related to the 1921 andirons he made for Coco Chanel (no. 33). What Lipchitz found particularly interesting about this sculpture was the "total integration of the man, the guitar, and the chair. All become part of one another. The guitar is also the torso of the man and the man's legs are those of the chair."[72]

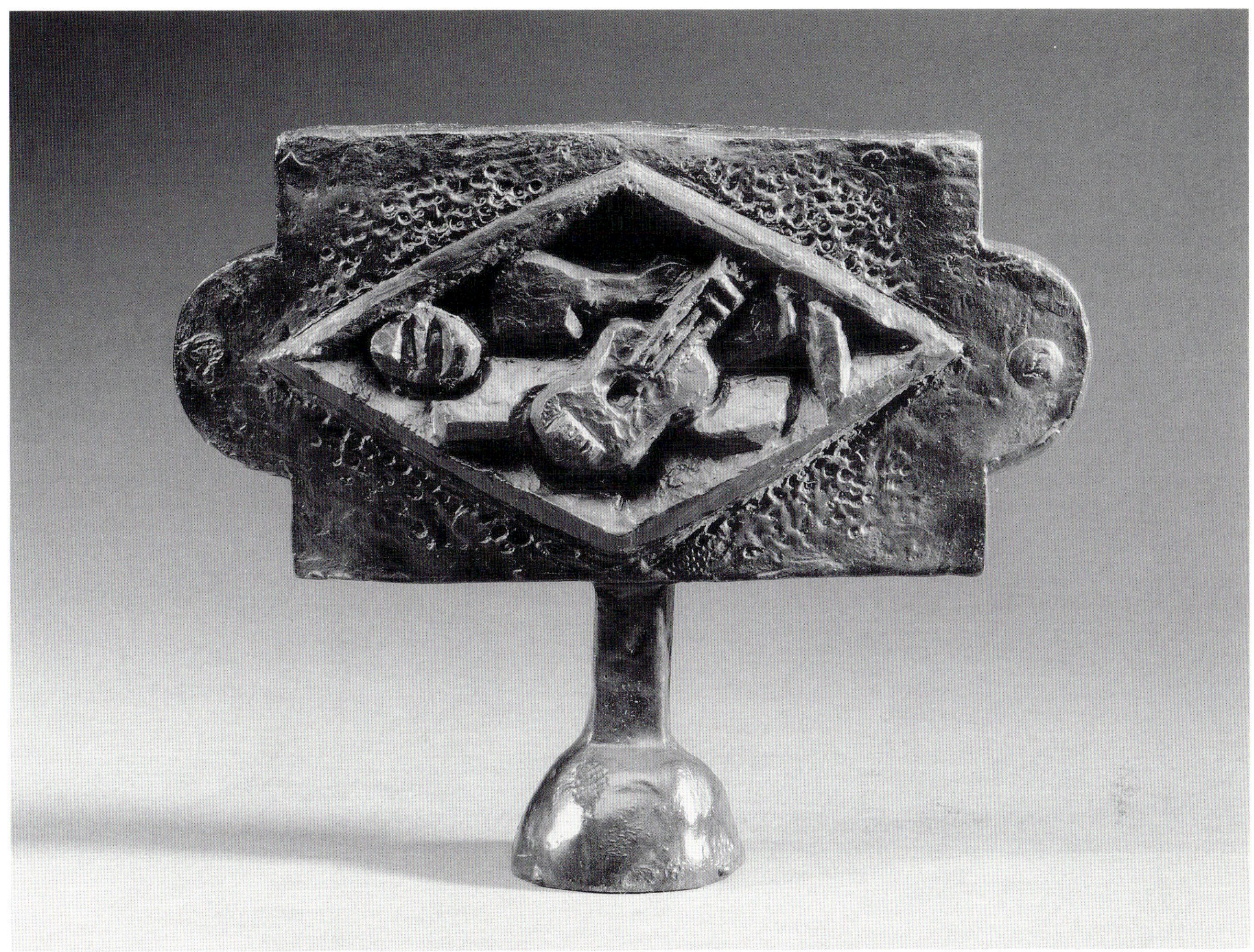

39 *Reclining Figure with Guitar* 1923
Bronze 3/7
L. 9½″/24.1 cm
The Estate of Jacques Lipchitz represented by Marlborough International Fine Art AG.

THE FINANCIAL DIFFICULTIES THAT LIPCHITZ EXPERIenced after he left Rosenberg's gallery in 1920 continued until 1922, when he met Dr. Alfred Barnes, a wealthy American collector who had arrived in Paris late in the year. At Dr. Barnes's insistence, the dealer Paul Guillaume brought him to meet Lipchitz at his studio. It was, according to Barnes's biographer, Howard Greenfeld, "an enormously successful meeting – surprisingly, because Lipchitz's work was greatly influenced by the very Cubists Barnes had earlier scorned – and in the course of it Barnes startled the artist by purchasing eight of his sculptures. Lipchitz was further stunned when, at a dinner following their meeting, Barnes not only paid for his purchases in full but also asked the sculptor to design five reliefs for the niches on the facade of the museum he was having built in Merion [Pennsylvania]."[73] Initially Lipchitz refused, because he did not think his Cubist work would fit in with the French Renaissance style of Paul Phillipe Cret's building. At Barnes's insistence, however, Lipchitz agreed, on condition that he be given the complete freedom in realizing the project.

> There were five locations for the reliefs and the serious problem was the architectural shapes of these places. The wall spaces to be filled were an awkward and rather ugly shape, a rectangle with protruding curves at each end. I finally resolved the problem by creating a powerful inner lozenge-shaped frame within which I set the sculptural figures.[4]

Reclining Figure with Guitar is one of a number of preliminary maquettes for the Barnes commission. The figure with guitar crowds into the lozenge-shaped frame described above. Again Lipchitz has achieved total integration of figure and object, so that as he said, "the result would be a figure-guitar rather than simply a figure holding a guitar."[75]

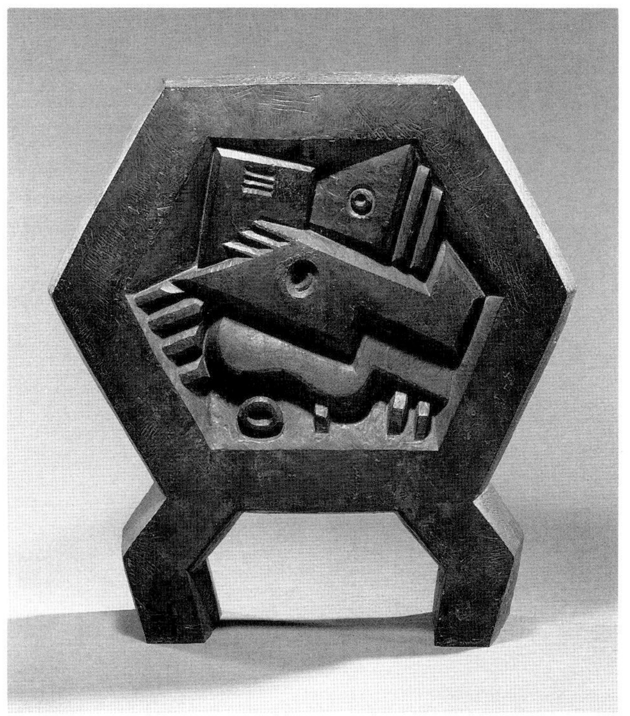

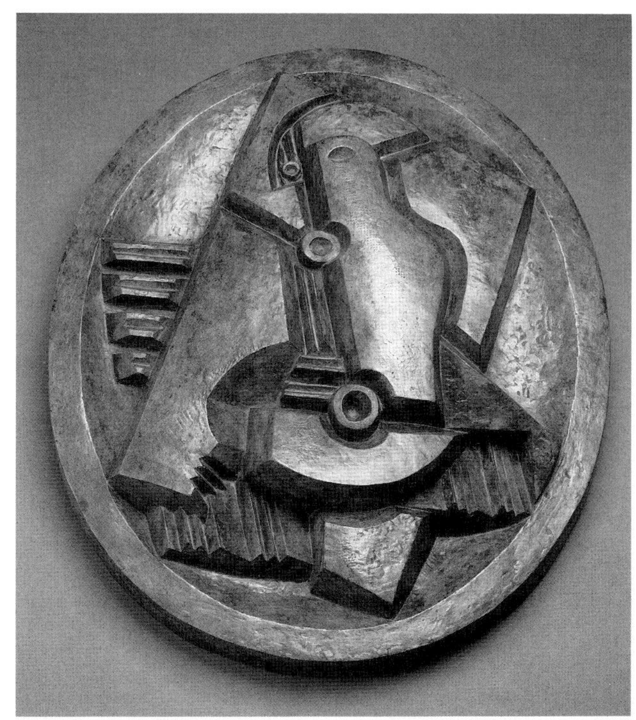

40 *Musical Instruments (Pentagonal Shape)* c.1923–26
Bronze 1/7
19⅜ x 18¾ x 3⅝"/49.2 x 47.6 x 9.2 cm
The Estate of Jacques Lipchitz represented by
Marlborough International Fine Art AG.

41 *Harlequin with Mandolin in Oval* 1923
Bronze 3/7
49½ x 41¾ x 9½"/125.7 x 106.1 x 24.1 cm
The Estate of Jacques Lipchitz represented by
Marlborough International Fine Art AG.

The dating of this work is problematic. The relief is obviously connected to the Barnes commission, to such preliminary sketches as the 1923 terra-cotta *Étude pour un bas-relief (Study for a Bas Relief)* in the Centre Georges Pompidou.[76] The Tate Gallery's plaster *Musical Instruments, Standing Relief*, identical to no. 40 but without the legs, has been dated 1924.[77] Hammacher has given the dates 1923–26 for the plaster version of no. 40, entitled *Standing bas relief*, in the Rijksmuseum Kröller-Müller.[78] It is conceivable that Lipchitz added the legs to no. 40 in 1926, in order to prop up the relief, as he had done in the *Ploumanach* sketches of that year (see fig. 18).

The Barnes commission and related reliefs represent Lipchitz's last series of undiluted, purely Cubist sculptures, the final resolution and consolidation of the disciplined vocabulary that had informed his work, with very few exceptions, since 1915. Here again, in this superb relief, figurative elements, musical forms and abstract shapes fit together like an irregular jigsaw puzzle comprising relatively few individual pieces. In the reliefs of 1923 Lipchitz said he was striving for "a completely integrated design involving a wide range of curving volumes contrasted with straight lines and rectangular masses."[79] The harlequin, with the head and eye shown in profile to the left, is wedged in among the abstract forms and the dislocated parts of the mandolin. The pun on the harlequin/bottle form is evident, while the largest of the two round holes is also suggestive of a navel. The oval format, and the way in which the harlequin is placed diagonally between flat, abstract forms on either side are features so remarkably close to Laurens's carved and painted relief *Bottle, Pipe and Glass* of 1919 as to suggest a direct influence.[80]

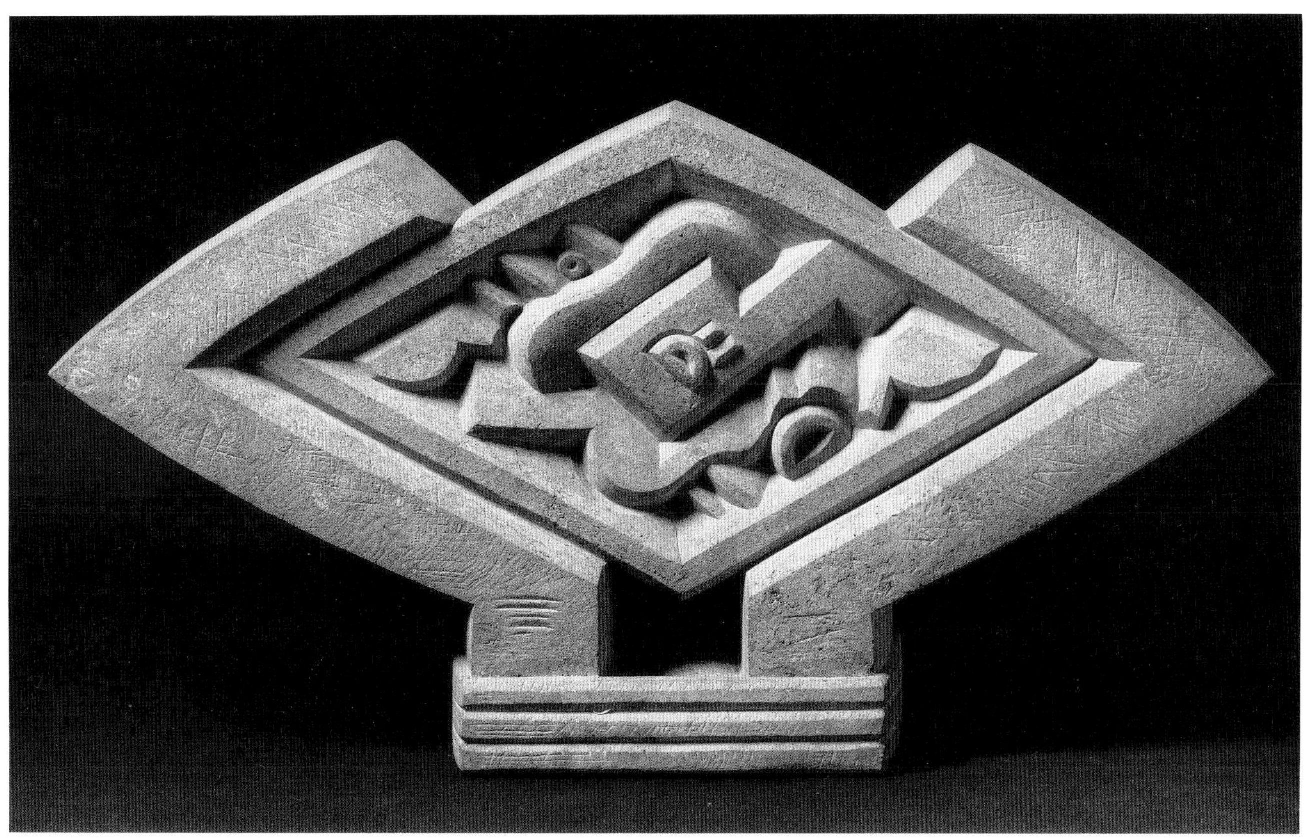

42 *Musical Instruments* 1923
Stone (unique)
19⅛ x 34¾ x 6⅝"/48.6 x 87.3 x 16.8 cm
The Estate of Jacques Lipchitz represented by Marlborough International Fine Art AG.

The inner lozenge shape is very closely related to studies for the Barnes Foundation commission (see no. 39). While a guitar is clearly legible at the centre of the composition, the other musical instruments are less obviously recognizable. Lipchitz has eliminated the reclining figure that in most of the Barnes reliefs is tightly integrated with the guitar.

The way in which the relief is partially framed is a feature found in the paintings of Picasso, Braque and Gris. For example, in Gris's 1917 *Still Life with Plaque* (fig. 37) the artist has painted at the top of the picture a trompe l'oeuil frame on which he has inscribed his name and "12–17," the month and year that the work was executed.[81]

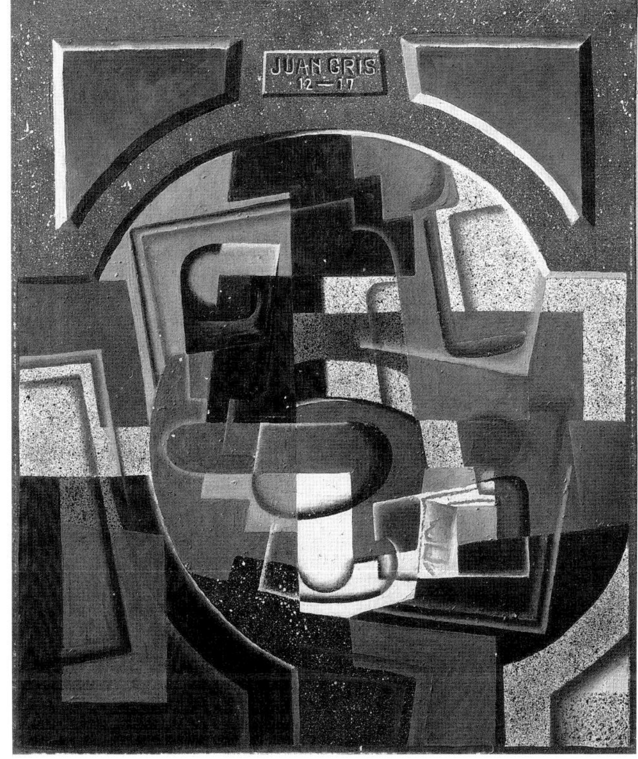

fig. 37 Juan Gris, Still Life with Plaque, *1917, oil on canvas, 25.7 x 31.8"/65.5 x 81 cm. Öffentliche Kunstsammlung Basel, Kunstmuseum.*

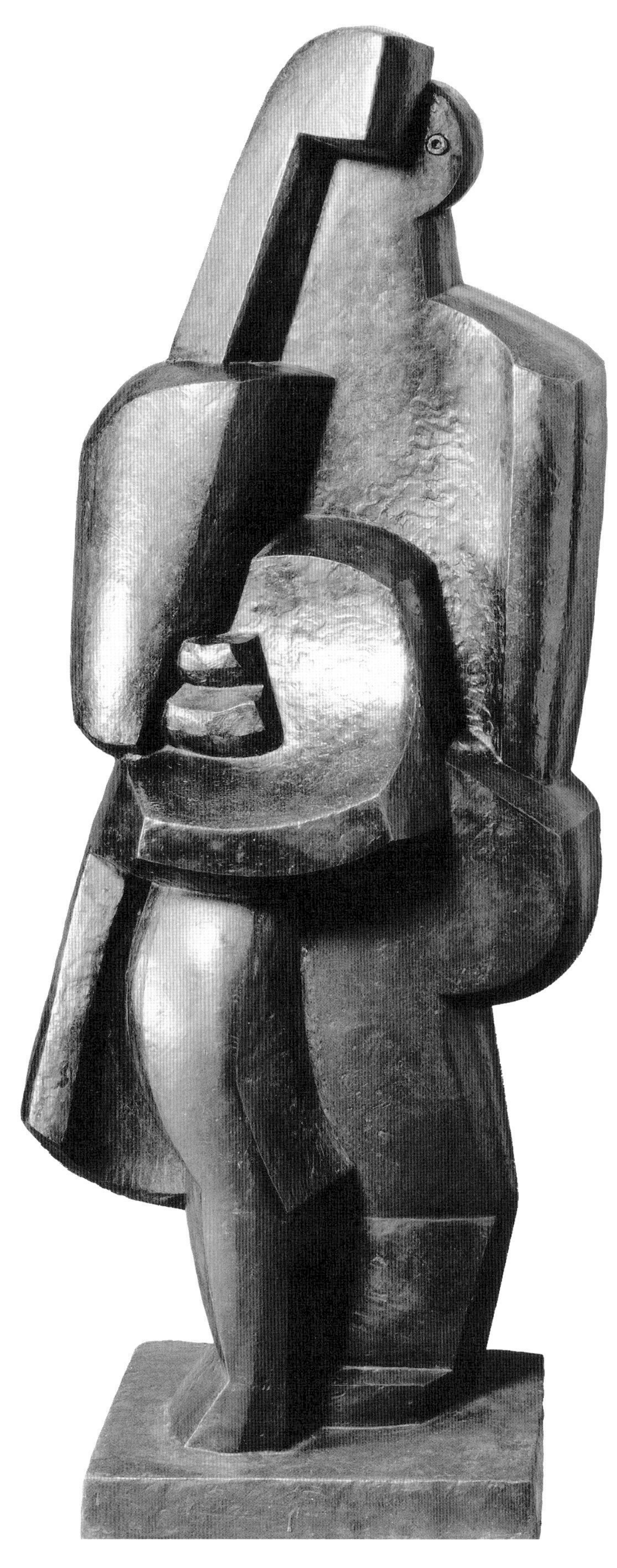

43 *Bather* 1923–25
Bronze 3/7
H. 78⅜″/199.0 cm
The Estate of Jacques Lipchitz represented by Marlborough International Fine Art AG.

THE FREESTANDING CUBIST FIGURES LIPCHITZ MADE between 1915 and 1922 were modest in scale, the tallest of them probably the 1915 *Sculpture* (no. 15). *Bather* was by far his largest fully three-dimensional sculpture to date. It is a confluence of many features already discussed in the notes above. Before abandoning the rigid discipline of his Cubist heritage, Lipchitz must have wanted to make a final statement on a monumental scale. Of the standing *Bather*, he said:

> ... I was returning to the problem of creating a cubist figure, free-standing in surrounding space, creating that space by its axial pivot. The legs are placed firmly at right angles to each other, and the circular movement is suggested by the curvilinear forms of the drapery enclosing the arm, actually enclosing space. In its final form, I think it is a successful work, despite and perhaps because of the long period of struggle that went into its making; but, at the same time, it was in a sense my farewell to literal cubism, the record of the moment when it was no longer necessary for me to concentrate on the vocabulary of forms, when I could move on to a sculpture of themes and ideas.[82]

44 *Man Leaning on Elbows* 1925
Bronze 6/7
H. 5″/12.8 cm
The Estate of Jacques Lipchitz represented by Marlborough International Fine Art AG.

Man Leaning on Elbows AND *Meditation* (NO. 45) ARE THE first of Lipchitz's gestural sculptures focusing on relationships between the head and the hands or arms. The theme is taken up again in a number of works of the early 1930s (see nos. 70–72).

Stylistically, this small maquette heralds a complete and radical break with the monolithic massiveness of Lipchitz's Cubist work. As he explained:

> This is simply a skeleton figure, a framework of elongated torso, inclined legs and arms folded up over the head, in which every tradition of solid and void in sculpture is reversed.[83]

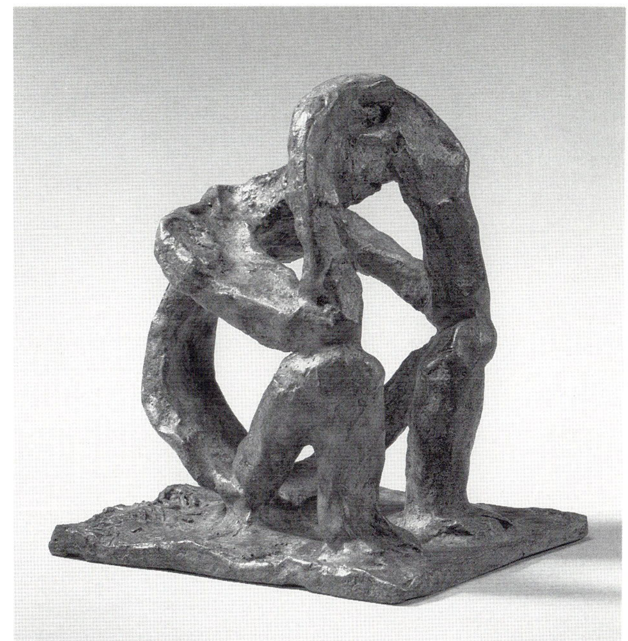

44

In its open, airy structure, in which the negative space in and around the figure is as vital an element as the spindly solid forms themselves, *Man Leaning on Elbows* signals a significant new departure in Lipchitz's development, anticipating the remarkable series of transparents of 1926–27 (nos. 48, 49 and 52). The gesture and pose alone (rather than facial features) evoke a range of moods from contemplation to despair. Any similarity is surely fortuitous, and yet this little figure recalls in an uncanny way van Gogh's two famous 1882 drawings entitled *Sorrow*.

45 *Meditation* 1925
Bronze 6/7
H. 8¼″/21.0 cm
The Estate of Jacques Lipchitz represented by Marlborough International Fine Art AG.

AS WE HAVE SEEN, LIPCHITZ'S DESCRIPTIONS OF HIS purely Cubist work of 1915–25 focused almost exclusively on formal considerations. In his comments on the larger, onyx version of no. 45, entitled *Seated Man (Meditation)*,[84] he was also very much aware of a totally new dimension to his work, the way in which bodily gestures create a mood, a personality, or an attitude.

> As a form, we have simply the block of the head with suggestion of a half-closed eye, the S curve that is the reclining

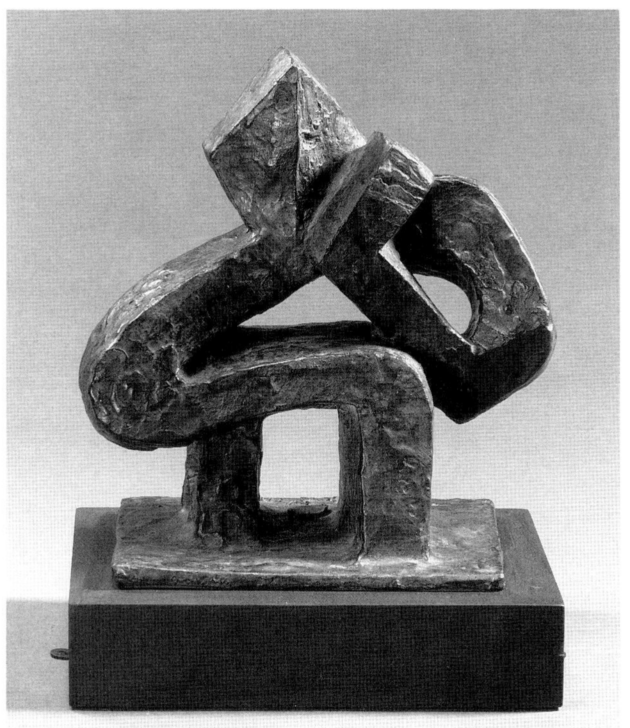

45

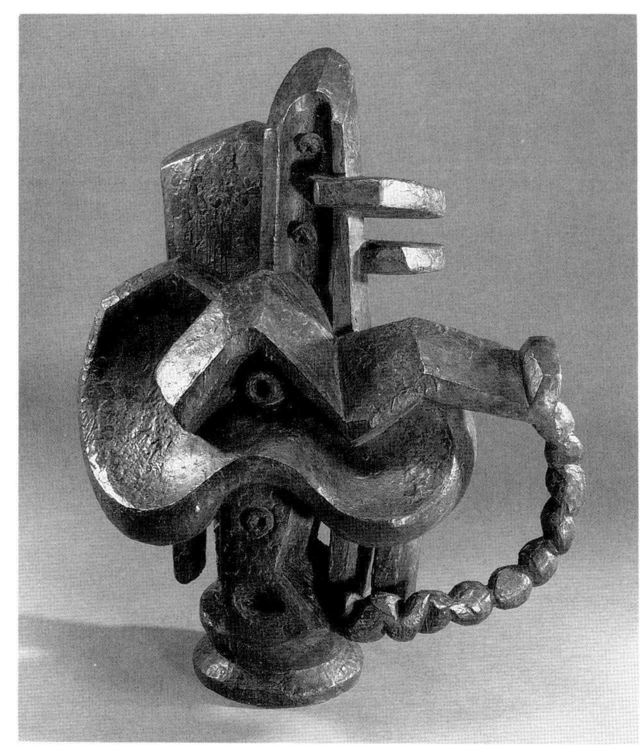

torso and one leg, the contrasting curve and diagonals of the arm, and the vertical mass of the other leg. All of this translates into a weary man, slumped in a chair, his arms supporting his nodding, drowsy head. The personification involves a deliberate element of humor. I recall a business man I knew who, when he saw this piece, exclaimed, "My God, that's exactly how I feel at the end of the day."[85]

Lipchitz described as a most significant departure purely in terms of form and structure "the opening up of the spaces to the point where not only are the intervals between the legs and arm completely interpenetrated, but the torso is actually a void encompassed by the S curve of the solid stone or bronze. Here we can see the first stage in the concept of the transparents, of sculpture as space, as air or spirit rather than as solid mass."[86]

46 *Musical Instruments* 1925
Bronze 6/7
H. 32½″/82.6 cm
The Estate of Jacques Lipchitz represented by Marlborough International Fine Art AG.

In *Musical Instruments*, Lipchitz has taken the traditional Cubist objects found in his 1923 reliefs and arranged them in a looser, more transparent structure, in keeping with the new spatial concepts discussed in no. 45 above. In that solid forms predominate, the sculpture is closer in spirit to the earlier Cubist reliefs than to a work such as *Meditation*. And yet, as Lipchitz wrote, "it is cubism with a difference, extremely free, open, interpenetrated, and dynamic. The guitar or mandolin becomes a dancing figure and both figure and guitar become a kind of architecture."[87] Yet again musical and figurative forms become interchangeable. The vertical clarinet becomes an upright figure, while the horizontal, curvilinear form of the guitar, like that of the andiron he made for Coco Chanel (no. 33), suggests a reclining woman. *Musical Instruments* was to be the last of the important transitional works that formed a bridge between the sculpture of a decade of unbending commitment to the austerity and discipline of Cubism and the sudden appearance, in 1925–26, of the transparents, startling and innovative small bronzes that were to change forever the direction of his art.

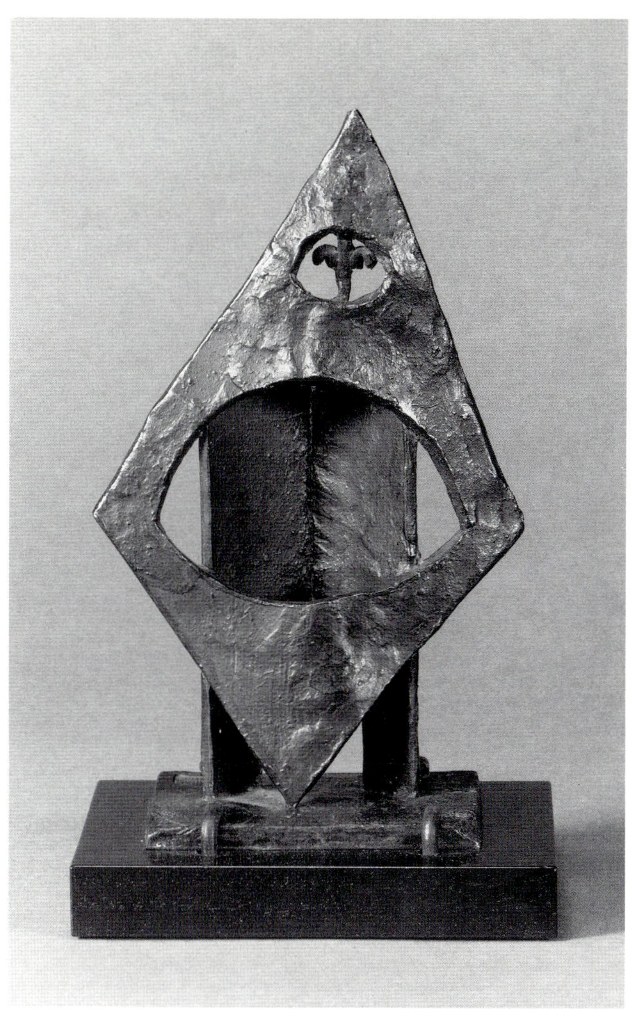

47 *Pierrot* 1925
Bronze (unique)
H. 7¾"/19.7 cm
The Estate of Jacques Lipchitz represented by Marlborough International Fine Art AG.

Pierrot WAS THE FIRST OF LIPCHITZ'S TRANSPARENTS, AS he called the series of small sculptures executed between 1925 and 1927. We have seen how in *Meditation*, also of 1925 (no. 45), he had made the spaces within the sculpture a feature as important as the solids that enclosed them. Now, as Lipchitz told Stott, he not only wanted to introduce space and light into sculpture, he wanted to "make it as quick as the inspiration comes."[88] Up to this point Lipchitz had maintained his loyalty to the traditional materials of sculpture: modelling in clay and carving in wood or stone. *Pierrot* heralds a complete break with his previous work method. The idea evolved in the following way.

While attending a lecture at the Sorbonne, Lipchitz found himself unable to concentrate and began thinking

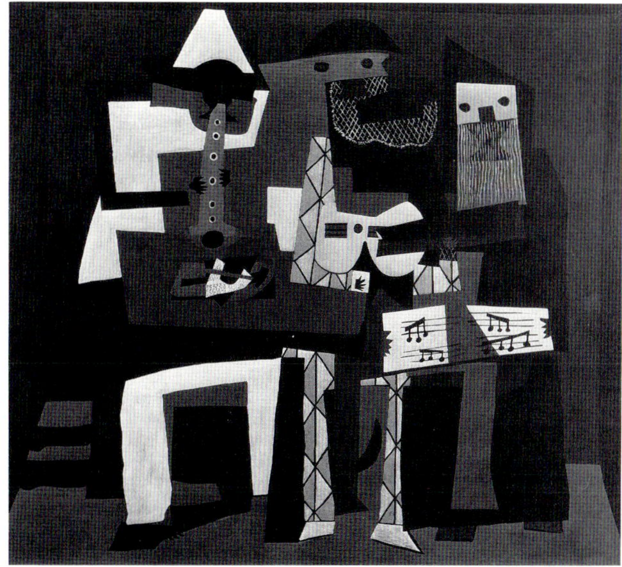

fig. 38 Pablo Picasso, Three Musicians, *1921, oil on canvas, 6'7" x 7'3¾"/227 x 222.9 cm. The Museum of Modern Art, New York, Mrs. Simon Guggenheim Fund.*
© Picasso/ VIS-ART Inc. 1989.

about his own work. According to Lipchitz, suddenly "I saw how to make something that I had apparently been longing to make for a long time. So I left the lecture and went home. There I built it from cardboard the same evening."[89] He took it to the Valsuani foundry the following day, made it in wax and had the little *Pierrot* cast in bronze. In first making the sculpture in cardboard, Lipchitz used a working method identical to that of the Russian-born Constructivist Naum Gabo when he had made his 1915 *Model for 'Constructed Head No. 1'* (lost) in the same material.[90]

A lozenge-shaped hood and cloak partially hide the standing Pierrot behind. The way in which the flat forms of the figure are set behind the hood is distinctly reminiscent of Picasso's 1921 *Three Musicians*, in the Museum of Modern Art, New York (fig. 38). Stott has described the way in which the transparents gave Lipchitz a spontaneous, lyrical means of expression that freed him at last from the materiality of traditional sculpture:

> In the transparencies of 1925-1928, the twin ideas of economy and spiritualization unite to produce sculpture whose volume is indicated by thin planes and lines of material, sculpture whose core is no longer irresistible mass, but space, a transparent suggestion of volume, a volume which is "a construction of the spirit."[91]

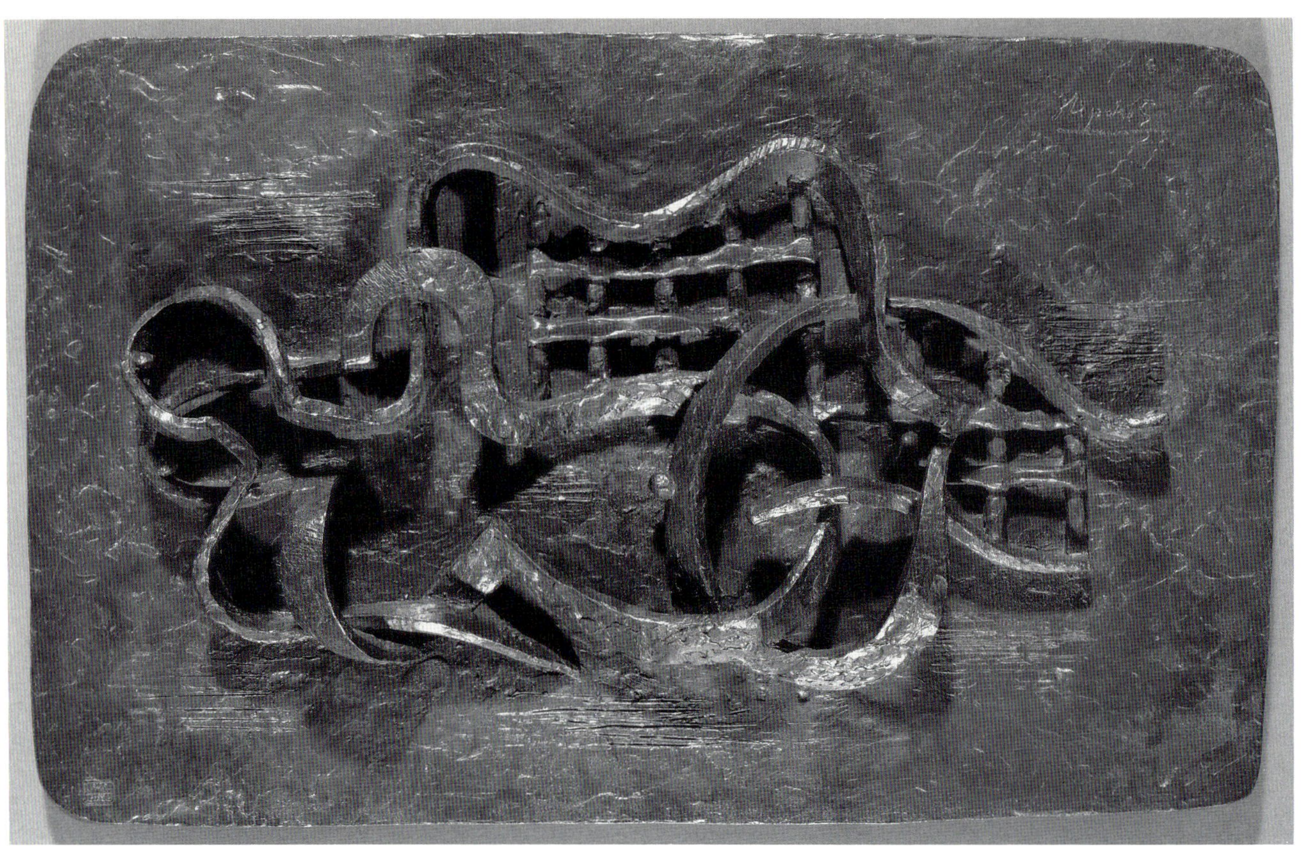

48 *Reclining Woman* 1926
Bronze (unique)
11¾ x 18⅜ x 3″/29.7 x 46.6 x 7.5 cm
Art Gallery of Ontario, Purchase, 1988.

This is Lipchitz's only known transparent in which the thin, wiry forms are attached to a flat surface. In this lyrical transparent, the beautifully resolved curvilinear forms suggest two figures intertwined in an embrace, rather than a single reclining woman, as the title indicates. Two heads are clearly legible at the left. The thin strips of bronze curve and bend, passing over and under as if the two figures are knotted together in a tight embrace. The vertical and horizontal fretwork suggests the back of a chair or sofa, against which the figures recline.

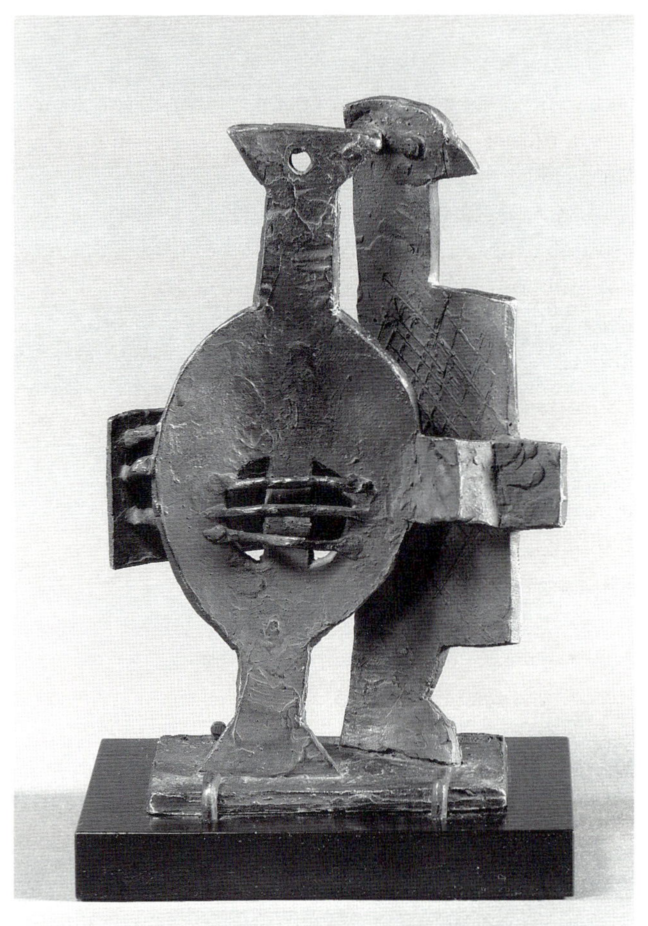

49 *Harlequin with Mandolin* 1926
Bronze (unique)
H. 7¾″/19.7 cm
The Estate of Jacques Lipchitz represented by Marlborough International Fine Art AG.

This delightful sculpture can surely be read as two figures as well as a single figure at the back holding a

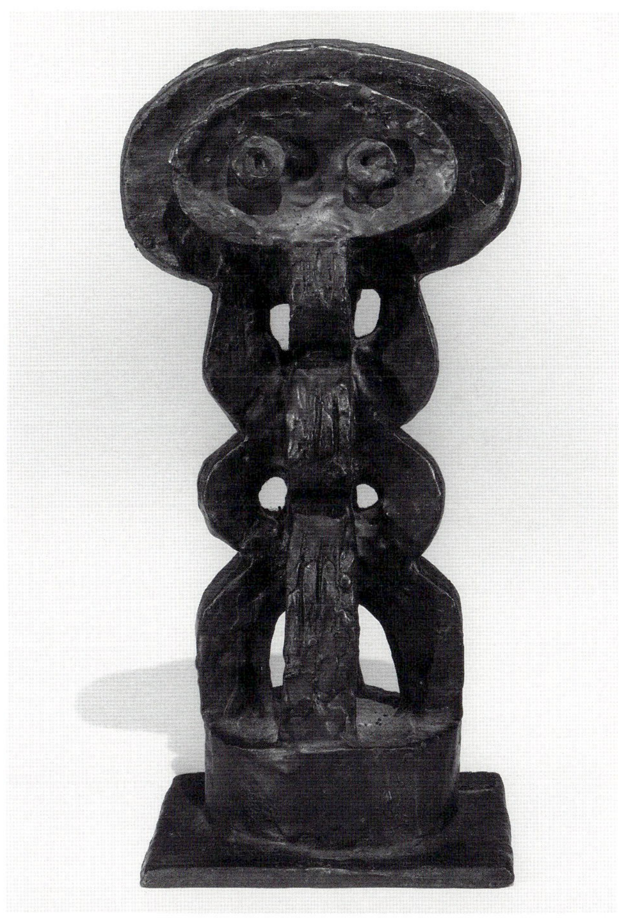

50

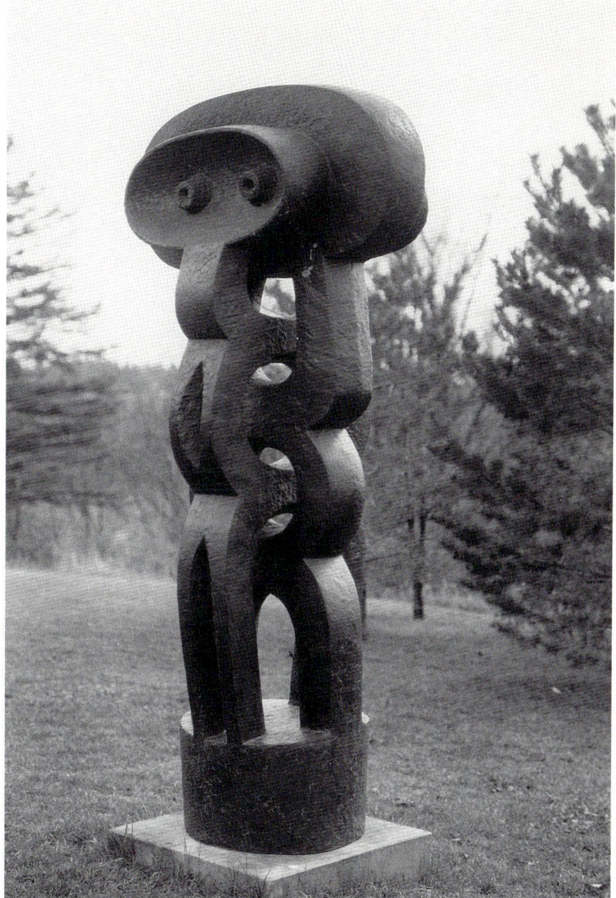

51

mandolin. As we have come to expect in Lipchitz's depictions of musical instruments, the shape of the mandolin is interchangeable with the form of a standing figure. Certain features found in *Harlequin with Mandolin*, such as the circular eyehole, the cross-hatchings and the rigid geometry of the figure behind, again suggest the influence of Picasso's 1921 *Three Musicians*, in the Museum of Modern Art, New York (fig. 38).

50 *Study for Figure* 1926
Bronze
H. 9½″/24.2 cm
Yulla Lipchitz, New York.

This maquette evolved from a sculpture entitled *Ploumanach* (fig. 18), the name of a resort on the Brittany coast, which Lipchitz visited in the summer of 1926. He was intrigued by the rock formations in the water offshore, where large stones balanced on other stones that had been eroded by water. The supported rocks moved and swayed in the wind. In the initial study inspired by the rock formations, a reclining figure, related to the Barnes reliefs, appears on the upper form.

Study for Figure is related both to *Ploumanach* and to the small 1921 *Study for Garden Sculpture* designed for Coco Chanel. In the first *Study for Figure*, Lipchitz noted, "there is still a reclining figure in the top part, but I must have begun to see this as a primitive totem, for in the next sketch [no. 50] I transformed the upper part into a head with an indication of staring eyes."[92] The large *Figure* of 1926–30 (no. 51) evolved directly from this second maquette.

51 *Figure* 1926–30
Bronze 6/7
H. 7′3″/216.6 cm
Walter Carsen
(Shown in Toronto only)

In 1930 Lipchitz was asked by a Madame Tachard, who wanted a sculpture for the entrance to her house, if he would enlarge the terra-cotta sketch she had seen (see no. 50). This marked the first instance when the sculptor decided to develop, on a very large scale, a work that had been conceived on a small scale and, as he later said, "seemed to me to be complete as it was."[93]

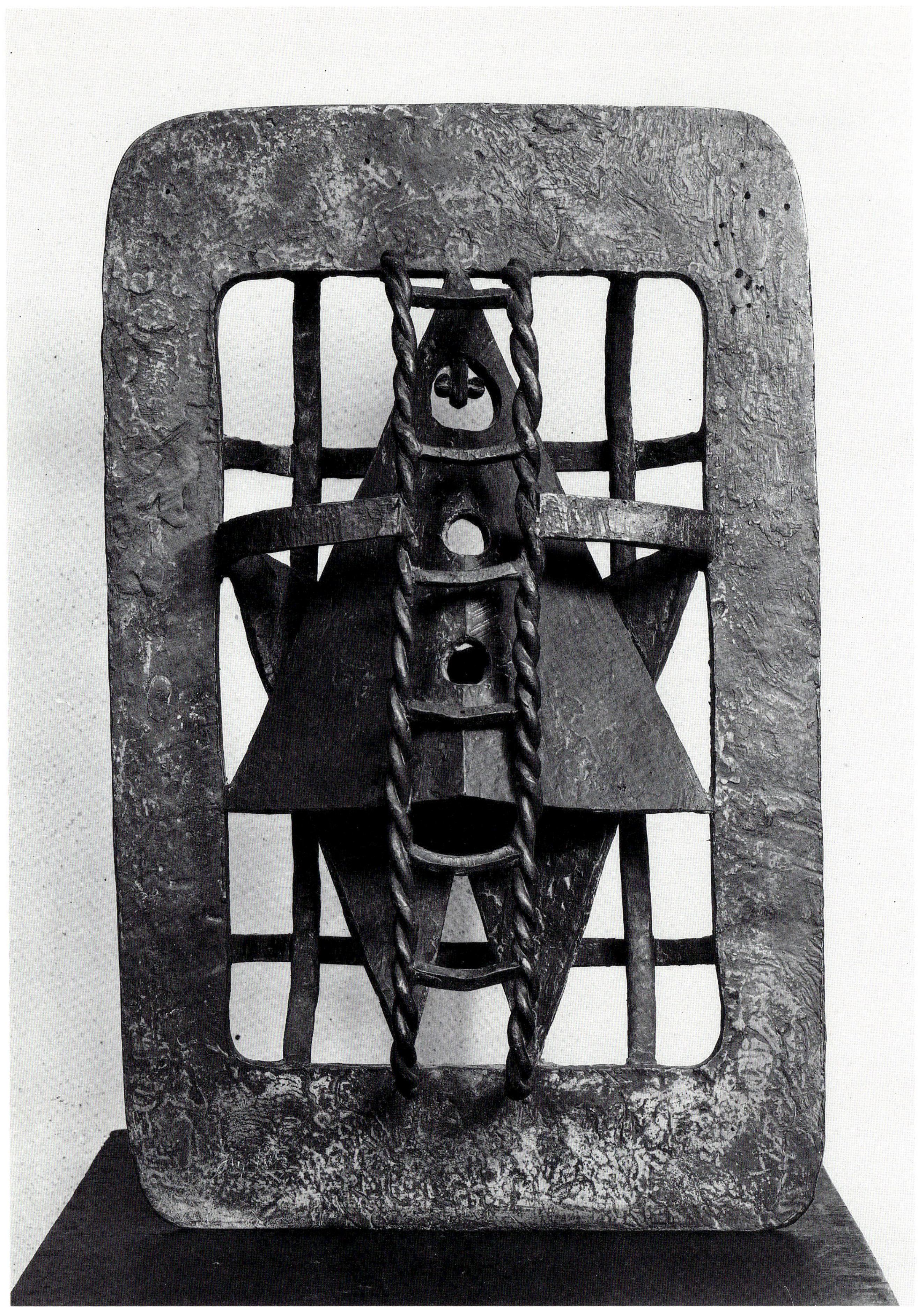

52

As often happens when a sculpture is enlarged, certain changes were made. In this large version of *Figure*, Lipchitz has eliminated the three sets of vertical, parallel lines that appear on the central axis of the maquette. They have been replaced by two deeply incised areas. The lower section suggests divided legs, while the incised gash above it almost certainly represents the female sex. It is interesting to compare this central, vertical form with that found in the 1915 *Sculpture* (no. 16). Indeed, Lipchitz himself saw *Figure* as a summation of his ideas dating back to 1915:

> Specifically, it pulled together those different directions of massive, material frontality and of aerial openness in which I had been working during the 1920s. It is also very clearly a subject sculpture, an image with a specific and rather frightening personality. Although the *Figure* has been associated with African sculpture and the resemblance is apparent, it is now evident to me that it emerged, step by step, from findings I had made in my cubist and postcubist sculpture over the previous fifteen years.[94]

Of all Lipchitz's sculptures that reflect affinities with tribal art, *Figure*, with the hypnotic, staring eyes, comes closest to the demonic presence found in Picasso's work of 1907–08. It is possible that the projecting cylindrical eyes derive from Grebo masks from the Ivory Coast, an example of which Lipchitz had almost certainly seen in Picasso's collection of African sculpture.[95] Both the proportions of *Figure* and the symmetrical, transparent interlocking loops between the head and the base are remarkably close to the Cook Islands staff god in the Cambridge University Museum of Archaeology and Anthropology.[96]

Figure should be seen as a confluence of various influences from his previous work, as well as from various affinities with tribal art. Along with Moore's *Glenkiln Cross* of 1955–56, *Figure* is one of the greatest totemic images in twentieth-century sculpture.

52 *Pierrot Escapes* 1927
Bronze (unique)
H. 19⅓"/49.0 cm
Kunsthaus, Zürich.

In *Pierrot Escapes*, one of his earliest purely autobiographical sculptures, Lipchitz proclaims his liberation from the taboos and restrictions of Cubism. He felt he had had enough: "it bothers you instead of giving you a lift, so you try to escape from it... And I started immediately to make subjects."[97] Symbolically, *Pierrot Escapes* represents Lipchitz's escape:

> This is a flat construction, almost like a relief in effect, although it is a free- standing work. Pierrot is shown within a wide metal frame behind bars but with a ladder in front of him with which he is escaping from his prison. The whole idea is extremely personal, a reflection of my excitement in the discovery of the transparents. Pierrot is myself escaping from the iron rule of syntactical cubist discipline, from all the taboos, regulations, and restrictions we had set up for ourselves, to become a free man.[98]

Lipchitz had indeed escaped, but in doing so he had brought with him the formal vocabulary of Cubism, which he continued to alter and reshape and build on for the rest of his working life. As he told Stott in 1969: "I have always been a Cubist."[99]

53 *Reclining Nude with Guitar* 1928
Bronze
L. 29⅝"/75.3 cm
Hirshhorn Museum and Sculpture Garden, Smithsonian Institution. Gift of Joseph H. Hirshhorn, 1966.

Reclining Nude with Guitar is a traditional Cubist subject in a new reclining pose, subjected to the openness of the transparents, a style best described as lyrical, spatial Cubism. Lipchitz described the work as follows:

> The subject is a reclining figure with a guitar; the curved shape of the right leg is also the shape of the guitar. This is again a total assimilation of the figure to the guitar-object; even the left arm reiterates the shape of the guitar. The work is massively conceived in curvilinear volumes, with a strong sense of frontality, but involving a movement in and out of depth. Thus, the lower, or right, leg is composed at a diagonal directing the eye through the space below the left leg. Similar planar diagonals under the head and the left arm emphasize the opening void. This sculpture is a development of the 1925 *Seated Man (Meditation)* [see notes for no. 45], and is a transitional figure in the entire sequence of reclining, embracing groups of the next decade.[100]

Abstraction and representation are harmoniously balanced in this work, which, like *Meditation* (no. 45) evokes bodily sensations of what it actually *feels* like to recline with one's head propped up by one's arm.

The first version of this sculpture was carved in black basalt. As this was too small for the client, a Madame de Moudrot, who wanted it for the garden of her summer

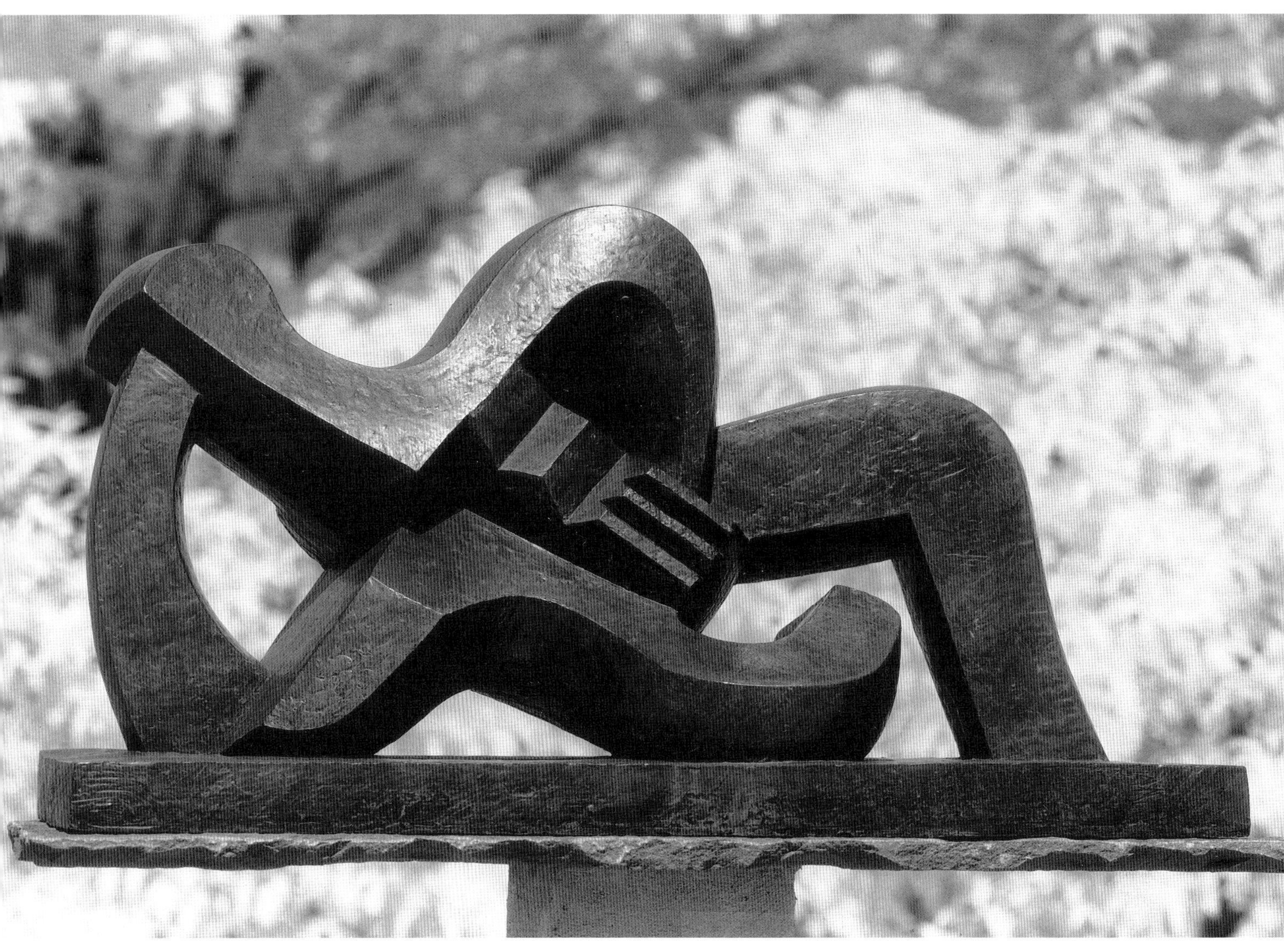

53

house at Le Pradet, designed by Le Corbusier, Lipchitz made a larger version in white stone. The basalt version is in the Museum of Modern Art, New York. The white stone version is in the Kunsthaus, Zürich.

54 *The Cry (The Couple)* 1928–29
Bronze 2/7
L. 63⅜″/161.0 cm
The Estate of Jacques Lipchitz represented by Marlborough International Fine Art AG.

Lipchitz could not have chosen a more provocative subject in his transition from the emphasis on formal values to the concentration on content than this rather brutal, impersonal image of a copulating couple. The work also reflects, as did the *Joy of Life* of 1927 (see fig. 19), a deeply felt emotional reaction to events in his own life. As in so many subsequent sculptures, the creative process became for Lipchitz a cathartic experience, a vehicle to reflect on the meaning of life and death:

> This is clearly a sexual work of two lovers embracing. The idea for it actually arose from my despondency at the deaths of my sister and father. [They both died in 1928, his friend Gris in 1927.] I was filled with a terrible sorrow and depression, but, since I am not a pessimist by nature, I made this sculpture as a kind of release, a defiance to show that in the midst of tragedy life must continue, that we must live and multiply. In the midst of death there is love and procreation and birth. This is how the sculpture came about, as a hopeful and optimistic reaction to tragedy.[101]

The original title, *The Couple*, emphasized the provocative subject, and so Lipchitz renamed it *The Cry*, since the two heads combine to give the effect of a single screaming head.

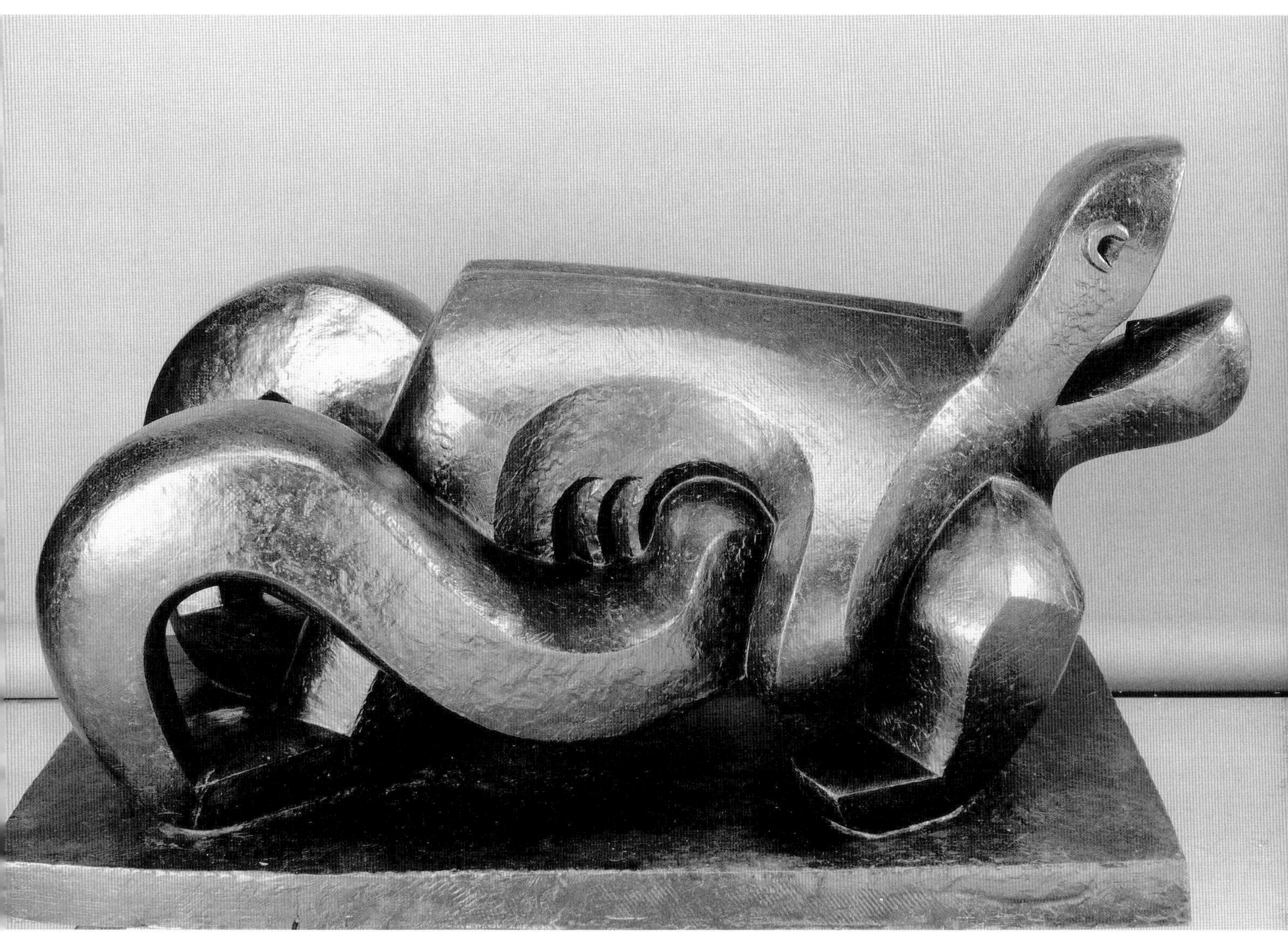

54

The Couple was based on a small study of which the plaster is in the Musée National d'Art Moderne, Centre Georges Pompidou.[102] In the latter the heads are joined, forming a strange head that is more animal than human. The sweeping, curving rhythms of the legs of the woman, who is propped up on her elbows beneath the male figure, recall *Reclining Nude with Guitar* of 1928 (no. 53). Like *Figure* of 1926–30 (no. 51), the work has a symmetrical rigidity in the way in which the forms of the body lock together that is less interesting from a purely sculptural point of view than the asymmetry of, for example, *Reclining Nude with Guitar*.

In terms of subject matter, *The Cry*, as Lipchitz explained, announced an extremely important new theme in his work: "I became intrigued with the idea of a loving embrace which was also a kind of conflict, a sort of love-hate relationship."[103] The embrace, in many forms and in many subsequent works, encompasses the full range of human contact and relationships, as in *Encounter* 1929 (no. 56), *The Return of the Prodigal Son* 1931 (no. 66) and in *The Last Embrace* 1971 (no. 132), a work completed near the end of his life.

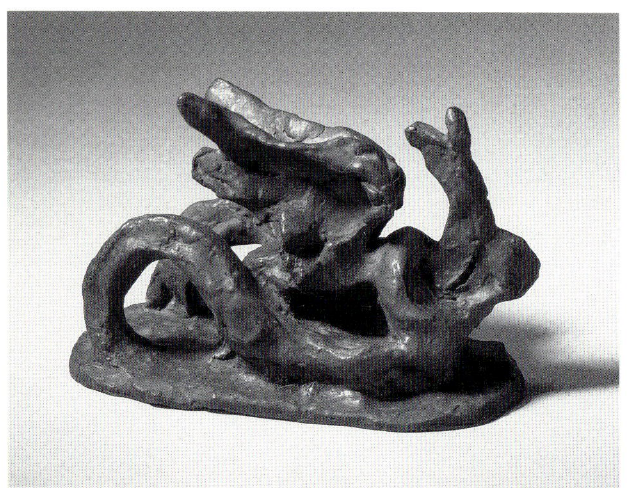

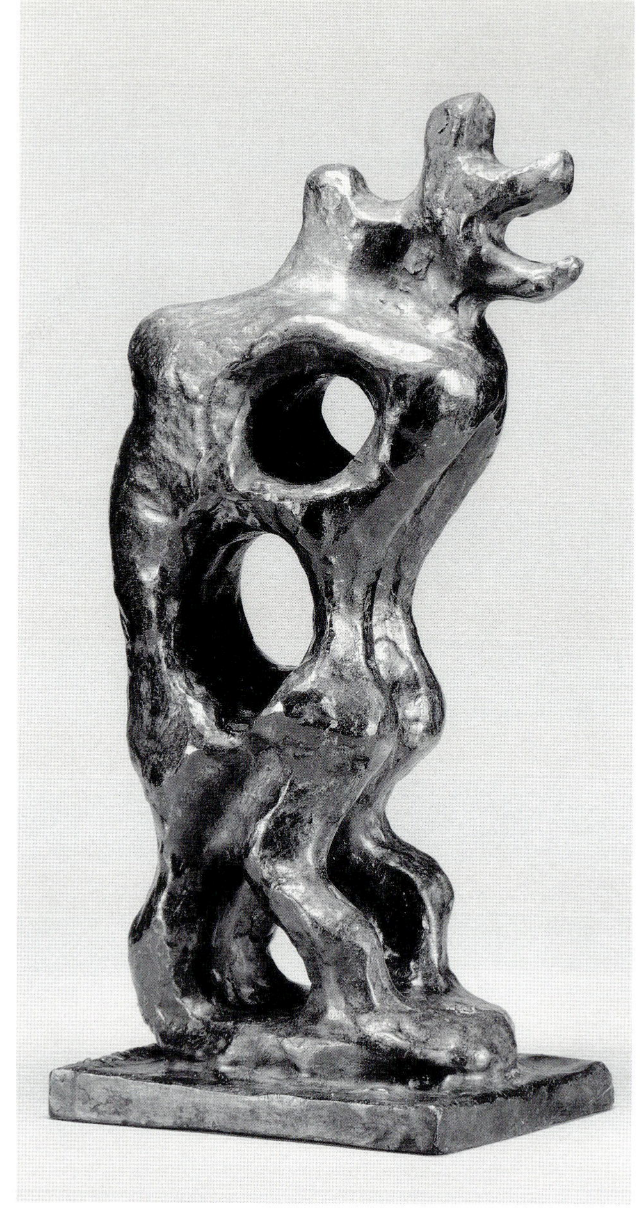

56

55 *Study for Leda and the Swan* 1929
Bronze 2/7
H. 4″/10.2 cm
The Estate of Jacques Lipchitz represented by Marlborough International Fine Art AG.

THIS MAQUETTE IS RELATED TO *The Cry* (NO. 54) IN THE way the legs of the reclining Leda arch upward, like the woman's, and the way the beak of the swan is open in a cry of passion. For what was almost certainly his first sculpture based on classical mythology, Lipchitz chose an erotic subject, very much in keeping with his personal obsessions during the late 1920s.

> I think it is only natural that with my ever-increasing interest in sculptural subject and idea should have led me to the great reservoirs of classical myth as well as the Old and New Testaments.[104]

Compared to the somewhat rigid composition of *The Cry*, *Leda and the Swan* has a feeling of great spontaneity in the lyrical, flowing movement of the interlocking forms.

56 *Encounter* 1929
Bronze 5/7
H. 9¾″/24.8 cm
The Estate of Jacques Lipchitz represented by Marlborough International Fine Art AG.

EROTIC THEMES WERE THE SUBJECT OF SEVERAL OF Lipchitz's maquettes of 1929. For example, *The Couple*[105] relates in a general way to *The Cry* of 1928–29 (no. 54), but the two horizontal figures have been penetrated and partially separated by three large voids or holes. *Encounter* is really an upright version of the maquette *The Couple*. The two heads meet and form a strange single head with a gaping mouth that becomes a recurring motif in a number of subsequent works depicting double figures (see *The Embrace* 1933 [no. 73]).

> This theme of the encounter has always had a special significance for me and at this moment in the late 1920s and early 1930s emerged in a number of different contexts. In my sculpture I think continually of the idea of encounter... I sometimes think that the idea of encounter is central to the vast proportion of my sculpture. Whatever the specific subject, I continually think of the sculpture itself as an encounter between the artist, the material, and the forms he is using.[106]

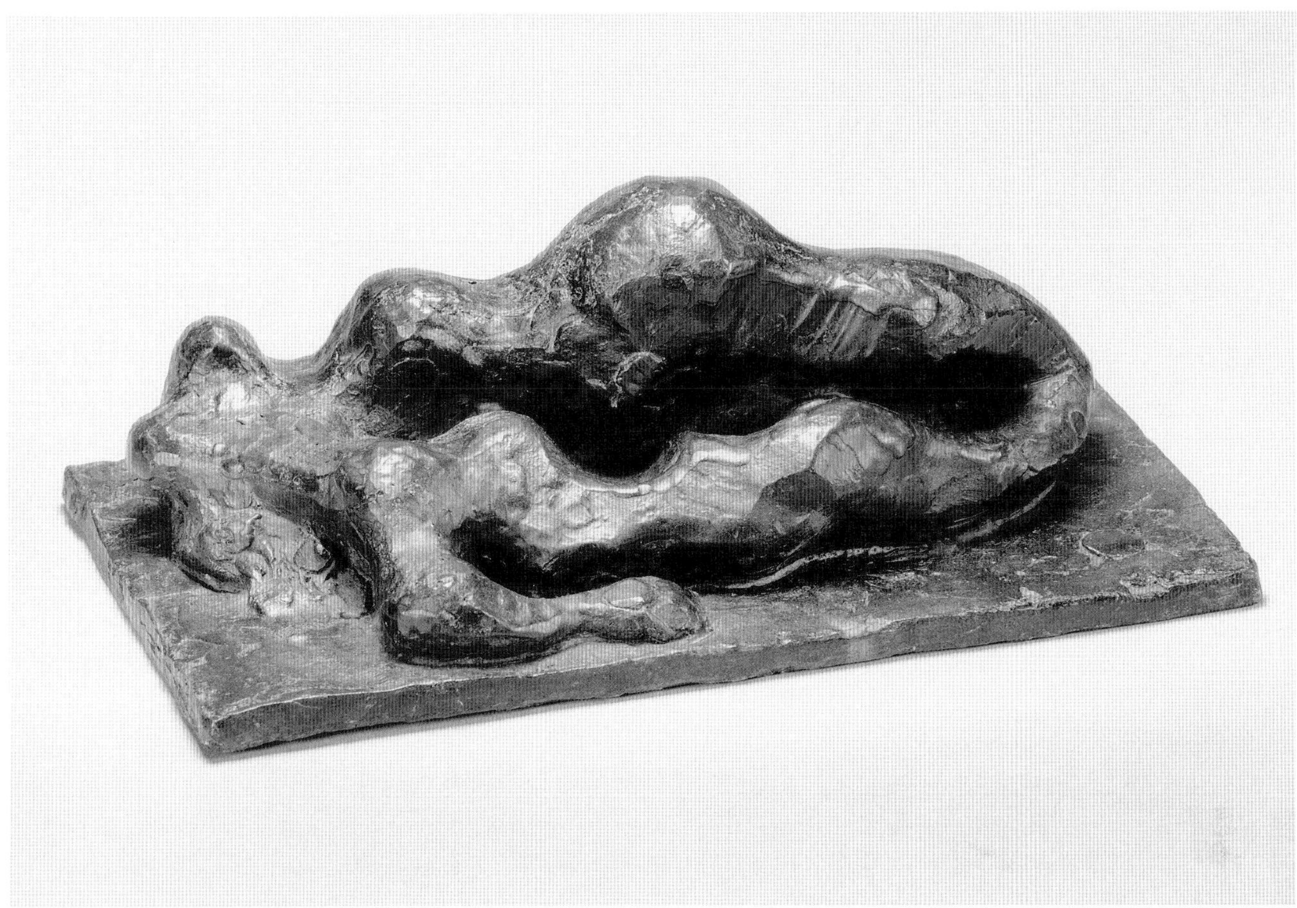

57

By 1929 Lipchitz established the terms of reference that were to inform his art for the rest of his life: the formal vocabulary of Cubism and the transparents and a new focus on Biblical, mythological and personal themes. If his subsequent art lacked the purity and strict discipline of his Cubist years (1915–25), it gained in its humanity and in its links with the great tradition of European sculpture from Bernini to Rodin.

57 *Reclining Woman* 1929
Bronze 5/7
L. 12″/30.5 cm
The Estate of Jacques Lipchitz represented by Marlborough International Fine Art AG.

"Sculptural energy is the mountain,"[107] declared the French sculptor Gaudier-Brzeska. This concept was taken up by Henry Moore, whose first title for his 1930 stone *Reclining Woman*, in the National Gallery of Canada, was simply *Mountains*. Between 1913 and 1934 Gaston Lachaise, too, created numerous reclining female "mountain" figures.

This powerful *Reclining Woman* is almost unique in Lipchitz's oeuvre in the way the female figure is used as a metaphor for landscape. There are few obvious figurative references, apart from the right arm and the hair. The gash down the centre of the figure suggests a deep valley between rolling hills. *Reclining Woman* may well have been inspired by prehistoric fertility goddesses, such as the Venuses of Lespugue and Willendorf, which were much admired by many artists of Lipchitz's generation, Picasso and Moore among them.

58 *Chimène* 1930
Bronze (unique)
H. 14½″/36.8 cm
The Estate of Jacques Lipchitz represented by Marlborough International Fine Art AG.

Chimène, one of the last transparents, announces an important new motif in Lipchitz's work. It is the first in a series of gestural motifs of the head resting or balancing on the hand or arm. This was the subject of a number of innovative sculptures made during the next several

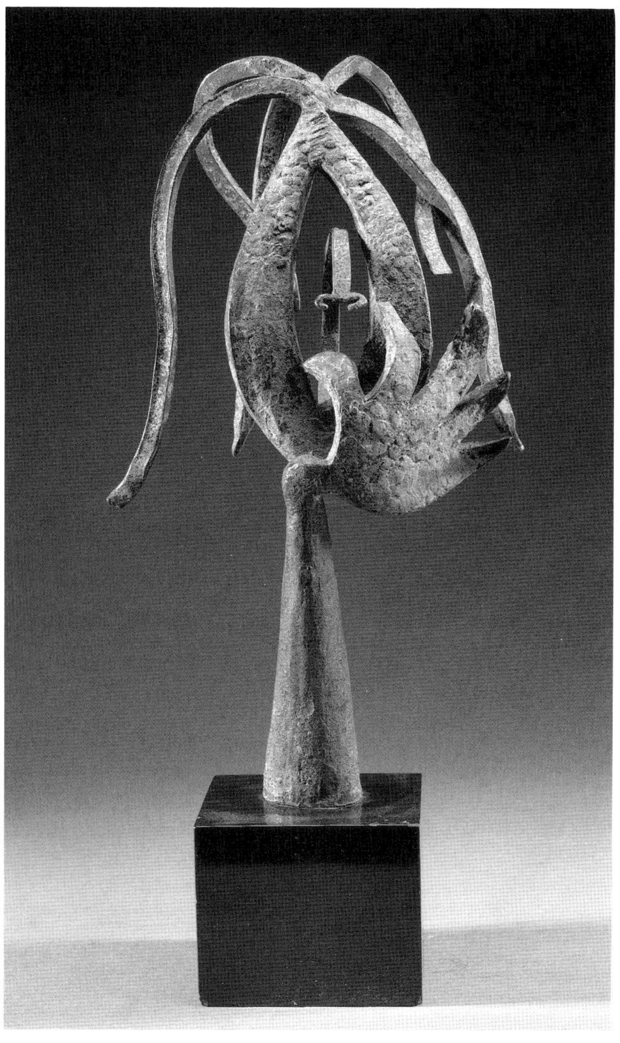

58

years. Throughout his career, Lipchitz often suddenly embarked on new ideas and stylistic innovations that had no apparent connection with what had gone before.

Increasingly, Lipchitz's sculpture was inspired by deeply felt emotions related to his personal life. Indeed, he was to become one of the most autobiographical sculptors of the twentieth century. He has described in some detail the circumstances that gave rise to this work:

> *Chimène* is a woman's head and hand, like a plant or a flower... It was inspired by a particular woman, someone who fascinated me for several years. She attracted me very much but there was nothing between us. Among other things, she was the wife of a friend. But it is obvious that I had some kind of an obsession about her and the sculpture was a way of possessing her. This head and hand reflected a gesture of hers that impressed itself deeply on me...[108]

The head is an ingenious open construction, with the nose and nostrils arching through the pierced space. The five strands of hair that splay from a single point at the top of the head are reminiscent of the spiky hair in several of Picasso's sculptures of the period, such as *Woman in a Garden* 1929–30.[109] It is possible that at this time Picasso and Lipchitz borrowed freely from each other's work.

59 *Transparent* 1930
Bronze (unique)
H. 15″/38.1 cm
Yulla Lipchitz, New York.

This is one of the few sculptures in Lipchitz's entire oeuvre that do not suggest or even hint at a recognizable subject. Is it some sort of cloaked figure, or a figure and its shadow (see no. 114, *The Tower and Its Shadow* 1962)? In Picasso's 1931 *Construction* (Musée Picasso)[110] the metal wire, twisted around an armature, relates closely to Lipchitz's transparents. The work of both sculptors anticipates to a remarkable degree the welded steel sculptures of David Smith and Anthony Caro.

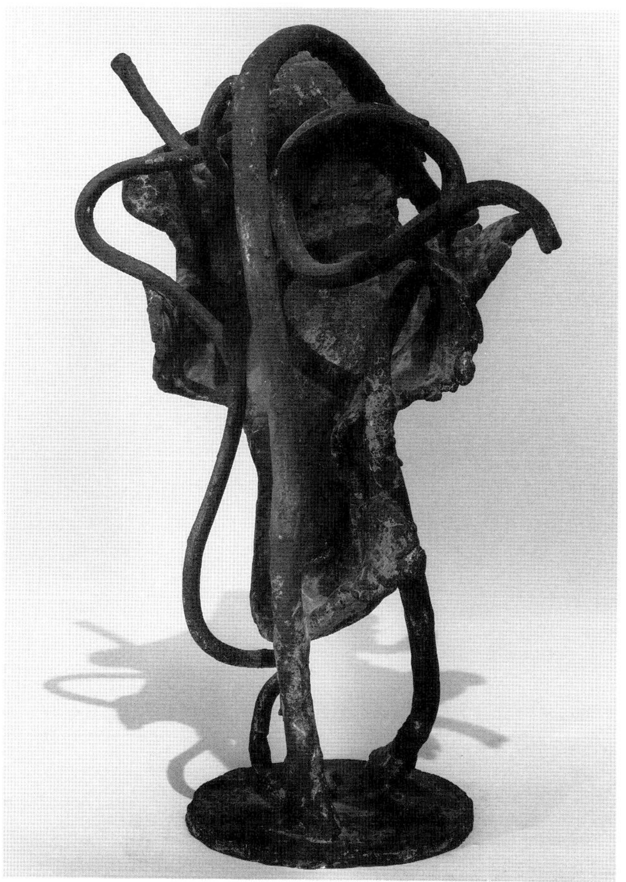

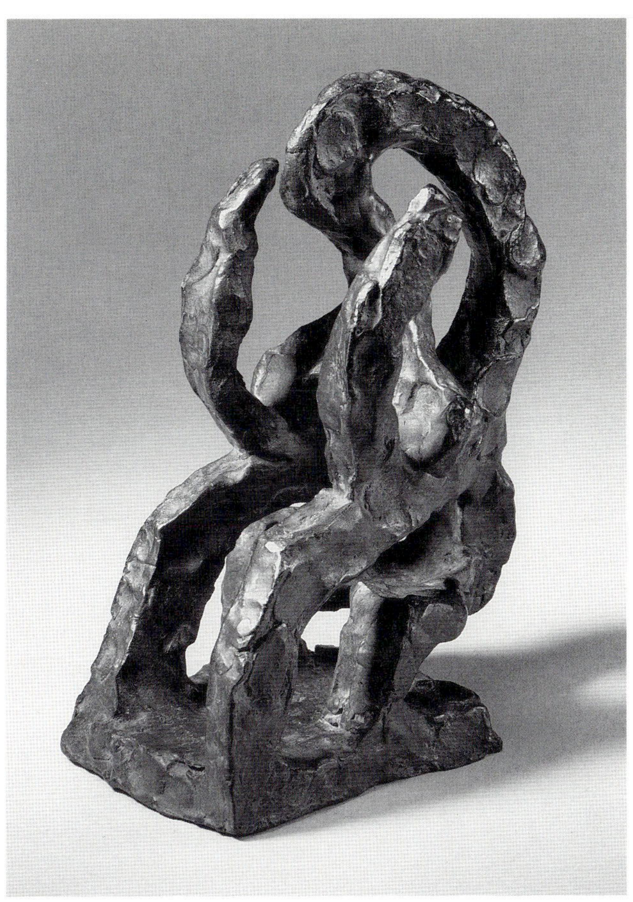

60 *Seated Woman* 1930
Bronze 1/7
H. 7½″/19.11 cm
The Estate of Jacques Lipchitz represented by Marlborough International Fine Art AG.

The transparents of 1925–30, like the Cubist work of the previous decade, provided a vocabulary of open, airy constructions that Lipchitz returned to periodically for the rest of his career. In *Seated Woman*, one of two closely related versions, the negative space in and around the figure is as important as the solid forms themselves. As in the 1922 *Guitar Player in Chair* (no. 38), the figure and the chair are totally integrated.

61 *Return of the Prodigal Son* 1930
Bronze 4/7
H. 7¼″/18.5 cm
The Estate of Jacques Lipchitz represented by Marlborough International Fine Art AG.

In the early 1930s Lipchitz began producing preliminary maquettes – sometimes one, but more often a

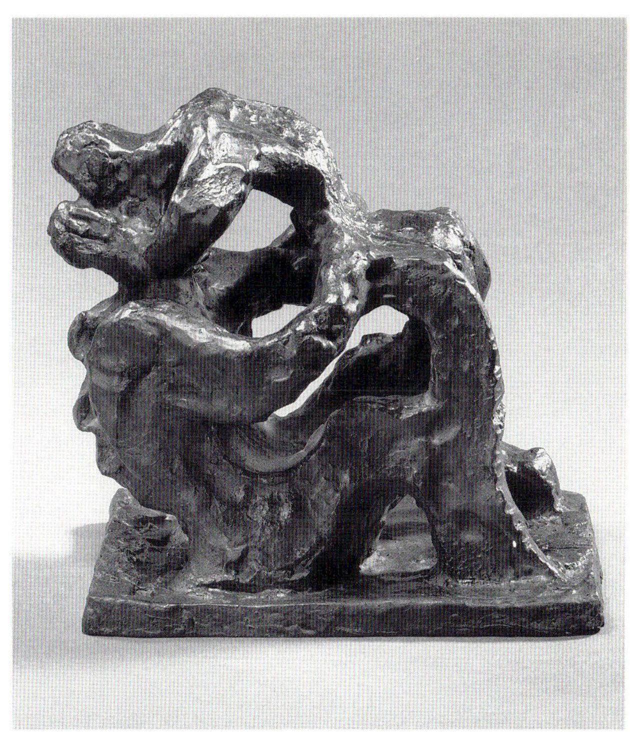

series – before embarking on the large version of a work. This work is one of at least two studies for the large *Return of the Prodigal Son* 1931 (no. 66). Although, as Lipchitz pointed out, this is one of his first Biblical subjects, it had a special significance for him. As he said:

> It had a very personal association to me, the idea of the son who is returning home, the artist who is returning to nature; it is a continuation of the *Pierrot Escapes* [no. 52] a longing for nature rather than abstraction. In the Biblical story the son returns to his father, but here I have come back to his mother, Mother Nature.[111]

Lipchitz's maquettes, modelled in clay, have a fluidity and spontaneity that are difficult to reproduce in the enlarged versions. In this study the heads of the mother and her son merge and become one. Tunnels of space open out in all directions. As the sculptor pointed out, the relationship of the two figures, one directly above the other, recalls *The Cry* 1928–29 (no. 54). Interlocking figures was a motif to which Lipchitz returned again and again. The humanity and intensity of feeling in this brilliant little maquette are conveyed by the roller-coaster rhythms created by the mother embracing her son. Despite Lipchitz's personal interpretation of the story, this is the moment as described in Luke 15:20:

> And he arose, and came to his father. But when he was yet a great way off, his father saw him, and had compassion, and ran, and fell on his neck, and kissed him.

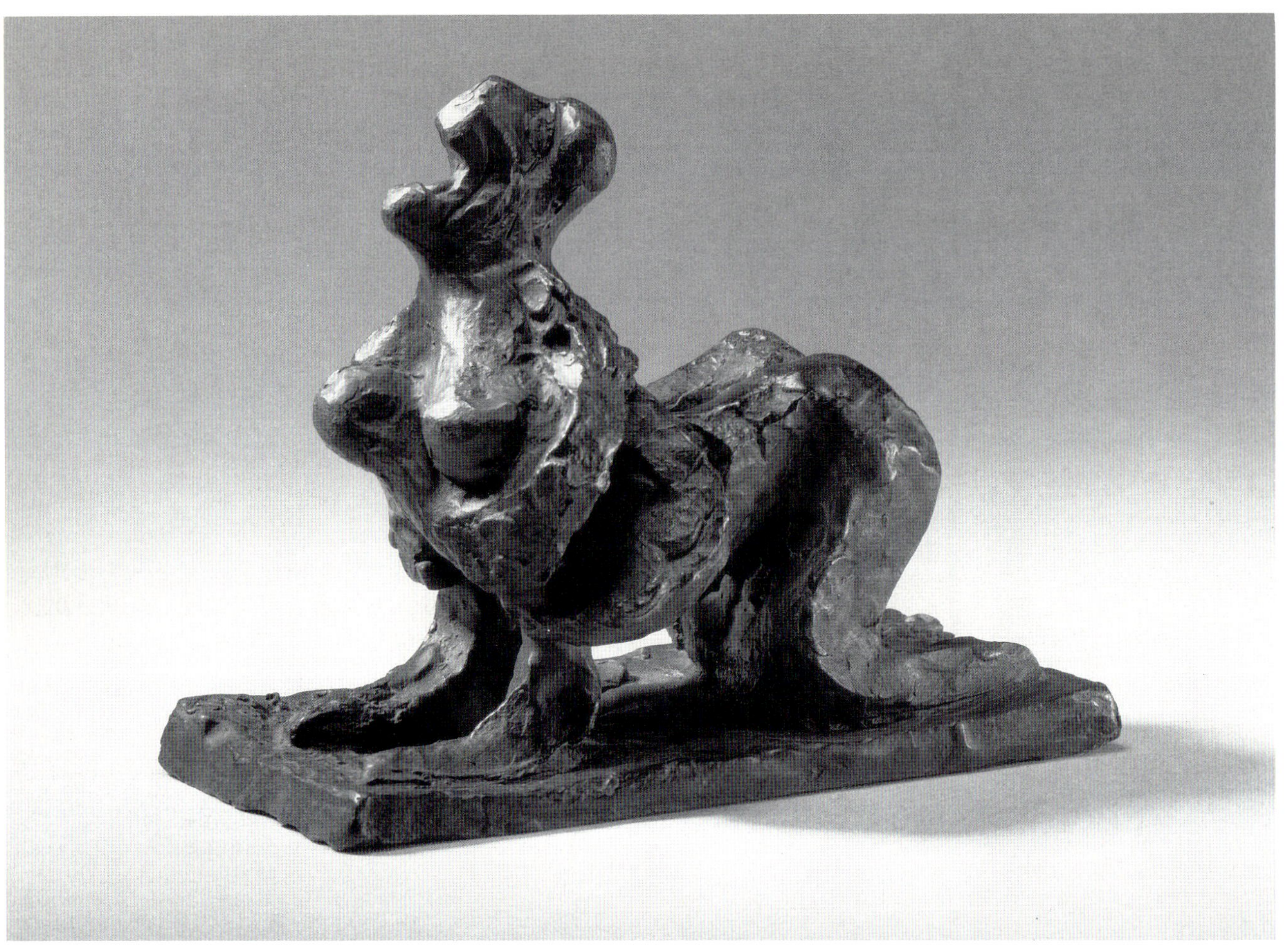

62 *Mother and Child* 1930
Bronze 5/7
H. 5″/13.0 cm
The Estate of Jacques Lipchitz represented by Marlborough International Fine Art AG.

NOTHING IN LIPCHITZ'S EARLIER WORK PREPARES US FOR the unbearable pain expressed in this little bronze. It is clearly related to another maquette of the same title made in 1929 in which the mother is squatting, her arms free to hold the child. Here the mother kneels on hands and knees, so that the child must cling to her chest. The mother's head and neck strain back, with the large, gouged-out mouth releasing a cry of anguish. Whereas in *The Cry* (no. 54) the deliberately misleading title was derived from the gap formed between the faces of the lovers, this small maquette could with good reason be entitled *The Cry*. The great, gaping mouth and the featureless face establish a motif that appears many times in subsequent works, such as *Jacob Struggling with the Angel* 1932 (no. 68) and *The Embrace* 1933 (no. 73).

The mother and child was one of the major themes throughout Lipchitz's career. Most of his varied interpretations of this subject related to events in his own life. This *Mother and Child*, Lipchitz said, was made during "a very difficult time for me, with the death of my father and my sister, and I was questioning many things. 'For what am I born? For what did I come on this earth?' "[112] Both the 1929 and 1930 maquettes "involve a cry of anguish that resulted from the tragedy that had befallen me."[113] They reflected a moment of pessimism, a period of angry questioning.

Mother and Child, despite its small scale, is one of the most anguished and deeply felt expressions of despair in twentieth-century sculpture. It is a timeless, primordial cry of mankind. Could this little bronze, as Ziva Amishai-Maisels has suggested, have been the source for the mother holding the dead child in Picasso's *Guernica*?[114]

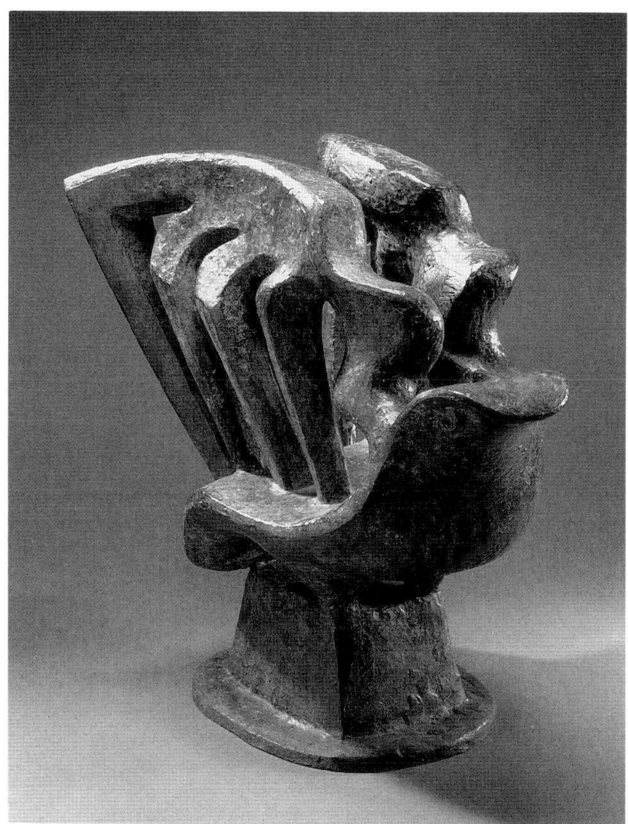

63 *The Harpists* 1930
Bronze 4/7
H. 21¾″/55.2 cm
The Estate of Jacques Lipchitz represented by Marlborough International Fine Art AG.

THIS WORK IS RELATED TO THE 1928 *The Harpist*, ONE OF Lipchitz's most successful transparents.[115] The latter sculpture was inspired by harp players the artist had seen at the symphony in Paris. He described this version as follows:

> The 1930 bronze I entitled *The Harpists* since I seemed to see more than one figure. Also, there was a curious visual metamorphosis of the harp player and her instrument into a bird form.[116]

64 *Mother and Child* 1930
Bronze
H. 51¼″/142.2 cm
The Cleveland Museum of Art, The Norman O. Stone and Ella A. Stone Memorial Fund, with a contribution from Bernard J. Reis.
(Shown in Toronto only)

ALTHOUGH LIPCHITZ HAS WRITTEN THAT THIS SCULPTURE emerged from the very small mother-and-child maquettes discussed in no. 62 above, it has no direct stylistic connections with the earlier works. The truncated arms of the mother were based on a 1929 maquette entitled *Form Seen in a Cloud*, which was inspired by a cloud formation that suggested the shape of a bird.[117] Apart from the mother's head, turned sharply to her right, the sculpture has the rigid frontality and symmetry that characterize a number of Lipchitz's large works. He discussed with great candor the personal significance this work had for him:

> This is also a strangely brutal piece in the manner in which the child digs his fingers into his mother's breasts. I know that I identified myself with the child, but I cannot explain the brutality except as something arising from this time of extreme misery, something in which I felt a passionate need for support. I know that my own mother was the one who always supported and encouraged me and that for her I felt the deepest love. It may be that there was some kind of guilt involved in this image, some feeling that I had not sufficiently repaid her love.[118]

Indeed, the disproportionately large figure on the mother's back seems more like a young, aggressive adolescent than a small child.

Lipchitz remarked on the somewhat simple volumes of this work and others of the period. "It is as though, having worked with the greatest freedom in the sketches, I felt a need to discipline myself in their final realization."[119] This often resulted in somewhat monotonous surfaces with none of the lively modelled textures found in the maquettes.

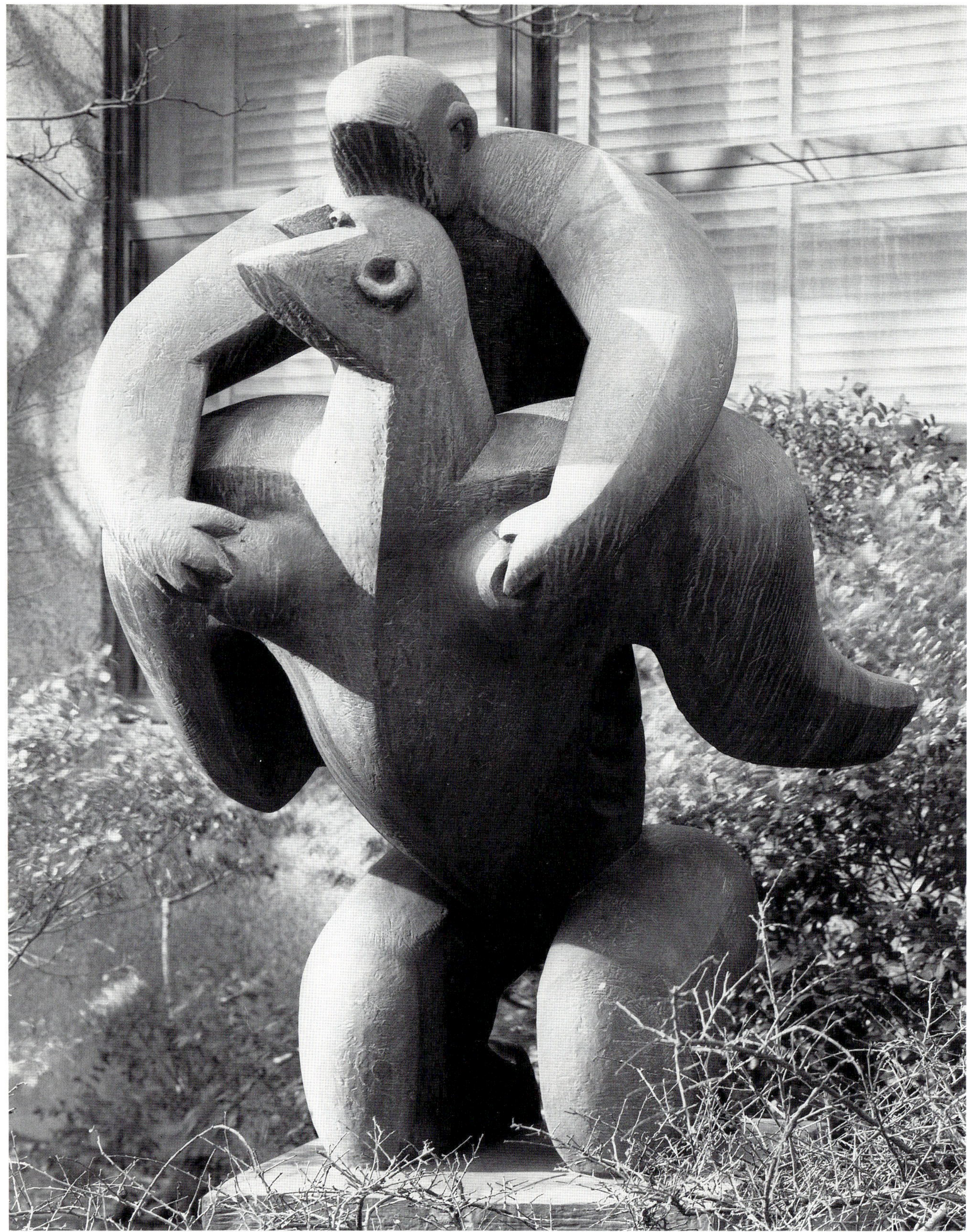

64

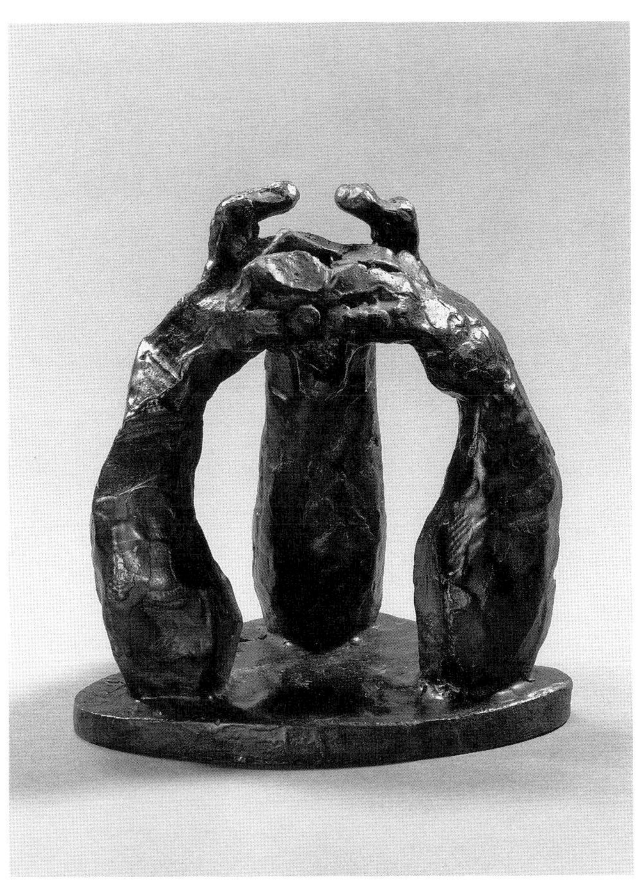

65 *Meditation* 1931
Bronze 3/7
H. 7½″/19.0 cm
The Estate of Jacques Lipchitz represented by Marlborough International Fine Art AG.

IN LIPCHITZ'S FIRST SCULPTURE ENTITLED *Meditation* 1925 (no. 45), the entire figure is represented. In this work the focus on the theme is even more intense because all body parts that are superfluous to the subject have been eliminated. The arms, neck and head rise vertically from the base as separate elements and arch inward to lock together at the head. The fingers cover most of the face, leaving only the nose exposed. The index fingers are raised above the head, like two budding horns. Rodin, in his sculpture *The Walking Man* 1877–78, eliminated the head and arms to focus the viewer's attention exclusively on the basic movement of walking. Likewise, Lipchitz has used only those parts of the human anatomy necessary to create an intensely focused, self-sufficient representation of meditation.

66 *Return of the Prodigal Son* 1931
Bronze
H. 42″/106.7 cm
The Nelson-Atkins Museum of Art, Kansas City, Missouri (Gift of Mrs. R. C. Kemper, Sr., through the R. C. Kemper, Sr., Charitable Trust).

ALTHOUGH THIS SCULPTURE FOLLOWS THE COMPOSITION established in the maquette (no. 61) a number of significant changes have occurred. The overall rhythm of both figures is more rigid, with crisp angles defining, as in the arms of the child, where two planes meet. The way in which the two heads have been separated creates a V shape between them, reminiscent of the heads in *The Cry* of 1928–29 (no. 54). The loosely flowing hair in the maquette has been replaced by three pronounced projections running down the entire length of the mother's back. Again, Lipchitz felt the need to abandon the spontaneous, lively modelling of the maquette in favour of a more disciplined, regular surface texture.

67 *Jacob and the Angel* 1931
Bronze 7/7
H. 9¼″/23.5 cm
The Estate of Jacques Lipchitz represented by Marlborough International Fine Art AG.

THE THEME OF THE STRUGGLE OF JACOB AND THE ANGEL (Gen. 32:24–32) began to obsess Lipchitz in 1931. He paraphrased the story as follows:

> Jacob was sleeping and the angel came to him and woke him and challenged him to do battle, so that Jacob began to fight. Although the angel was a messenger of the Lord, and Jacob could not overcome him, he did fight nevertheless, and after that, the Lord rewarded him for having fought and named him Israel. To me, this meant that God wants us to fight with him.[120]

This maquette, as one has come to expect, is much freer and more spontaneous than the large version (no. 68). Jacob (shown here on the right) stands on his left leg and leans far forward locked in combat with the angel. Where the two heads meet a deep gouge is formed, creating the now-familiar cry of pain, which was becoming a common feature in sculptures dealing with embracing or combative figures.

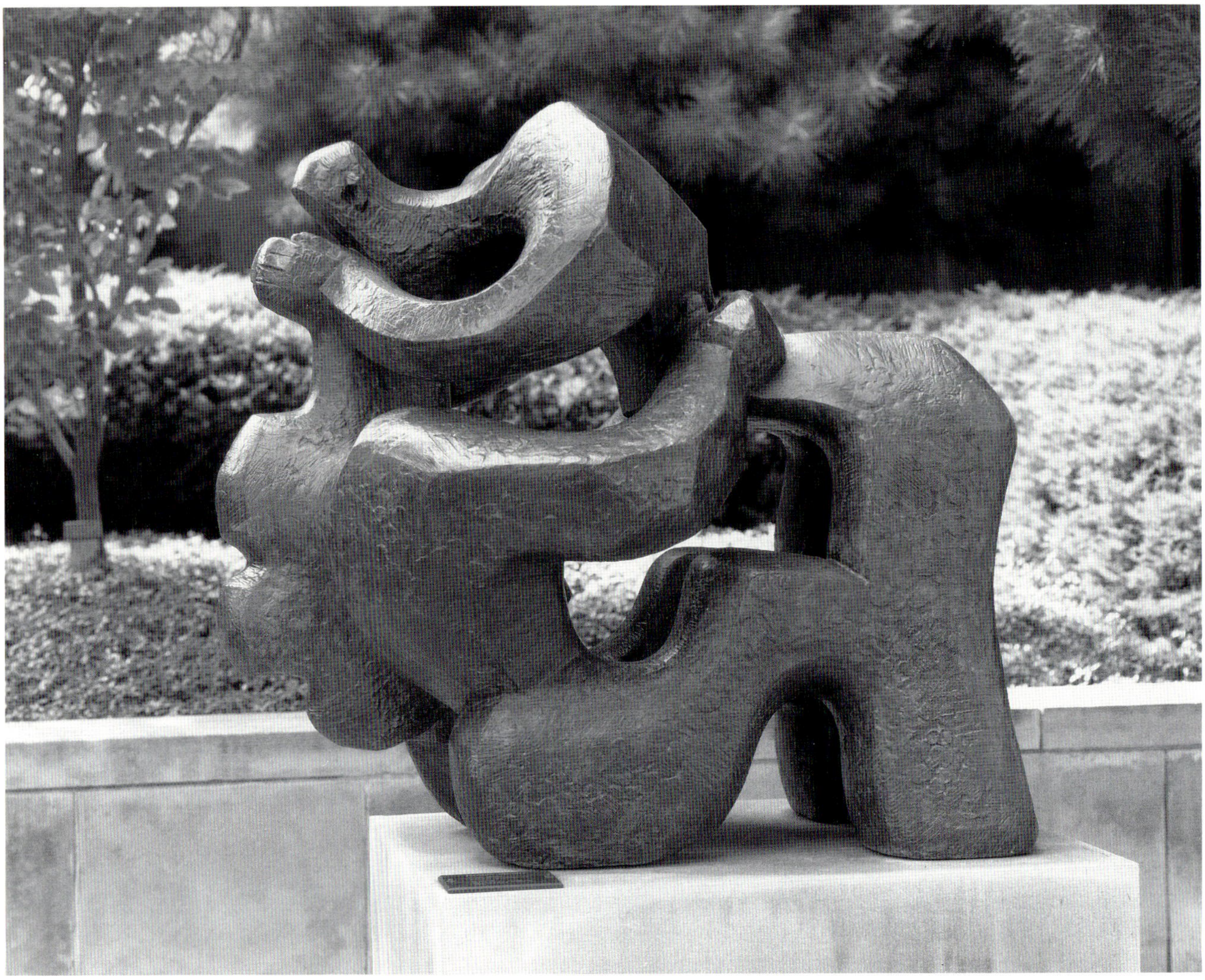

66

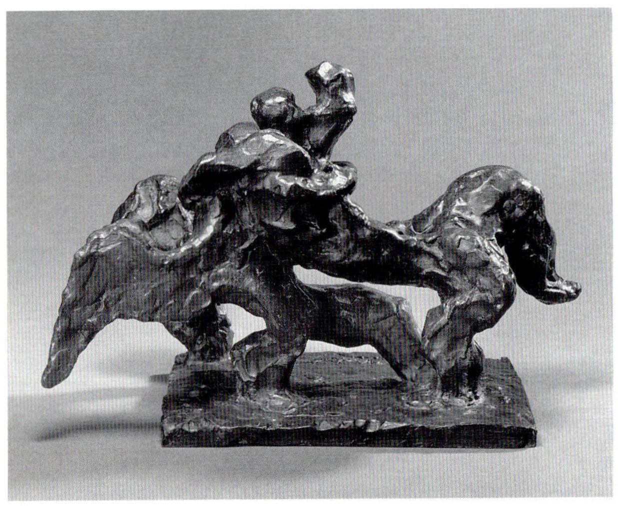

67

68 *Jacob Struggling with the Angel* 1932
Bronze, edition of 7
L. 50″/127.0 cm
The Estate of Jacques Lipchitz represented by Marlborough International Fine Art AG.

In this large version, based on no. 67, the forms of the two figures are heavier, more compact and more clearly defined. Jacob, shown here on the right, seems to be mounting the angel, as the figures are locked together in combat. Whereas in the maquette the wings are clearly legible, in this sculpture one of the wings looks more like Jacob's extended right leg.

In the early 1930s the subjects represented by interlocking figures – the rape, the embrace, combat, even strangulation – become, in a sense, interchangeable. In 1933, in his *David and Goliath* (no. 75), Lipchitz used the theme of struggle as a vehicle of protest against the growing threat of Hitler and the onset of the Nazi era.

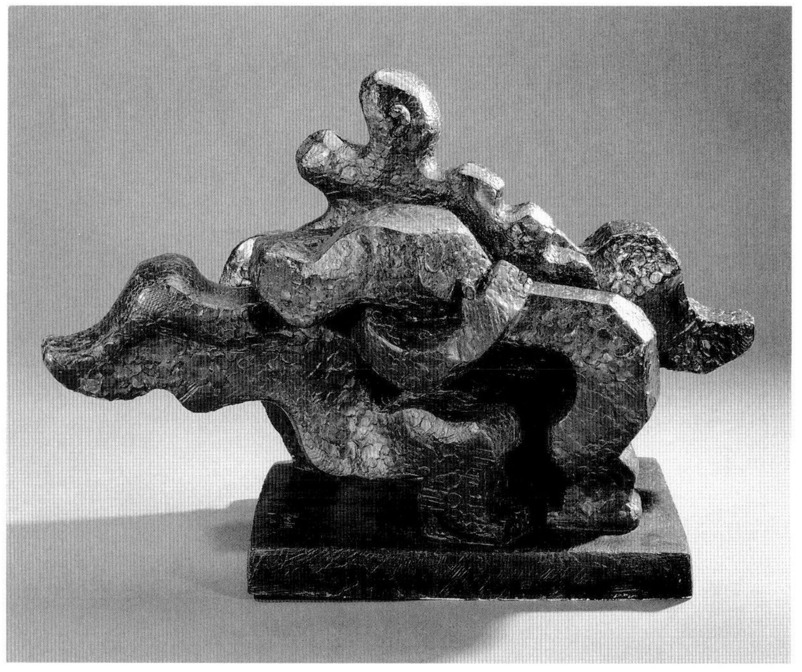

68

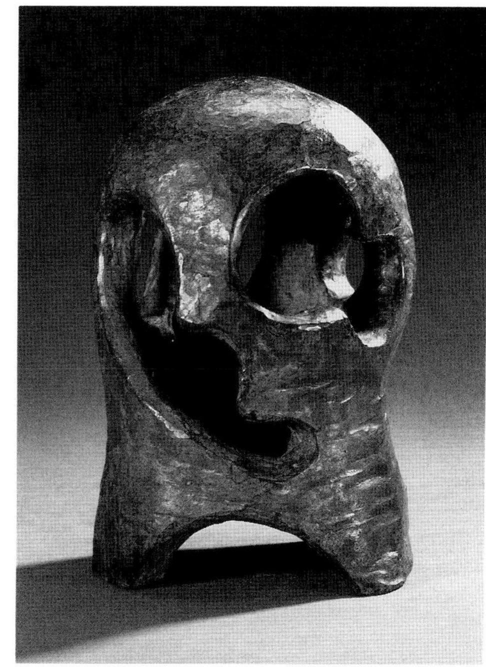

69

69 *Head* 1932
Bronze 4/7
H. 8⅝″/21.9 cm
The Estate of Jacques Lipchitz represented by Marlborough International Fine Art AG.

LIPCHITZ'S OBSESSION WITH THE HEAD, OFTEN RESTING on the hand, culminated in a series of sculptures executed in 1932–33.

> Some of these studies of head and hands were formal explorations of interior or negative sculptural space, and the interest in this problem led me in 1932 to a series of sketches of helmet or skull heads in which the interior space is open and enveloped by a skin or bone structure pierced with great eye holes.[121]

Head is one of two versions of this theme, both of which were made in 1932. Here, the counterbalance between the outer shell of the skull and the large, curvilinear voids seems perfectly judged. The view shown here suggests a very large left eye, and the single void beside it seems to depict the right eye, the profile of the nose and the mouth.

Those familiar with the work of Henry Moore will be reminded of his 1964 *Maquette for Atom Piece* (see fig. 20). Although the striking similarities between *Head* and *Maquette for Atom Piece* might suggest a direct influence, the Moore bronze was almost certainly inspired by the large elephant skull that Moore owned. That one associates images of helmet heads and hollowed-out skulls with the sculpture of Moore – and not Lipchitz – is simply indicative of our lack of familiarity with the latter's work.

70 *Woman Leaning on Hand* 1932
Bronze 4/7
H. 6″/15.3 cm
The Estate of Jacques Lipchitz represented by Marlborough International Fine Art AG.

IN *Meditation* 1925 (NO. 45) THE HEAD RESTS AGAINST the blocklike left hand and arm, which are supported by the continuous S curve formed by the right arm and left leg. In this work the head and left arm create a single self-sufficient entity detached from the rest of the body. The way the head leans back, away from the viewer, suggests that the woman may be sleeping. The head, shown in profile to the right, is wedged between the hair and the massive left arm and hand. The face is comprised of two planes, one receding back to the top of the head, the other down to the chin. Even though the head is in profile, the entire right eye is depicted. This is a Cubist device found in early works such as *Woman with Braid* 1914 (no. 8). Lipchitz has managed to convey, with broad gestures rather than with anatomical detail, the very essence of sleep and relaxation. This pose appears again in the 1942 bronze *Head of a Sleeping Man (Marsden Hartley Sleeping)* (no. 87).

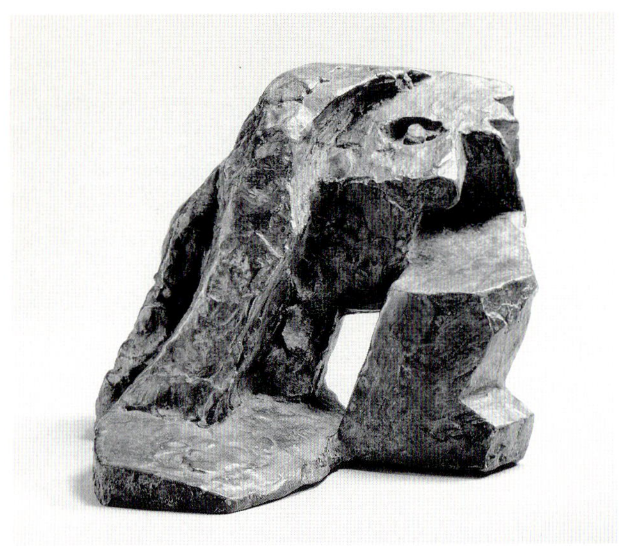

70

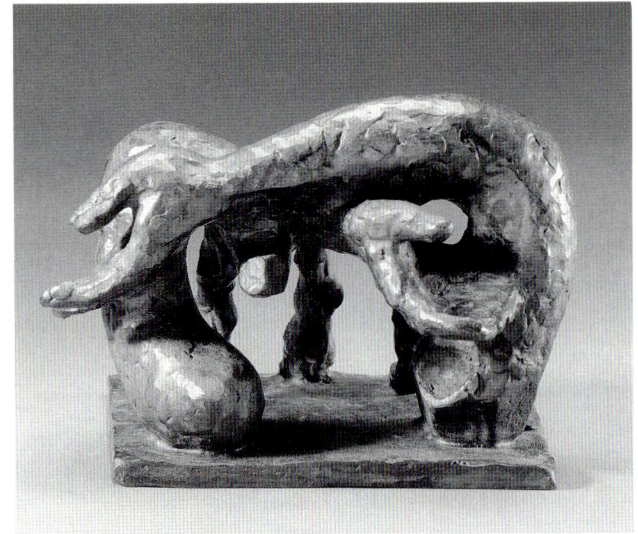

71

71 *The Arms* 1933
Bronze 5/7
L. 9½″/24.1 cm
The Estate of Jacques Lipchitz represented by Marlborough International Fine Art AG.

Rodin's numerous studies of hands and arms, of which *The Cathedral* 1908 is the best known, are an obvious precedent for these lyrical, intertwining arms. The three struts at the back, like flying buttresses, seem to have an architectural, structural function. The protruding form just left of centre suggests a nose (as in no. 65), as if the arms were raised in front of the forehead.

72 *Head and Hand* 1933
Bronze 2/7
H. 31″/78.7 cm
The Estate of Jacques Lipchitz represented by Marlborough International Fine Art AG.

This is one of several sculptures in the head-and-hand series in which, in Lipchitz's own words, "the head takes on a brutalized animal form that is even suggestive of the Minotaur, a subject I was to explore some years later."[122]

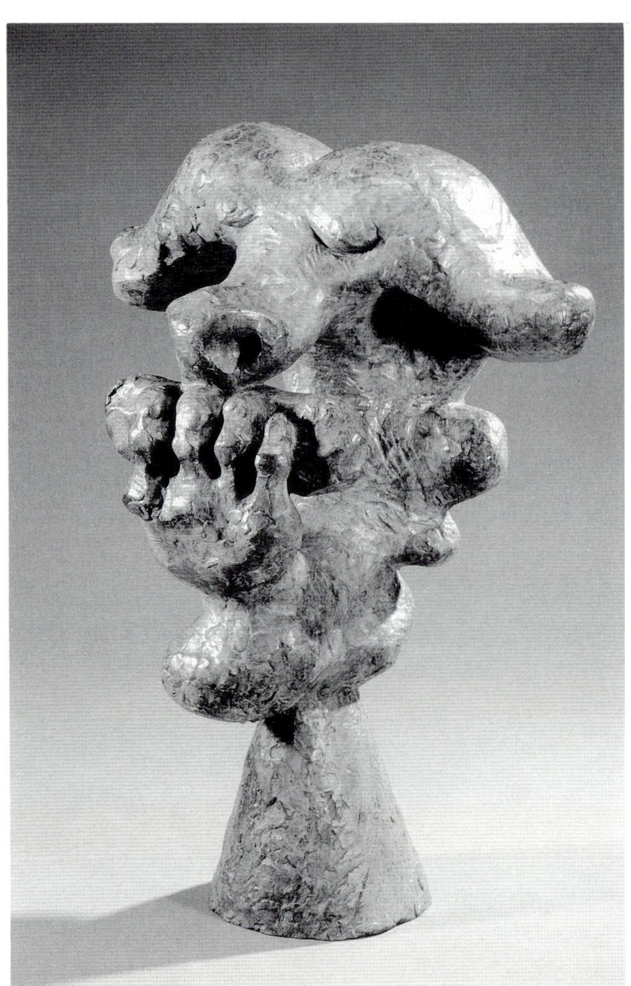

72

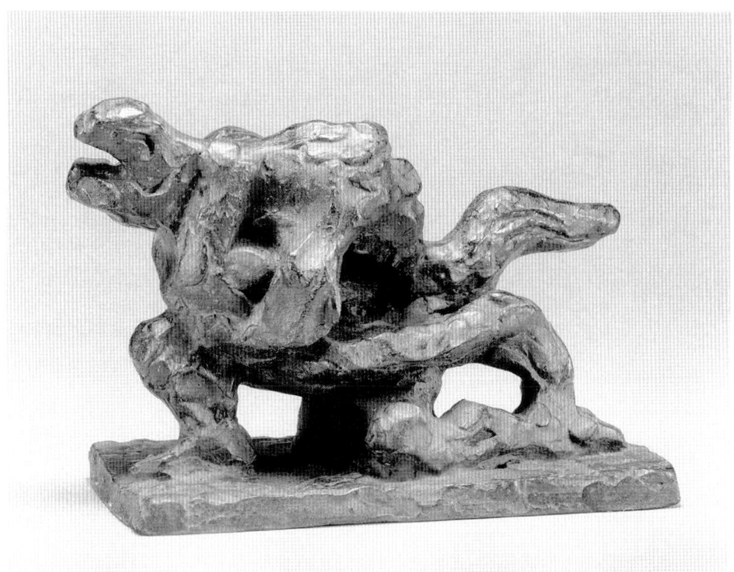

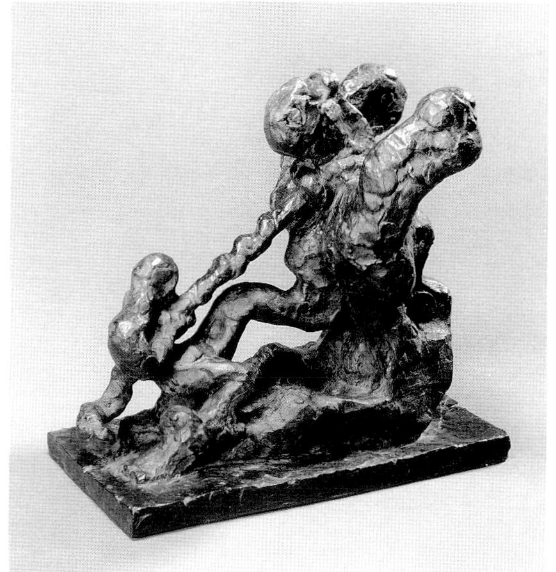

73 *The Embrace* 1933
Bronze 7/7
L. 5″/12.7 cm
The Estate of Jacques Lipchitz represented by Marlborough International Fine Art AG.

Sexual love, sexual violence and murder were the subjects of three small maquettes of 1933 (*The Embrace*, *The Rape* and *The Strangulation*). Whereas the theme of *The Embrace* is closely related to that of *The Cry* 1928–29 (no. 54), the forms and flowing modelling are stylistically akin to the maquette *Jacob and the Angel* (no. 67). Yet again, the gap between the two heads produces a cry, as if from a single figure. This was one of several sketches of 1933–34 focusing on erotic love, which, Lipchitz said, "seem to have been some sort of release for me."[123] And yet the sexuality seems as violent and brutal as that depicted in the maquette entitled *The Rape* of 1933.[124]

In 1934 Lipchitz made a larger version of *The Embrace* based on a maquette similar to no. 73.[125]

74 *David and Goliath* 1933
Bronze 7/7
L. 10½″/26.7 cm
The Estate of Jacques Lipchitz represented by Marlborough International Fine Art AG.

Lipchitz's art reflected the threat of fascism as early as 1931 in the small maquette entitled *First Study for Prometheus*,[126] for which he borrowed a theme from classical mythology to express, he said, his thoughts "about the intellectuals who were moving into a period of darkness and persecution."[127]

For his first blatant attack against Hitler's Germany, Lipchitz chose the story, told in 1 Sam. 17, of David, the young shepherd who defeated and killed the Philistine champion, the giant Goliath. He adapted the Old Testament story to fit the political climate of the day, and specifically, he said, to show "my hatred of fascism and my conviction that the David of freedom would triumph over the Goliath of oppression."[128]

This is one of four preliminary studies made in 1933.[129] In the first maquette David stands over the recumbent Goliath, twisting a rope around his neck. In the other three, including this work, Lipchitz said, "the figures are reversed, with the huge Goliath rising up vertically and David pulling back with all his strength on the great cable cord which he has twisted around the throat of the giant."[130] Here, Goliath, with his left arm bent back, is trying to free the rope around his neck. The upward thrust of his arms anticipates *Mother and Child II* 1941–45 (no. 84). David is kneeling on his right leg, with the left leg almost fully extended and pressing against the back of Goliath. That a swastika is incised on Goliath's chest indicates that Lipchitz wished there to be no doubt about his intent.

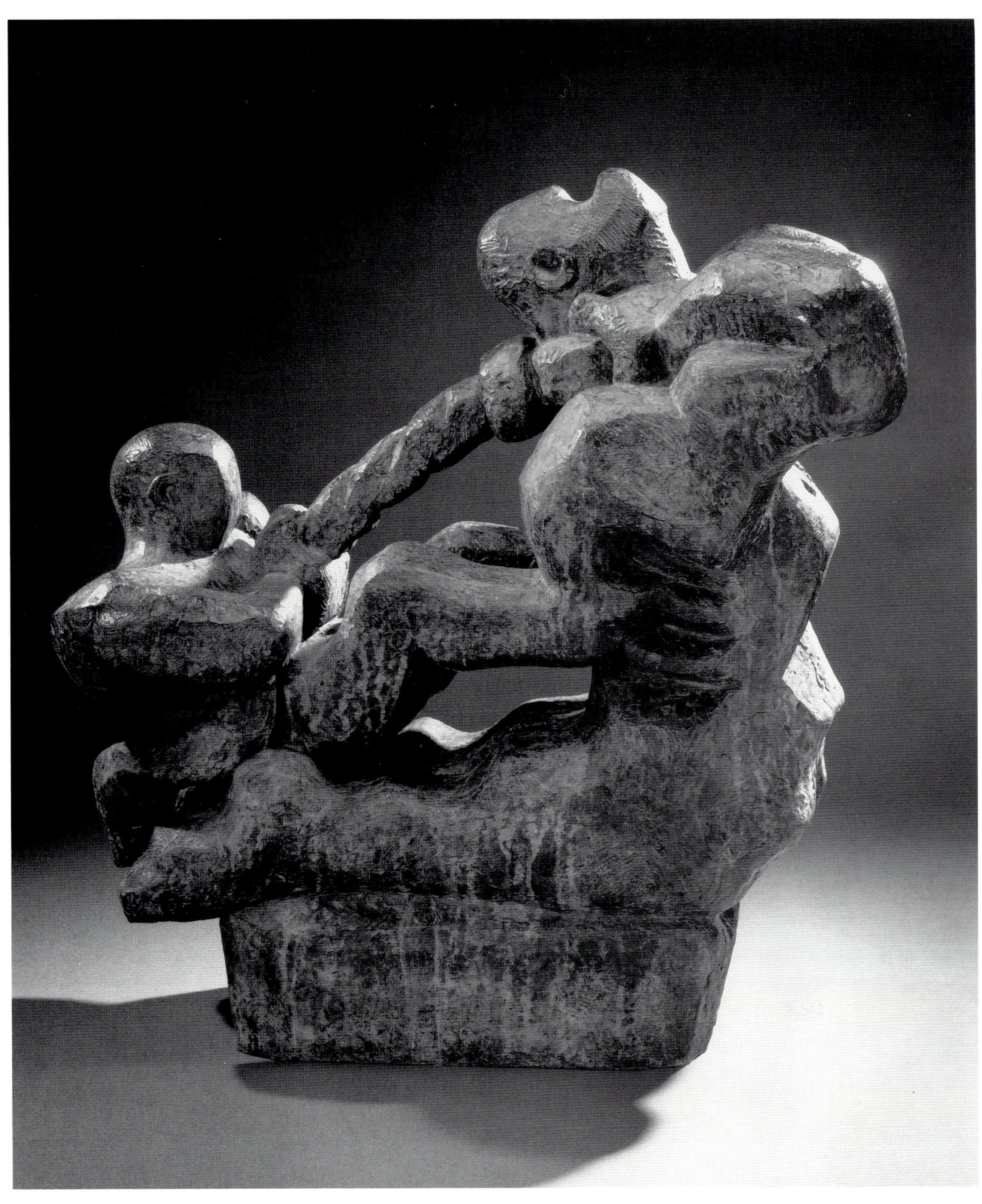

75 *David and Goliath* 1933
Bronze 1/7
H. 33″/83.8 cm
The Estate of Jacques Lipchitz represented by Marlborough International Fine Art AG.

Of all Lipchitz's large-scale sculptures of the 1930s based on preliminary studies, *David and Goliath* is the most successful for a number of reasons. The scale seems perfectly judged to contain the sheer energy and tension of the two figures. The surface texture and modelling are more varied, less repetitive, than in works such as *Return of the Prodigal Son* (no. 66). The composition is more symmetrical than that of the maquette (no. 74). Here both of David's legs are extended with the feet pressing against Goliath's back. Goliath's rib cage is gouged out at the front, with ribs indicated at each side. (See similar features in *Mother and Child II* 1941–45, no. 84). Goliath's head strains back under the tension of the rope, which he tries in vain to release with both hands. Another cry of anguish and pain, like those found in so many other works of the period, issues forth from his large, gouged-out mouth. As in the earlier maquette, a swastika appears on Goliath's chest.

76 *Head of Géricault* 1933
Bronze 7/7
H. 11⅜″/28.9 cm
The Estate of Jacques Lipchitz represented by Marlborough International Fine Art AG.

This is one of four known portraits Lipchitz made in 1933 of the French painter Théodore Géricault (1791–1824), which were followed by a larger bronze of which there is a cast in the Musée des Beaux-Arts, Rouen. Among his portraits executed in 1932–33, Lipchitz said, he found his studies of Géricault the most interesting:

> I have always been a great admirer of this painter, a genius who died young, and I have some paintings of his. There exists a death mask of Géricault of which I acquired a cast. I wanted to make the portrait as realistic as possible, so I checked documents and existing portraits of him. This was my homage to a great artist whom I loved very much. I think it is a good portrait.[131]

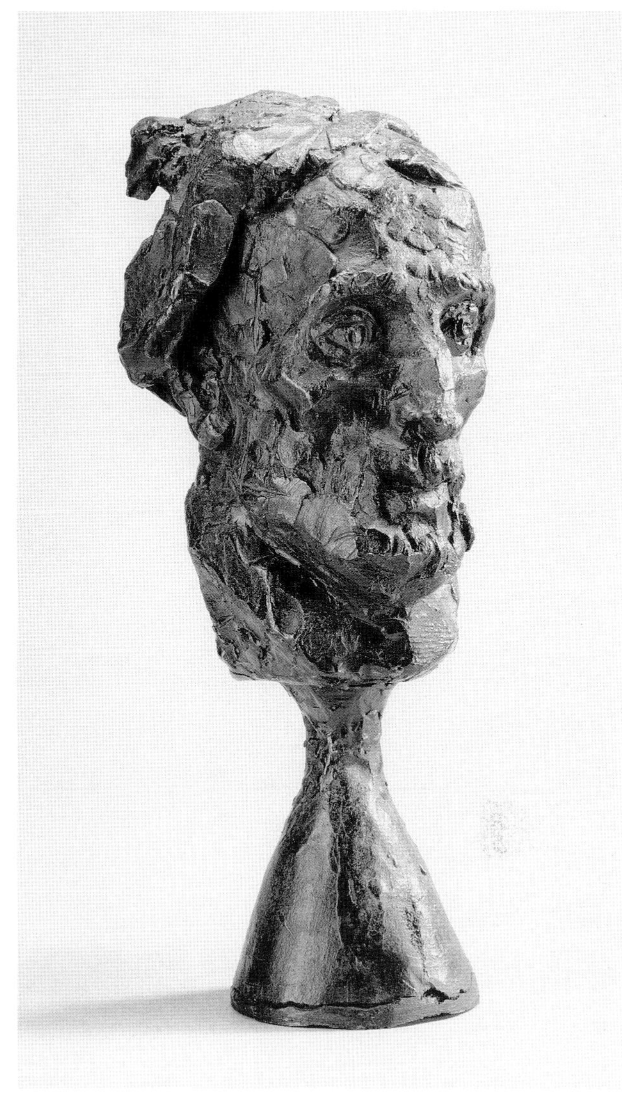

76

77 *Study for Prometheus* 1936
Bronze 5/7
L. 7½″/19.0 cm
The Estate of Jacques Lipchitz represented by Marlborough International Fine Art AG.

Lipchitz found in the legend of Prometheus a story that on a symbolic level could be adapted to contemporary life and political events. As a sculptor, Lipchitz may well have identified with Prometheus, the brilliant inventor who created man from clay and water. When he was commissioned by the French government to create a sculpture for the Palais de la Découverte at the 1937 Exposition Internationale in Paris, Lipchitz recalled that "the idea of Prometheus came to me because science is personified in Prometheus."[132] The Greeks saw Prometheus as the benefactor of mankind and the father of all the arts and sciences. This is one of two sketches of Prometheus

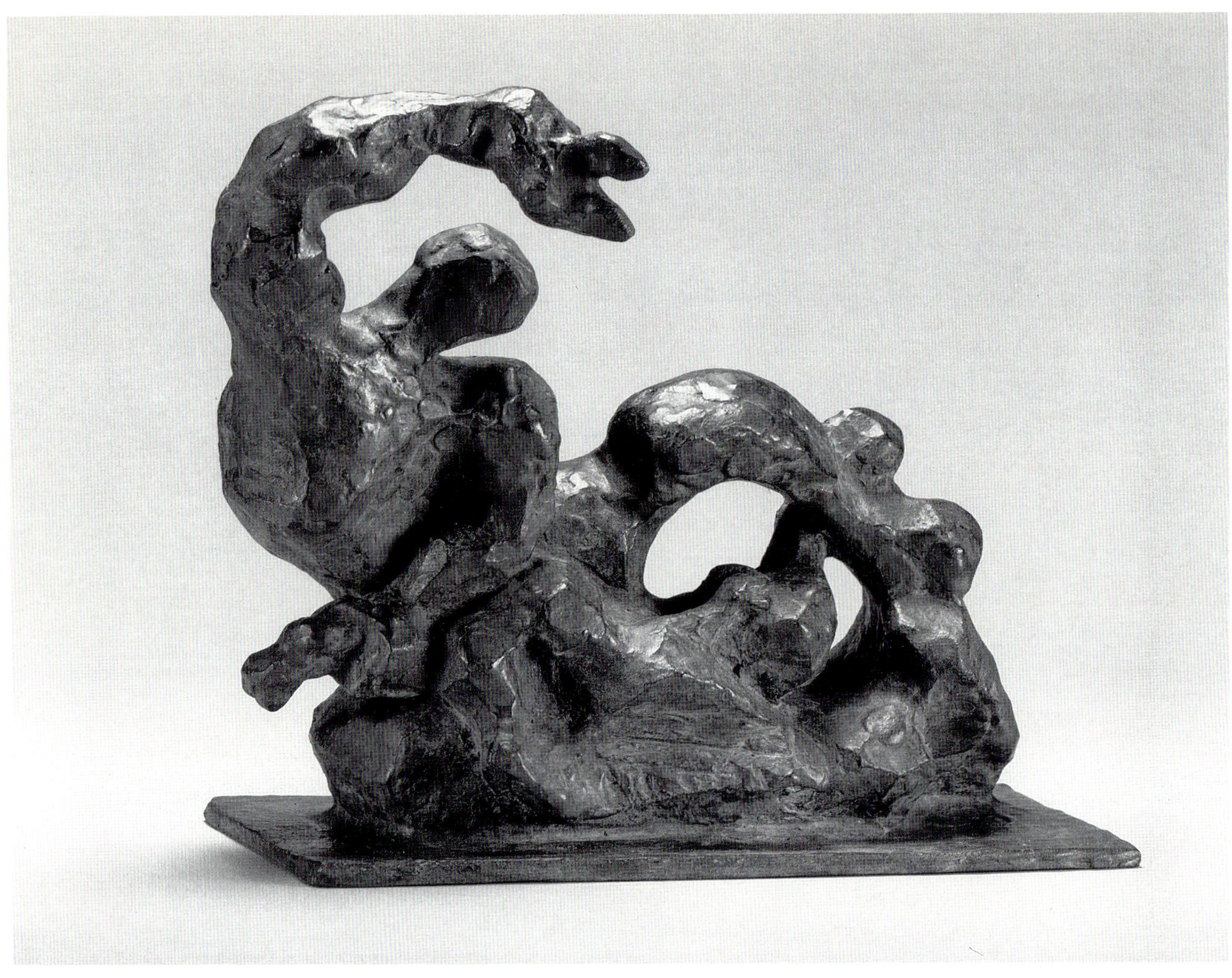

77

in chains, guarding the flame in his right hand while fending off the vulture, or eagle, sent each day by Jupiter to eat his immortal liver. As Lipchitz himself acknowledged, the two initial sketches, of which this is one, "are probably related to some of those earlier Laocoön images..."[133] Indeed, in this, one of Lipchitz's earliest Baroque compositions, the raised, curved right arm, the head, inclined to the left, and the tangled, interlocking forms of the left arm, the legs and the bird are so close to the Laocoön group as to suggest a direct influence.

78 *Study for Prometheus Strangling the Vulture* 1936
Bronze
H. 17½"/44.5 cm
Joey and Toby Tanenbaum, Toronto, Ontario
(Shown in Toronto only)

Lipchitz abandoned the aspect of the legend represented in no. 77 and embarked on studies showing Prometheus standing, strangling the vulture. He obviously wanted to present a more active struggle or conflict than that which could be represented by Prometheus helplessly chained to a rock with the vulture eating his liver. In this study Prometheus is shown with both hands clenched, as if strangling the vulture, whereas in the final version he chokes the bird with his right hand and with his left tries to wrench away the claw tearing at his vitals.

Lipchitz explained the didactic intent of the sculpture:

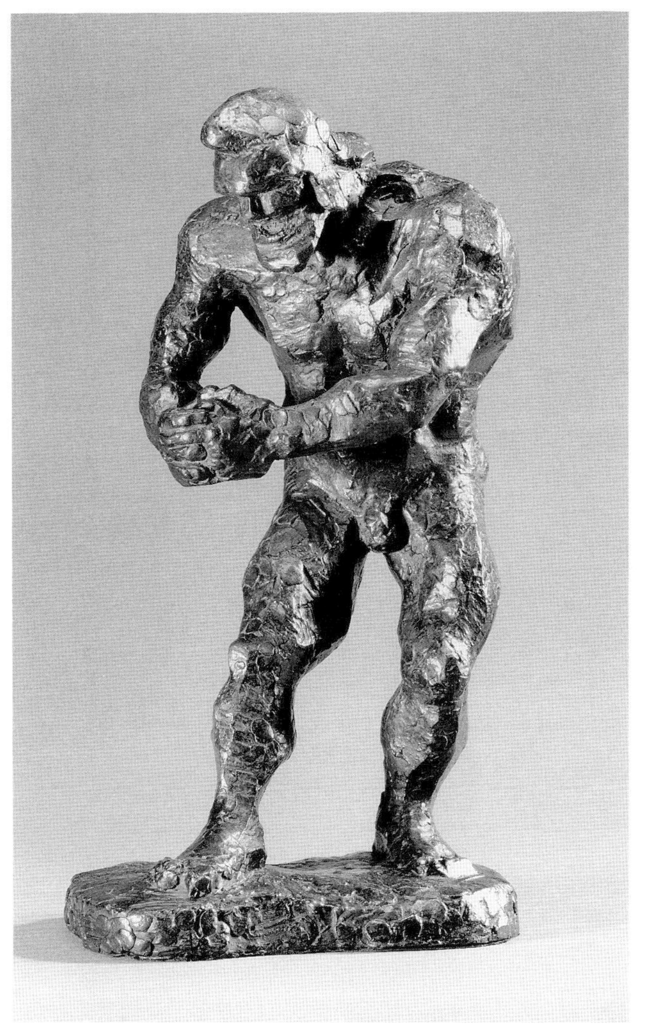

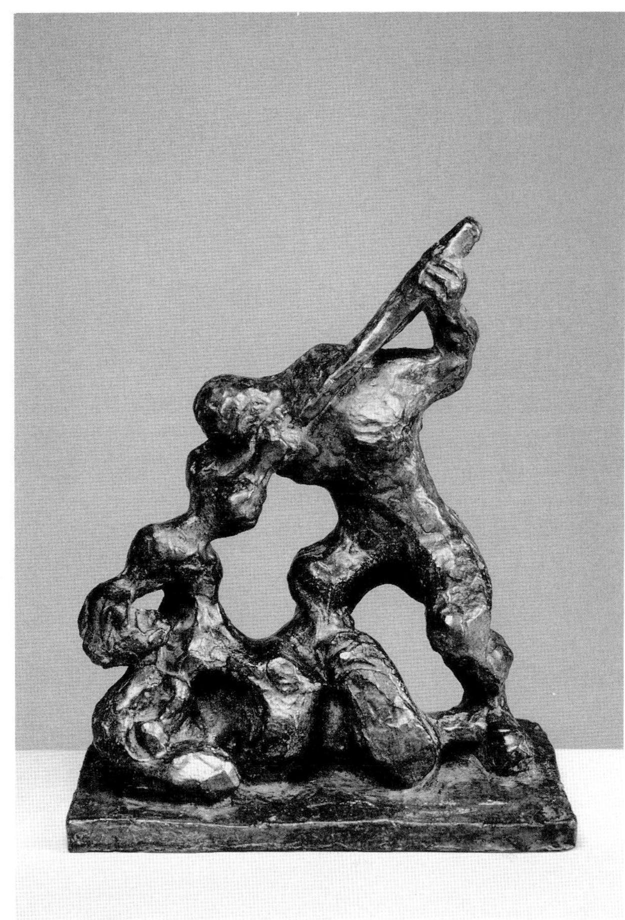

79 *Scene of Civil War* 1936
Bronze 2/7
H. 9¼″/23.5 cm
The Estate of Jacques Lipchitz represented by Marlborough International Fine Art AG.

> It was conceived as a struggle, not a simple conquest, in which light, education, science were struggling against darkness and ignorance, which had not yet been conquered... The Phrygian cap that I placed on Prometheus had a particular significance for me as a symbol of democracy; what I was trying to show was a pattern of human progress that to me involved the democratic ideal. So, in a certain way, this is a political sculpture, propaganda for democracy.[134]

In 1937, the thirty-foot-high (nine-meter) plaster *Prometheus and the Vulture* was installed over one of the entrances to the Grand Palais (which housed the Palais de la Découverte), some forty feet above the ground. (The Exposition Internationale ran from May to November.) After the exhibition closed, the sculpture was taken down and destroyed, in part because of attacks in the press. In 1943–44 Lipchitz returned again to the theme of Prometheus strangling the vulture in the commission for the Ministry of Education and Health building in Rio de Janeiro (see nos. 89 and 90).

TWO SMALL BRONZES OF 1936 CONTINUE TO REFLECT Lipchitz's state of mind as the political climate in Europe worsened. *The Terrified One* represents blind fear and terror, as a woman throws her head back and utters a cry.[135] In *Scene of Civil War*, the conflict in Spain is symbolized by a man with a gun hovering over a woman lying helplessly on the ground.

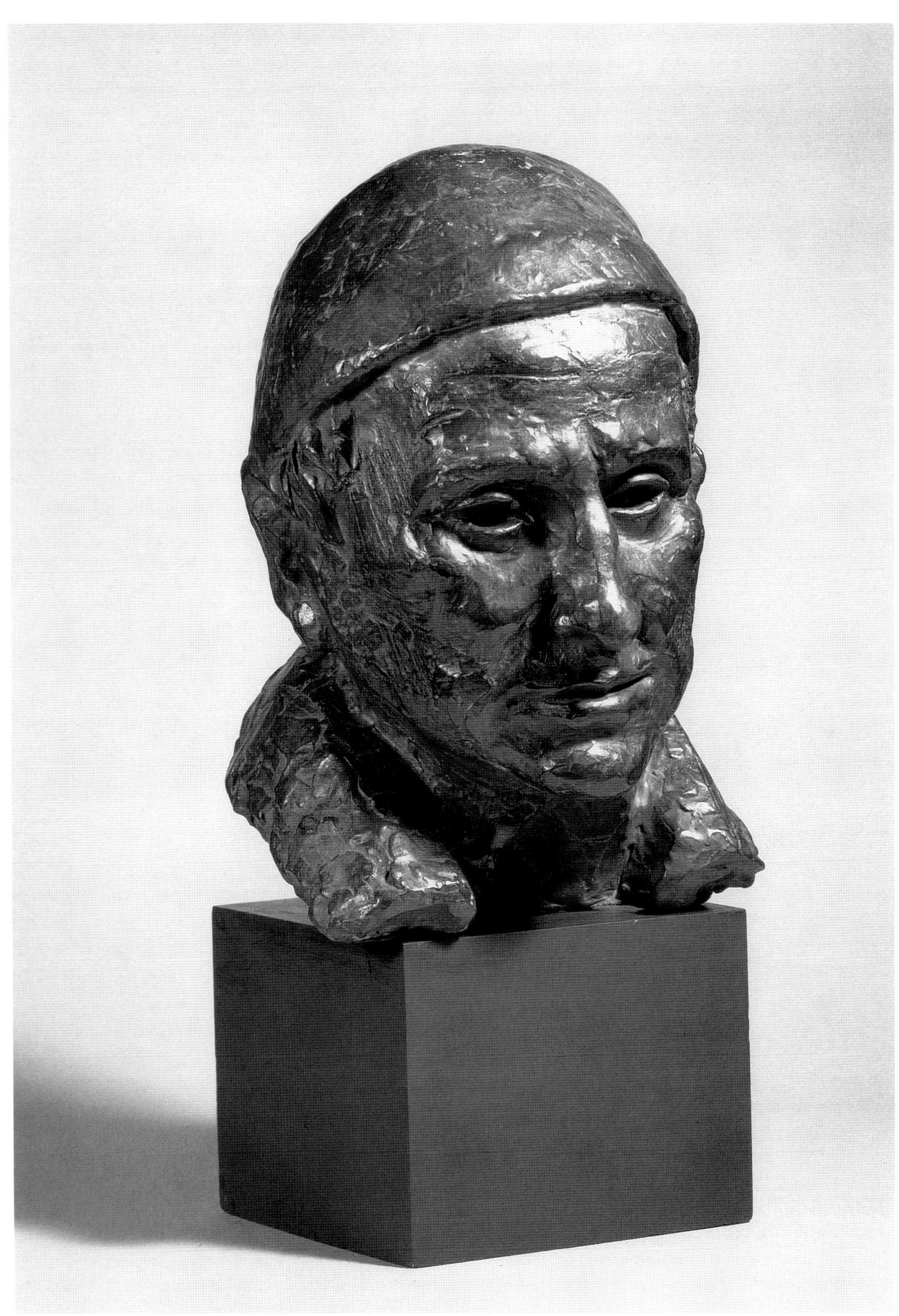

80 *Gertrude Stein* 1938
Bronze 3/10
H. 11¾″/30.0 cm
The Estate of Jacques Lipchitz represented by
Marlborough International Fine Art AG.

In his 1920 portrait of Gertrude Stein, (no. 32), Lipchitz depicted her, he said, "as a massive, inscrutable Buddha."[136] In 1938, after a long interval, they met again. Now, he remarked, she had lost a great deal of weight.

> She looked now like a shriveled old rabbi, with a little rabbi's cap on her head. I was so struck by the contrast that I asked if I could make another portrait of her. I made two different sketches, one with the cap [no. 80] and one without... The massive, self-confident Buddha has become a tired and rather tragic old woman.[137]

Perhaps this deeply moving study, one of Lipchitz's finest portraits, reflects something of the prevailing mood of gloom and pessimism among artists and intellectuals now that the outbreak of war seemed inevitable.

81 *Rape of Europa I* 1938
Bronze 6/7
L. 21″/53.3 cm
The Estate of Jacques Lipchitz represented by
Marlborough International Fine Art AG.

Among the last sculptures that Lipchitz made before the outbreak of war were three variations on the theme of the rape of Europa. In the Greek myth, Europa, the daughter of Phoenix, king of Phoenicia, was seduced by Jupiter. He changed himself into a beautiful white bull and approached her, breathing saffron from his mouth. She climbed on his back and wound flowers around his horns, whereupon the bull suddenly made off with her and swam to Crete. This bronze shows Europa clinging to the neck of the bull with her right arm; her left arm is on his raised left foreleg. The bull's tongue licks her face aggressively. Lipchitz remarked that "the appendages at the back suggest a fishlike form. In my collection there is an extremely rare bronze Coptic piece in which the bull takes on a different aquatic shape. I think that I may have been influenced by this."[138] Lipchitz was almost certainly aware of Picasso's numerous drawings, paintings and prints depicting bulls and minotaurs revelling in bacchanalian feasts.

In 1941 Lipchitz used the theme of the Rape of Europa in a quite different context (no. 85), with Europa a symbol for Europe and the bull as Hitler. In 1969–70, near the end of his life, Lipchitz returned again to this mythological subject, showing Europa being ravished by the bull (no. 125).

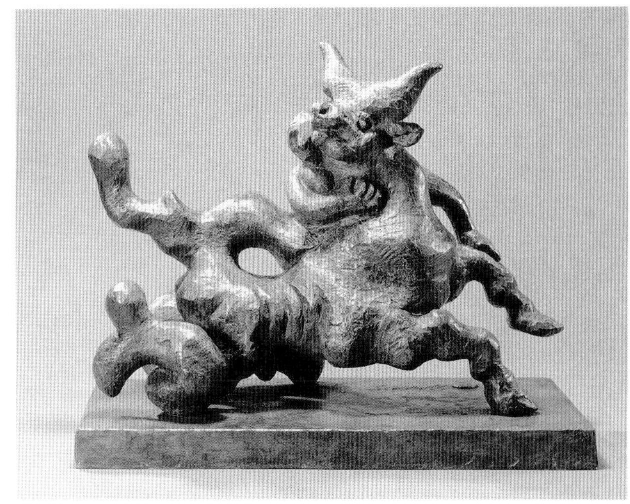
81

82 *Study for Return of the Child* 1941
Bronze 3/7
H. 11¾″/30.0 cm
The Estate of Jacques Lipchitz represented by
Marlborough International Fine Art AG.

In May 1940 Lipchitz and his wife, Berthe, fled Paris and settled in Toulouse. *Flight*, the only sculpture from his stay there to have survived, is the first of a number of intensely autobiographical works of 1940–41.[139] He has described this small sketch of a man and woman running as "very free and baroque in its organization, representing not only my emotions at this moment when I was fleeing with my family, but also a new and open expressionist type of composition."[140]

Through the assistance of Alfred Barr, director of the Museum of Modern Art, New York, and the American Rescue Committee, arrangements were made for Lipchitz and his wife to seek refuge in the United States. They sailed from Portugal and arrived in New York in June 1941. Soon after his arrival, Lipchitz made a companion piece, *Arrival*, in which the mother holds the child, who is saved.[141]

Study for Return of the Child is one of two maquettes from which the large bronze and the cast granite (Solomon R. Guggenheim Museum, New York) evolved. The theme is related to the 1914–15 bronze *Mother and Children*

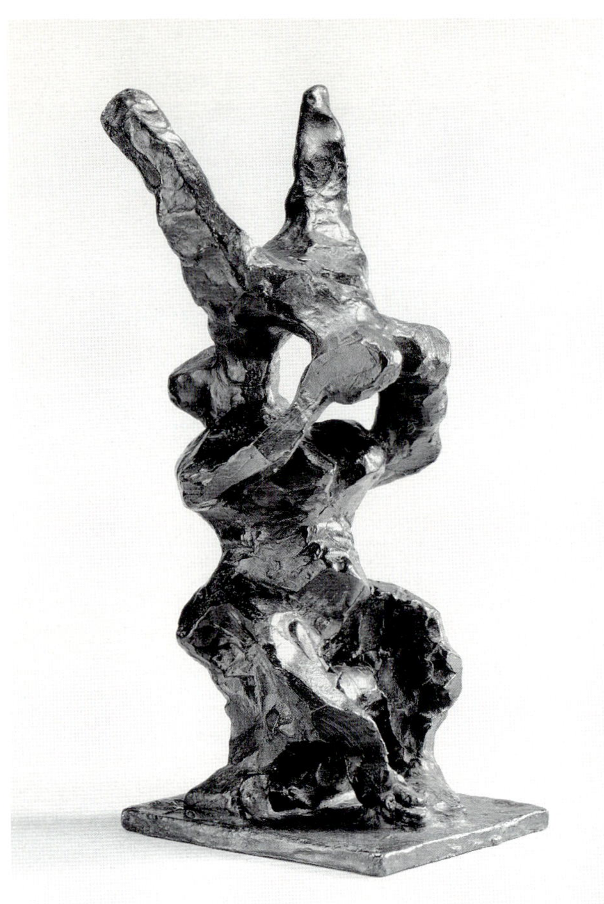

82

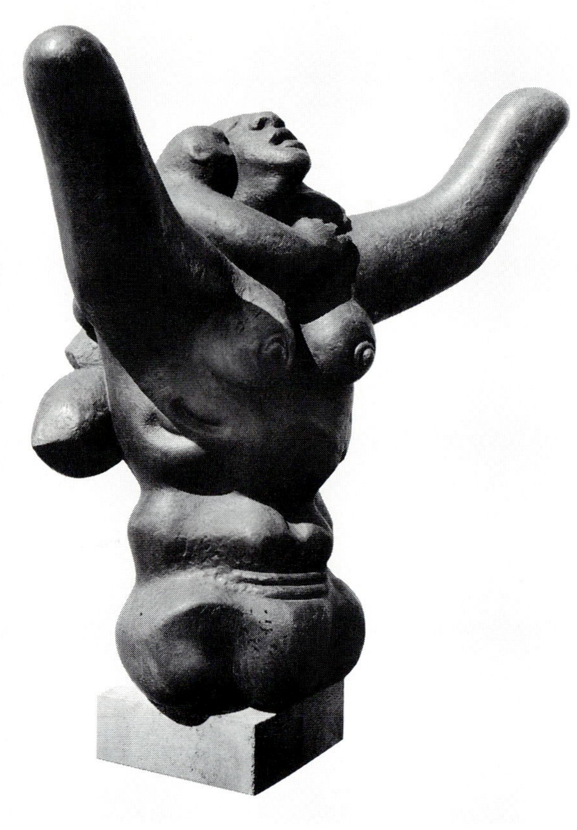

(no. 6) in which one of the children is held above the mother's shoulders. In *Return of the Child*, Lipchitz has written, "the child is a symbol of my sculpture that was returning to me."[142] It also expresses "the specific feeling of escape from the horror of the fascists to the refuge of the United States."[143]

83 *Return of the Child* 1941
Bronze 1/7
H. 45″/114.3 cm
The Estate of Jacques Lipchitz represented by Marlborough International Fine Art AG.

THIS WORK WAS BASED ON THE PRELIMINARY MAQUETTE (see no. 82 above).

84 *Mother and Child II* 1941–45
Bronze 6/7
H. 51½″/130.8 cm
Art Gallery of Ontario, Gift of Sam and Ayala Zacks, 1970.

Mother and Child II IS ANOTHER IMPORTANT WORK THAT Lipchitz began soon after his arrival in New York. He has described in great detail the genesis of the sculpture and its personal significance:

> There are many drawings for it which were originally made in Paris in 1939; but I could not begin on the actual sculpture until after I came to the United States. This to me is a frightening but at the same time a hopeful work that resulted from my feelings about the war. Although there are many obvious relationships with the previous versions of the mother and child, particularly that of 1930 [see no. 64], this one was really entirely different. The 1930 version grew out of the tragic period when I lost my father and sister and was questioning, "Why was I brought to suffer on this earth?" It is a very personal piece. The later version that I started in 1939 with the drawings I made in Paris and that I completed between 1941 and 1942 has to do with

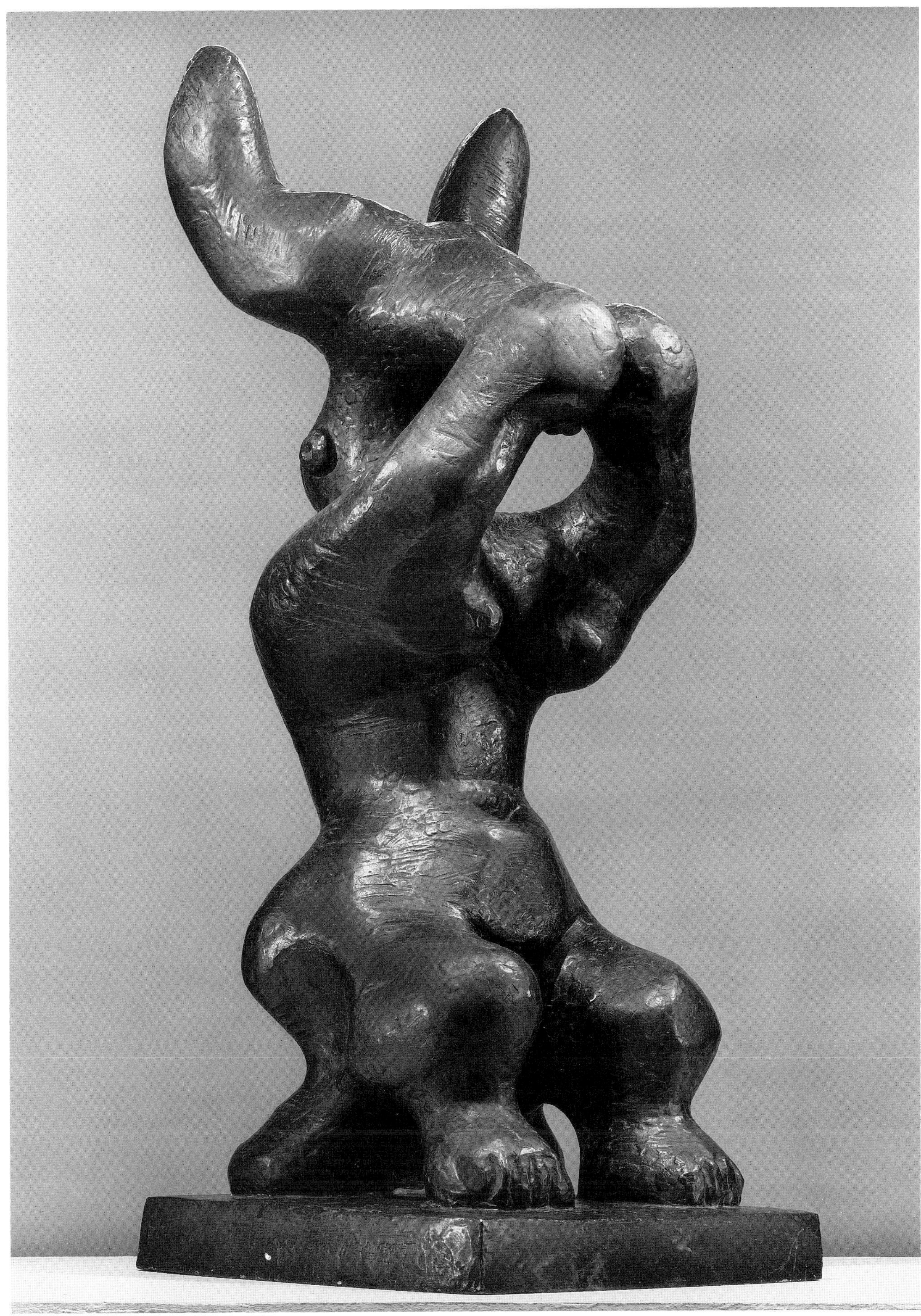

83

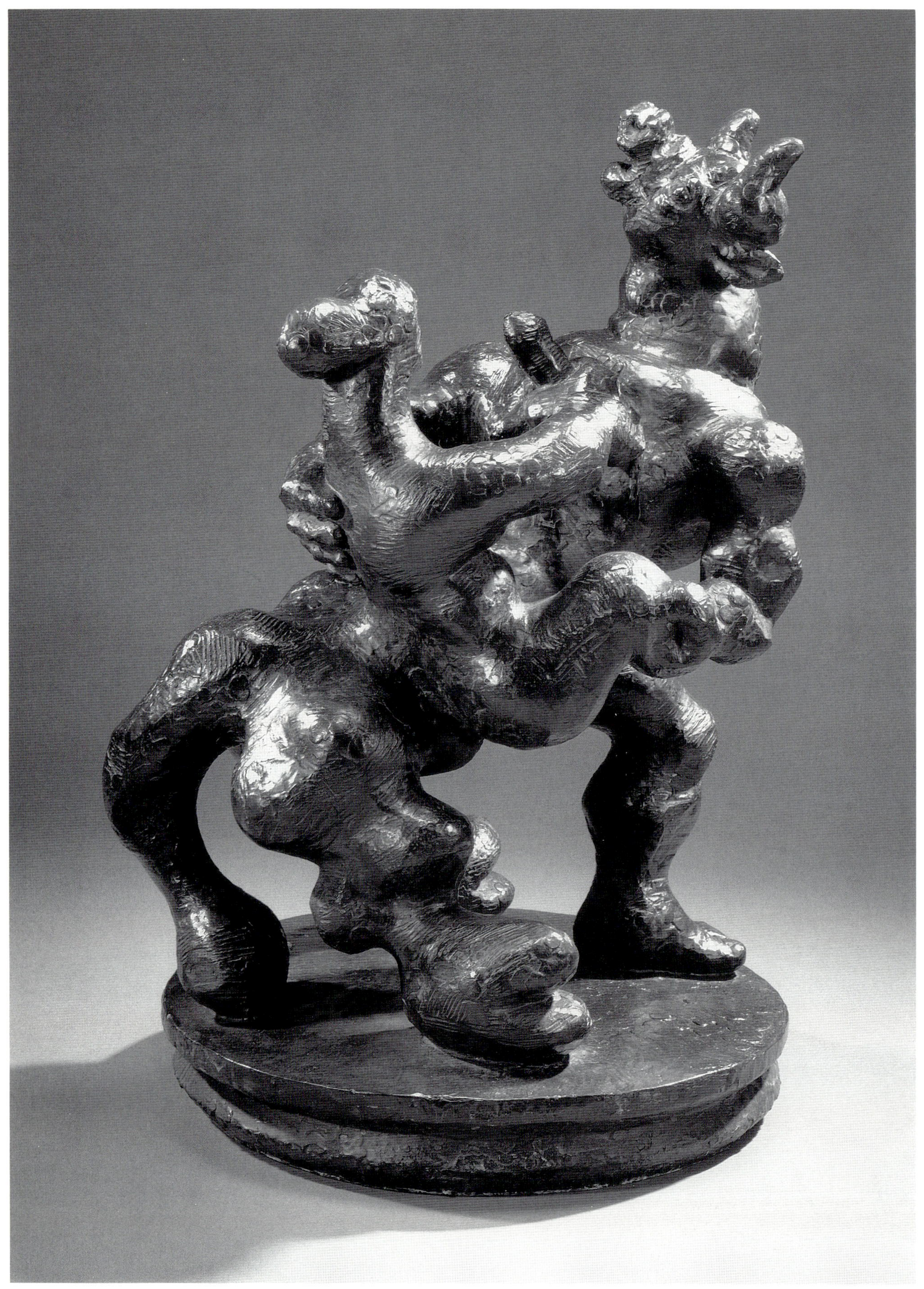

85

the Second World War. There is despair involved in this sculpture but also, I feel, a kind of hope and optimism and even a form of aggression. This piece has a curious history which I did not realize until after the fact. In 1935 I was in Russia and one night, when it was dark and raining, I heard the sound of a pathetic song. I tried to trace it and came to a railroad station where there was a beggar woman, a cripple without legs, on a cart, who was singing, her hair all loose and her arms outstretched. I was terribly touched by this image, but I only realized years later, when I made the *Mother and Child*, that it was this image that had emerged from my subconscious. Although the sculpture is obviously much changed, the woman is without legs and, in the final version, without hands. The winglike projections at the side are the legs of the child that I added. For some curious reason, the child's projecting legs and the woman's breasts seem to form themselves into the head of a bull, something that gave a quality of aggressiveness to the sculpture. That, I think, indicates my feelings at this time, in the midst of the war.[144]

85 *Rape of Europa* 1941
Bronze 1/7
H. 33½″/85.0 cm
The Estate of Jacques Lipchitz represented by Marlborough International Fine Art AG.

IN HIS 1938 *Rape of Europa I* (NO. 81), LIPCHITZ USED THE classical myth to express tender and erotic love. As he said of this 1941 version:

> I used the theme of the *Rape of Europa* later in a quite different context, the Europa as a symbol for Europe and the bull as Hitler, with Europe killing Hitler with a dagger. This reverses the concept to one of terror, whereas in the original sculptures of Europa the entire theme is tender and erotic love; the bull is caressing Europa with his tongue.[145]

86 *Myrah* 1942
Bronze (unique)
H. 22¾″/57.8 cm
The Estate of Jacques Lipchitz represented by Marlborough International Fine Art AG.

IN 1942, WHEN LIPCHITZ WAS WORKING AT THE MODERN Art Foundry, he suddenly had an urge to do open transparents such as he had done in Paris in 1926. By now he had mastered the technical problems, and this allowed him to work in a free, lyrical manner.

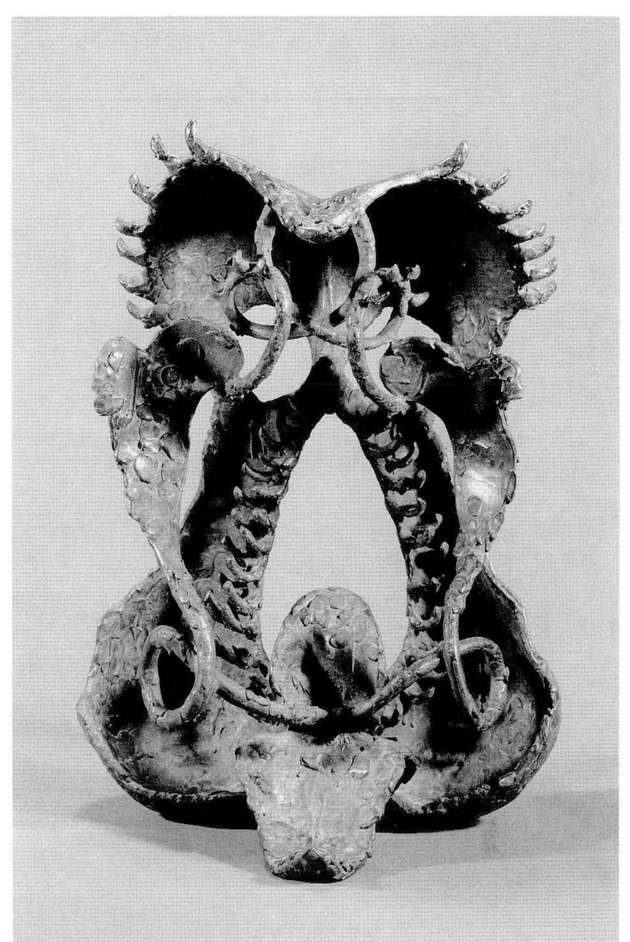

86

Nothing in Lipchitz's earlier sculpture prepares us for this terrifying image of a disemboweled female pelvic region. It is somewhat reminiscent of the skeletal structure of Giacometti's 1932 *Woman with Her Throat Cut* (Museum of Modern Art, New York), yet without the theme of sexual violence, mutilation and murder. It is difficult to determine the personal significance of this extraordinary creation. Lipchitz wrote of a group of works of 1942, of which *Myrah* would appear to be one:

> They also had a very close personal association, since they were related to someone with whom I was in love at the time. Most of them, thus, are made to express the sense of an exaltation of the woman.[146]

Certain features of *Myrah*, such as the pointed projections on each side at the top of the sculpture, are closely related to works such as *Blossoming* 1941–42 (Museum of Modern Art, New York). Perhaps, for Lipchitz, *Myrah* was an image of fertility and procreation.

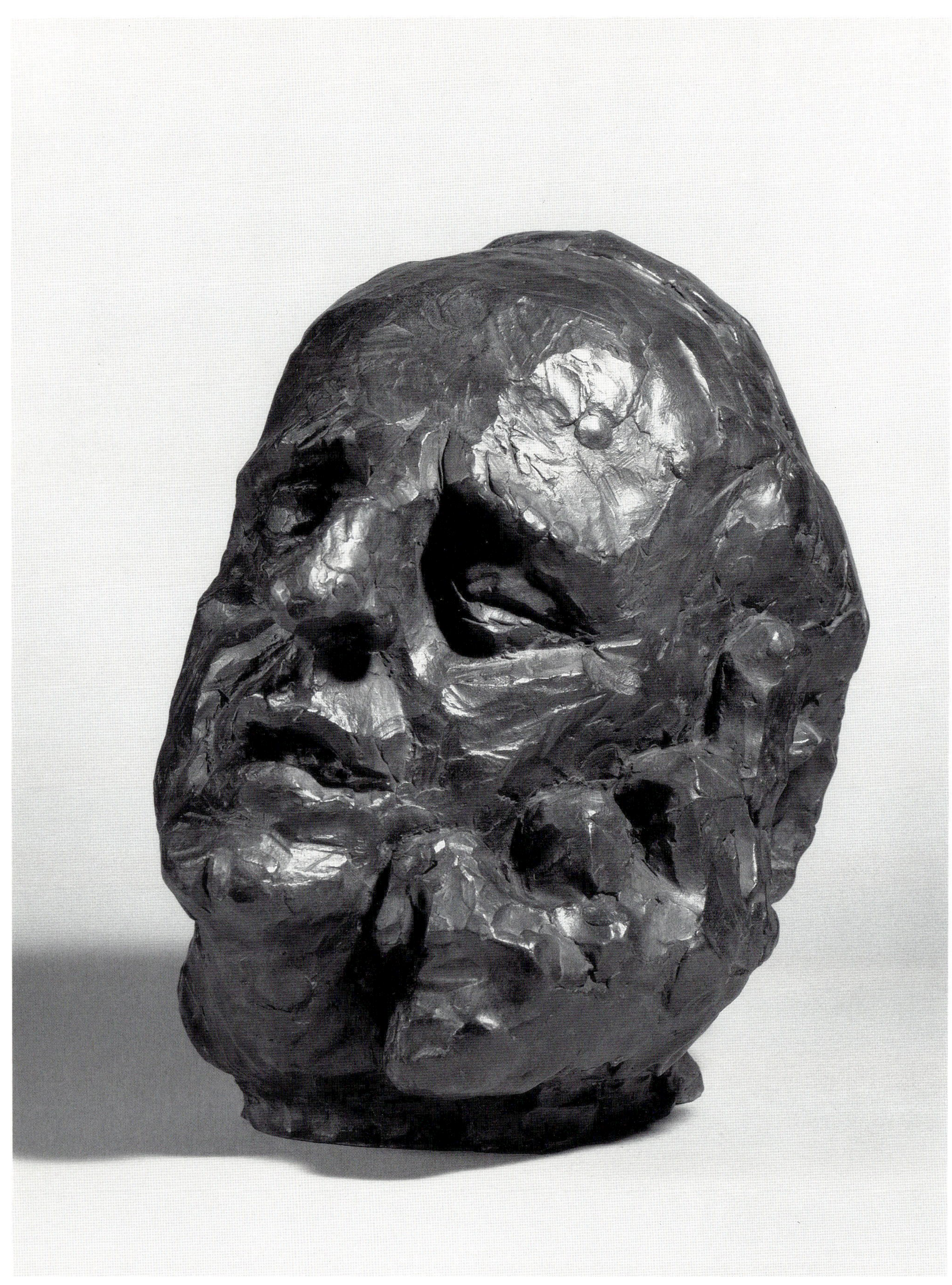

87 *Head of a Sleeping Man (Marsden Hartley Sleeping)* 1942
Bronze 4/7
H. 10¾"/27.3 cm
The Estate of Jacques Lipchitz represented by Marlborough International Fine Art AG.

Among Lipchitz's most successful portraits were his three studies of the American painter Marsden Hartley (1877–1943), made the year after his arrival in the United States. Portraiture, he thought, might bring in some much-needed income. In response to his new environment, Lipchitz thought it would be helpful to make "a new portrait of an American."[147] At the opening of an exhibition at Helena Rubenstein's, he recalled:

> ...I saw a man who seemed to me to have a typical American face. He was speaking to a lady whom I knew and speaking in French. As soon as possible I ran over to the lady and asked her if she would ask whether this gentleman would consent to pose for me...We were introduced (although I still did not know who he was), and he said he would be delighted to pose...One time, when he came to my studio, he said, "Jacques, I have just seen an old man sleeping on a bench, like this," and he assumed the pose of the sleeping man in such a graphic manner that I immediately said, "Marsden, will you hold that pose so I can make a sketch of you like that?"[148]

It was a fortuitous coincidence that the two should meet, for Hartley had long been an admirer of Lipchitz's work. In 1935, on seeing an exhibition of his work at the Brummer Gallery in New York, he had penned an open letter to the sculptor that was published in the catalogue of the 1948 exhibition held at the Buchholz Gallery in New York.

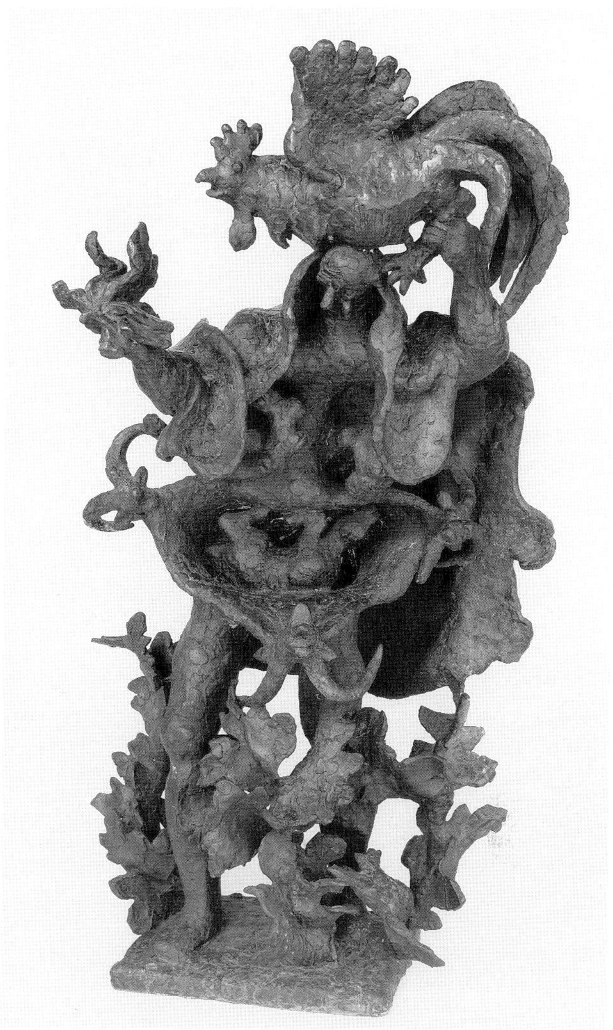

88 *The Prayer* 1943
Bronze (unique)
H. 42½"/108.0 cm
Philadelphia Museum of Art, Given by R. Sturgis and Marion B. F. Ingersoll.

The Prayer, like *The Pilgrim*[149] of the previous year, was first made directly in wax. "Technically," Lipchitz said, "it was extremely difficult and caused me terrible suffering when I was forming it and when it was being cast."[150] The extraordinarily delicate and varied forms and surfaces, with the complex interplay of projections, concavities and negative spaces seem to defy the casting process itself. In this sense, the sculpture anticipates the technical virtuosity of the 1958 series of bronzes entitled *To the Limit of the Possible* (see no. 108).

The Prayer was Lipchitz's most deeply felt and anguished statement of the horror he felt about Auschwitz and the other Nazi concentration camps:

> It was done at the most terrible moment of the war; it was a prayer, a Jewish prayer of expiation; you sacrifice the cock which has to take all your sins. In the left [*sic*] hand the man holds a book, in the right [*sic*] hand the cock; the man wears the Jewish prayer shawl. The cock is actually killed by a man who is trained to do this. The prayer takes place before the Day of Atonement. Actually the figure is not a rabbi; it is Everyman, every Jew who has to do this, who is asking for forgiveness. The figure is completely disembowelled; in the open stomach are heads of goats, and the innocent victim, a lamb. The entire subject is the Jewish people, whom I thought of as the innocent victims in this horrible war. I find this whole subject so difficult to explain because it emerged from so many different feelings. I was praying, I was crying when I made this work.[151]

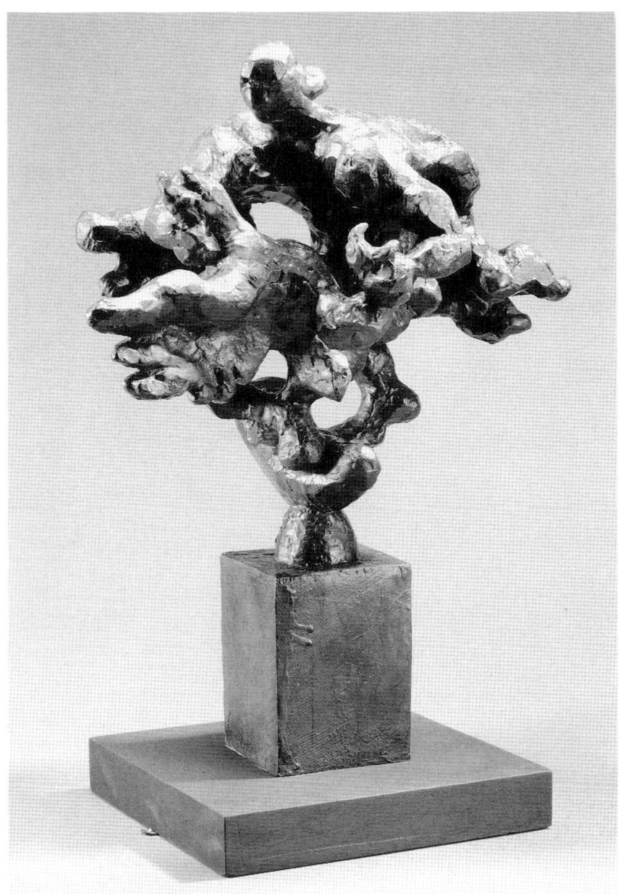

89 *Prometheus Strangling the Vulture* 1943
Bronze 7/7
H. 16½"/41.9 cm
The Estate of Jacques Lipchitz represented by Marlborough International Fine Art AG.

SOON AFTER LIPCHITZ'S ARRIVAL IN THE UNITED STATES, Nelson Rockefeller was instrumental in getting him a commission for the new Ministry of Education and Health building in Rio de Janeiro. Rockefeller told Lipchitz about the problems the architect, Oscar Niemeyer, was having in finding a suitable sculpture for the building. Lipchitz chose the theme of Prometheus and the vulture, the subject of the enormous commission he had done in Paris for the World's Fair of 1937 (see nos. 77 and 78). The Prometheus legend meant many things to Lipchitz, including, he said, "the victory of light over darkness, of education over ignorance..."[152] He produced a model about one-third the size of the projected sculpture, "but through some fantastic mistake the work was placed on the enormous wall in the reduced scale of the model rather than in the full scale intended. This was for me a terrible tragedy, and I simply deny it as a work of mine."[153]

In this study, Prometheus and the vulture are shown in profile to the left. In the enormous bronze (by far Lipchitz's largest sculpture to date) they are depicted in profile to the right. As in many of Lipchitz's enlargements, the rough modelling found in the study has been replaced in the large bronze by a much smoother, more uniform surface. Two casts of the large *Prometheus Strangling the Vulture* were made (H. 102"/259.1 cm). One is in the Philadelphia Museum of Art, the other in the Walker Art Center, Minneapolis.

90 *Prometheus Strangling the Vulture* 1943
Bronze
H. 37½"/95.3 cm
The Estate of Jacques Lipchitz represented by Marlborough International Fine Art AG.

THIS 1943 VERSION OF THE PROMETHEUS THEME IS MUCH closer to the 1936 treatment of the subject for the commission for the Paris World's Fair. Here, Prometheus, with a beak and tail, is half man, half bird. But the relationship of the figure to the vulture is very close to that in the 1936 composition.

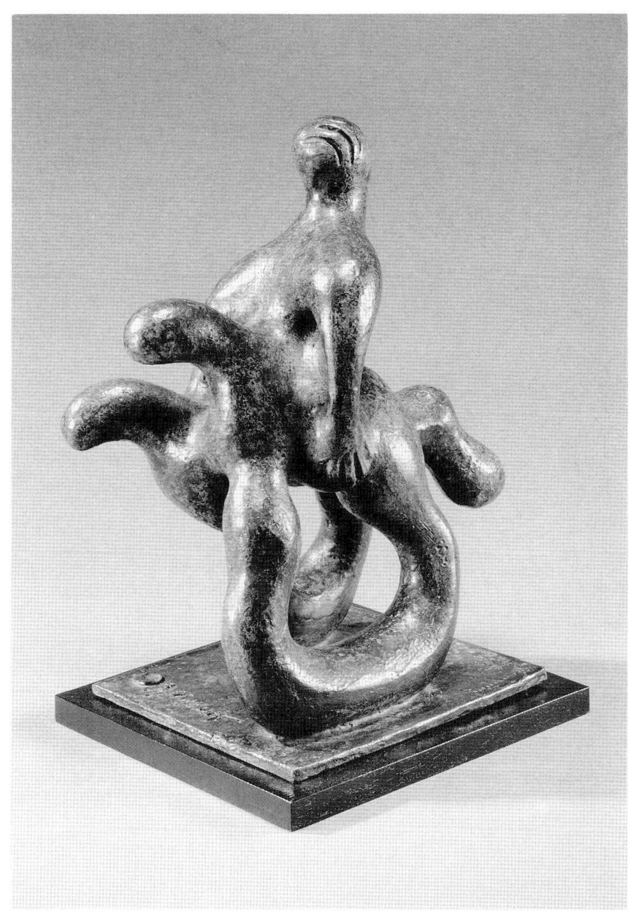

91

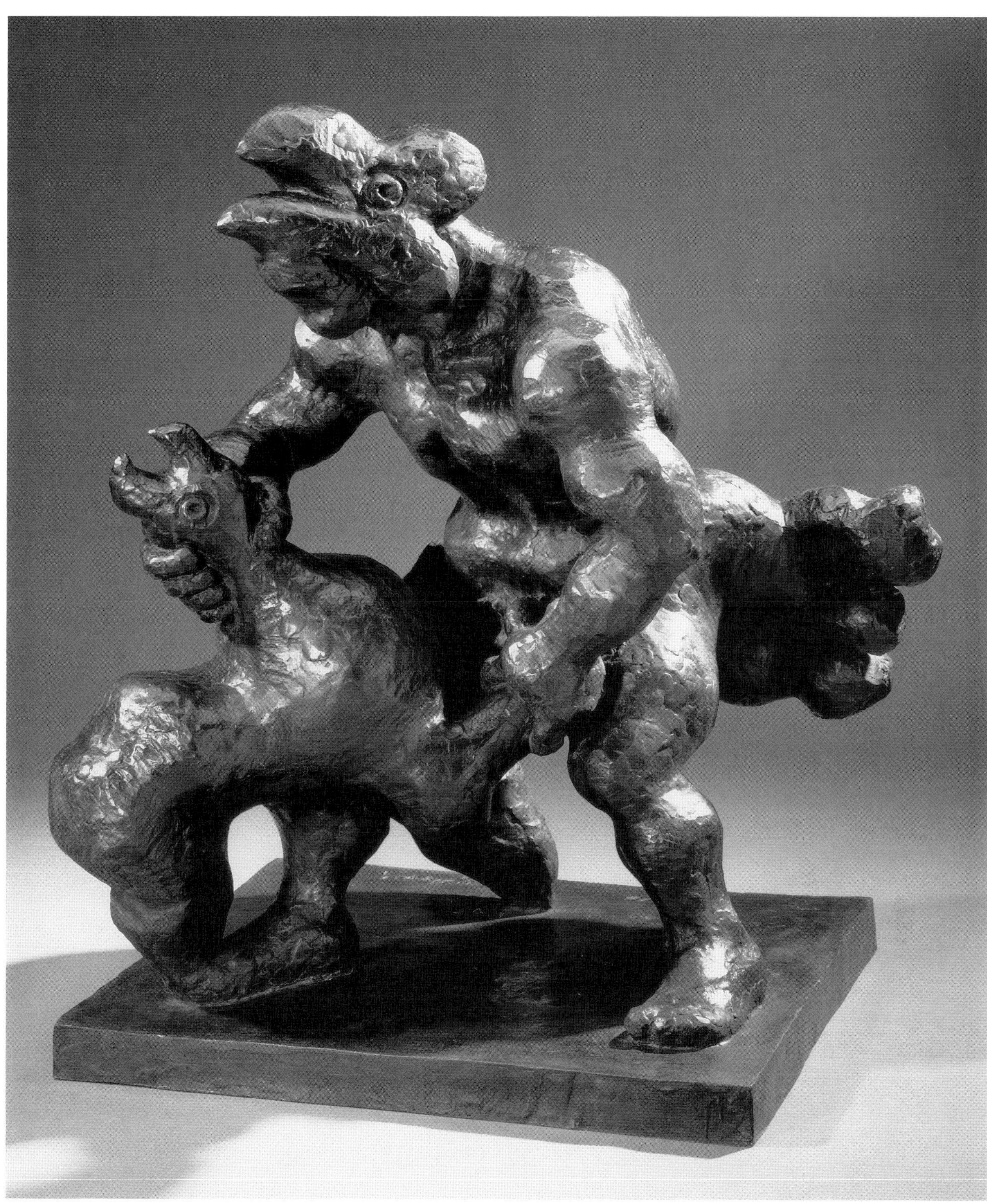

90

91 *The Rescue* 1945
Bronze 7/7
H. 15¾″/40.0 cm
The Estate of Jacques Lipchitz represented by Marlborough International Fine Art AG.

In *The Rescue* the child held aloft is no doubt symbolic of the sense of release and liberation the artist felt at the end of the war. The biomorphic, curvilinear rhythms in this work and in *Song of Songs* (no. 93) are reminiscent of the bulbous figures in Picasso's paintings of 1932, such as *Bather with Beach Ball* in the Museum of Modern Art, New York.

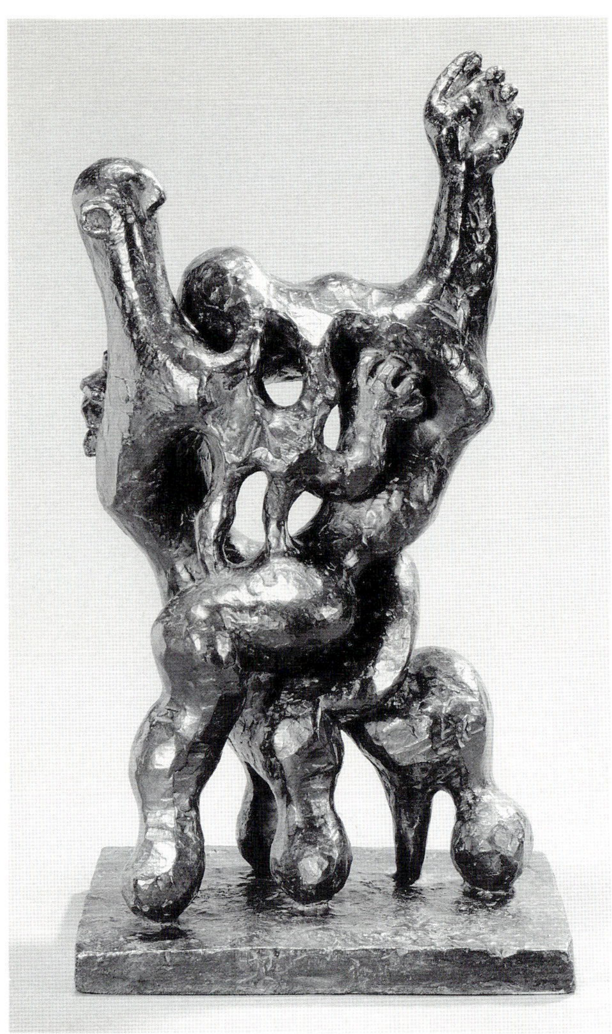

92 *Joy of Orpheus* 1945
Bronze 5/7
H. 18½"/47.0 cm
The Estate of Jacques Lipchitz represented by Marlborough International Fine Art AG.

THE *Joy of Orpheus* IS ONE OF LIPCHITZ'S MOST LYRICAL expressions of love between a man and a woman. Gone is the violence found in the erotic works of the early 1930s, such as *The Embrace* (no. 73). Lipchitz described the work as follows: "It has to do with the love of my wife. The woman is sitting on the man's lap. They are happy and her arm is raised in the air; and all of it takes on the form of a harp. I think of it as a very interesting sculpture, poetic and beautiful."[154]

93 *Song of Songs* 1946
Bronze 4/7
L. 36"/91.5 cm
The Estate of Jacques Lipchitz represented by Marlborough International Fine Art AG.

THIS WORK EVOLVED FROM A 1944 MAQUETTE OF AN embracing couple, which was followed by the small study *Song of Songs* 1945, of which there is a plaster in the Tate Gallery, London.[155] The dynamic horizontal thrust of the two figures suggests that they are suspended or flying through space, and as a result the work is reminiscent of *Prometheus Strangling the Vulture* 1943 (no. 89).

At the time, Lipchitz said, he was working on the maquette of the embracing couple:

> ... a friend of mine, an architect, told me that he wanted to give his wife a present, a sculpture for her music room. I looked at the apartment and felt that the idea involved in this piece might be appropriate; so I made a somewhat larger sketch in 1946, still rough and free, and finally the finished sculpture, which was first done in stucco to have it light for hanging on the wall. The forms as finally realized have a curvilinear flow appropriate to the musical theme... The title, *Song of Songs*, of course comes from the Old Testament, and the theme is a love song, extremely lyrical and tender, since it was made for a very loving couple.[156]

94 *Dancer with Braids* 1947
Bronze 2/7
H. 13¼"/33.7 cm
The Estate of Jacques Lipchitz represented by Marlborough International Fine Art AG.

IF *Song of Songs* (NO. 93) ECHOES THE FLOWING, BIOMORPHIC distortions of Picasso's work of the early 1930s, *Dancer with Braids* recalls, both in the twisting pose and in the full, ample body of the woman, Degas's sculptures of women at their toilet, such as *Seated Woman Wiping Her Left Hip*.[157]

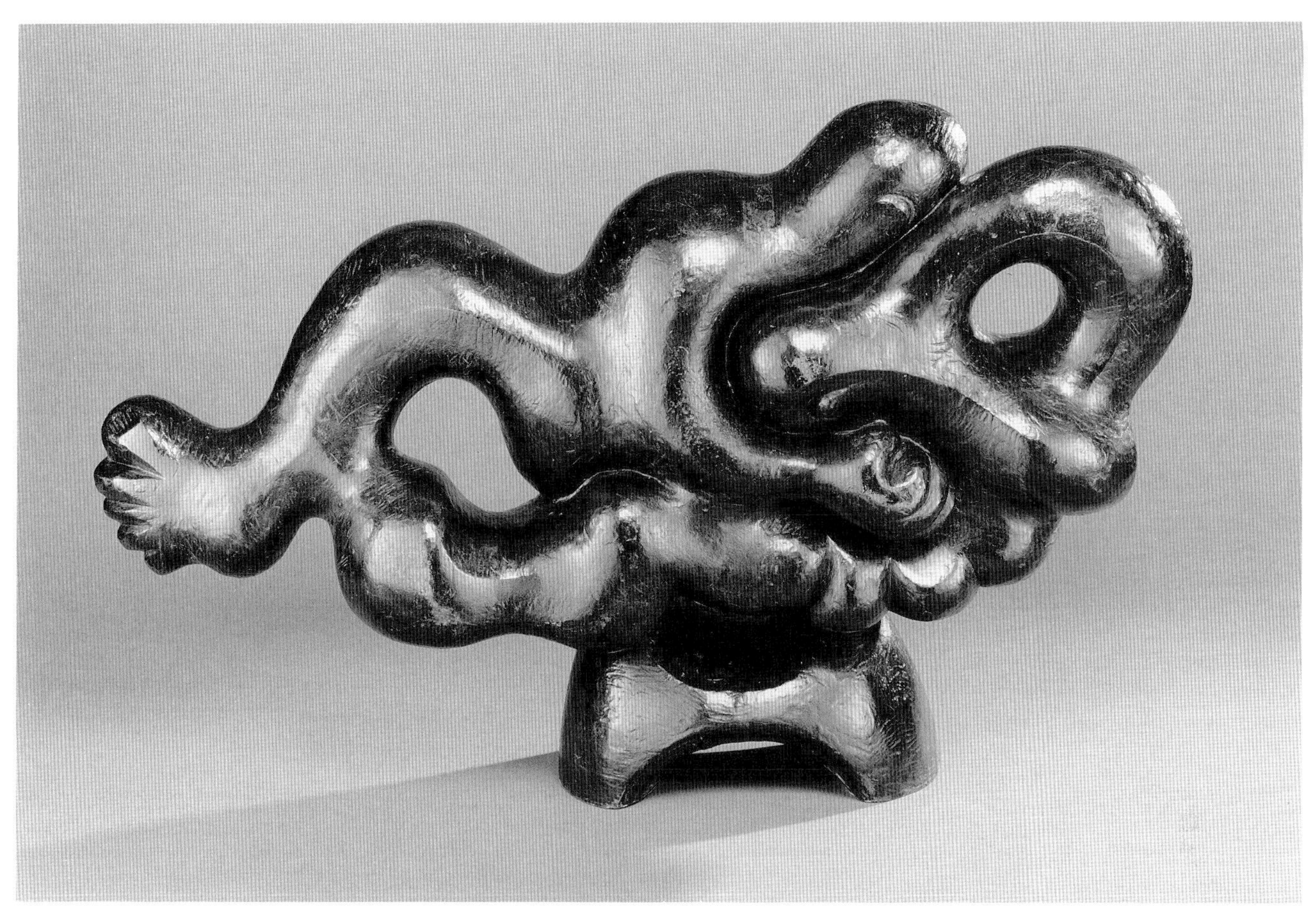

93

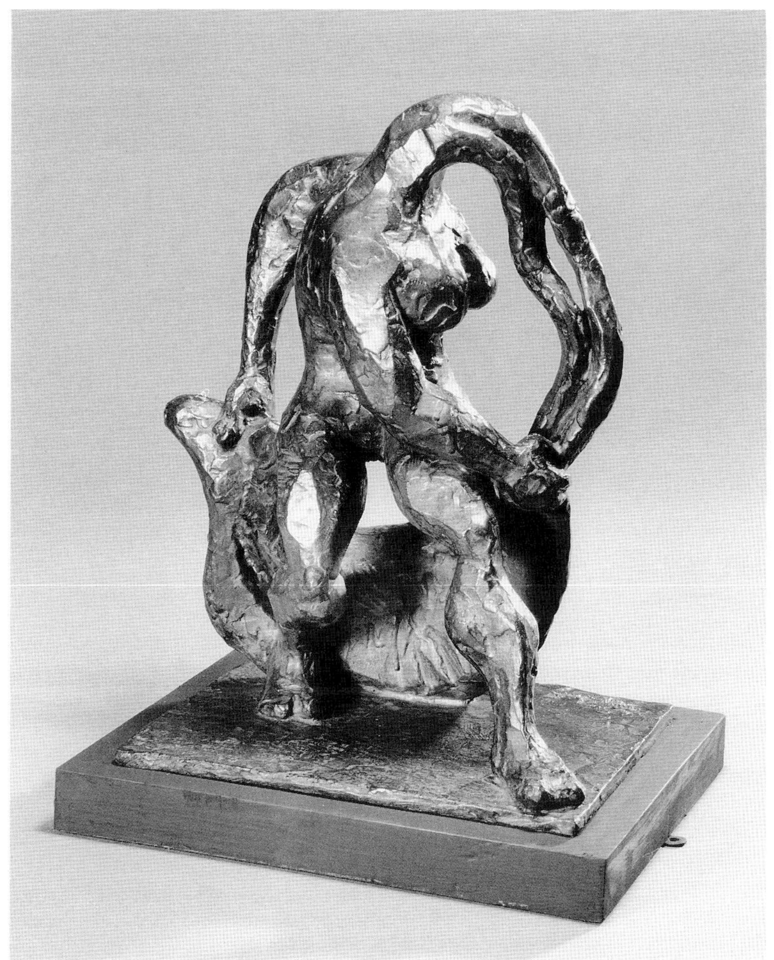

94

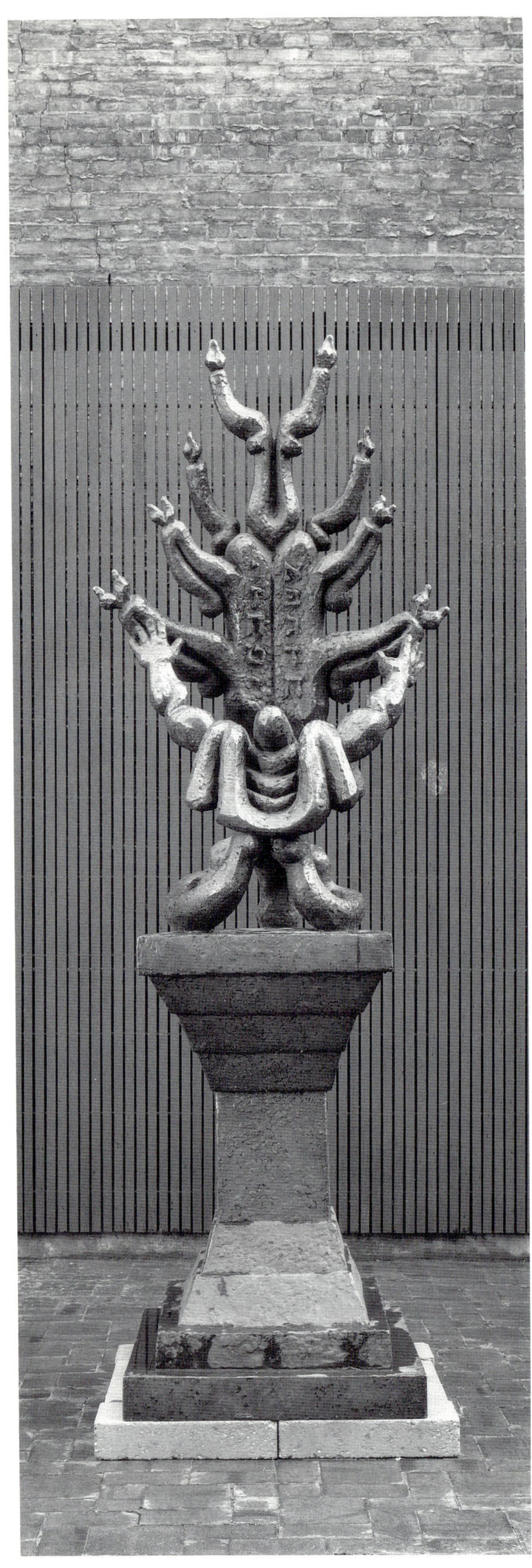

95 *Miracle II* 1948
Bronze 2/7
H. 110″/279.4 cm
The Estate of Jacques Lipchitz, represented by Marlborough International Fine Art AG.

THE DESTINY OF THE JEWISH PEOPLE LEADING UP TO THE creation of the state of Israel in 1948 and the birth of his daughter, Lolya Rachel, in the same year were the focus of Lipchitz's most important sculptures at the end of the 1940s. This piece is one of a series of works of 1947–48 that were collectively entitled *Miracle*. They evolved, as did so many of Lipchitz's Jewish subjects, from a passionate identification with contemporary events. In 1947, a shipload of Jewish immigrants aboard the *Exodus* arrived in Palestine, which was then under British mandate. The Jews were refused permission to disembark. "It was a terrible event, one that made me sick with anger and despair. There were many prayers and fasts among Jews for the safety of this ship, and I also fasted. It was during my fast that the idea for this sculpture appeared. I was certain that Israel would ultimately become a state, and the sculpture was in effect the birth of the new state of Israel, a candlestick with the Jew praying."[158]

Miracle I shows a figure praying in front of a menorah in the form of hands beseeching a miracle. This was followed by *Exodus 47*, "in which," Lipchitz said, "the forms in the middle of the candlestick reminded me of the Table of the Law; so this resulted in a third version, *Miracle II*, in which I consciously introduced the Tables... *Miracle II* was a prayer of Thanksgiving that Israel had officially become a state in 1948... On the tablets are written the numbers in Hebrew. The final version [no. 95] is large, some eleven or twelve feet high, on a monumental base modeled after one I saw in Israel that probably came down from Roman times.[159]

96 *Hagar I* 1948
Bronze 2/7
L. 31¼″/79.4 cm
Gift from The Women's Committee Fund, 1959.

Hagar I EMBODIES TWO CONCEPTS THAT PREOCCUPIED Lipchitz at the time the work was created: his feelings as a father (or father-to-be) for the mother-and-child theme and his deep concerns about the birth of Israel and the conflict between Jews and Arabs. "Despite my admiration for and love of Israel, I feel strongly that the Jews and the Arabs should make peace, that they should live

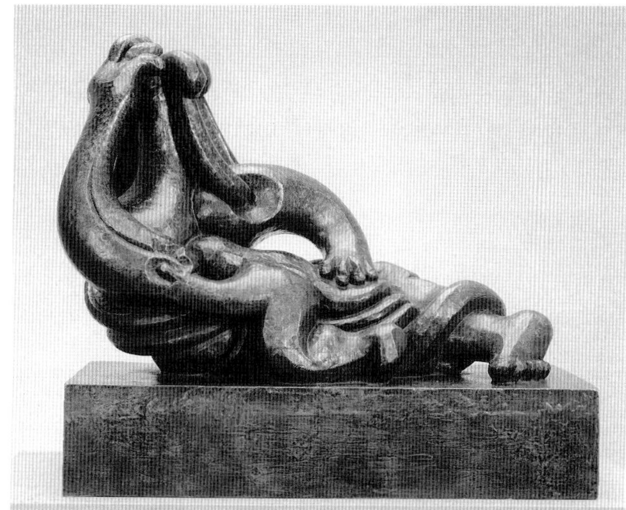

together as brothers, which they were able to do for many centuries."[160]

Lipchitz focused on one episode in the rather complicated story of Hagar as told in Genesis. Sarah at last had a son Isaac, born when Abraham, his father, was 100 years old. When Sarah saw Hagar's son, Ishmael (Abraham's illegitimate child), mocking her son, she said to Abraham: "Cast out this bondwoman and her son: for the son of this bondwoman shall not be heir with my son, even with Isaac" (Gen. 21:10). Abraham sent Hagar and Ishmael away with bread and a bottle of water. They wandered in the wilderness of Beer-sheba. When the water ran out Hagar feared for the life of her child, "And she sat over against him, and lift up her voice and wept" (Gen. 21:16). God heard the voice of the lad, and the angel of God said to Hagar:

> Arise, lift up the lad, and hold him in thine hand; for I will make him a great nation. And God opened her eyes, and she saw a well of water; and she went, and filled the bottle with water, and gave the lad drink (Genesis 21:18–19).

Again, Lipchitz has identified with a story from the Old Testament and used it to symbolize contemporary events:

> I wished to show my sympathy for Ishmael, who is thought of as the father of the Arabs in the same manner as the Hebrews are the sons of Abraham; so this is a prayer for brotherhood between the Jews and the Arabs. It is a concept which combines tragedy and suffering with tenderness and hope for the future.[161]

There are three plaster maquettes for Hagar in the Tate Gallery.[162] A bronze exhibited at the Buchholz Gallery, New York (May 1951, 22, repr.), includes the figure of Ishmael suckling at his mother's left breast. In the Toronto bronze, Ishmael lies face down against his mother's body. The figure of Hagar is more massive than the three studies in the Tate Gallery. Here Lipchitz has created heavy folds of drapery that accentuate the massive curvilinear rhythm of the figures, which merge to form an image of great tenderness and compassion.

97 *Mother and Child* 1948–49
Bronze 4/7
H. 15¼″/38.7 cm
The Estate of Jacques Lipchitz represented by Marlborough International Fine Art AG.

THE MOOD OF PESSIMISM AND ANGER THAT CHARACTERized *Miracle II* (no. 95) changed dramatically with the birth of Lipchitz's daughter, Lolya, in 1948.

> It was a fantastic experience at the age of fifty-nine [*sic*] finally to have my own child, particularly a daughter, which is what I wanted, partially because I wanted her to

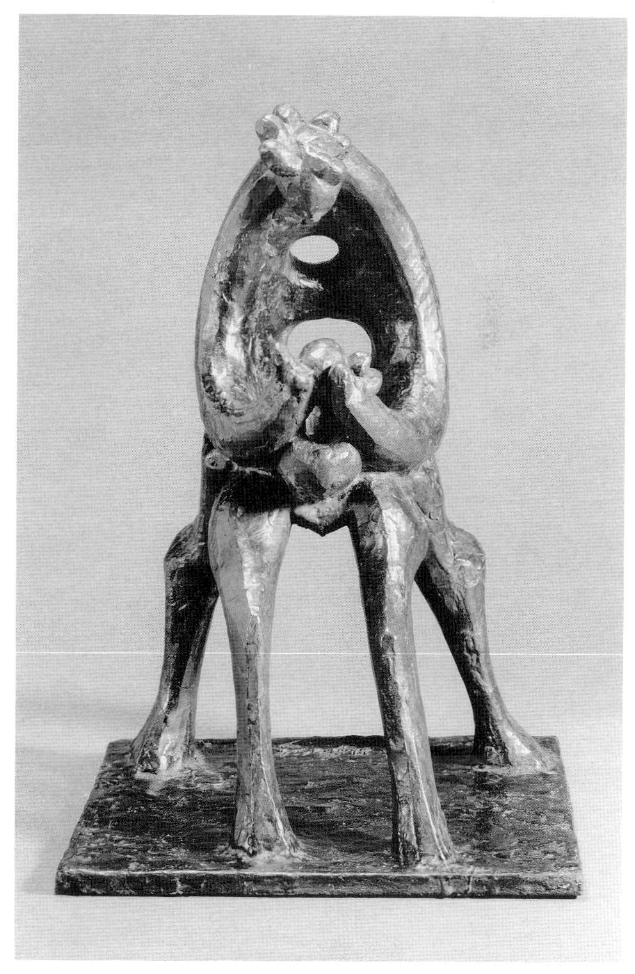

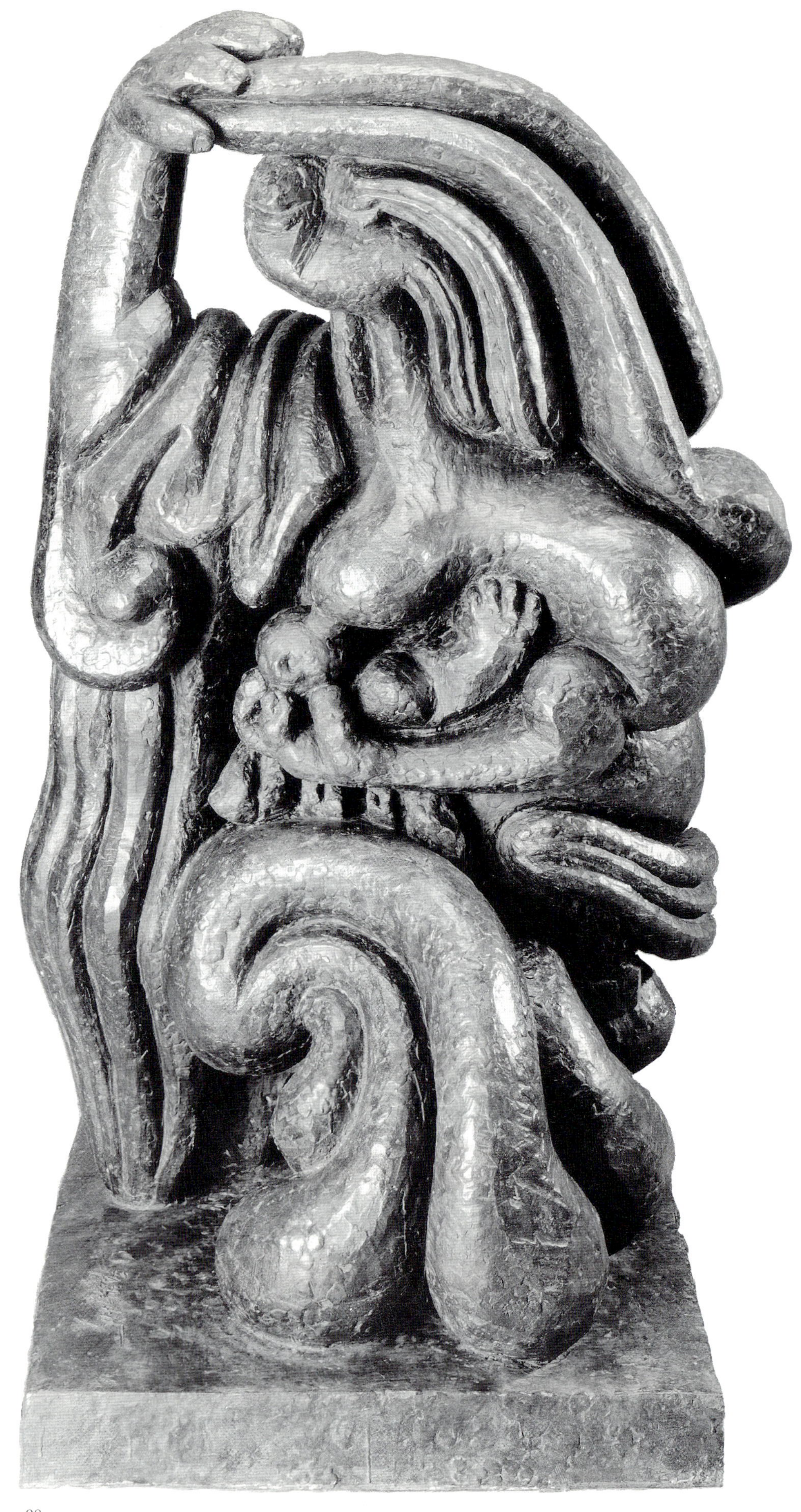

98

have my mother's name. The result in my sculpture was a series of extremely lyrical works on the theme of the mother and child.[163]

Here, the mother's small, Picasso-esque head looks down at the tiny child cradled in her lap. The arms and hollowed-out torso of the mother seem to envelop the child and focus our attention on the centre of the sculpture. The back of the figure is supported by an extra pair of legs joined to the buttocks. The anguish of Lipchitz's earlier depictions of the mother-and-child motif has been replaced by a beautifully resolved image of maternal love and protectiveness.

98 *Mother and Child* 1949
Bronze 2/7
H. 57″/144.8 cm
The Estate of Jacques Lipchitz represented by Marlborough International Fine Art AG.

Mother and Child, LIPCHITZ'S LARGEST AND MOST MONUMENTAL treatment of this subject to date, was, like the earlier *Mother and Child* (no. 97), inspired by his family life and his newfound happiness with his wife, Yulla, and their baby daughter. Held by the powerful left hand as she nurses at her mother's breast, the small child is totally integrated with and indistinguishable from the swollen, curvilinear forms and the deeply incised drapery but for her hand and head. Indeed, almost the entire surface is dominated by the surging flow of the "Baroque" drapery, and the work could be seen as a homage to Bernini.

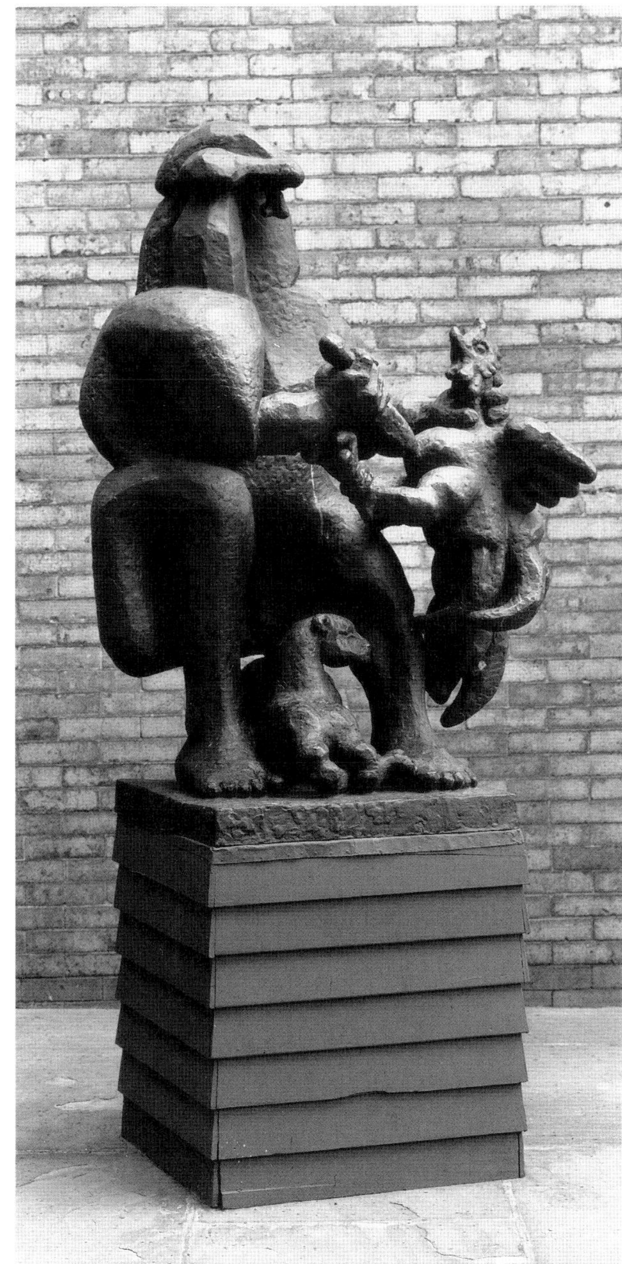

99

99 *Sacrifice* 1949–57
Bronze 7/7
H. 49½″/125.7
The Jewish Museum, New York, Gift of Mr. and Mrs. Albert A. List.

WITH THE HEROIC STRUGGLE OVER THE FOUNDING OF Israel still very much on his mind, Lipchitz turned his attention to the theme of sacrifice, a subject that related to *The Prayer* of 1943 (no. 88), in which the man holds the cock above his head. "For the prayer to be effective," Lipchitz said, "an animal must be sacrificed for one's sins."[164]

Whereas *The Prayer* is open and fragmented in structure, *Sacrifice* represents a change in direction in Lipchitz's work. "This is much heavier and forceful, even fierce, in concept."[165] *First Study for Sacrifice*, dated 1947–48, was followed by *Study for Sacrifice* 1948–49. In the former, "the man (he is not actually a rabbi but an individual specially ordained to perform the sacrifice) is killing the cock with his left hand, something that did not seem reasonable to me."[166] Why this should be so is unclear, but in the 1948–49 study, and in this work, the man stabs the cock with his right hand.

In this work a lamb – symbolizing Lipchitz's hopes for peaceful co-existence between Jews and Christians – is introduced between the legs of the figure. This is a radical new element in terms of the Jewish iconography of the subject. Lipchitz said:

Why I should have done this I cannot recall, since the lamb is rather a Christian than a Jewish symbol and is definitely not a victim of the sacrifice. I may have been thinking of the continuity of the Judeo-Christian tradition... Incidentally, the sacrifice is not portrayed in the actual manner of a ritual for which there are special ritual knives. The use of the dagger is deliberate, to heighten the sense of drama. I think this is one of my major works. It certainly is strong and complete, but it unquestionably comes out of some continuing feeling of anger."[167]

100 *Poet Woman with Crutches* 1952
Bronze (unique)
H. 8⅝"/21.9 cm
The Estate of Jacques Lipchitz represented by Marlborough International Fine Art AG.

THE INITIAL IDEA FOR THE CHISEL SCULPTURES CAME about in 1951, when Lipchitz was talking to a friend about painting and sculpture. The latter noticed a sculptor's chisel without its handle on a work bench. As Lipchitz recalled, "He looked at it and said, 'But that is a sculpture.' I said, 'No, it's not, but it could become one.' So I took a little plasticine and made a sort of figure of the chisel."[168]

A year later, following the disastrous fire in his studio on 23rd Street in New York on January 5, 1952, in which most of his work was destroyed, Lipchitz decided to make a sculpture every day with the wax chisels he had made at the foundry. In twenty-six days he made twenty-six sculptures and was cured of his depression. The small chisel pieces mark the beginning of a newfound freedom and spontaneity in Lipchitz's work that characterized his art for the last twenty years of his life. These "semi-automatics," as he called them, were "done rapidly and directly, without much conscious thought."[169] This approach, which had its roots in the Surrealist movement of the 1920s and 1930s, gave rise to a genuine late style in Lipchitz's oeuvre, a style that has yet to be fully understood or appreciated.

Among the series of chisel pieces made between 1951–52 are a group of ritualistic Hebrew objects, a *Begging Poet* and *Poet Woman with Crutches* (no. 100). In the latter, the figure has been built around a single vertical chisel, with two others forming the crutches. This ingenious little work is reminiscent of the actual drill incorporated into the original version of Epstein's 1913–14 *The Rock Drill.* Yet again Lipchitz's work reflects the events of his life: "These crippled, begging poets had a specific association because immediately after the fire... I began to receive letters of sympathy, many enclosing money, letters even from people I did not know."[170]

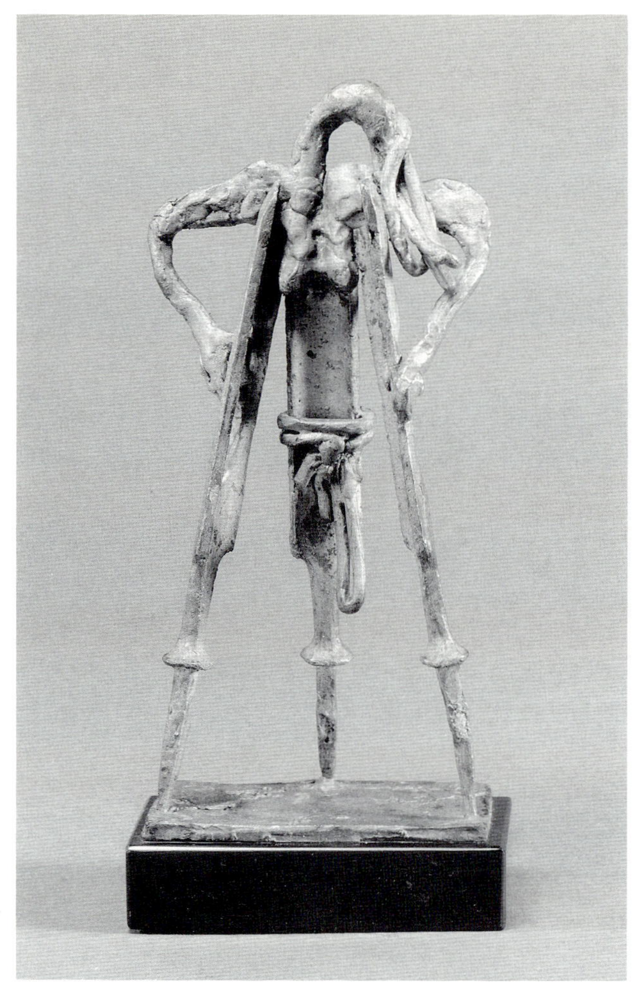

100

101 *Chisel Piece* 1952
Bronze (unique)
H. 8¾"/22.2 cm
The Estate of Jacques Lipchitz represented by Marlborough International Fine Art AG.

WHEN WORKING ON A SERIES OF SMALL, INNOVATIVE works such as the chisel sculptures, Lipchitz gave free rein to his imagination and created remarkable variations on a given theme. This delightful work could be retitled *Chisel Piece: Pas de Deux.*

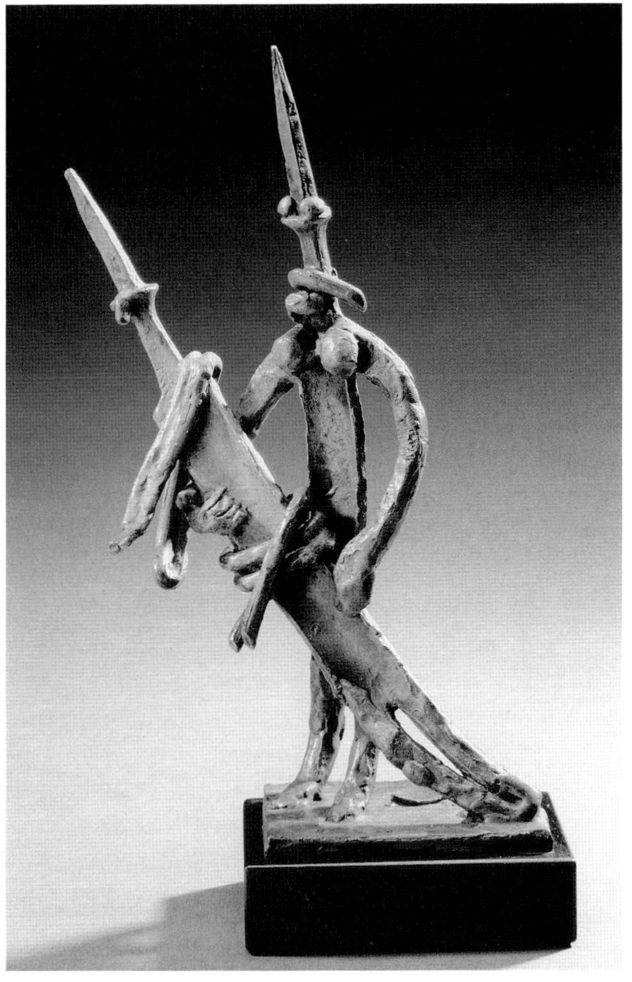

101

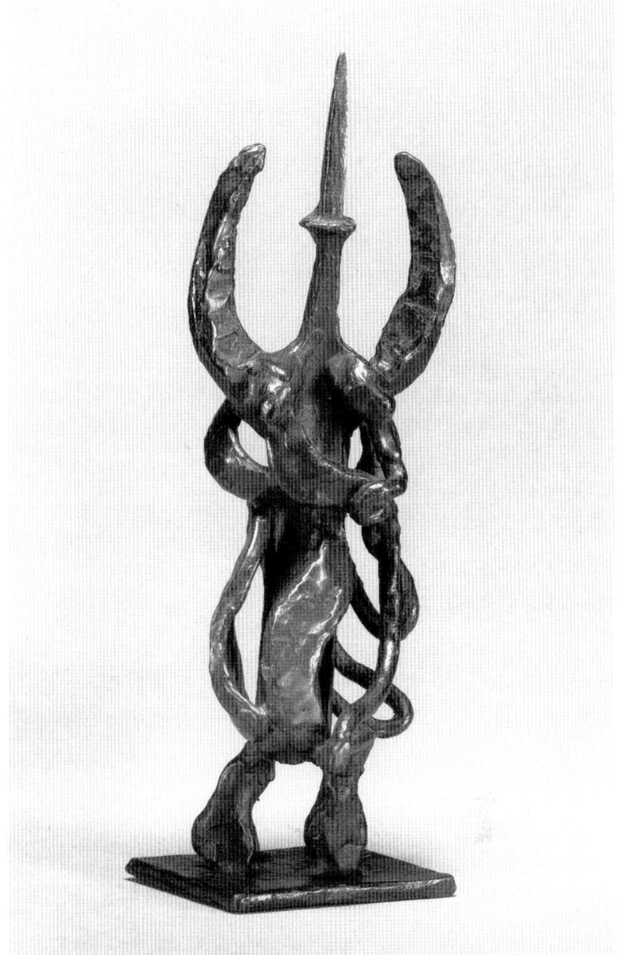

102

102 *Dancer* 1952
Bronze (unique)
H. 8½″/21.6 cm
The Estate of Jacques Lipchitz represented by Marlborough International Fine Art AG.

The chisel sculptures were followed by a series of dancers and centaurs composed of tangled and twisted linear forms. In *Dancer*, movement is conveyed by the twisting forms and open spaces surrounding the rigid, vertical chisel form of the body.

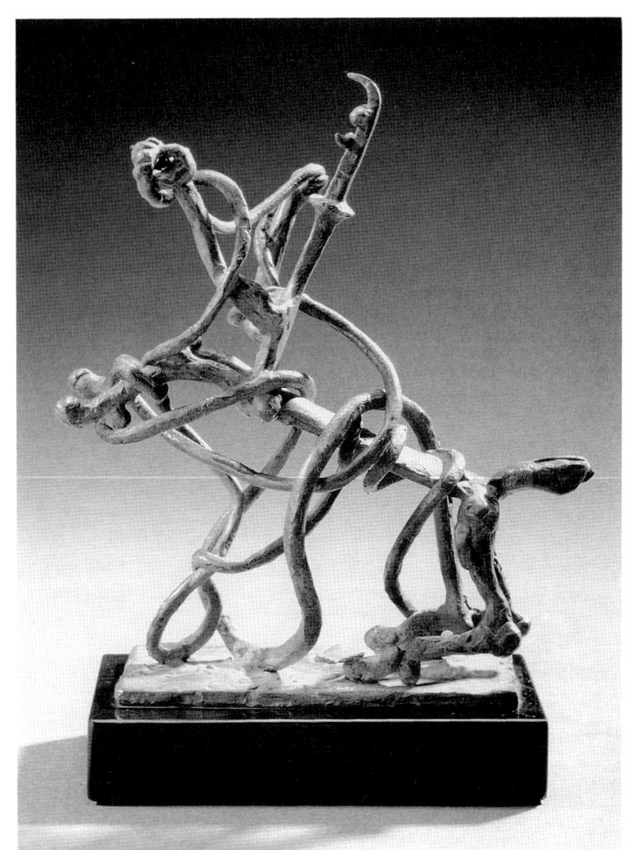

103

103 *Centaur Enmeshed* 1952
Bronze (unique)
H. 7½″/19.05 cm
The Estate of Jacques Lipchitz represented by Marlborough International Fine Art AG.

The series of enmeshed centaurs were more complicated than the chisel pieces in their linear entanglements, which are closely related to some of the transparents of the mid 1920s.

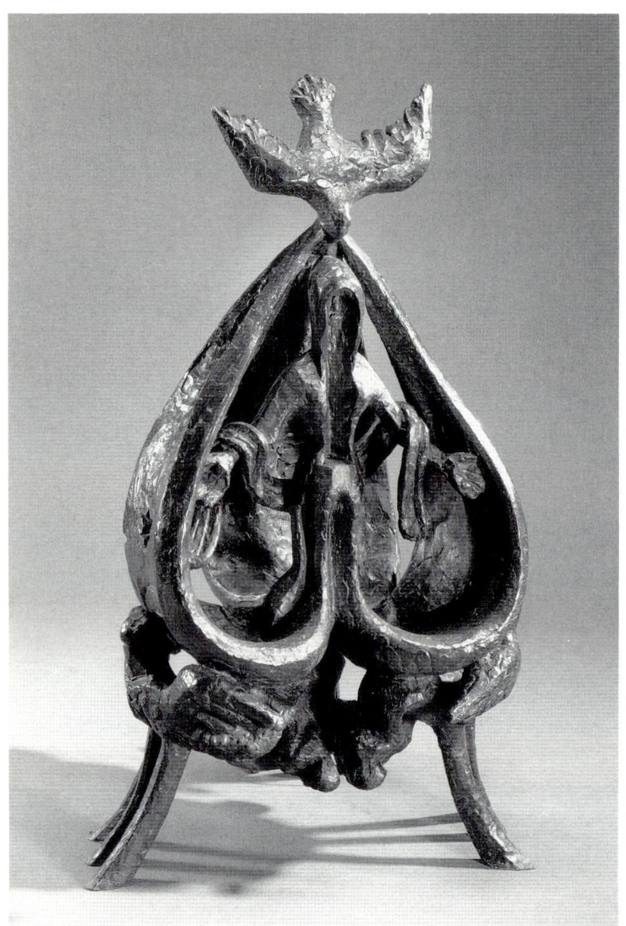

104 *Study for Nôtre-Dame de Liesse* 1953
Bronze, edition of 7
H. 33″/83.8 cm
The Estate of Jacques Lipchitz represented by
Marlborough International Fine Art AG.

THE INITIAL PROPOSAL FOR THIS WORK WAS DISCUSSED during Lipchitz's visit to France in 1946. At the opening of his exhibition at the Galerie Maeght in Paris, a man approached Lipchitz on behalf of Father Couturier and asked him if he would consider doing a sculpture of the Virgin for his church, Nôtre-Dame-de-Toute-Grâce, at Assy, in the Haute-Savoie. Lipchitz replied: "But you know I am Jewish?" The man said: "If it doesn't disturb you, it doesn't disturb us." I liked his answer and said that I would think about it. From this emerged my Virgin, which I feel to be one of the most important things I have ever done."[171]

When Lipchitz returned to New York, Father Couturier visited him and asked if he was still willing to make a sculpture of the Virgin for his church at Assy. The priest had, according to Lipchitz, commissioned artists such as Léger, Rouault, Bonnard and others to create religious works for his church. Lipchitz insisted on one condition: that to prevent any misunderstanding the following inscription appear with the work:

> Jacob Lipchitz juif fidèle à la foi de ses ancêtres a fait cette Vierge pour la bonne entente des hommes sur la terre afin que l'esprit règne.
> (Jacob Lipchitz, Jew, faithful to the religion of his ancestors, has made this Virgin for the better understanding of human beings on this earth so that the Spirit may prevail.)[172]

In the late 1940s Lipchitz produced a number of preparatory maquettes for *Nôtre-Dame de Liesse* (Our Lady of Joy),[173] and in 1951 the large model. The latter was destroyed in the devastating fire at his 23rd Street studio in January, 1952. Lipchitz has described the problems he had in realizing this commission of a Christian subject:

> The vision of the Virgin was extremely difficult. I had read a great deal about the Catholic religion in order to make myself familiar with the ritual and yet I could not somehow see it. Then one day, riding in the subway, I suddenly saw it and saw how to make it and quickly made a small drawing. I was frightened by the idea of making a Virgin, an image to which people would pray... As finally realized, she is placed in a *mandorla* with the dove, the Holy Spirit, above her and the lamb below, as a base.[174]

This work was almost certainly an intermediate stage in the realization of the final sculpture. In the definitive study, the 'legs' that support the mandorla in the present work have been replaced by kneeling lambs. Lipchitz also incorporated the Virgin motif in the 1958 bronze *Between Heaven and Earth* (see no. 111) and in the enormous 1967–69 sculpture *Peace on Earth*.

Three bronzes were cast of the final version of *Nôtre-Dame de Liesse*: one for the church at Assy; another for the Abbey of Saint Columba on the Hebridian island of Iona, off the west coast of Scotland; and a third for which Philip Johnson designed the Roofless Church in New Harmony, Indiana (fig. 25 and see no. 110).

105 *Study for the Monument to "The Spirit of Enterprise"* 1953
Bronze 5/7
H. 31⅝″/80.0 cm
The Estate of Jacques Lipchitz represented by
Marlborough International Fine Art AG.

DURING THE 1950S LIPCHITZ WAS INCREASINGLY ABLE TO work on a more monumental scale. In 1950 he was commissioned to create a large work for Fairmount Park in

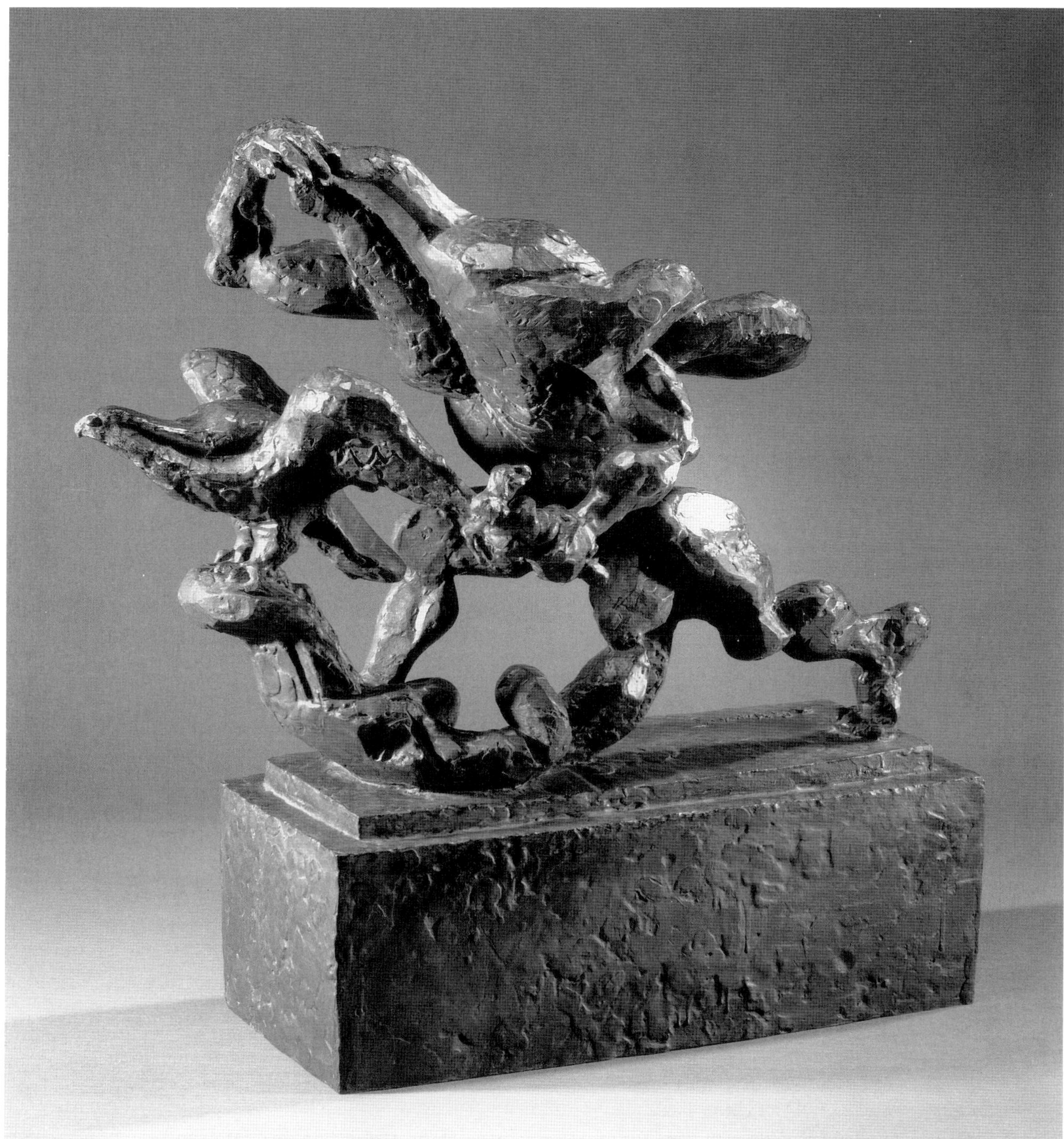

Philadelphia. For this collection of sculpture in the open air commemorating American history, Lipchitz chose as his theme American enterprise.

> In the first sketch I had a striding figure, very open and free in concept, who seemed to be stepping on an eagle and who carried a dove of peace as well as the caduceus, the winged staff with serpents twined around it that is the symbol of Hermes, or Mercury, the god of commerce and transportation, among other things. I wanted to combine the stories of the eagle with the dove of peace and the idea of progress. The committee refused this sketch for the curious reason that they thought Americans would object to the implication of someone stepping on the eagle, while in reality I wanted to make the figure in the steps of the eagle.[175]

Lipchitz altered the composition in a number of other studies that were destroyed when his studio burned down in January, 1952. When he returned to the project in 1953 in his new studio at Hastings-on-Hudson, he was able to retain his original concept, but in a form that in the final work showed the eagle perched on a stump; the eagle, according to Jenkins, is "apparently leading the pioneer in his westward journey across the giant prairies."[176]

This work was followed by a larger (H. 45″/114.3 cm) definitive study entitled *Model for Enterprise* 1953, in which the surface modelling of the figure is smoother and the deeply incised gashes more sharply defined. In addition, the eagle's features are much more detailed and realistic.

The Spirit of Enterprise was Lipchitz's first major American commission. In its personification of abstract national and patriotic values, it is a continuation of the nineteenth-century French tradition of public sculpture dedicated, as Albert Elsen has written, "to the celebration of the nation's heroes, institutions, and middle class values."[177] If his little bronze *Arrival* of 1941 celebrated Lipchitz's physical arrival in the United States, *Spirit of Enterprise* marked his assimilation of and identification with American values: "I now felt myself so completely an American..."[178]

The very large bronze, about three and a half metres high, was installed on a base of black marble in Fairmount Park in October, 1960.

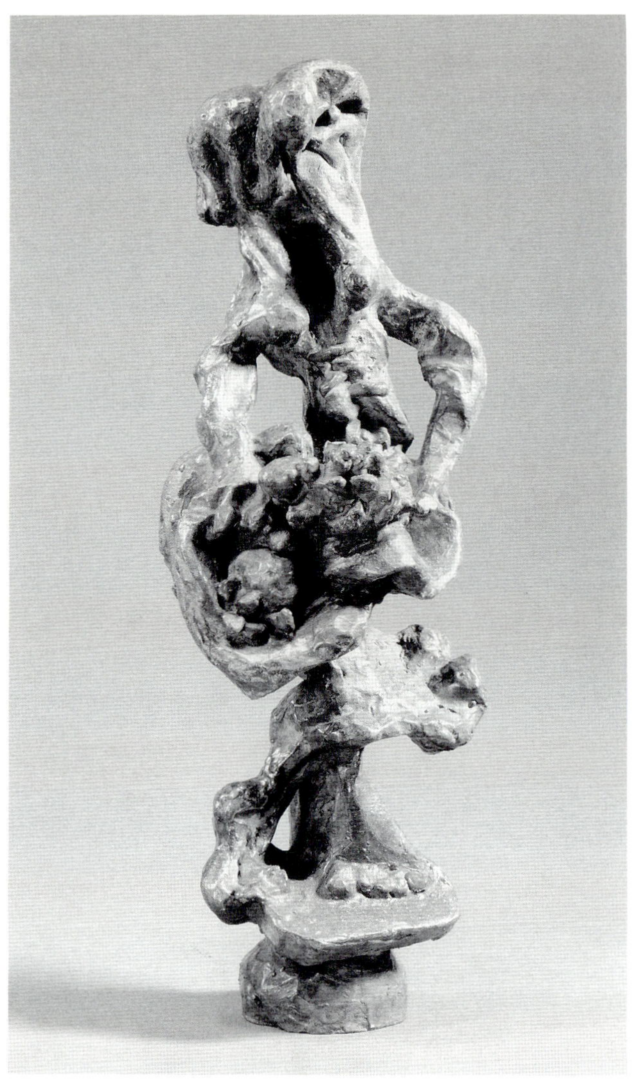

106 *Here are the Fruits and the Flowers* 1955–56
Bronze (unique)
H. 16¾″/42.5 cm
The Estate of Jacques Lipchitz represented by Marlborough International Fine Art AG.

As a reaction against the monumental commissioned sculptures of the early 1950s, such as *Nôtre-Dame de Liesse* and *The Spirit of Enterprise*, Lipchitz once again became absorbed in the private, spontaneous world of what he called his semi-automatics. The initial idea for these works was suggested when his assistant, Isadore Grossman, told him that a girl had asked their teacher, who had been discussing modern sculpture, what he thought of the sculpture of Lipchitz. The teacher had a lump of clay in his hand that he let fall to the floor and splatter, declaring that that was a Lipchitz. Lipchitz later described his reaction:

> That is a rather interesting idea. I think I might try to make some such sculptures. So arose the idea of the semi-automatics, in which I would just splash or squeeze a piece of warm wax in my hands, put it in a basin of water without looking at it, and then let it harden in cold water.[179]

This method is akin to the automatism of the Surrealists from the mid 1920s on. In 1924 Breton defined Surrealism as "Pure psychic automatism, by which one intends to express verbally, in writing or by any other method, the real functioning of the mind. Dictation by thought, in the absence of any control exercised by reason, and beyond any aesthetic or moral preoccupation."[180] This could obviously be achieved far more spontaneously in painting, and particularly in drawing, than in modeling in plaster, wax or clay, or the painfully slow method of direct carving in stone or wood. The first stage of Lipchitz's semi-automatics, begun with highly malleable soft wax squeezed and shaped in water, with no conscious subject in mind, is closer to the automatism advocated by the Surrealist painters than to the early Surrealist work of Arp and Giacometti.

The second stage in the creation of Lipchitz's semi-automatics involved a conscious effort to interpret and develop images suggested by the wax forms that emerged from the water. As he said: "Up to this point my acts were purely automatic; from here on they were completely conscious."[181] In *Here are the Fruits and the Flowers*, it would appear that the general proportions and distribution of mass of the figure were formed underwater and that the image that emerged suggested the subject. Details such as the eye, the ribs, the fruit and flowers and the toes were then modelled in a conscious effort to give definition to this free, poetic image. A work such as this anticipates to a remarkable degree de Kooning's bronzes of the early 1970s, such as *Floating Figure* of 1972.

107 *Sketch for Yulla Lipchitz* 1956
Bronze 5/7
H. 12⅛″/30.8 cm
The Estate of Jacques Lipchitz represented by
Marlborough International Fine Art AG.

This charming study of Lipchitz's wife, Yulla, captures her delicate, chiseled features. It is one of Lipchitz's most spontaneous portraits; the rough modelling enhances the sense of immediacy.

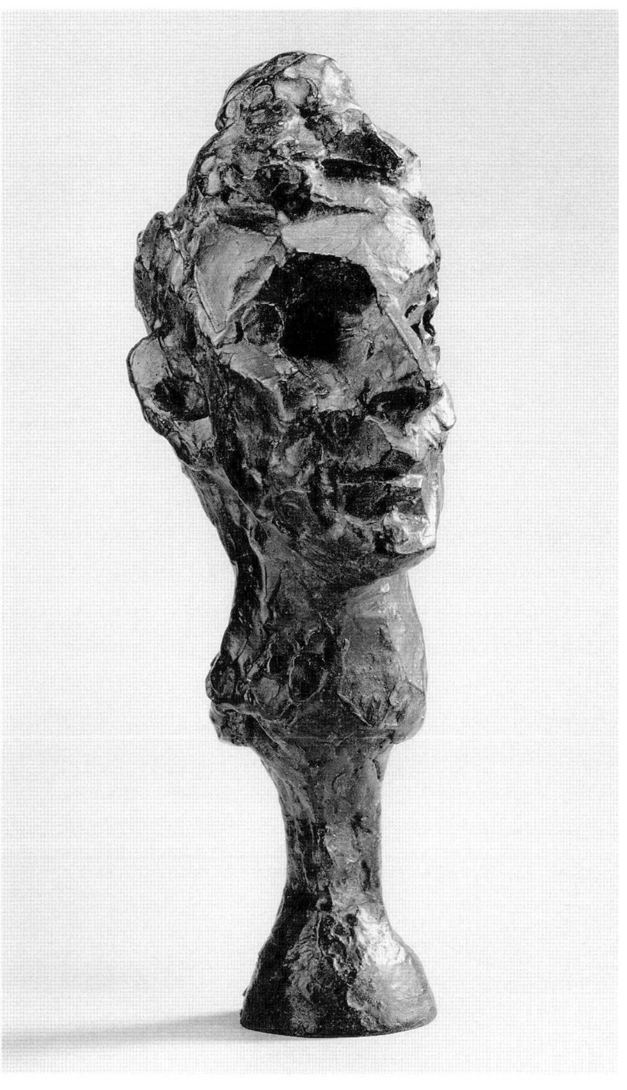

107

108 *Freedom* (à la limite du possible) 1958
Bronze (unique)
H. 26″/66.0 cm
The Estate of Jacques Lipchitz represented by
Marlborough International Fine Art AG.

In 1956 or 1957 Lipchitz built on the technique of his semi-automatics by introducing found objects, yet another link with the working methods of the Surrealists. For example, in an untitled work of c.1957 he attached a real flower to a figure of a woman with swirling robes, which, he said, "actually came out in the bronze. I was enormously excited by this innovation, something about which I had been thinking for a long time, and it inspired me to go on with the series that I called *To the Limit of the Possible*."[182]

Freedom, by its very title, indicates the sense of release and the boundless inventiveness opened up by this newfound technique. The bird cage may well be a readymade found object. Chains are clearly visible above and beneath the cage. One can only speculate on the other objets trouvés that Lipchitz may have incorporated into this sculpture. The multiwinged birds alighting on and below the cage are poetic fantasies rather than literal interpretations of known species. One can only marvel that it was possible to cast in bronze such intricate and fragile forms.

109 *Galapagos I* (à la limite du possible) 1958
Bronze (unique)
H. 19½″/49.5 cm
The Estate of Jacques Lipchitz represented by
Marlborough International Fine Art AG.

Among the 1958 series entitled *À la limite du possible*, Lipchitz created three works that he called *Galapagos I, II* and *III*. They were directly inspired by photographs and paintings that appeared in the September 8, 1958, issue of *Life* magazine, in the lengthy article "Darwin's World of Nature: Part II: The Enchanted Isles," an account of the scientist's expedition to the Galapagos Islands in 1835. In *Galapagos I* it would appear that most of the sculpture was cast directly from a branch or gnarled root of a tree. The sculpture was almost certainly a free adaptation of the photograph in the *Life* article of a land iguana climbing a tree in search of greenery.

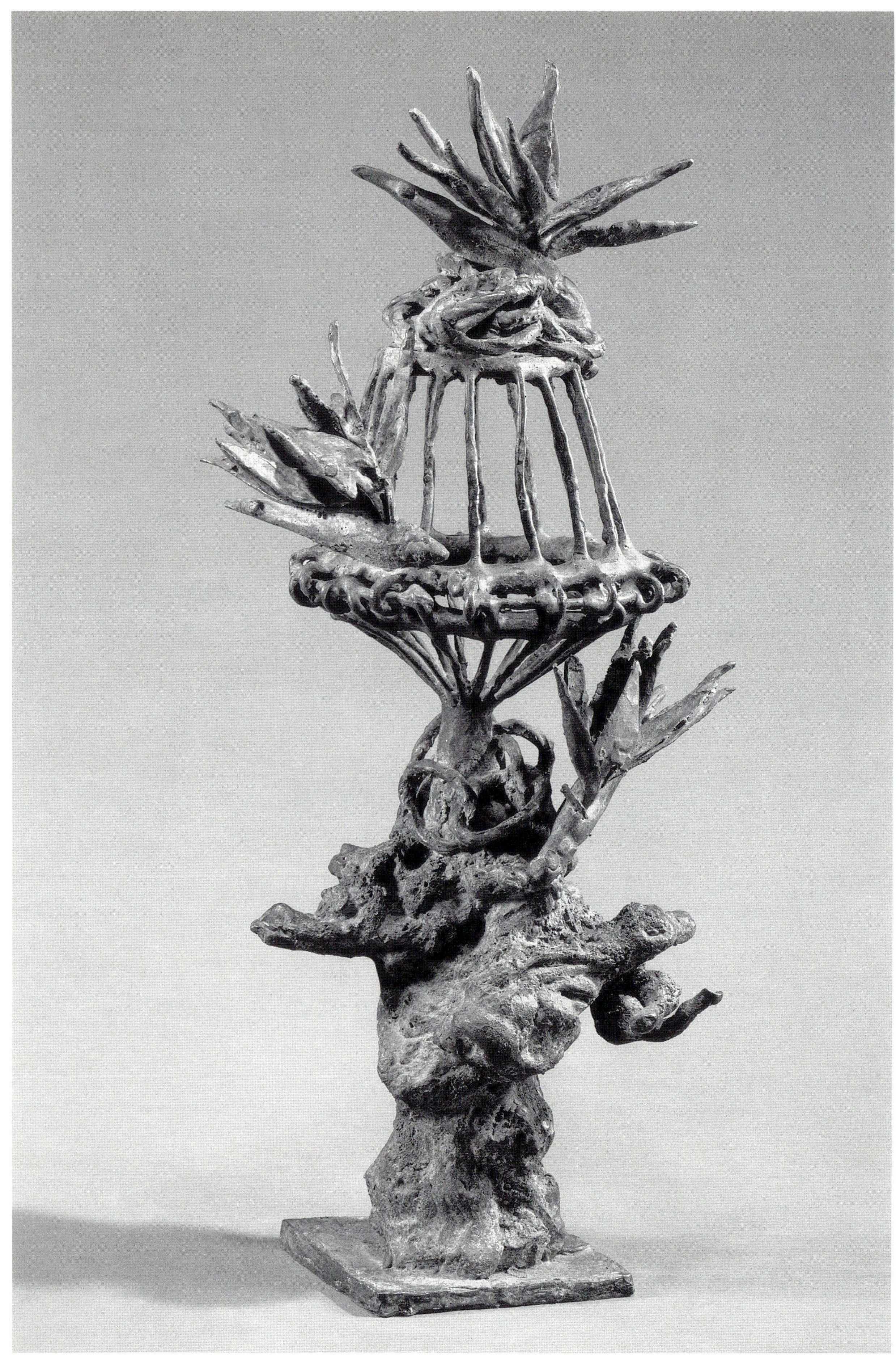

108

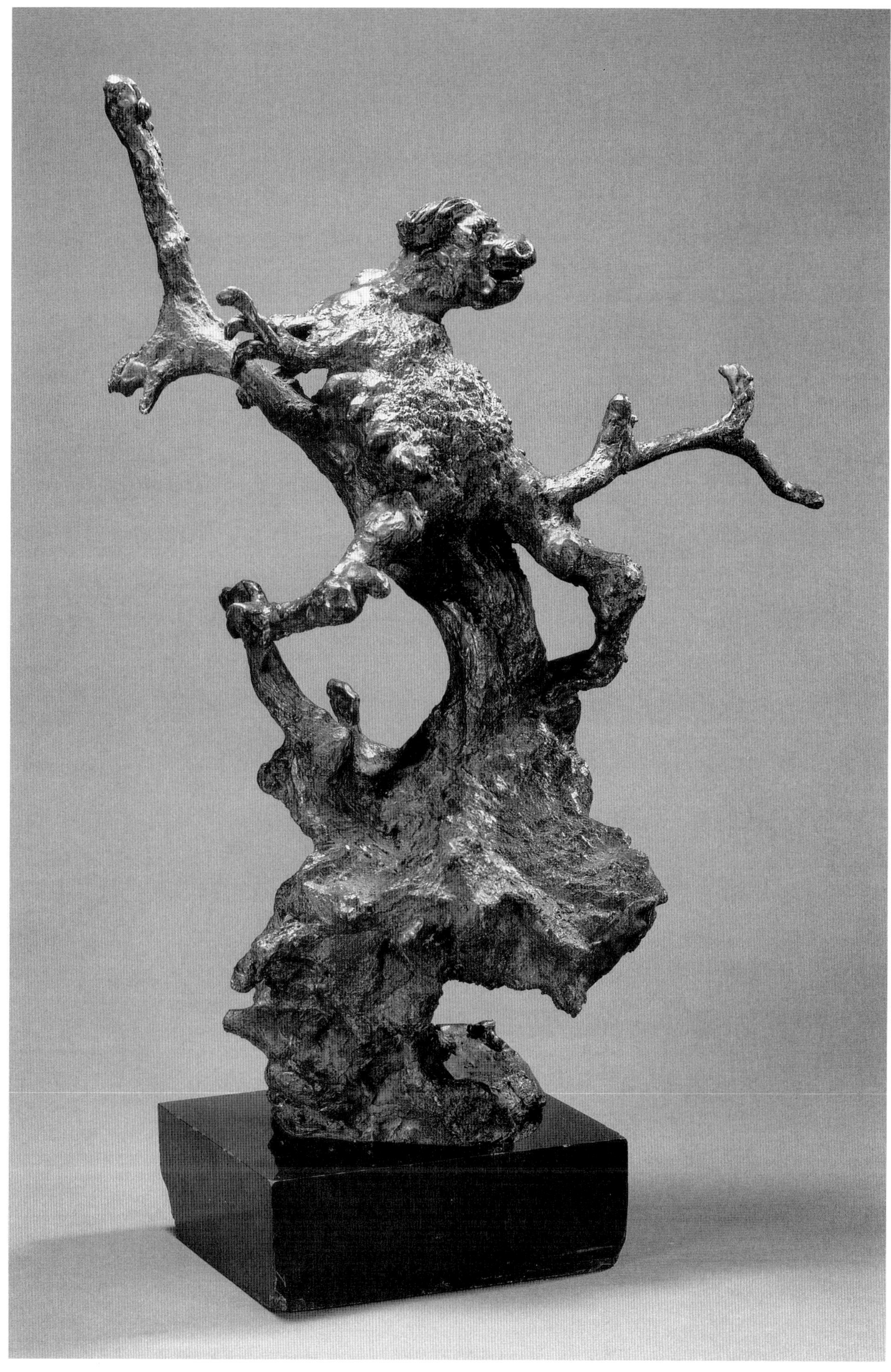

109

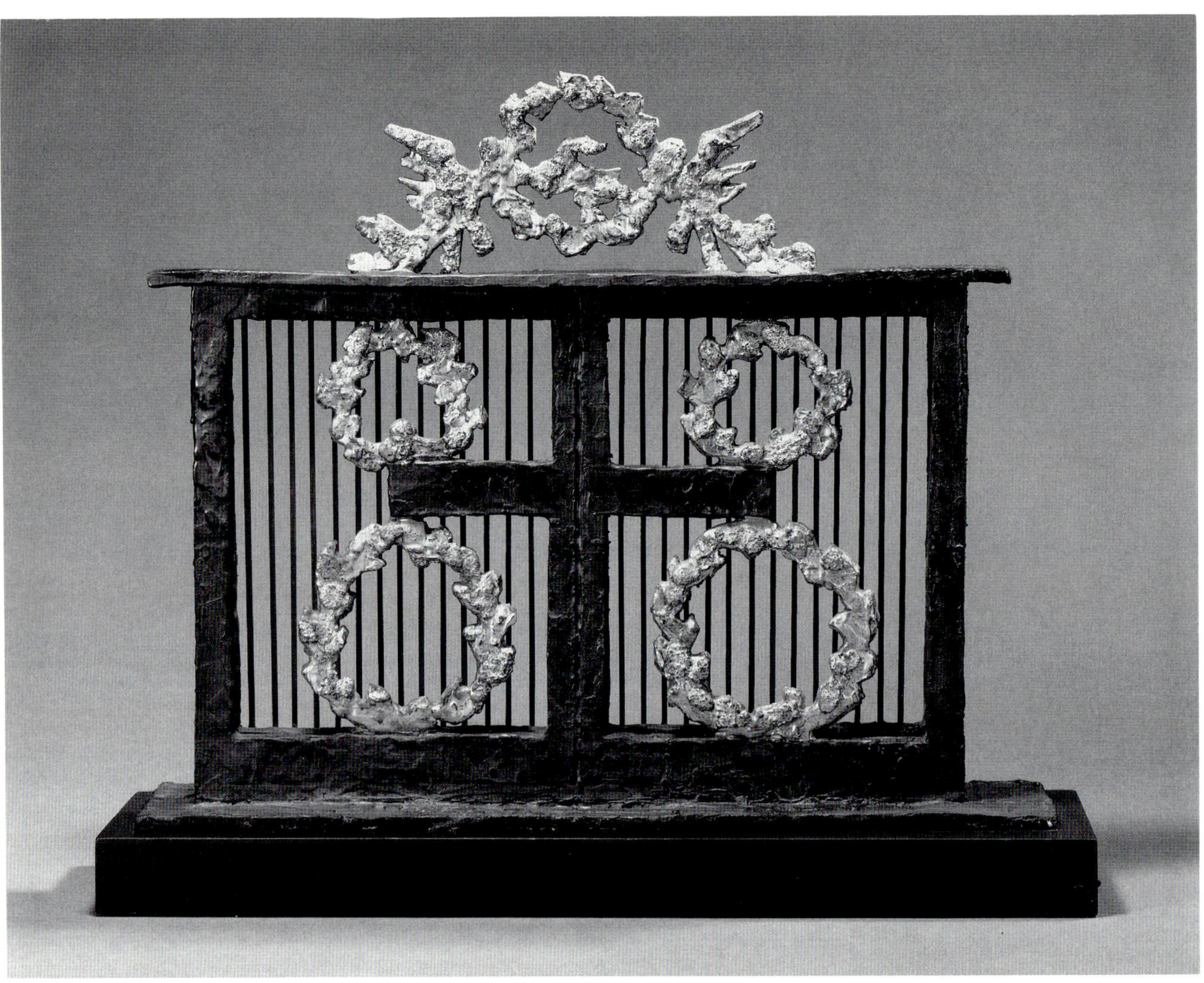

110 *Sketch for the Gate of the Roofless Church* 1958
Bronze
17 x 20¾ x 3½″/43.2 x 52.7 x 8.9 cm
The Estate of Jacques Lipchitz represented by Marlborough International Fine Art AG.

It was in the late 1940s, according to Mrs. Jane Blaffer Owen, that she saw one of Lipchitz's preliminary maquettes for the Nôtre-Dame de Liesse commission reproduced in a magazine.[183] She wanted to acquire a religious work for the town of New Harmony, Indiana. Through her husband she was related to Robert Owen, the nineteenth-century Welsh-Scottish industrialist and philanthropist who had bought the town in 1824 from the Rappites, a German religious sect that had settled there in 1814. Through the Robert Lee Blaffer Trust, Mrs. Owen commissioned Lipchitz to make a cast of *Nôtre-Dame de Liesse* for New Harmony; the cast was given to the Episcopal diocese of Indiana. She then commissioned Philip Johnson to design the Roofless Church

lamb of God, with two angels supporting a wreath of leaves. Below this are two circles of roses. The two larger circles represent thorns. In the monumental gate itself (no. 110), enclosed within the circles of thorns are the Greek letters alpha and omega.

111 *Between Heaven and Earth* 1958
Bronze 2/3
H. 46″/116.8 cm
The Estate of Jacques Lipchitz represented by Marlborough International Fine Art AG.

The genesis of this work dates from 1953, when Lipchitz was working on *Nôtre-Dame de Liesse* at the for Lipchitz's Virgin. The Roofless Church and the sculpture were dedicated in 1960.

Johnson had also designed a large courtyard leading up to the church. In 1958 Lipchitz made this study for the gate opening onto the courtyard. At the top is the

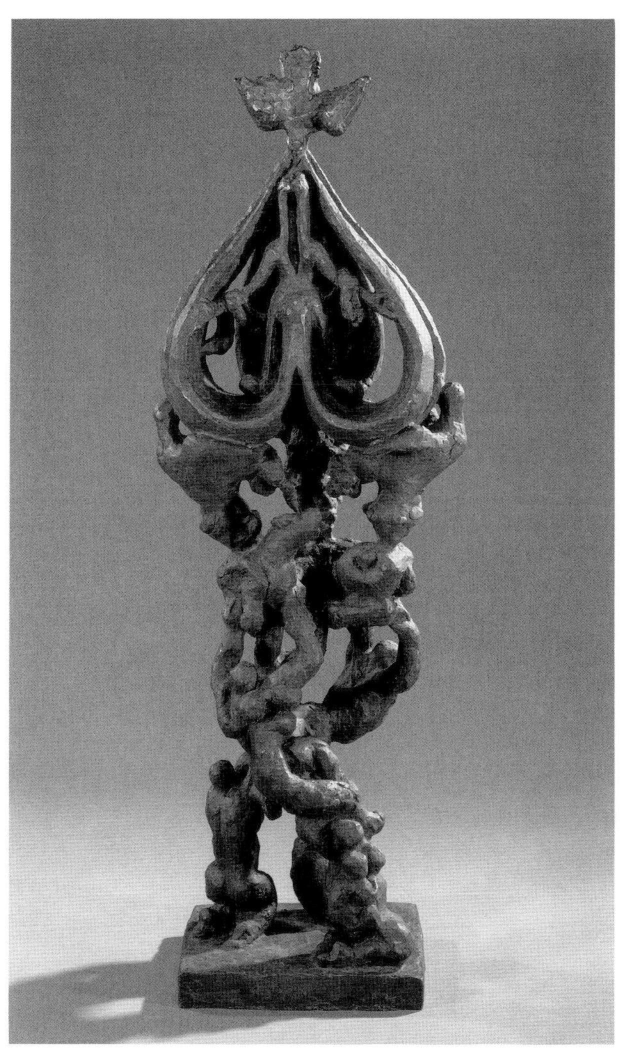
111

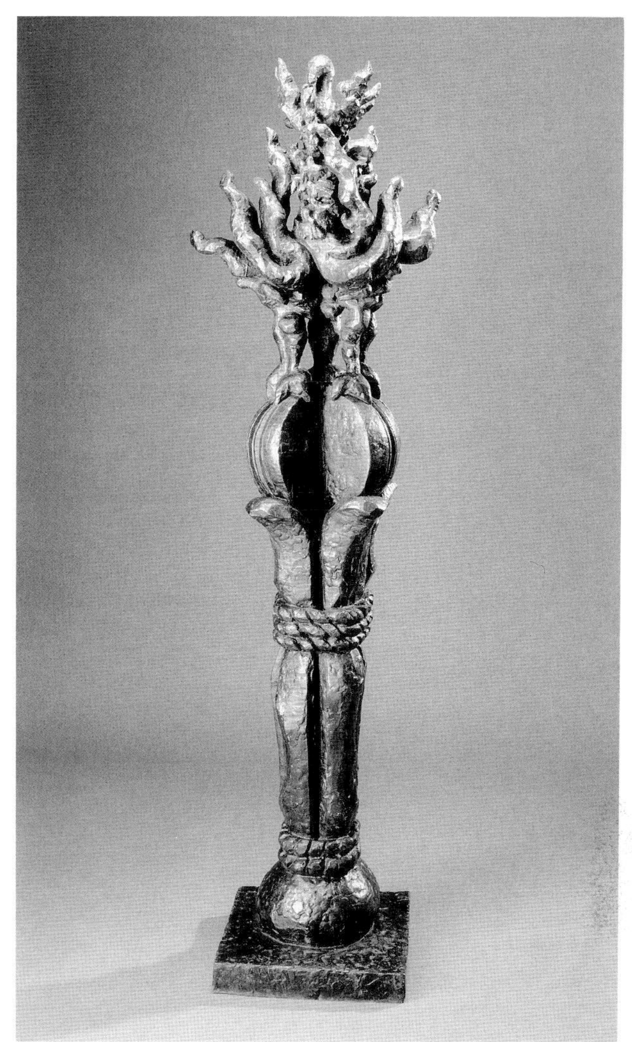
112

foundry (see no. 104). He said:

> ...the bronze was suspended in the air; suddenly, as I looked at it, I had the impression that if it were continued at the bottom it could be like a chalice...As I conceived it, the figures below constituted humanity receiving the Virgin. The idea has something to do with the songs and rituals of primitive people and also, curiously, in my mind about some of the regulations and taboos involved in the beginning of cubism. This later fact pushed me further in the direction of freedom and lyrical expression, away from the dictatorship even of ideas, toward images of the unity of humanity.[184]

Lipchitz's intention was to integrate the Christian imagery of the dove and the Virgin with symbolic ideas of all humanity. "There are many elements involved in it: the mother and child, a pair of lovers...In its final form I do not consider it a specifically religious or Christian sculpture; rather, it becomes religious in a universal sense."[185]

Between 1967–69 Lipchitz made two large variations of *Between Heaven and Hell* that he entitled *Peace on Earth*. A cast of the ten-foot-seven-inch-high version of *Peace on Earth* is in the collection of the Nelson-Atkins Museum of Art, Kansas City. In May 1969 the forty-five-foot-high bronze *Peace on Earth* was unveiled at the Los Angeles County Music Center (see fig. 24).

112 *Working Model for Lesson of a Disaster* c.1961–70
Bronze 2/7
H. 71″/180.3 cm
The Estate of Jacques Lipchitz represented by Marlborough International Fine Art AG.

THIS BRONZE, AND THE LARGER (144″/365.3 CM) VERSION of *Lesson of a Disaster*, developed from a series of sculptures made after the devastating fire in Lipchitz's New York studio in January 1952. In the fire, his *Nôtre-Dame de Liesse* was destroyed. His first reaction was to make a small sketch entitled *Virgin in Flames* 1952, which was followed by a related work entitled *Lesson of a Disaster*.[186] In the late 1950s and 1960s Lipchitz returned to the theme of the lesson of a disaster, an idea that he felt could be made into a monumental sculpture. He described the work as "a curious structure that is like a growing plant on the legs of an animal... The concept is difficult to explain. There is a phoenix at the top which is feeding a nest of small birds, and the flames are transformed into a blossoming flower. I think the whole idea had to do with hope and renewal after the disaster."[187]

113 *The Cup of Atonement* (Images of Italy) 1962
Bronze 2/7
H. 15″/38.1 cm
The Estate of Jacques Lipchitz represented by
Marlborough International Fine Art AG.

LIPCHITZ VISITED ITALY FOR THE FIRST TIME IN 1962. He began working at the Tommasi Foundry in Pietrasanta on a series entitled *Images of Italy*. *The Cup of Atonement* (or *The Cup of Expiation*) was, he said, "a personal prayer for forgiveness because I had been unpleasant in some context."[188] Like his 1955–56 bronze *Remembrance of Loie Fuller*,[189] this work has a strong art-nouveau flavour. Lipchitz, always interested in explaining techniques and creative processes, describes the work as follows:

> It is a semi-automatic like the earlier ones in which I took a sheet of wax [see no. 106 above] softened it in hot water, and then twisted it to see what happened. This series is perhaps more deliberate than the earlier group, *To the Limit of the Possible*, because in most cases I had a specific idea in mind before I began.[190]

114 *The Tower and Its Shadow* (Images of Italy) 1962
Bronze 7/7
H. 11¾″/29.8 cm
The Estate of Jacques Lipchitz represented by
Marlborough International Fine Art AG.

THIS INTRIGUING WORK, LIPCHITZ SAID, "IS A CURIOUS mixture of the leaning Tower of Pisa and a tool designed to make macaroni [more likely a ravioli cutting pin]."[191] The shadow is not, in fact, that of the tower, but that of a draped woman standing behind it. As in a number of Lipchitz's earlier Cubist works, figure and object are integrated. The woman holds the tower with both hands. Dislocated breasts project from the top of the tower. In some of Medardo Rosso's sculptures, such as *Kiss Under the Lamppost* (1882), the figure becomes an extension of the environment and the physical surrounding fuses with the figure.

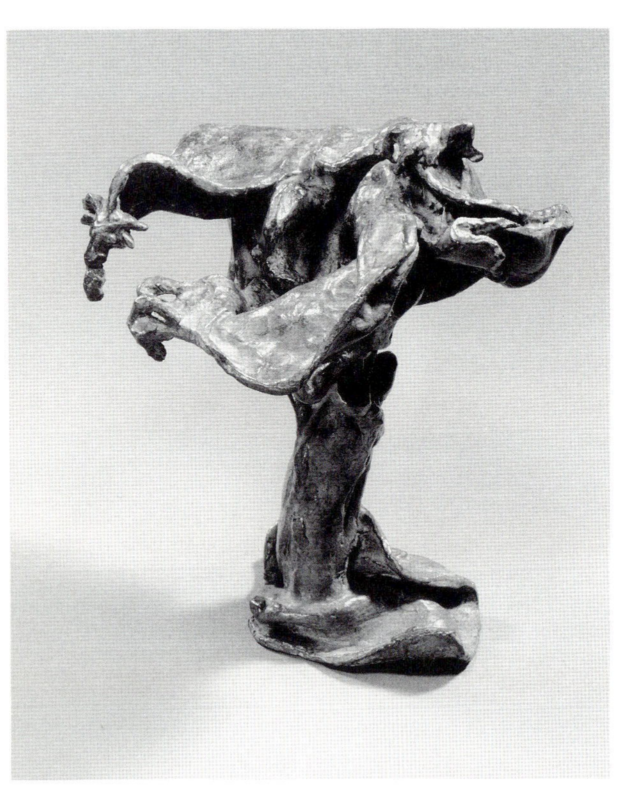

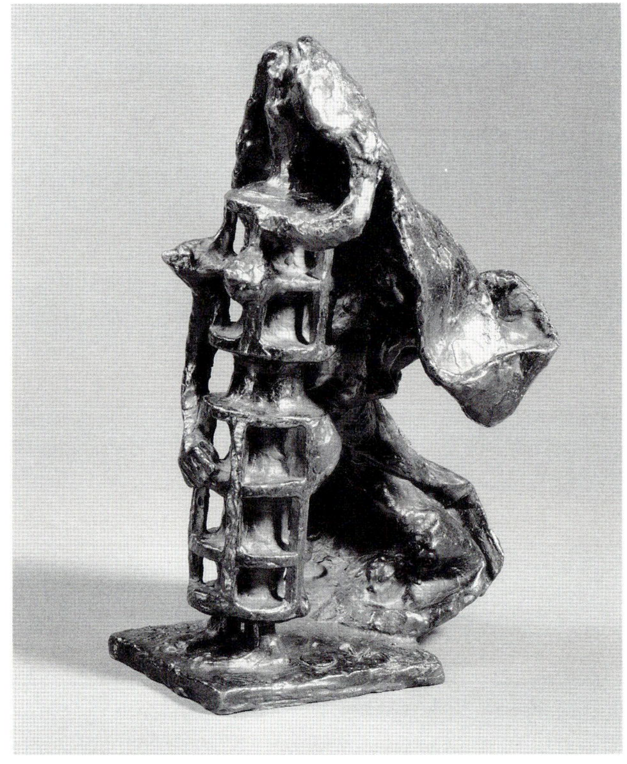

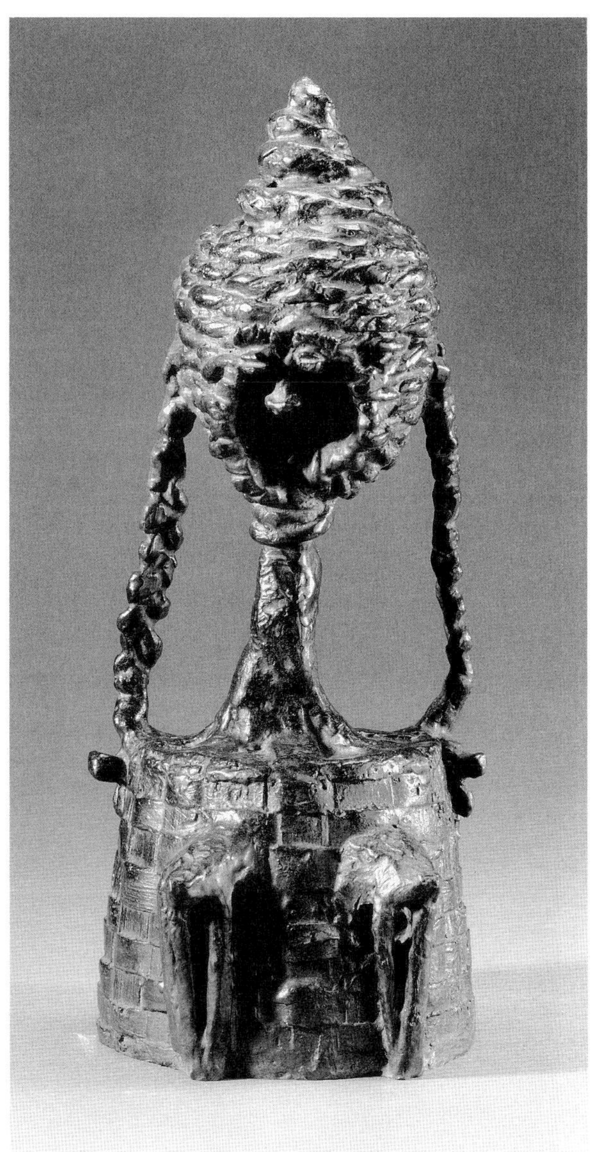

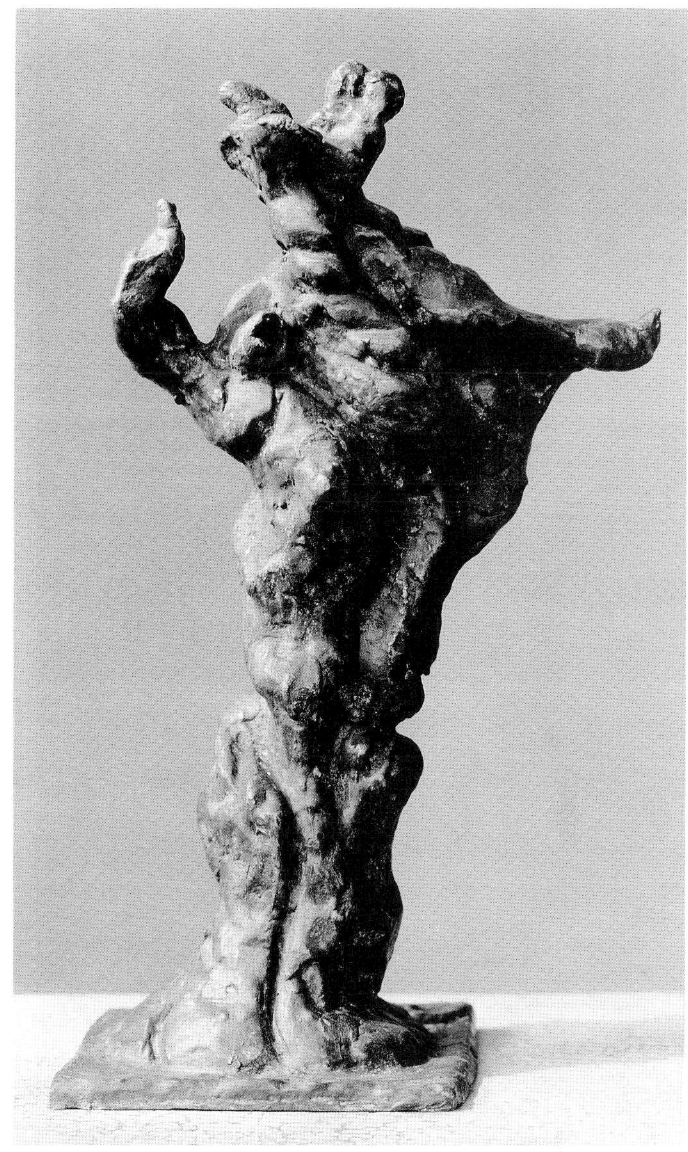

115 *The Beautiful One* (Images of Italy) 1962
Bronze 5/7
H. 12½″/31.3 cm
The Estate of Jacques Lipchitz represented by Marlborough International Fine Art AG.

THIS CHARMING SCULPTURE WAS, LIPCHITZ SAID, INSPIRED by a girl he had seen on the beach at Forte dei Marmi: "... she had small breasts, was wearing a little chemise. The sculpture is made of two baskets and some rope. The neck is some kind of a tool, I do not remember exactly what."[192] The little face is defined for the most part by the negative space, at the top of which are two small eyes and tiny nose. This ingenious metamorphosis of found objects is, in its playfulness and charm, reminiscent of Picasso's 1951 bronze *Baboon and Young* (Museum of Modern Art, New York).[193]

116 *The Geisha* 1963
Bronze 4/7
H. 13½″/34.3 cm
The Estate of Jacques Lipchitz represented by Marlborough International Fine Art AG.

LIKE THE SEMI-AUTOMATICS OF THE MID 1950S, SUCH AS *Here are the Fruits and the Flowers* (no. 106), this work may well have been modelled in wax underwater. The title was no doubt suggested by the gesture of the figure which, despite the extreme liberties taken with the human anatomy, evokes in an uncanny way the dress and Oriental dancing movement of a Japanese geisha.

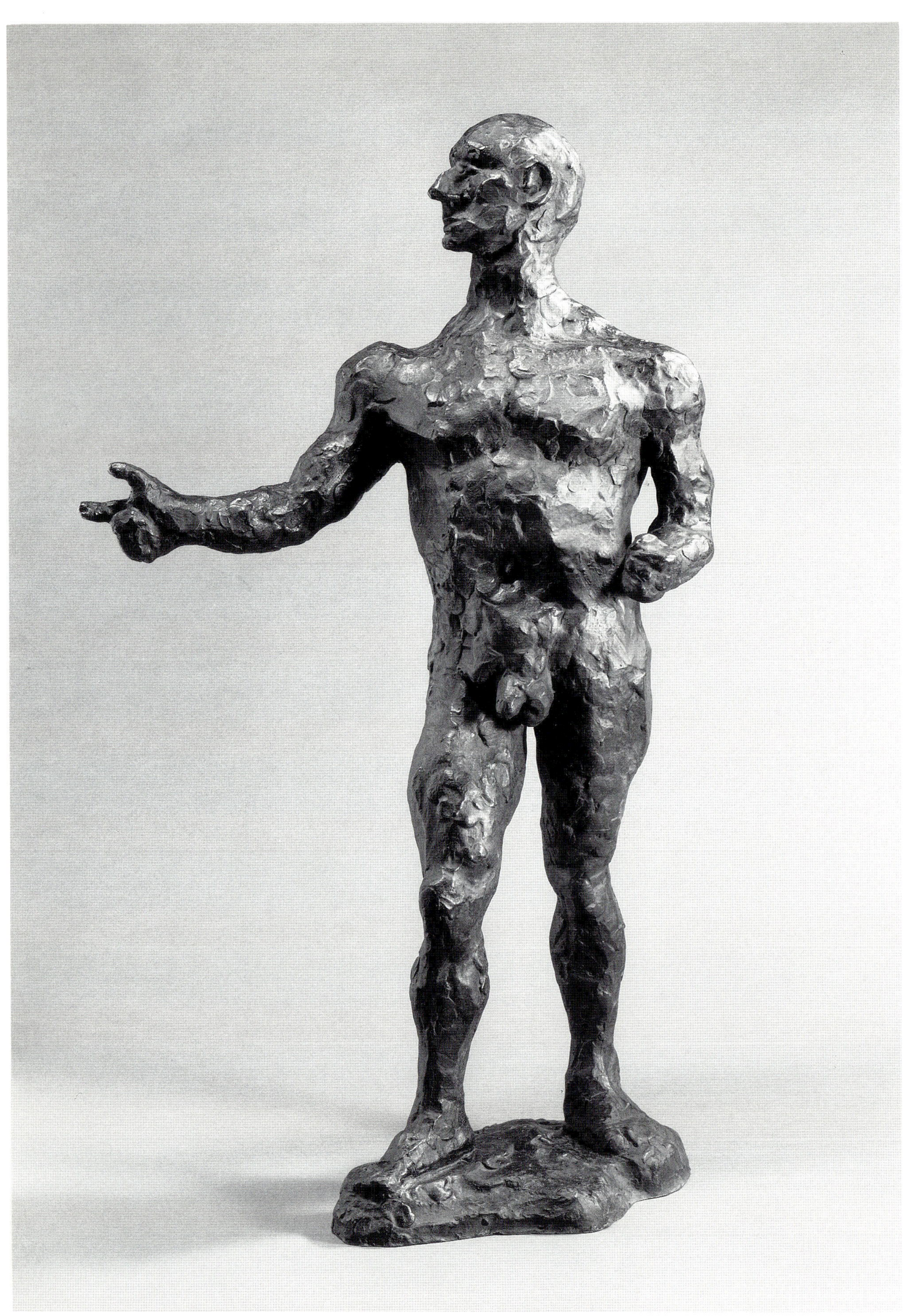

117 *Study for Duluth Monument* 1963
Bronze 1/7
H. 26″/66.0 cm
The Estate of Jacques Lipchitz represented by Marlborough International Fine Art AG.

In late 1961 or early 1962 Lipchitz became involved with a commission for the Tweed Museum of Art, University of Minnesota, Duluth, for a sculpture of Daniel Greysolon, Sieur Duluth (1636–1710), the great seventeenth-century French explorer after whom the city was named. At first Lipchitz declined, because the proposed bronze would be too large for the Modern Art Foundry in New York. Once he had established a working relationship with the Tommasi Foundry in Pietrasanta, Italy, which was able to cast on a very large scale, the project went ahead. He described the commission as follows:

> The Duluth monument was interesting because it was a portrait of a man of whom no portraits existed. Therefore, I had to create an idea of the explorer rather than a specific portrait. The result was that I made a great number of sketches, including a nude model [no. 117] for which a man at the foundry posed one morning.[194]

This study of Giuliano, the Italian model, is reminiscent of Rodin's preparatory nude studies for *The Burghers of Calais*, which preceded the clothed figures. The pose established here, with the right leg forward and the right arm gesturing, was followed fairly closely in the nine-foot-high final version, which was installed at the University of Minnesota in 1964.

118 *Sketch for Daniel Greysolon, Sieur Duluth* 1963
Bronze 7/7
H. 22½″/57.0 cm
The Estate of Jacques Lipchitz represented by Marlborough International Fine Art AG.

Lipchitz made a number of preparatory sketches of the clothed figure of Duluth. Lipchitz explained that the site for the sculpture and the high column on which it was to be placed dictated the exaggerated proportions of the figure:

> The sculpture was designed to be placed on a high pedestal in a rather narrow courtyard between buildings. So I actually distorted the figure in order to correct the perspective from which it would normally be seen, with the upper part of the body larger than would be natural.[195]

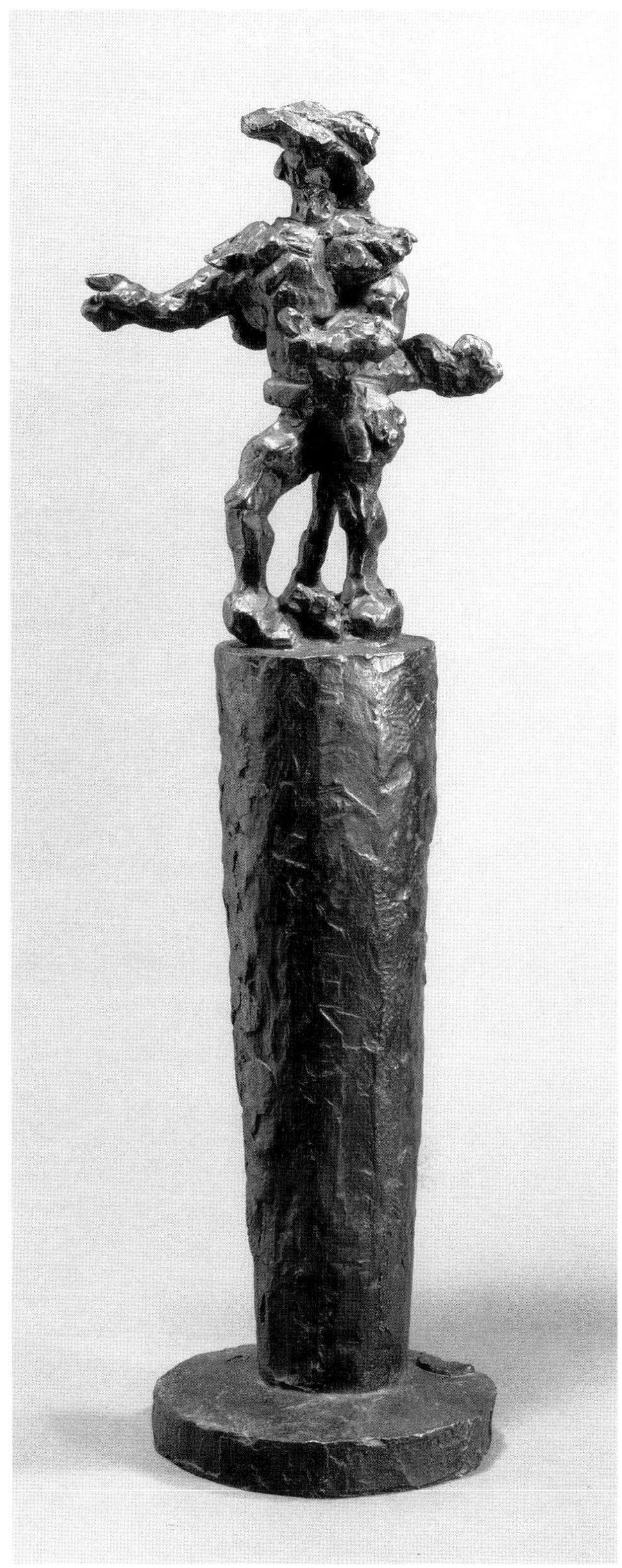

Even in this very rough and spontaneous little sketch, Lipchitz is beginning to consider such details as the hat. Indeed, in the final version the hat and clothing of the explorer are essential elements in giving the figure historical credibility.

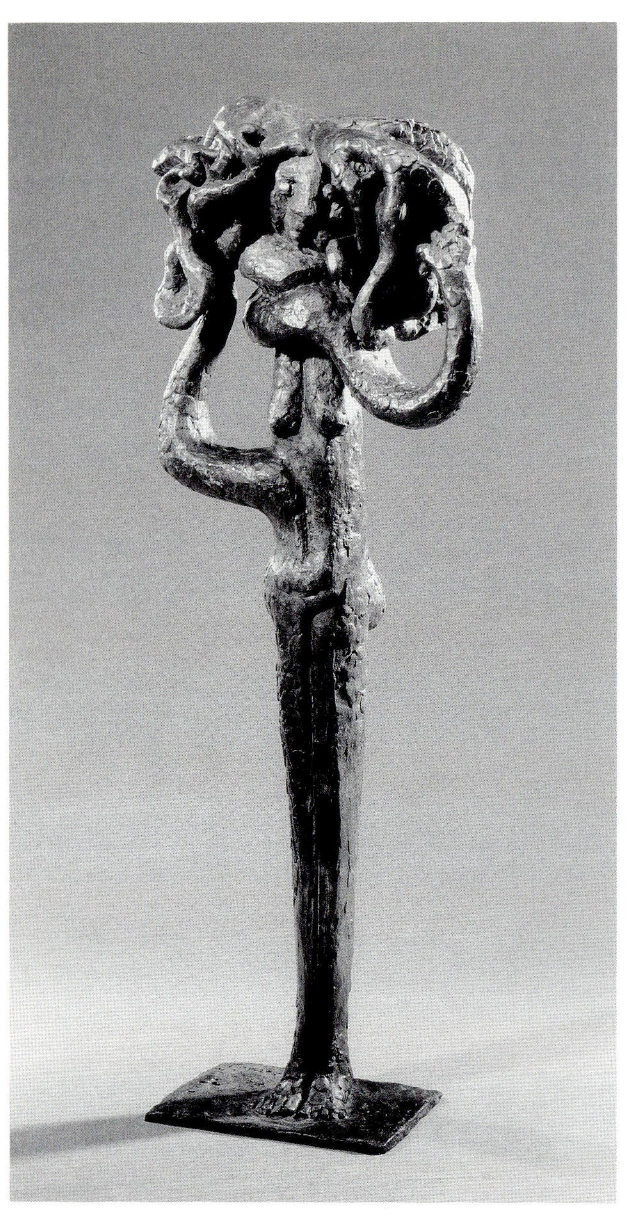

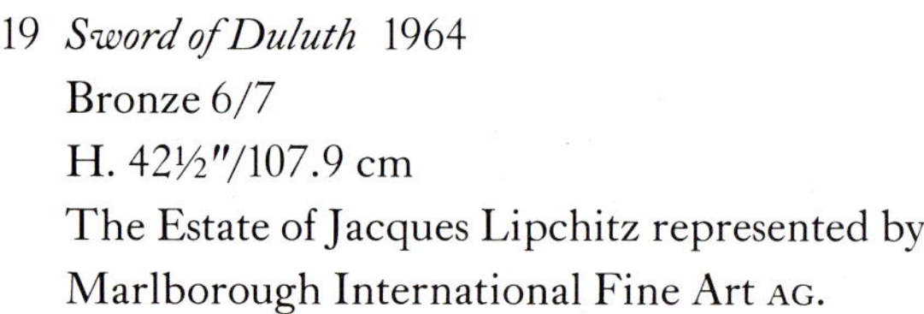

119 *Sword of Duluth* 1964
Bronze 6/7
H. 42½″/107.9 cm
The Estate of Jacques Lipchitz represented by
Marlborough International Fine Art AG.

THE SWORD THAT HANGS BEHIND THE FIGURE OF DULUTH was cast separately. "When I was given the wax, I suddenly saw a figure in it, a familiar figure, so I made a separate sculpture based on the sword."[196] No doubt the curved basket or knuckle bow of the hilt of the sword suggested an arm. With the addition of the feet, the small breasts and the buttocks, Lipchitz has transformed the sword into a thin, elongated female figure with arms raised. Her face apears in profile to the right, near the top of the sculpture.

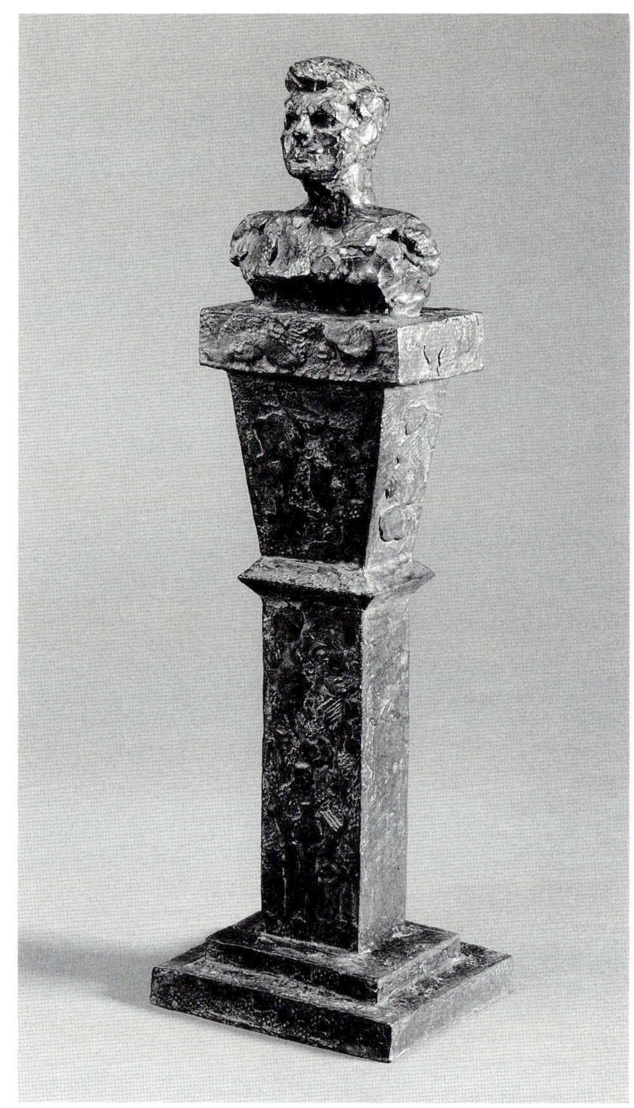

120 *Sketch for John F. Kennedy* 1964
Bronze 17/21
H. 17¾″/45.1 cm
The Estate of Jacques Lipchitz represented by
Marlborough International Fine Art AG.

LIPCHITZ MADE POSTHUMOUS PORTRAITS OF TWO AMERICAN politicians: Senator Robert Taft and President John F. Kennedy. Of the latter, he wrote:

> First of all a student organization in London asked me to make a sculpture of Kennedy after his death and, since I had great admiration for the President, I made it, even though it was a posthumous bust. Then I was asked to make a larger version for Newark, New Jersey. I had never seen the President, but I had a model who was supposed to look very much like him and Pierre Salinger sent me photographs. Members of the Kennedy family came and made suggestions about my sculpture. Nevertheless, I was never

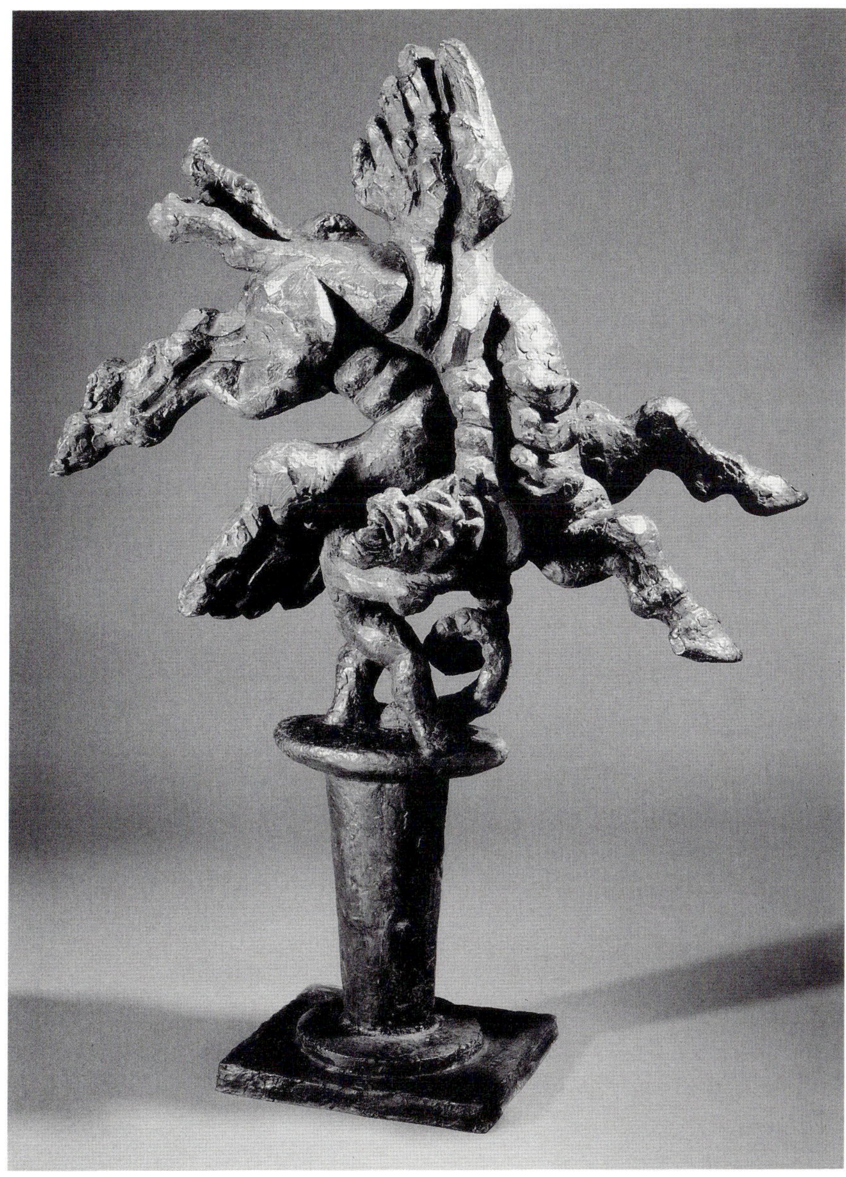

121

satisfied with it and I will never do such a posthumous sculpture again.[197]

The rough, lively surface of this bronze study reflects the obvious spontaneity of Lipchitz's modelling technique. A recognizable likeness has been achieved, despite the sketchy quality of this work. Two thirty-one-inch-high versions of the bust of John F. Kennedy were installed at the International Students House, London, and in Newark, NJ.

121 *Study for Bellerophon Taming Pegasus* 1964
Bronze 5/7
H. 60"/152.5 cm
The Estate of Jacques Lipchitz represented by Marlborough International Fine Art AG.

In 1964 Lipchitz was invited to make a sculpture for the Columbia University Law School in New York City, one of the most important commissions he undertook during the last decade of his working life.

One day I received a letter or a telephone call from Dean Warren of the Columbia Law School, who invited me to a meeting with the architect Max Abramovitz. Abramovitz had designed a building for the Law School and they wanted a sculpture over the entrance. I immediately said: "Don't expect a blinded lady with a scale and all those things from me. I will try to think of something else."[198]

Something horizontal was needed for the space over the entrance. This led Lipchitz to consider returning to the theme of the horse and the legend of Pegasus, the subject of the large 1944–50 bronze, *Birth of the Muses*:

Then I thought about Bellerophon because Bellerophon is a symbol of man dominating nature. In the myth, Bellerophon was a human being who fell in love with the daughter of Zeus. When he asked for her hand, Zeus was not happy about it and gave him terrible deeds to do, hoping that he would perish, but Bellerophon, an intelligent man, tamed Pegasus, the winged horse who represents the wild forces of nature, and with the help of Pegasus he was able to accomplish all the tasks that were required of him.[199]

Characteristically, Lipchitz was able to interpret the Greek myth to fit in with his purpose. The story seemed to him to reflect somehow the rule of law: "You observe nature, make conclusions, and from these you make rules, and these rules help you to behave, to live, and law is born from that."[200]

Bellerophon taming the winged horse Pegasus is indeed a far cry from the traditional blinded lady with a scale. The small figure of Bellerophon is overwhelmed, engulfed as he attempts to capture the monstrously large flying horse by tying a rope around its neck. If Pegasus represents the wild forces of nature, man, in attempting to tame it, seems to be facing insurmountable odds. An aspiring law student could be forgiven for thinking that the sculpture suggested that man, in his struggle against the wild forces of nature, is at a grave disadvantage.

Lipchitz made at least five sketches for the commission, ranging in height from 11¾ inches to 20¾ inches.[201] This work was followed by a twelve-foot-high version and finally the approximately thirty-eight-foot-high final monument at Columbia University, which was unveiled in November 1977, four years after Lipchitz's death.

122 *L'Arno Furioso* 1967
Bronze 4/7
H. 11″/27.9 cm
The Estate of Jacques Lipchitz represented by Marlborough International Fine Art AG.

In 1967 Lipchitz made four small sculptures to record his reaction to the terrible floods in Florence in the spring of 1966. One, a kind of offering of sympathy to the city, is entitled *Flowers for Florence* (*Fleurs pour Florence douloureuse*) and depicts a seated woman, her head down, with arms extended, holding flowers. *Lamentation*, a standing figure with the arms above the head and hands clasped, was, Lipchitz said, "a lamentation for the Christ of Cimabue, so damaged that it could not be restored."[202] In *L'Arno Furioso* (*The Furious Arno*), Lipchitz transformed the raging power of the river in flood into what he described as "an animal who is spitting or foaming at the mouth like a dog with rabies. It is very ugly."[203] River gods in human form have been depicted often enough in European sculpture, but has the churning energy of water itself? This extraordinary flight of the imagination recalls Leonardo da Vinci's visionary drawings of storms and tempests.

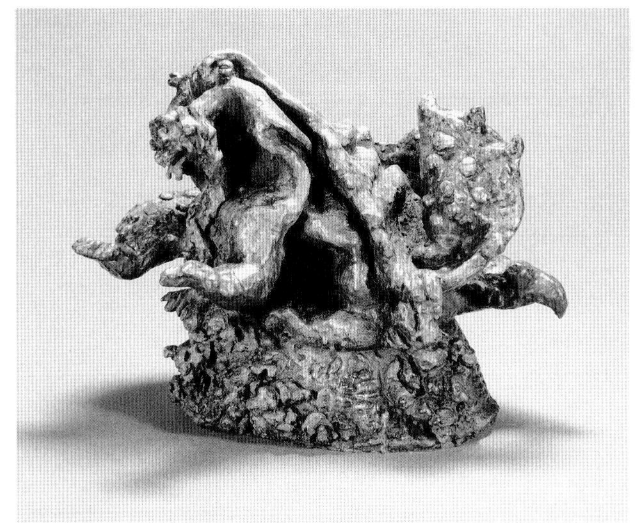

122

123 *Le Ponte Vecchio* 1967
Bronze 1/7
H. 12″/30.5 cm
The Estate of Jacques Lipchitz represented by Marlborough International Fine Art AG.

In another image of Florence of great originality, Lipchitz has, as he said, "translated the bridge into an old woman with a cap and crutches, but still standing erect."[204] As always in Lipchitz's work, the human spirit is defiant and courageous in the face of adversity. The veiled protective form, arching above the vulnerable figure of the woman, is a reworking of a motif that first appeared in *Dancer with Hood* 1947.[205]

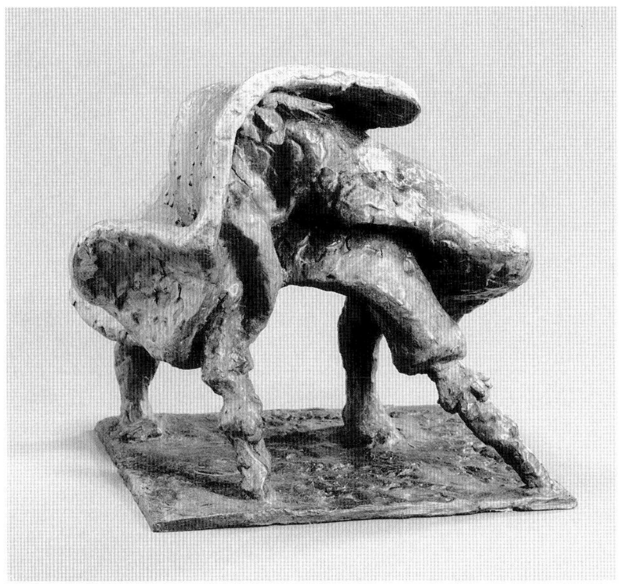

123

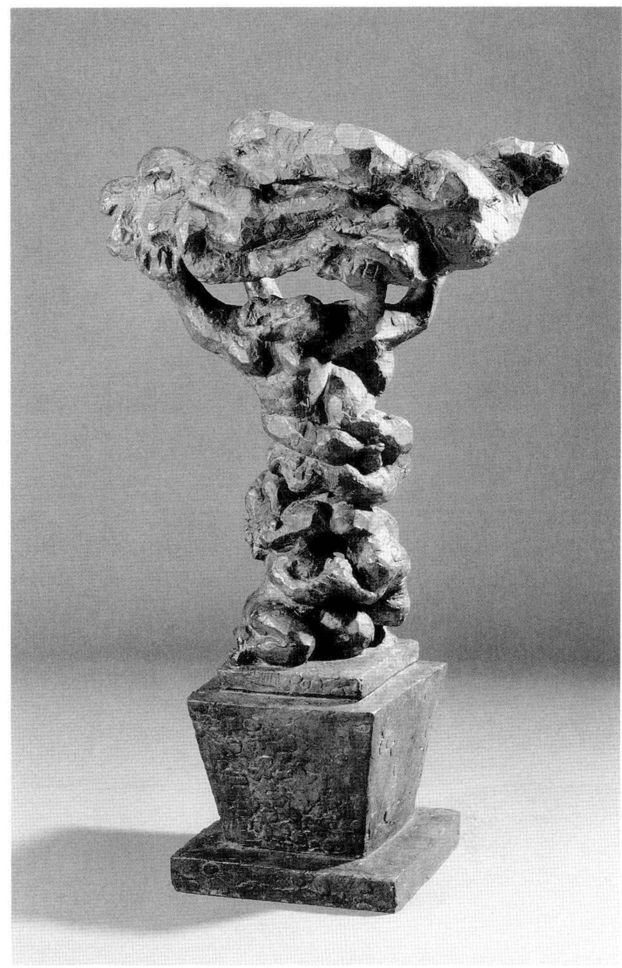

124

124 *Study for Government of the People* 1967
Bronze 1/7
H. 48½″/123.2 cm
The Estate of Jacques Lipchitz represented by Marlborough International Fine Art AG.

IN 1967 LIPCHITZ WAS AWARDED HIS LAST MAJOR AMERICAN public commission, to create a monumental sculpture for the Municipal Plaza in Philadelphia. He described the project as follows:

> The Plaza involves in addition to the City Hall, a modern building and a number of heterogeneous nineteenth-century buildings; the original City Hall, nineteenth-century Victorian, is very interesting with the sculptural decorations done by Alexander Milne Calder, the grandfather of the sculptor Alexander Calder. So it has been quite a job to create a work that would unite these different buildings. I was not given a specific commission or theme but simply asked to make a monumental work. I did a sketch which was a sort of totem pole. At the base there is a couple, and then another couple, and this develops in groups to a climax of the Philadelphia city flag. So those concerned entitled it *Government of the People*.[206]

Whereas *Bellerophon Taming Pegasus* (see no. 121) embodies a specific theme directly related to the commission for the Columbia University School of Law, the symbolism of *Government of the People* seems to be more private and personal. Does the sculpture symbolize civic life or government? In the final version at Municipal Plaza in Philadelphia the forms of the bodies are much more clearly defined than in this study. As David Fraser Jenkins has written:

> Three pairs of nudes are represented, in three tiers: at the base a couple are touching heads and hands; at the centre two nudes turn in a spiral, reaching upwards; at the top, designed to be seen only from below, the figures are indistinct but lie horizontally.[207]

Just as Lipchitz, in his interpretation of mythological subjects, tried to make them reflect the political climate or events in his own life, the focus on human contact in *Government of the People* perhaps symbolizes in a general way the City of Brotherly Love.

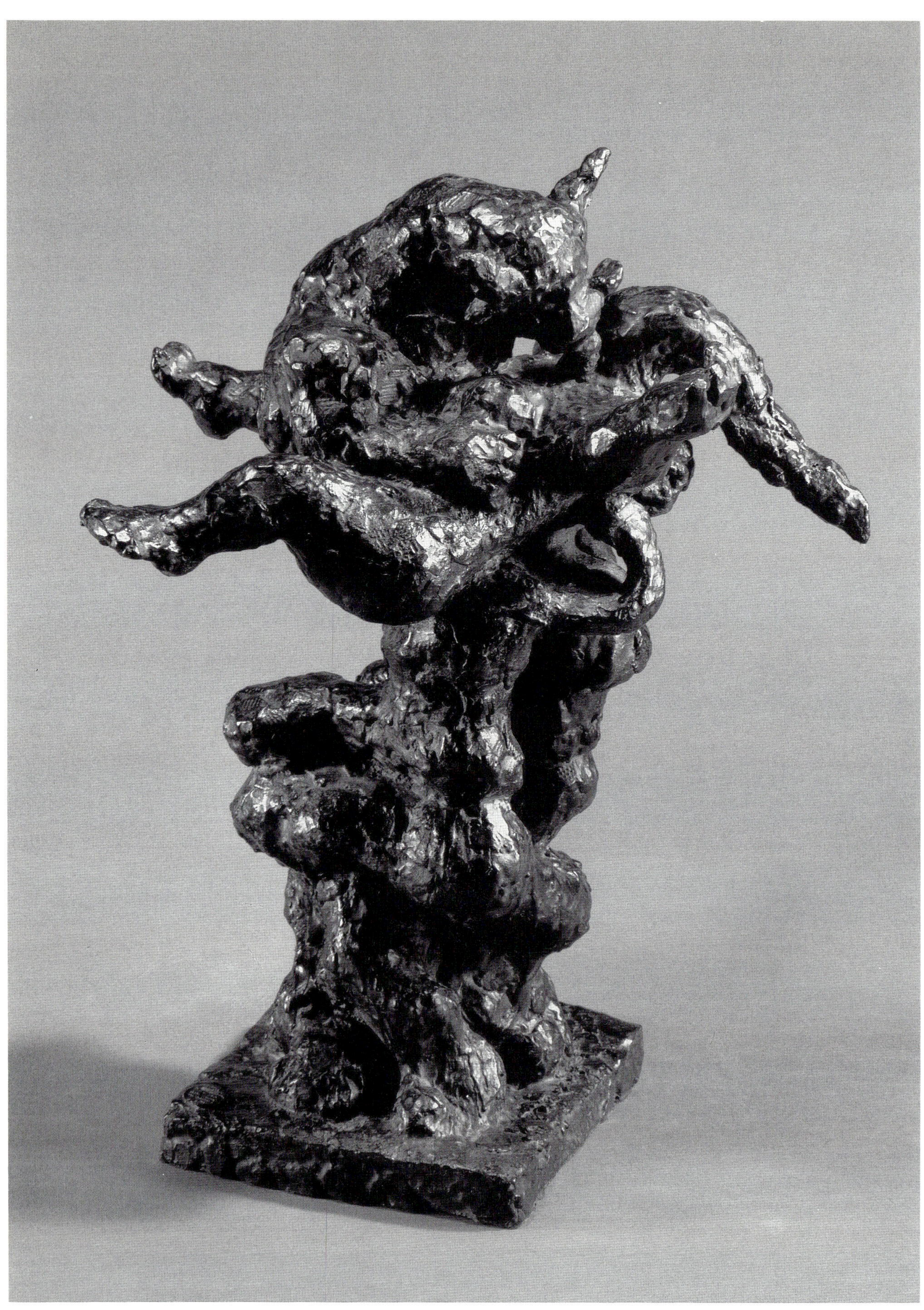

125 *Rape of Europa* 1969–70
Bronze 1/7
H. 21¼"/54.0 cm
The Estate of Jacques Lipchitz represented by Marlborough International Fine Art AG.

Two earlier sculptures of this subject are included in this exhibition. In the 1938 *Rape of Europa I* (no. 81), the bull carries off Europa and swims with her to Crete. In the 1941 version (no. 85) Europa is fighting against her rapist Hitler, whom she stabs in the chest. In this 1969–70 *Rape of Europa*, one of his last mythological sculptures, Lipchitz has returned to the theme of erotic love.

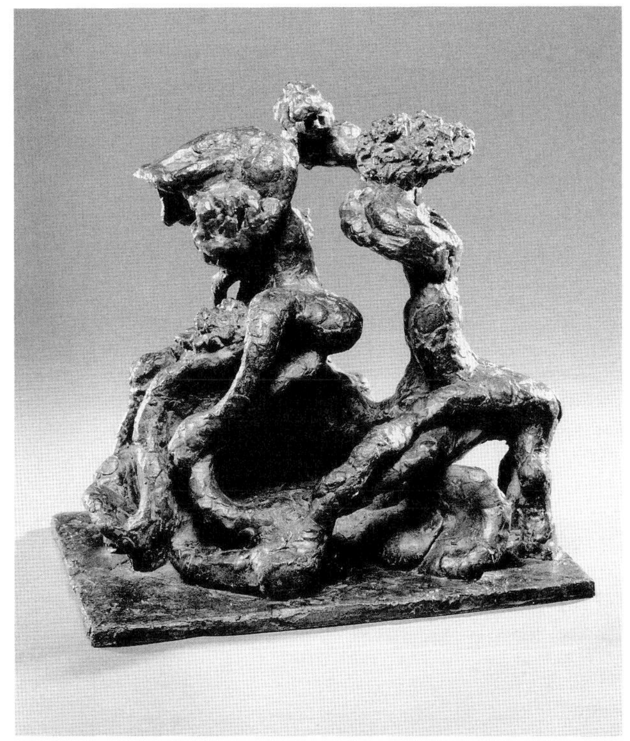

126

126 *Homage to Dürer* 1970
Bronze 3/7
H. 15¾"/40.0 cm
The Estate of Jacques Lipchitz represented by Marlborough International Fine Art AG.

In 1971, to mark the 500th anniversary of the birth of Albrecht Dürer (1471–1528), a number of exhibitions were held in Germany. For one of these, Lipchitz said, "I was invited to contribute a piece, and for this I designed a bronze that I entitled *Melancholia* in honor of Dürer's wonderful engraving of that name. This was a bronze of the lost-wax process, very free in execution, embodying many of my ideas about automatism and the relations of the unconscious to the conscious in sculpture."[208] This bronze is almost certainly the work Lipchitz refers to above – a very free interpretation of Dürer's *Melancholia*.

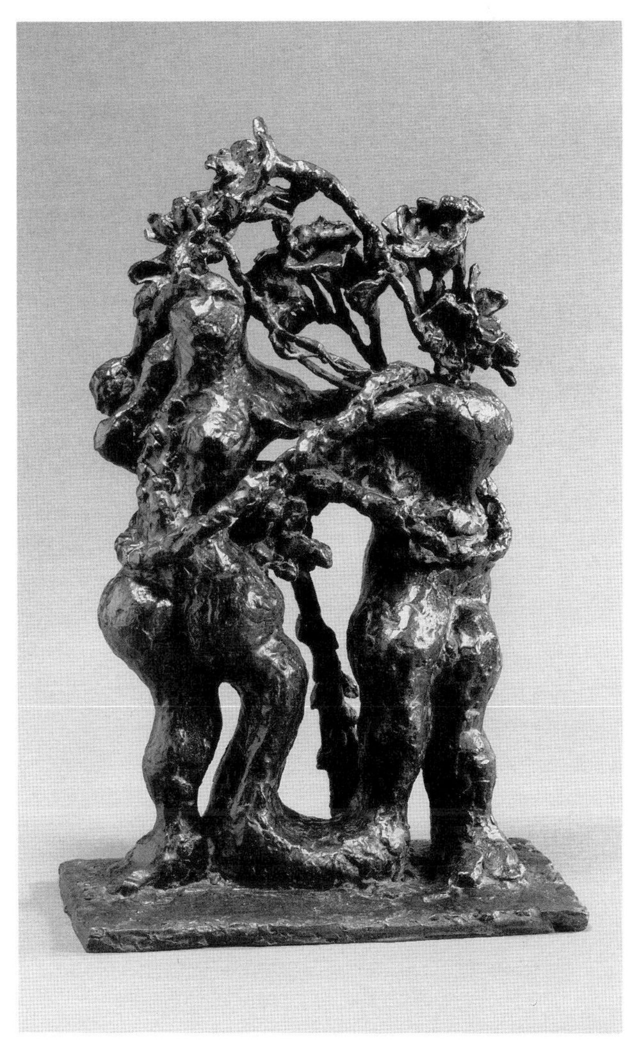

127

127 *The First Meeting (La première rencontre)* 1970–71
Bronze 1/7
H. 17½"/44.5 cm
The Estate of Jacques Lipchitz represented by Marlborough International Fine Art AG.

In 1970–71 Lipchitz worked on a series of sculptures based on themes from the commedia del l'arte, a form of comedy popular in Italy from the sixteenth to the eighteenth centuries, using improvised dialogue and masked characters such as Harlequin, Columbina and Scaramouche. Although *The First Meeting* is part of this series, the subject may derive from the meeting of Adam and Eve in the Garden of Eden, in Gen. 2:22–24:

> And the rib, which the Lord God had taken from man, made he a woman, and brought her unto the man. There-

fore shall a man leave his father and his mother, and shall cleave unto his wife: and they shall be one flesh. And they were both naked, the man and his wife, and were not ashamed.

Where the heads should be are clusters of flowers and vines. The anatomy of the woman is subjected to a completely illogical structure, with the breasts and buttocks on the same vertical plane. In this work and the other small bronzes of 1971 included in the exhibition, Lipchitz has given free reign to his imaginative powers, creating poetic images of great originality. These small bronzes excited him very much, he said, "in the move from the unconscious or automatic gesture to the conscious sculptural structure and back to a final unconscious realization."[209] In these works, Lipchitz has achieved a genuine late style that, like Picasso's late work, is characterized by a total freedom of expression and lack of stylistic constraints.

128 *The Death of a Harlequin (La Mort d'Harlequin)* 1971
Bronze 1/7
L. 17¾"/45.0 cm
The Estate of Jacques Lipchitz represented by
Marlborough International Fine Art AG.

This was the final sculpture in the commedia del l'arte series. In his autobiography, all Lipchitz says about this sculpture (referred to as *The Death of Pierrot*, but presumably the same work) is that it was "a theme that has a very personal significance for me."[210] His 1927 *Pierrot Escapes* (no. 52) had signified for the sculptor an escape from the discipline of Cubism. In this late work, the splayed-out, contorted body of the harlequin, a nail through his heart, is supported by a kneeling figure with a musical instrument in the right hand. At the right of the composition a small, rather plump woman kneels and leans forward. The harlequin, one of the central subjects of Lipchitz's art, is dying.

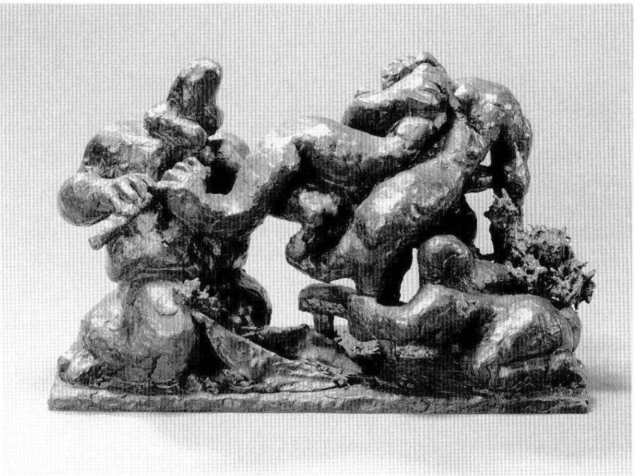

129 *Homage to Arcimboldo* 1971
Bronze (unique)
H. 21½"/54.6 cm
The Estate of Jacques Lipchitz represented by
Marlborough International Fine Art AG.

In discussing the way in which he incorporated natural forms – actual flowers or bones – in his 1958 series *À la limite du possible*, Lipchitz mentioned the name of the sixteenth-century Milanese painter Giuseppe Arcimboldo (1527–1593). Arcimboldo, whose fantastic heads were composed of fragments of landscape, fruit, vegetables and flowers, was claimed as a precursor by the Surrealists. This work is a very free evocation of Arcimboldo's heads, no doubt incorporating actual flowers, fruit and vegetables. As in *The Beautiful One* 1962 (no. 115), the head is mounted on a basket. Once again, Lipchitz has taken the technical skill of bronze casting to the limit of the possible.

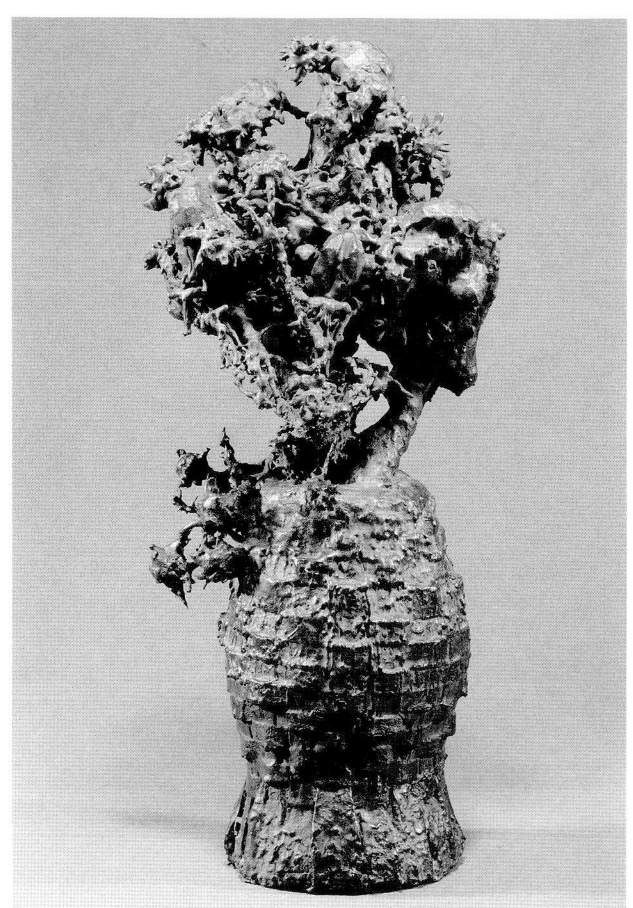

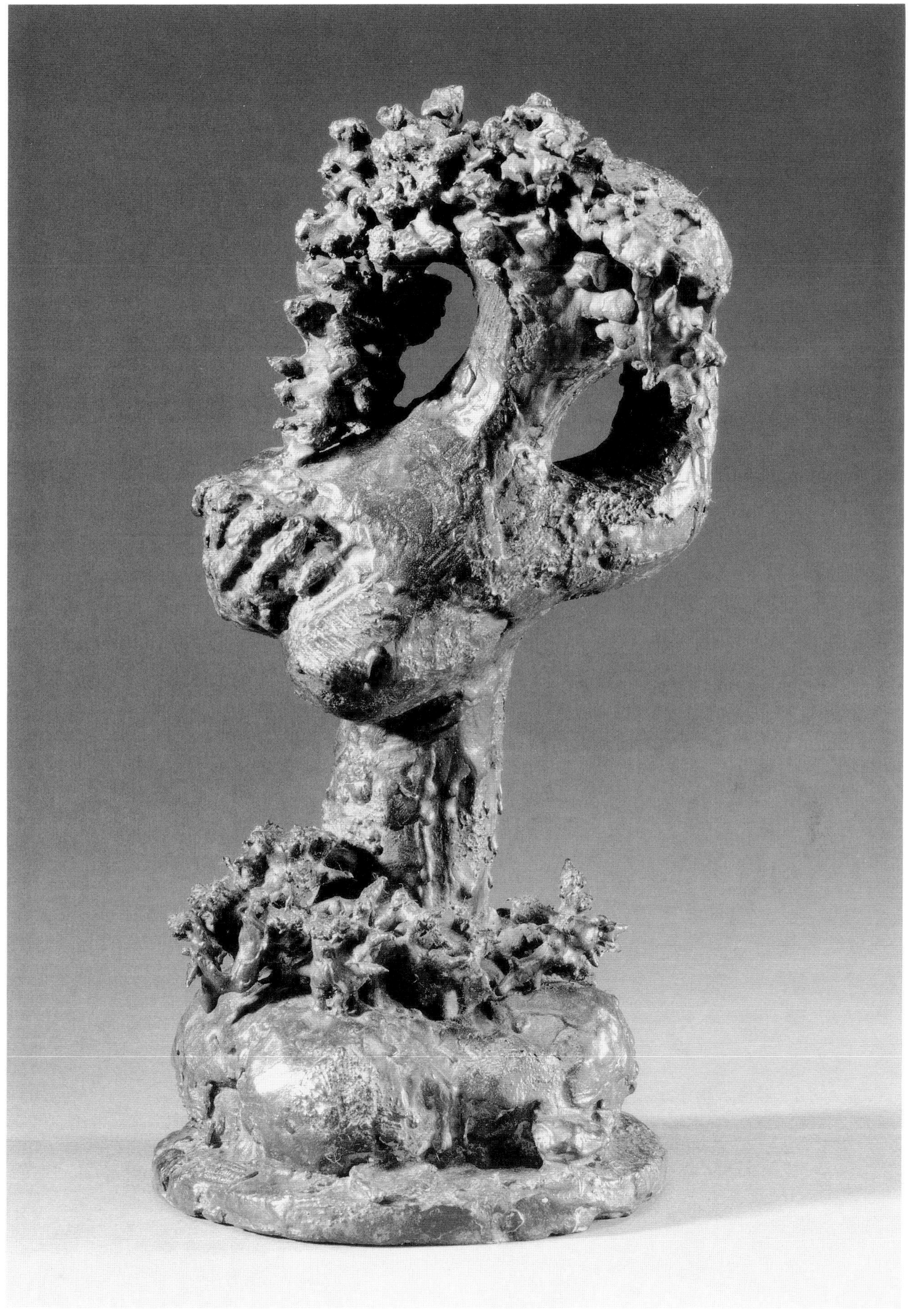

130

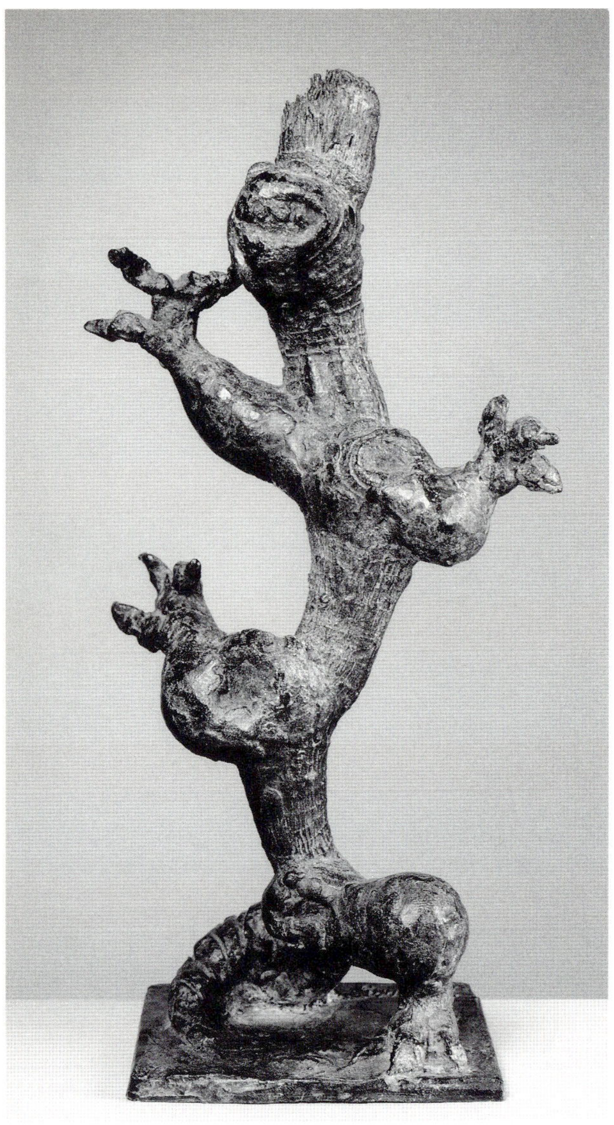

131

130 *The Beautiful One (La Belle)* 1971
Bronze (unique)
H. 12¼″/31.1 cm
The Estate of Jacques Lipchitz represented by
Marlborough International Fine Art AG.

At least eight closely related variations on this subject are among Lipchitz's last series of works entitled, *À partir de*. Each of the bronzes is a unique cast. A tubular torso rises from the base of the sculpture, suggestive of a mound of earth. The woman's right hand holds one of her full breasts; the left arm is raised with the hand placed against the side of the head. Devoid of facial features, the head and hair appear to be enveloped by a garland of flowers. In *The Beautiful One*, Lipchitz has created an image of eroticism and fecundity in which woman is an extension of the natural world. She seems to belong to an idyllic vision like that of Andrew Marvell's poem "Thoughts in a Garden":

> Ripe apples drop about my head;
> The luscious clusters of the vine
> Upon my mouth do crush their wine;
> The nectarine and curious peach
> Into my hands themselves do reach;
> Stumbling on melons, as I pass,
> Ensnared with flowers, I fall on grass.[211]

131 *La danse érotique* 1971
Bronze (unique)
H. 17¾″/45.0 cm
The Estate of Jacques Lipchitz represented by
Marlborough International Fine Art AG.

The shape and texture of this work suggest that Lipchitz based it on a piece of gnarled wood that reminded him of a dancing figure. If so, he no doubt made a cast in plaster and possibly added a few rudimentary anatomical details, such as the truncated fingers and toes.

132 *The Last Embrace* 1971
Bronze 2/7
L. 48″/122.0 cm
The Estate of Jacques Lipchitz represented by
Marlborough International Fine Art AG.

The titles of *The Death of a Harlequin* (no. 128) and *The Last Embrace* suggest that Lipchitz somehow knew that they would be the final expression of two of the major themes of his art: the harlequin as the symbol of his great Cubist sculptures of 1915–25; the embrace as a vehicle to express the emotionally charged personal, mythological, Biblical and political subjects that dominated his work from the mid 1920s until his death in 1973. In the context of Lipchitz's sculpture, the embrace should be seen as physical encounters capable of expressing such diverse subjects as the mother and child (no. 64), lovers (no. 54), violent contact or struggle (no. 75), rape, even strangulation. Indeed, in Lipchitz's treatment of such themes, the line between love and affection, violence and death is not always clear.

In *The Last Embrace*, two massive figures lock together, in a manner reminiscent of Rodin's tortuous *Les Damnées* 1885–95 (fig. 39). The man, standing, his head thrown back, provides the vertical thrust. The woman lies hori-

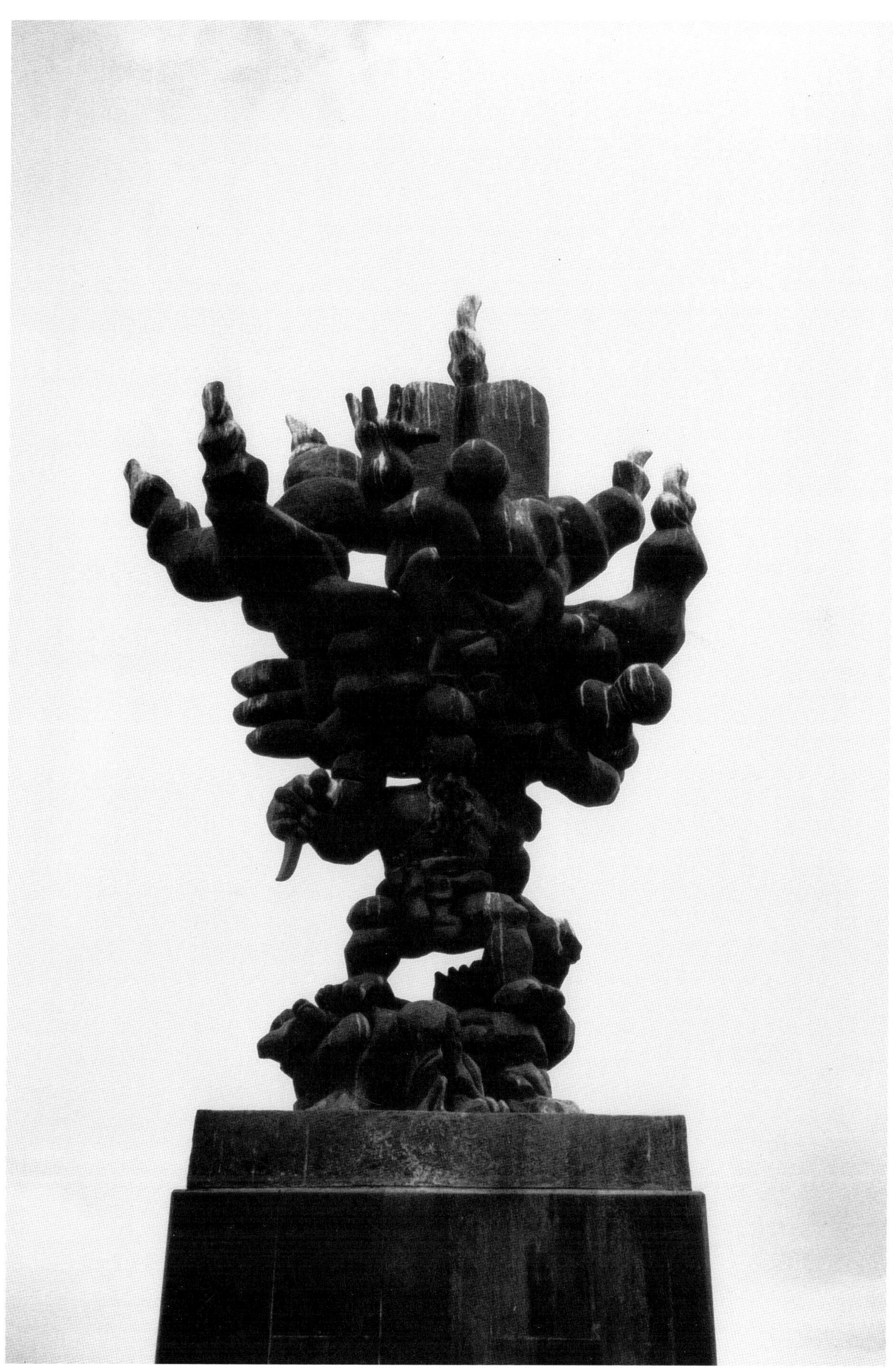

fig. 40 Our Tree of Life, *Mount Scopus, Jerusalem.*

Drawings

■

All the drawings have been lent by
The Estate of Jacques Lipchitz represented by Marlborough
International Fine Art AG.

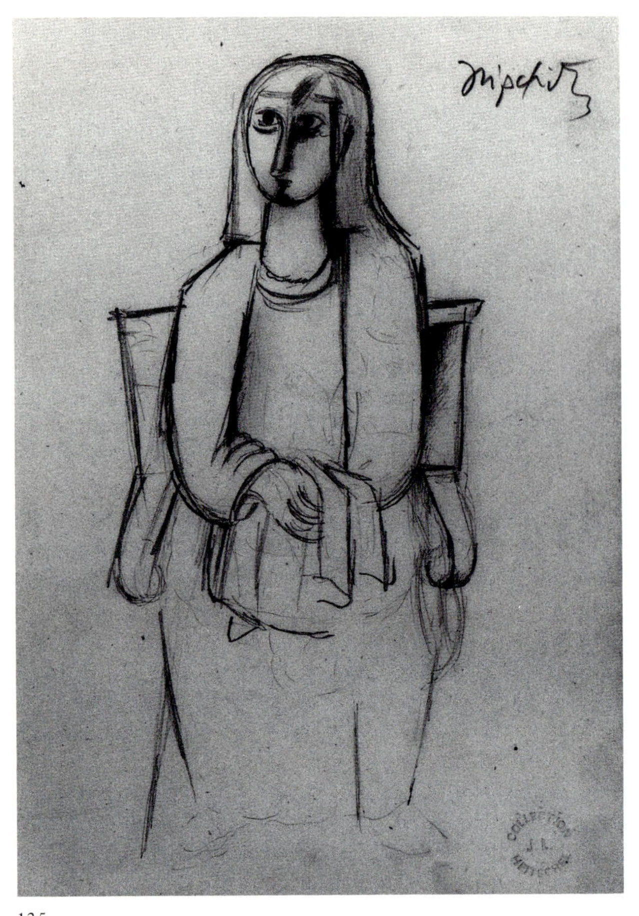

135

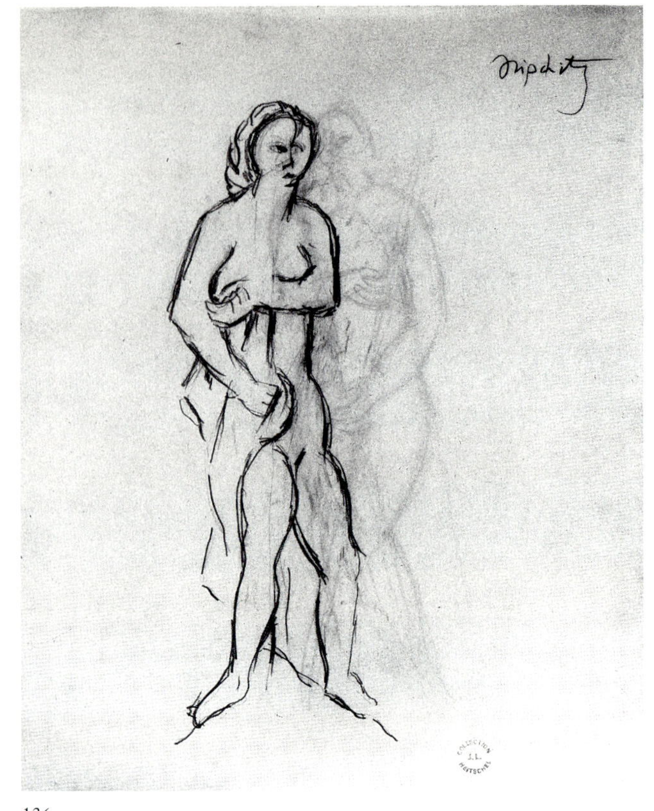

136

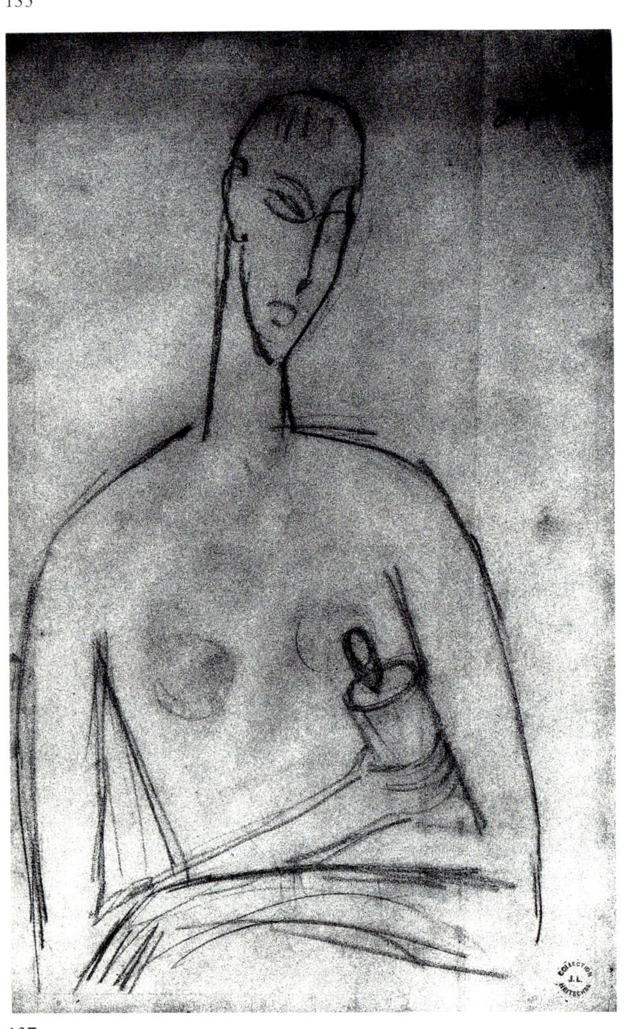
137

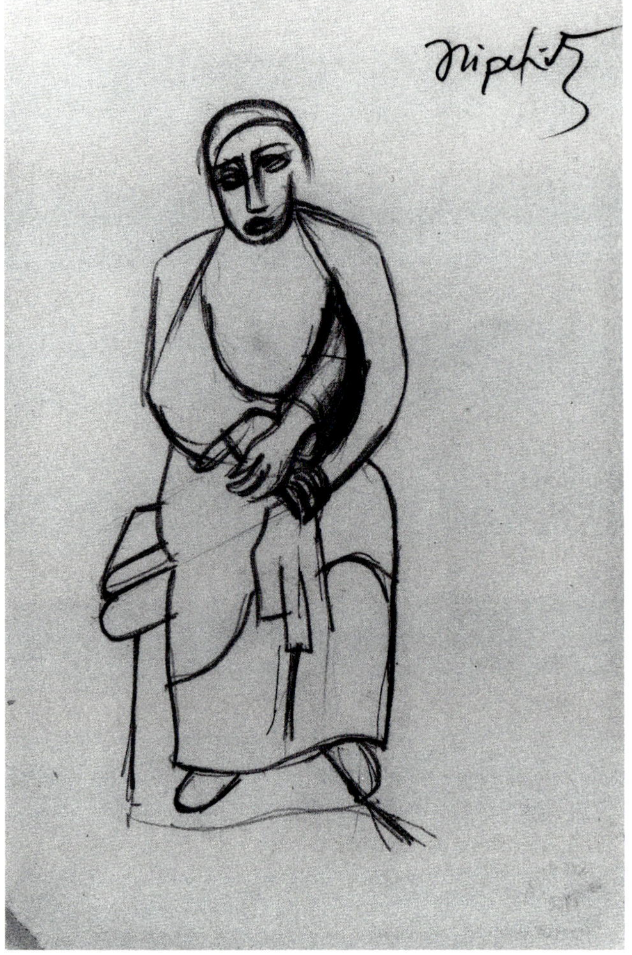

138

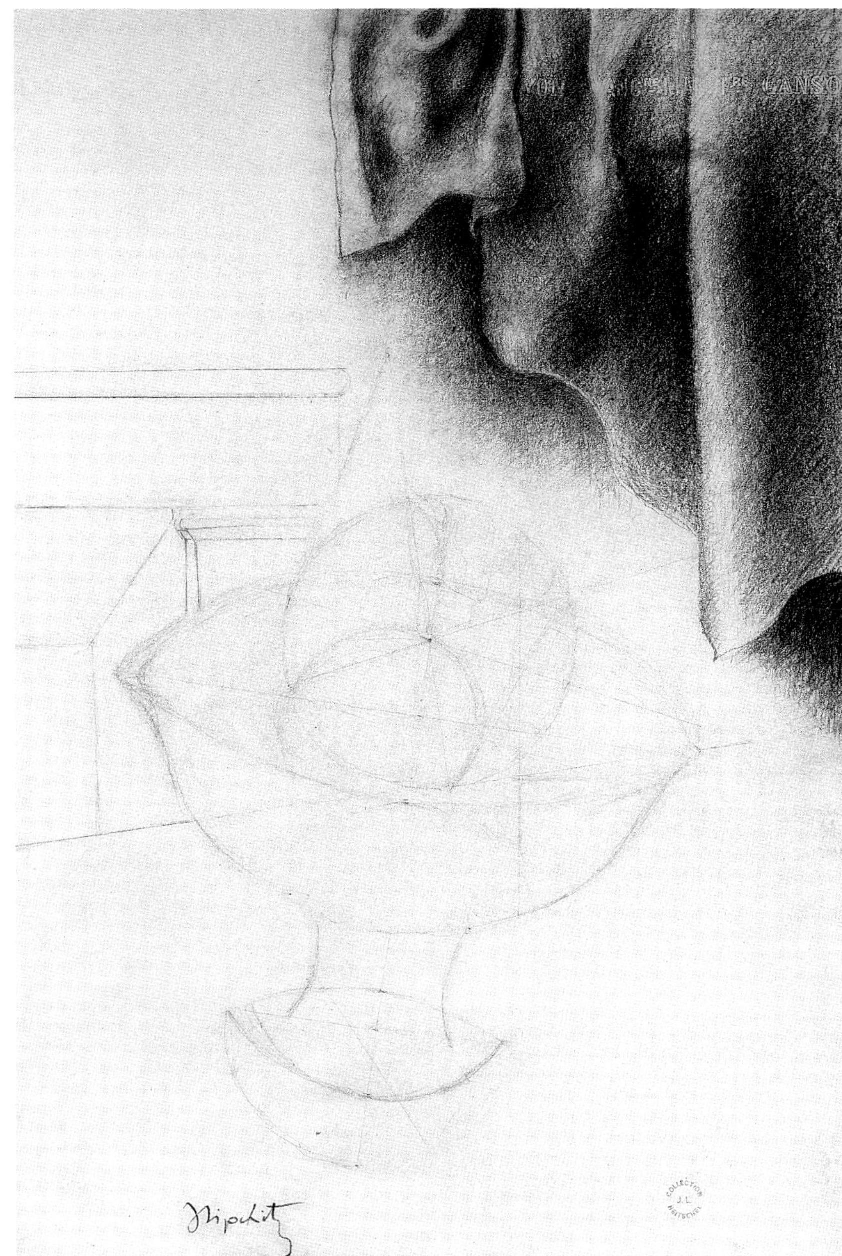

139

135
Young Girl Seated 1912
Graphite
7⅝ x 5¼"/19.4 x 13.5 cm
Signed upper right: Lipchitz

136
Bather 1912–13
Graphite
13¼ x 10¾"/33.7 x 27.2 cm
Signed upper right: Lipchitz

137
Seated Personage 1913
Graphite
16⅝ x 10⅜"/42.3 x 26.2 cm
Signed upper right: Lipchitz

138
Bather (Seated Personage) 1913
Graphite
7 x 4½"/17.9 x 11.4 cm
Signed upper right: Lipchitz

139
Study of Drapery 1914
Graphite and charcoal
19⅜ x 12⅝"/49.3 x 32.1 cm
Signed lower left: Lipchitz

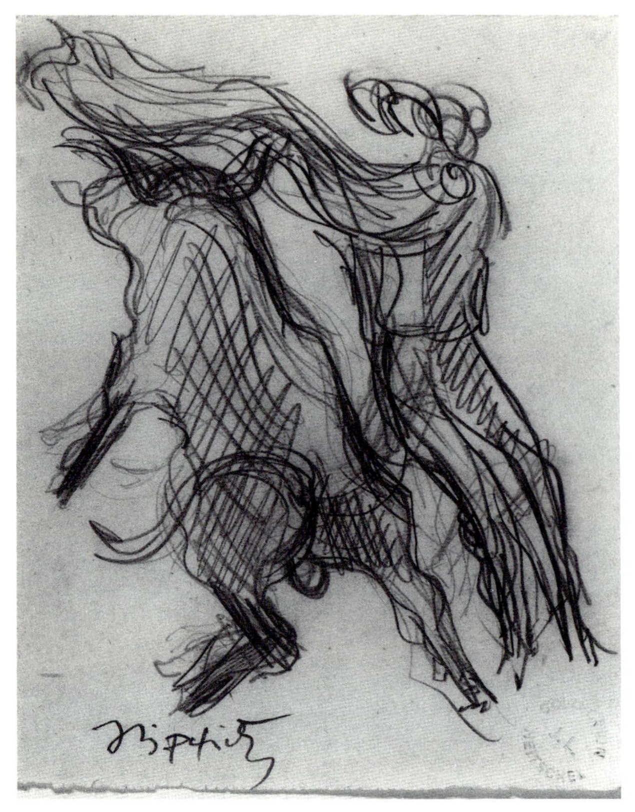

140

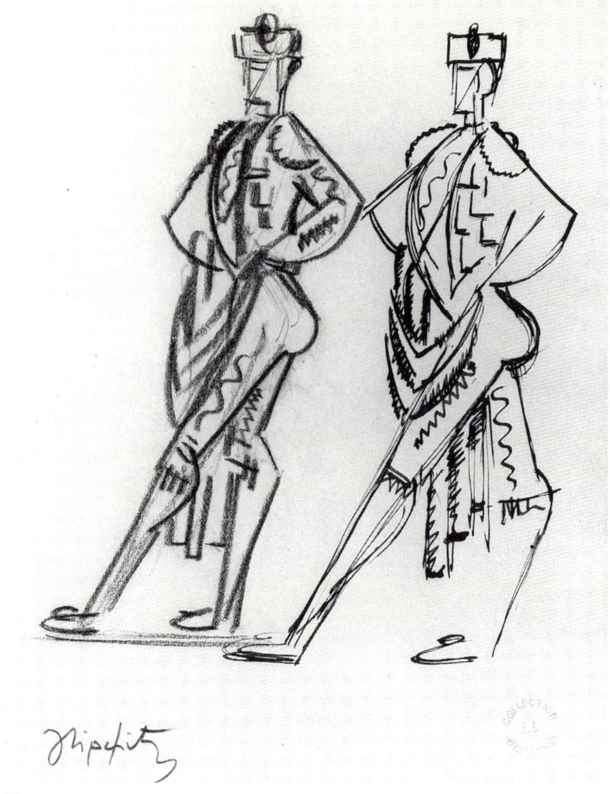

141

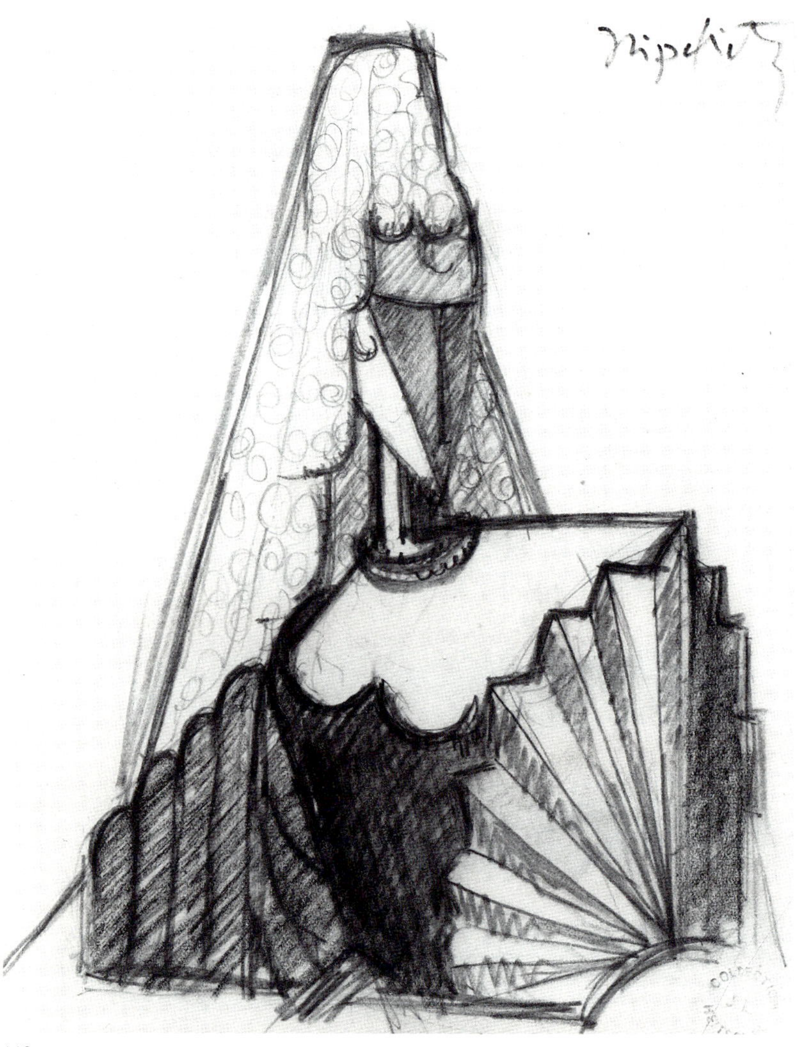

142

140
La Corrida 1914
Graphite
5¼ x 4⅛″/13.4 x 10.5 cm
Signed lower left: Lipchitz

141
Studies for "Toreador" (The Matador)
1914
Charcoal and ink
8 x 6″/20.3 x 15.2 cm
Signed lower left: Lipchitz

142
Spanish Woman with Fan 1914
Graphite and coloured pencils
8 x 6″/20.4 x 15.8 cm
Signed upper right: Lipchitz

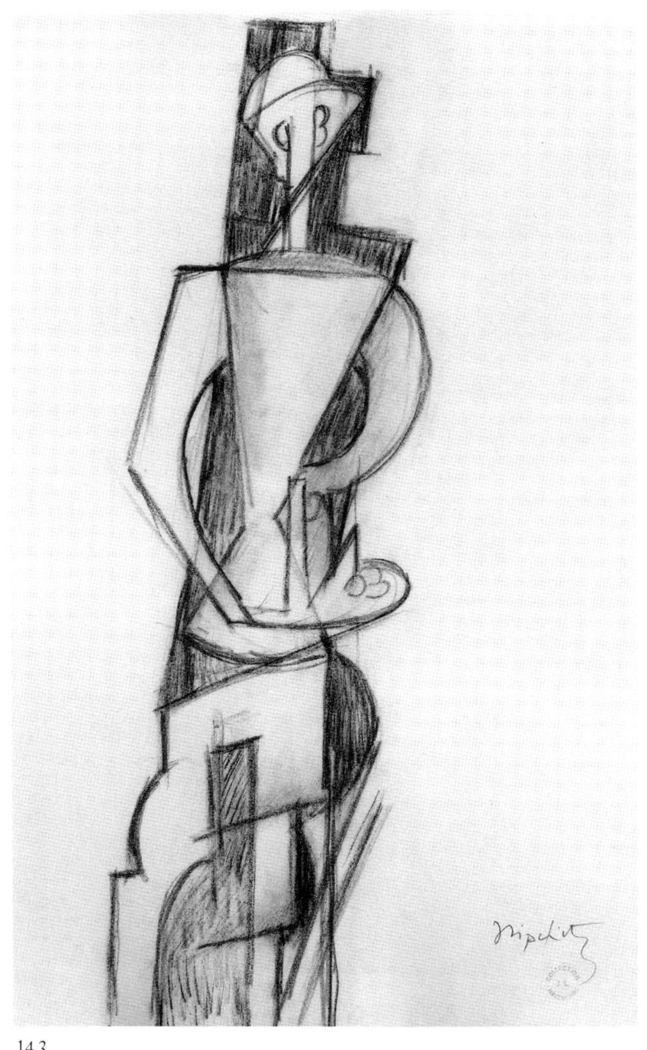

143

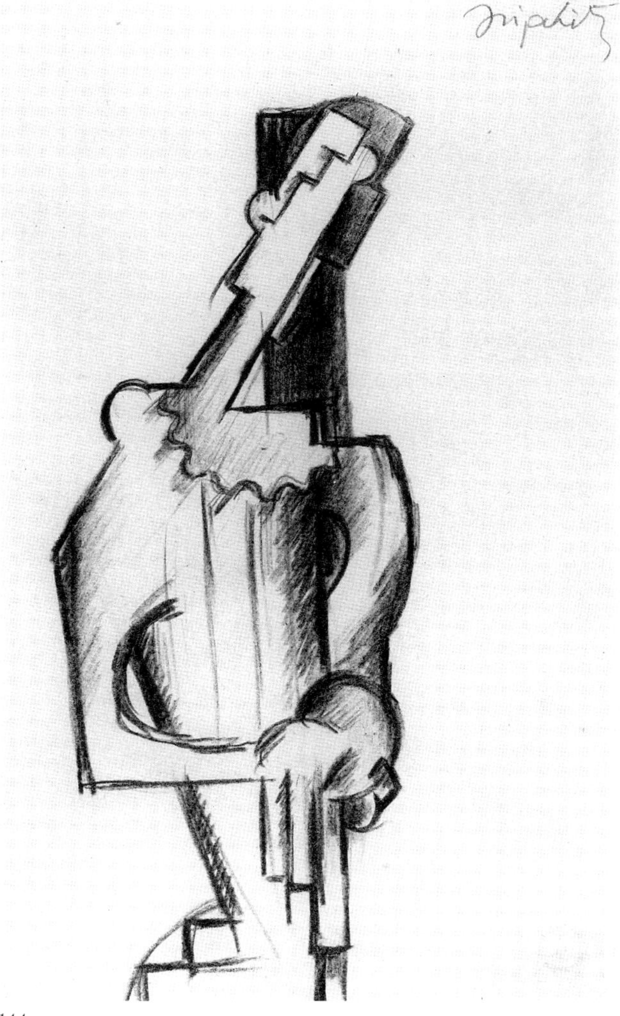

144

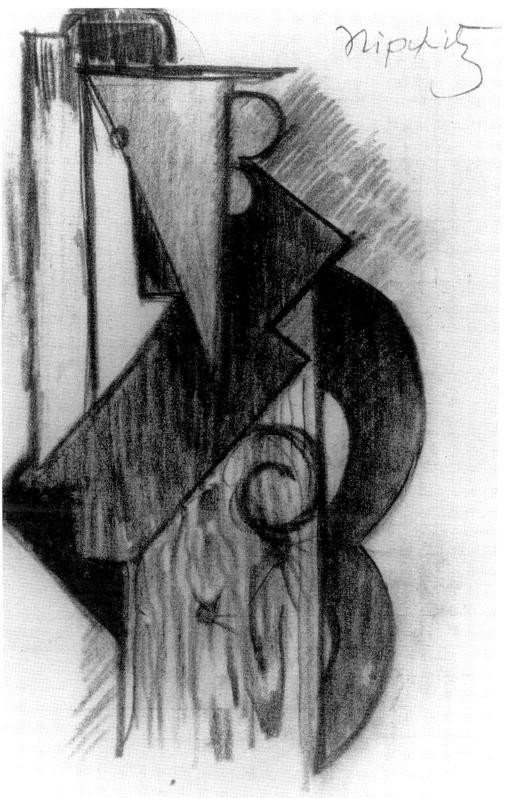

145

143
The Waitress 1914
Charcoal and chalk
16⅞ x 10⅜″/42.9 x 26.4 cm
Signed lower right: Lipchitz

144
Spanish Servant Girl 1915
Blue pencil
11⅝ x 7″/29.6 x 18.0 cm
Signed upper right: Lipchitz

145
Study for Sculpture 1915
Black chalk and coloured pencil
8⅜ x 5¼″/21.2 x 13.4 cm
Signed upper right: Lipchitz

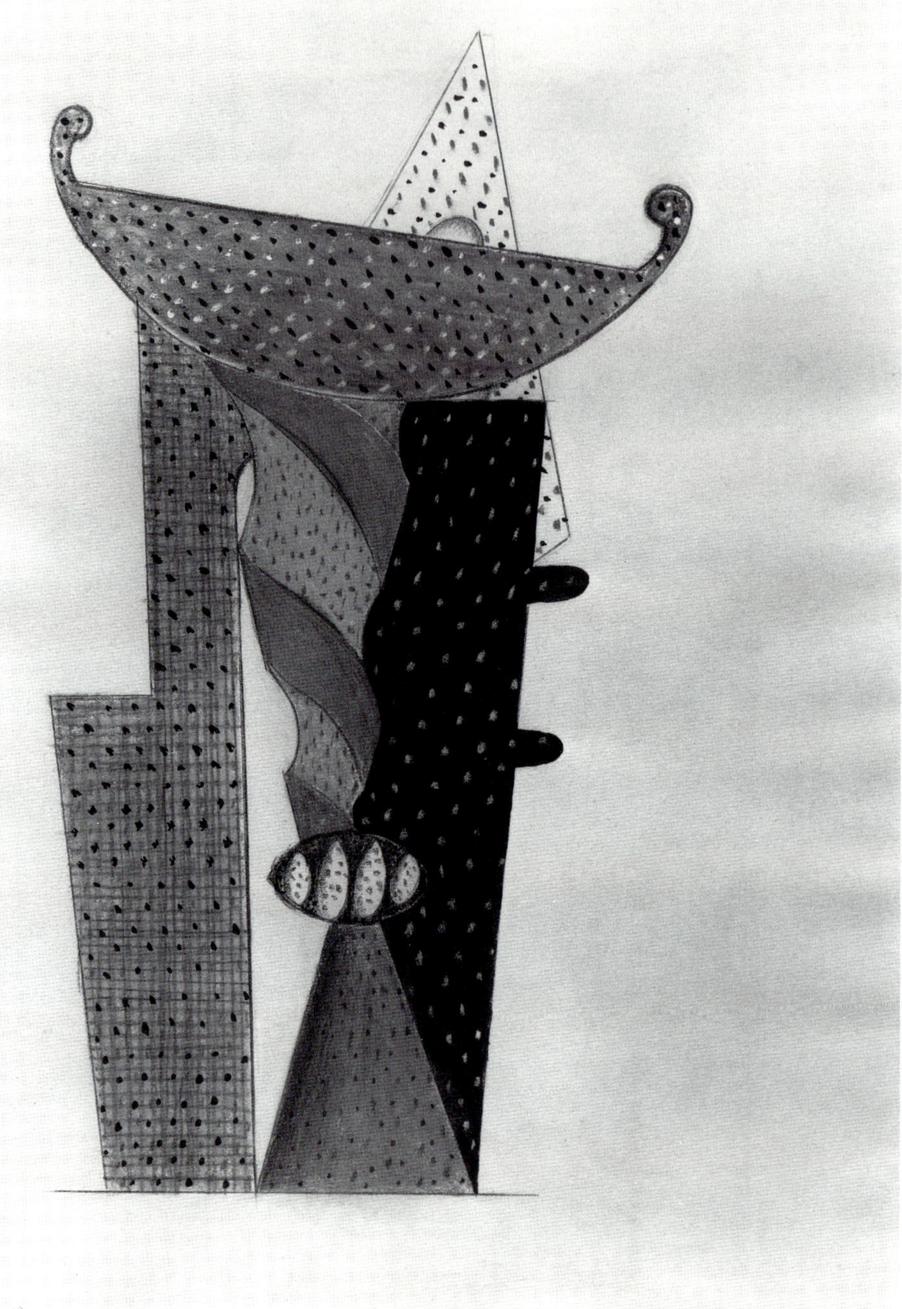

146
Study for Head 1915
Ink, graphite, charcoal and chalks
19¼ x 12⅝″/48.9 x 32.0 cm
Signed upper left: Lipchitz

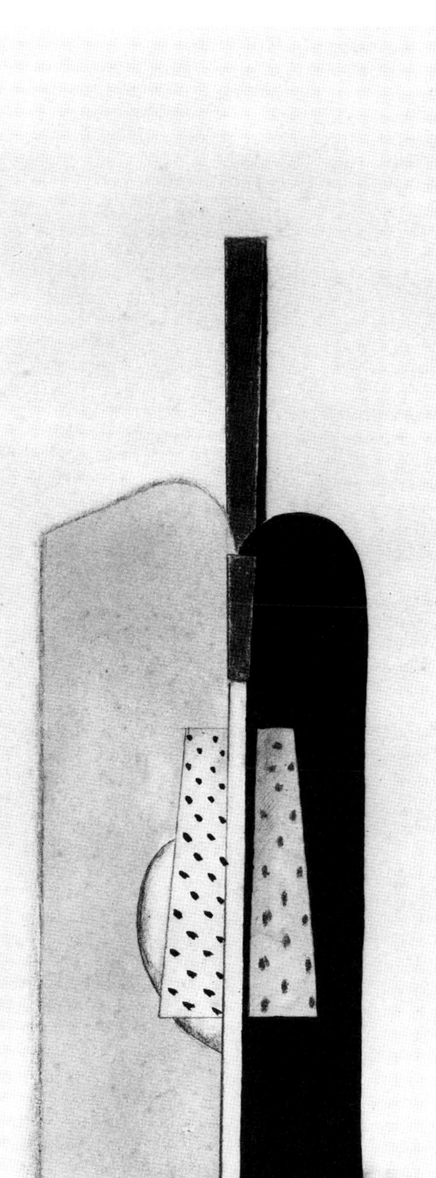

147
Head 1915
Ink and chalks
19½ x 12⅝″/49.6 x 32.1 cm
Signed upper right: Lipchitz

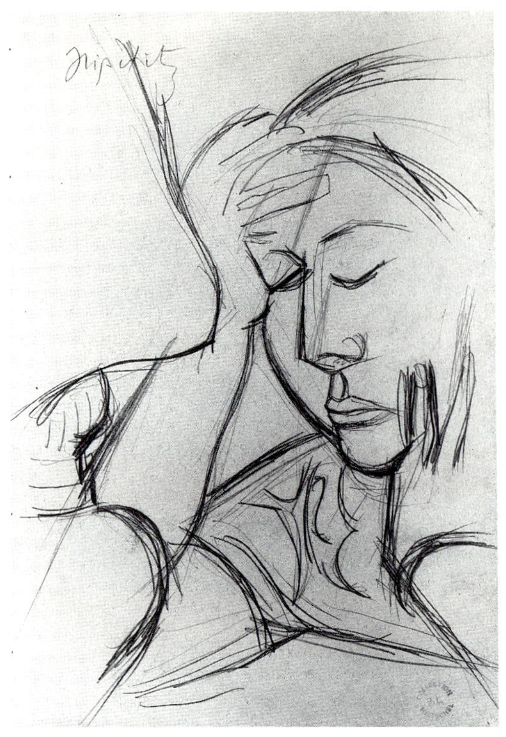

148

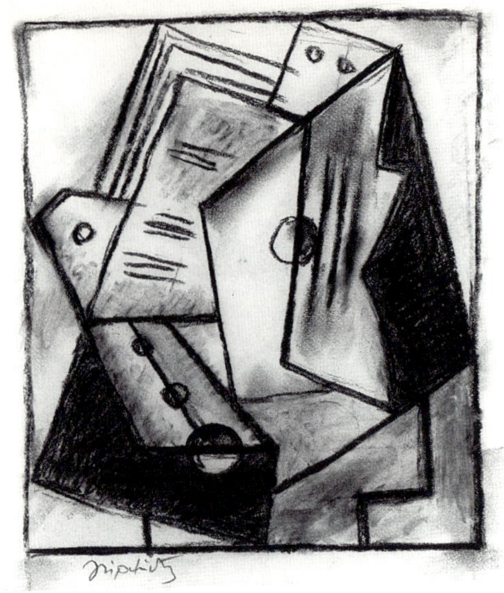

150

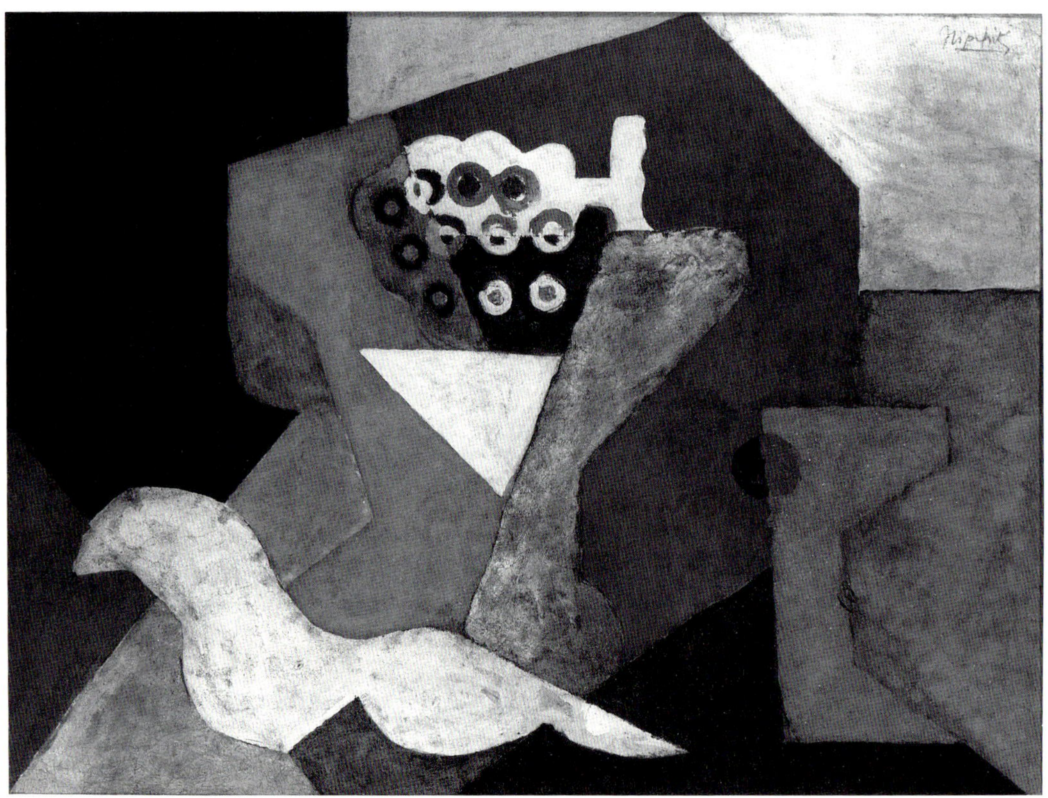

149

148
Portrait c.1915–16
Graphite
11⅛ x 7¾"/28.3 x 19.7 cm
Signed upper left: Lipchitz

149
Fruit Dish with Grapes 1918
Oil and sand on board
14¼ x 18⅛"/36.1 x 46.1 cm
Signed upper right: Lipchitz

150
Study for a Relief 1918
Charcoal
12 x 10½"/30.3 x 26.7 cm
Signed lower left: Lipchitz

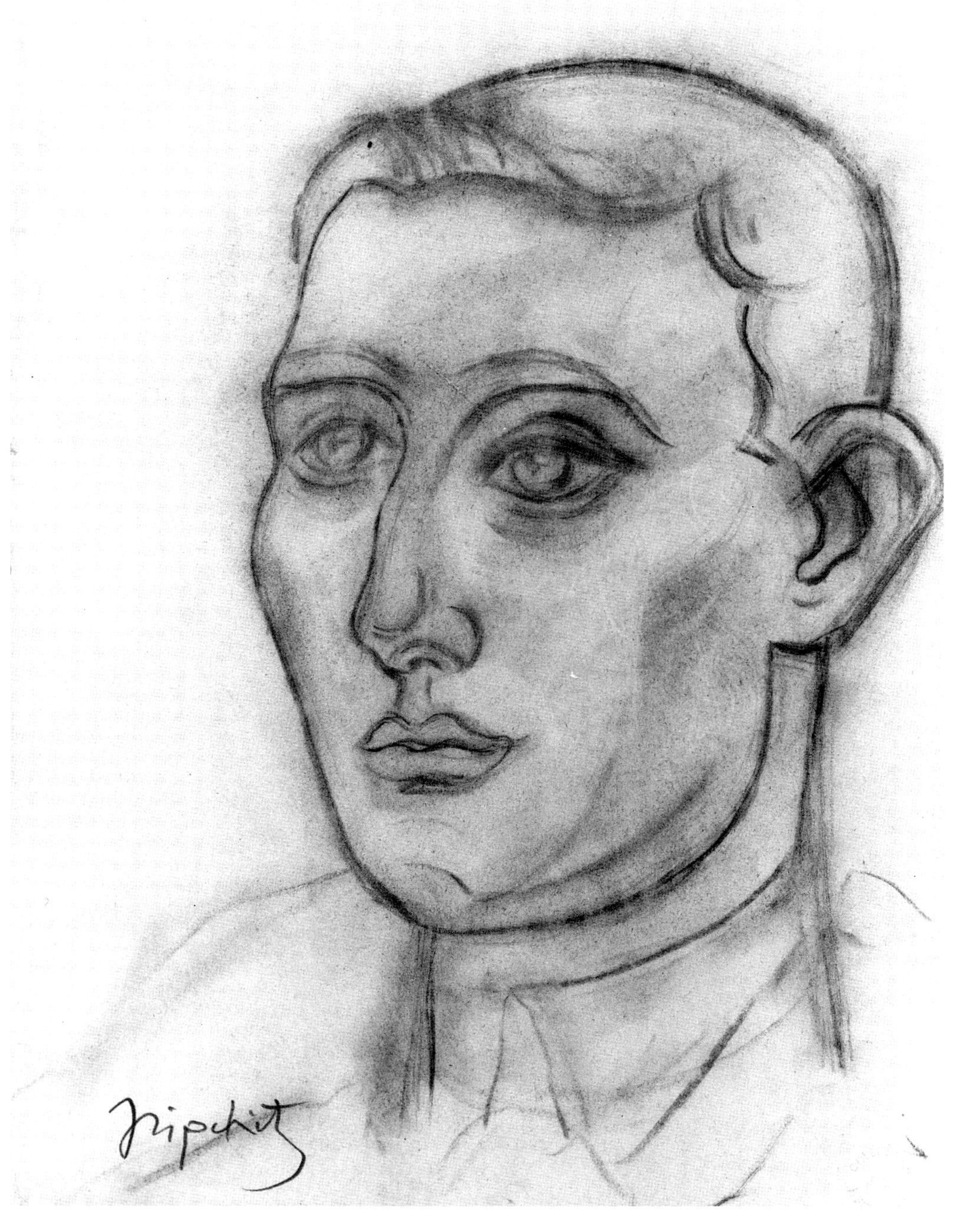

151
Study for "Portrait of Raymond Radiquet"
1920
Charcoal
10½ x 8″/26.6 x 20.5 cm
Signed lower left: Lipchitz

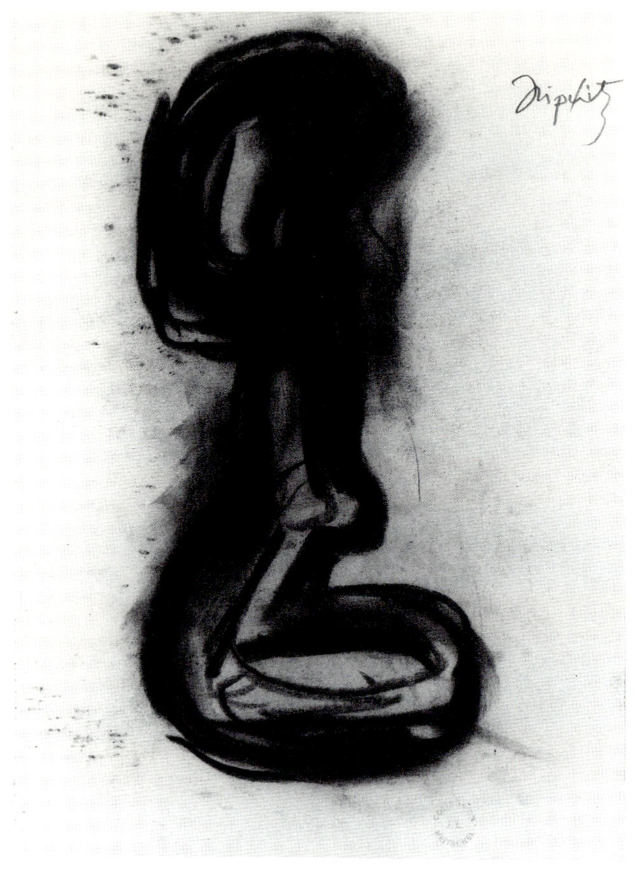

152

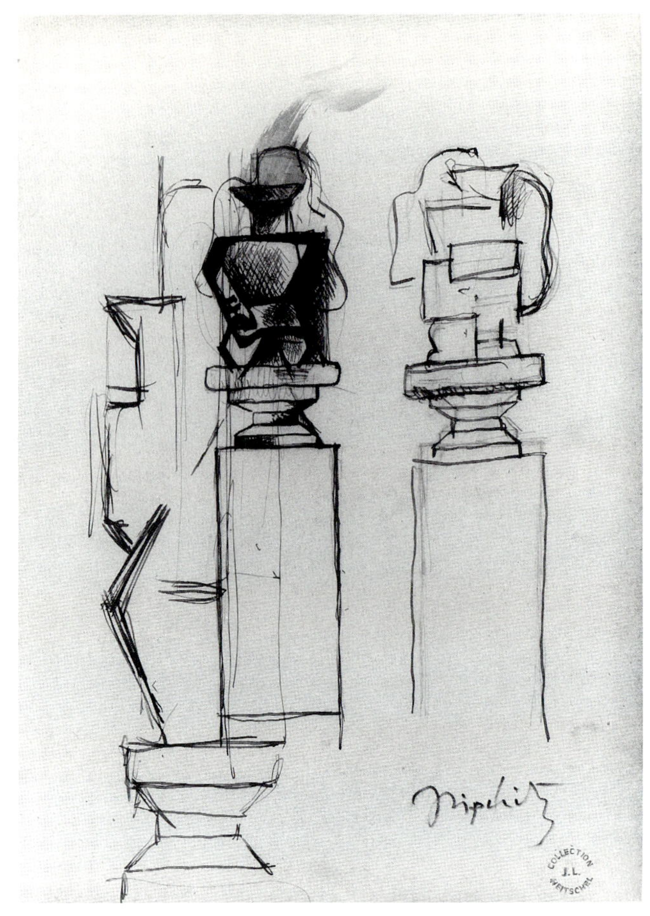

153

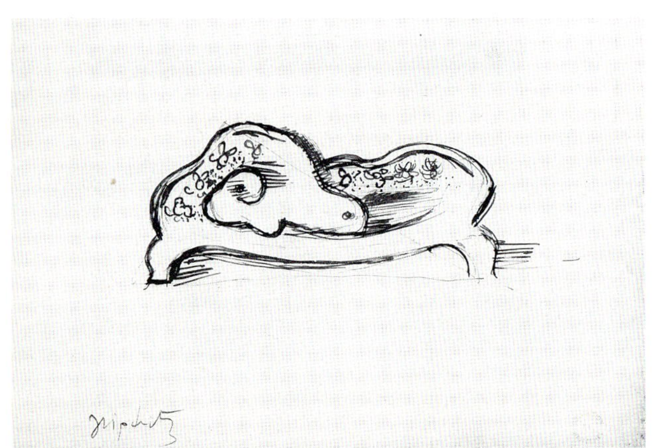

154

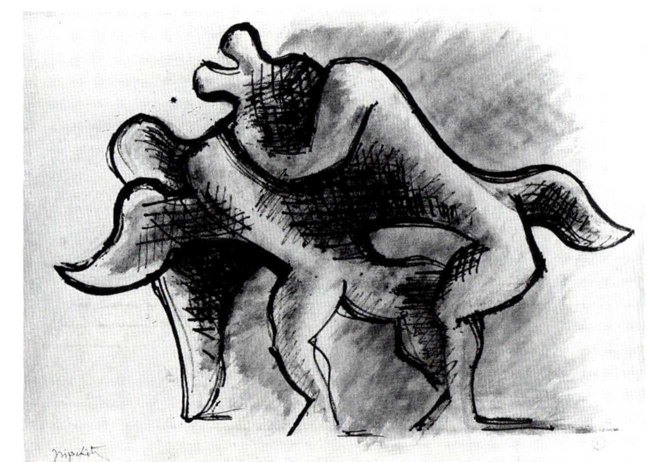

155

152
Kneeling Figure 1920
Charcoal
10⅞ x 7¾″/27.6 x 19.8 cm
Signed upper right: Lipchitz

154
Study for an Andiron 1921
Ink
7¾ x 11⅛″/19.6 x 28.3 cm
Signed lower left: Lipchitz

153
Study 1920
Ink and graphite
11⅛ x 7⅝″/28.4 x 19.5 cm
Signed lower right: Lipchitz

155
Study for Jacob and the Angel 1931
Ink and sepia wash
18¾ x 24⅞″/47.7 x 63.2 cm
Signed lower left: Lipchitz

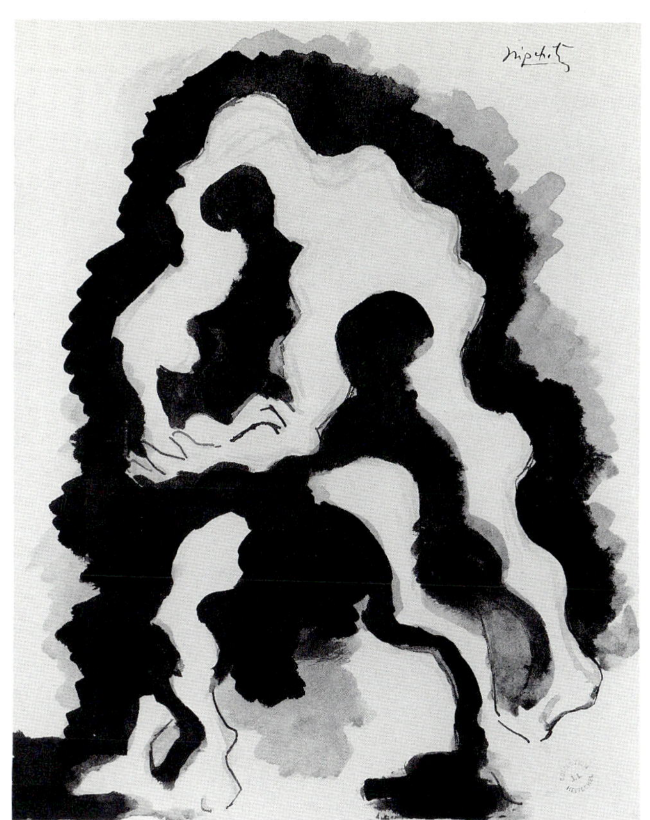

156
Couple 1933
Ink and watercolour
13¾ x 10½"/35.0 x 26.9 cm
Signed upper right: Lipchitz

157
Combat (Scène de guerre) 1936
Blue ink
7⅛ x 8¼"/18.1 x 21.0 cm
Signed upper right: Lipchitz

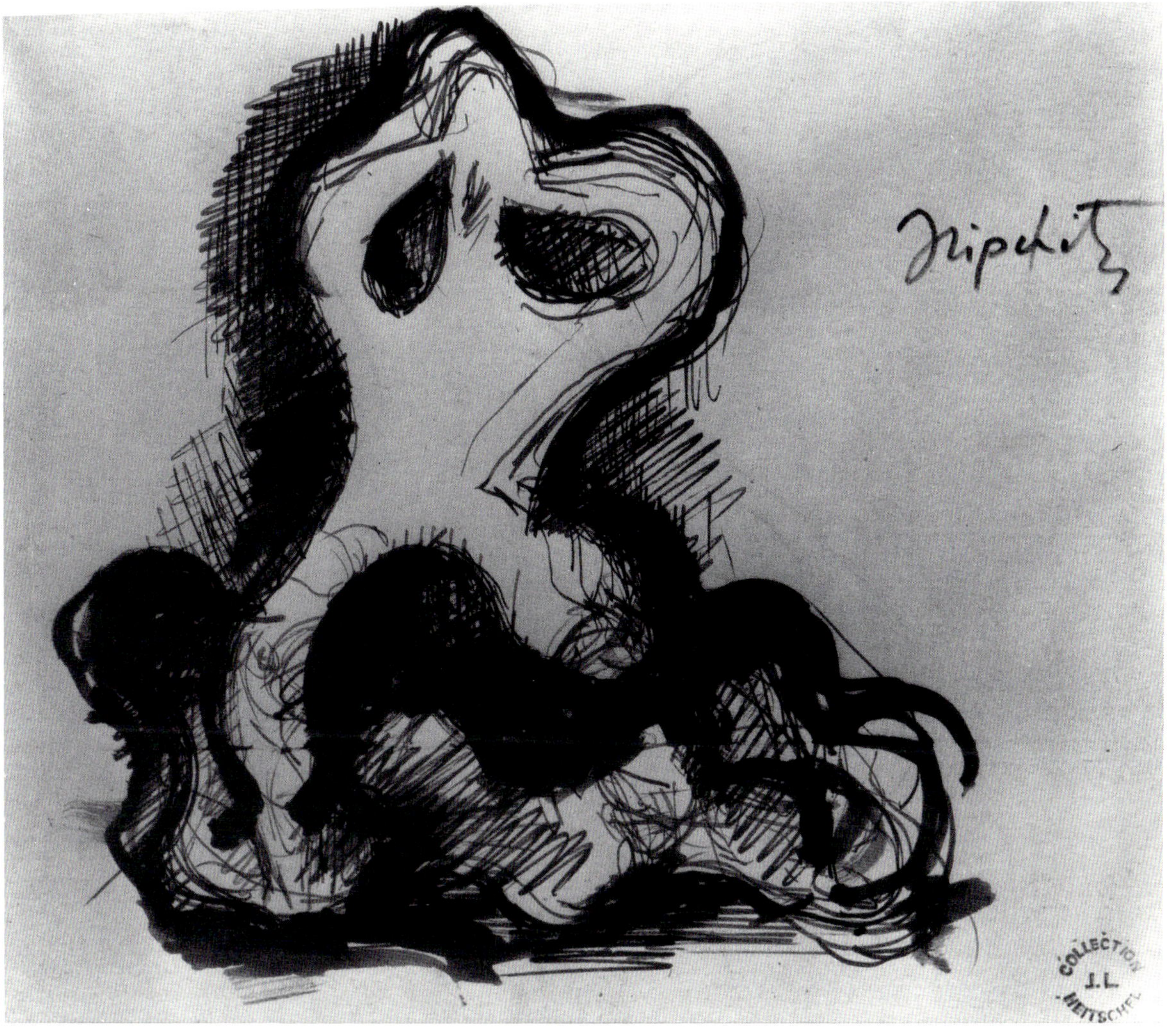

157

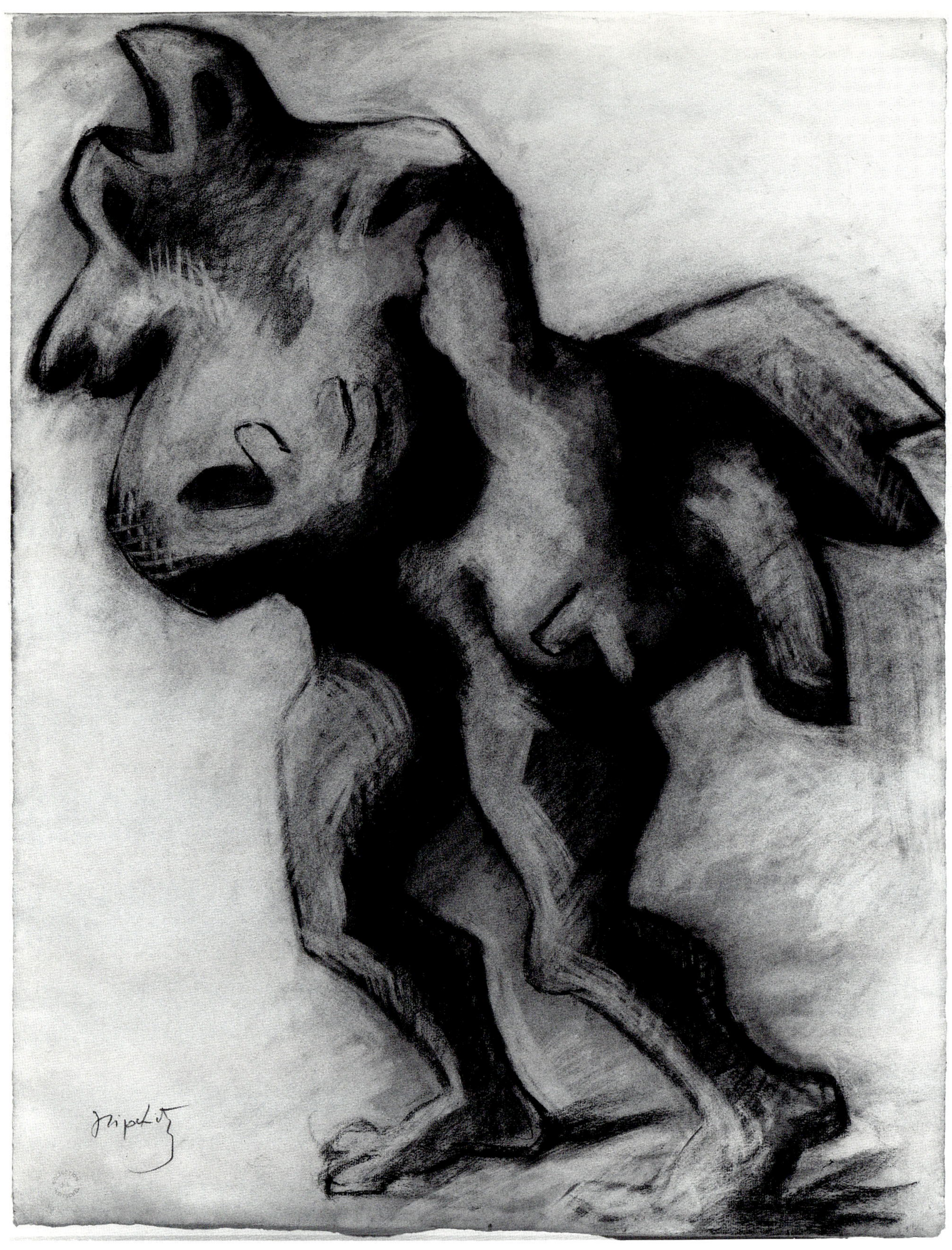

158
Study for Sculpture 1938
Charcoal
24¾ x 19″/63.0 x 48.1 cm
Signed lower left: Lipchitz

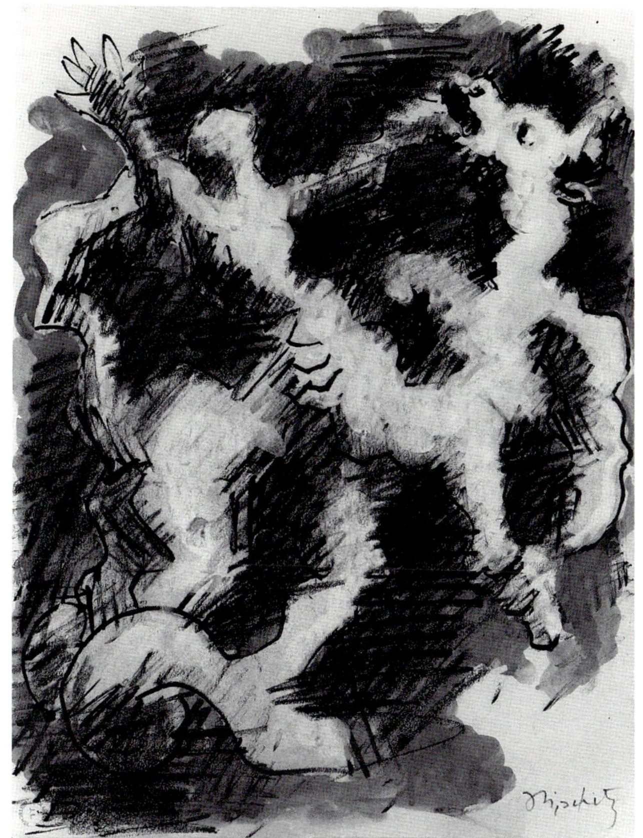

159

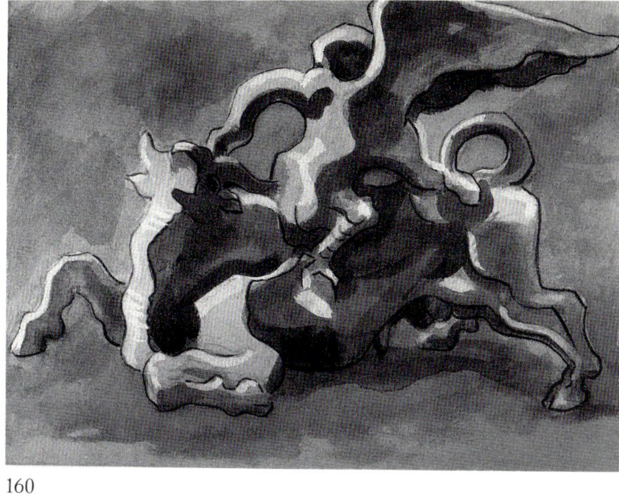

160

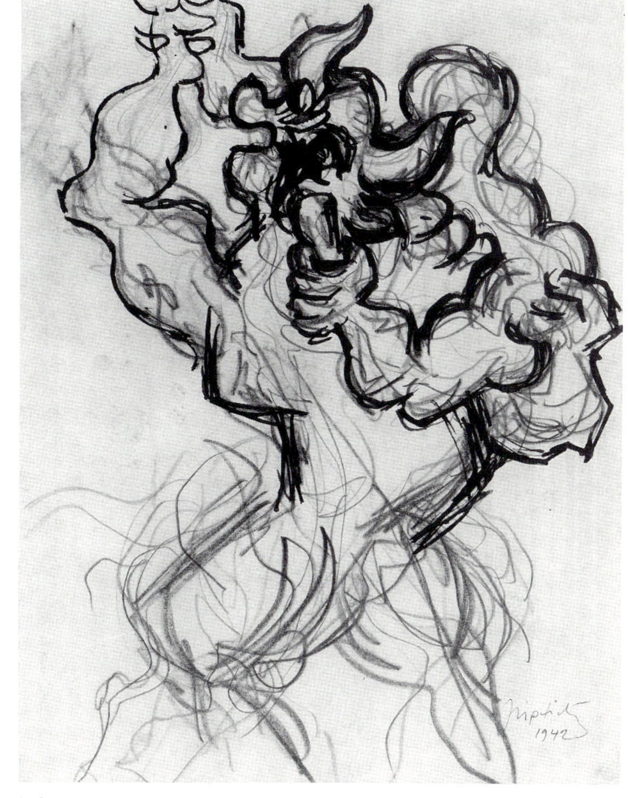

162

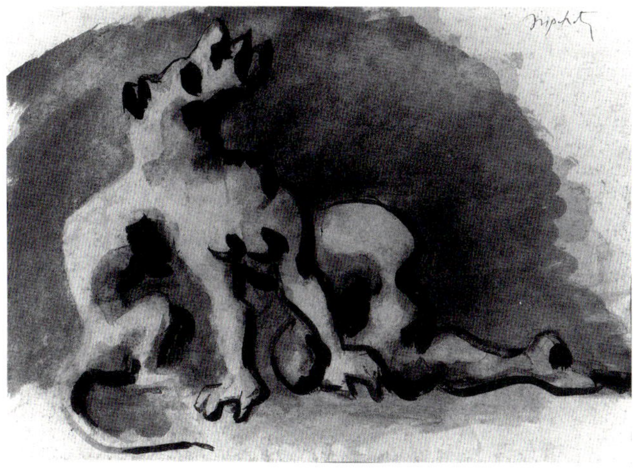

161

159
Study for the Rape of Europa II 1938
Ink, gouache and chalks
17¼ x 12¾"/43.7 x 32.3 cm
Signed lower right: Lipchitz

161
Study for Sculpture 1939
Ink, chalk and watercolour
11¾ x 16⅜"/29.9 x 41.5 cm
Signed upper right: Lipchitz

160
Sketch for Bull and Condor 1938
Black crayon, watercolour and gouache
9½ x 12¼"/24.0 x 31.2 cm
Unsigned

162
Study for Theseus and the Minotaur 1942
Ink and graphite
13¾ x 10½"/35.0 x 26.6 cm
Signed and dated lower right: Lipchitz

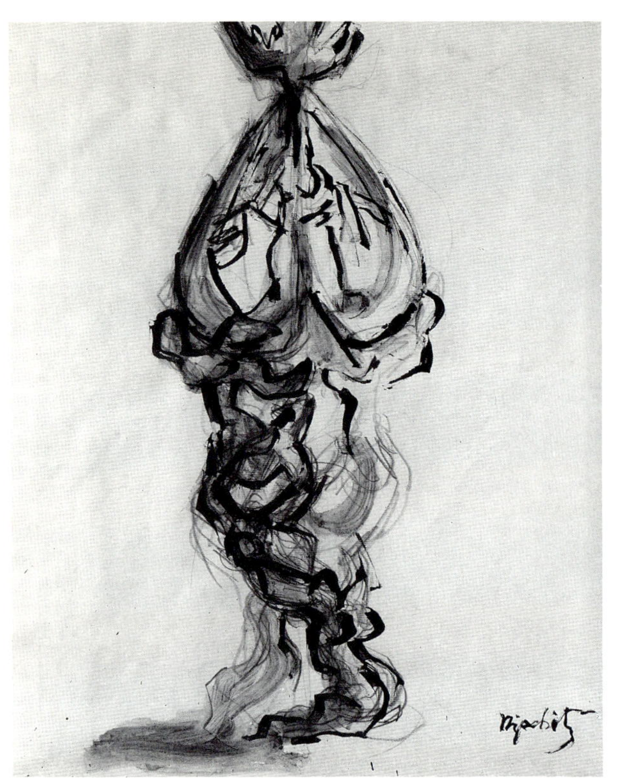

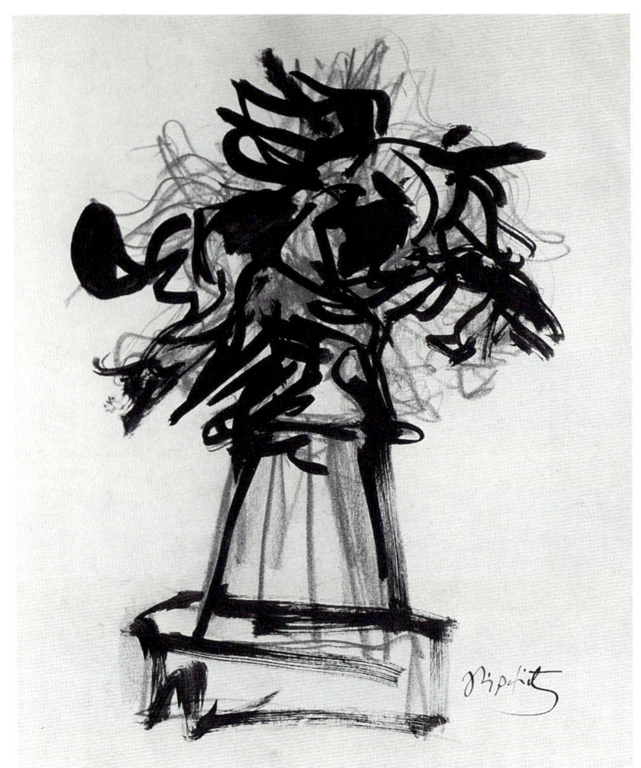

163
Study for Between Heaven and Earth 1958
Ink and graphite
21⅜ x 17"/54.2 x 43.2 cm
Signed lower right: Lipchitz

164
Study for a Monument 1962
Ink and chalk
16⅞ x 13½"/42.9 x 34.5 cm
Signed lower right: Lipchitz

165
Study for Our Tree of Life c.1962
Felt-tipped pen, graphite and chalk
12 x 8⅞"/30.3 x 22.5 cm
Signed lower right: Lipchitz

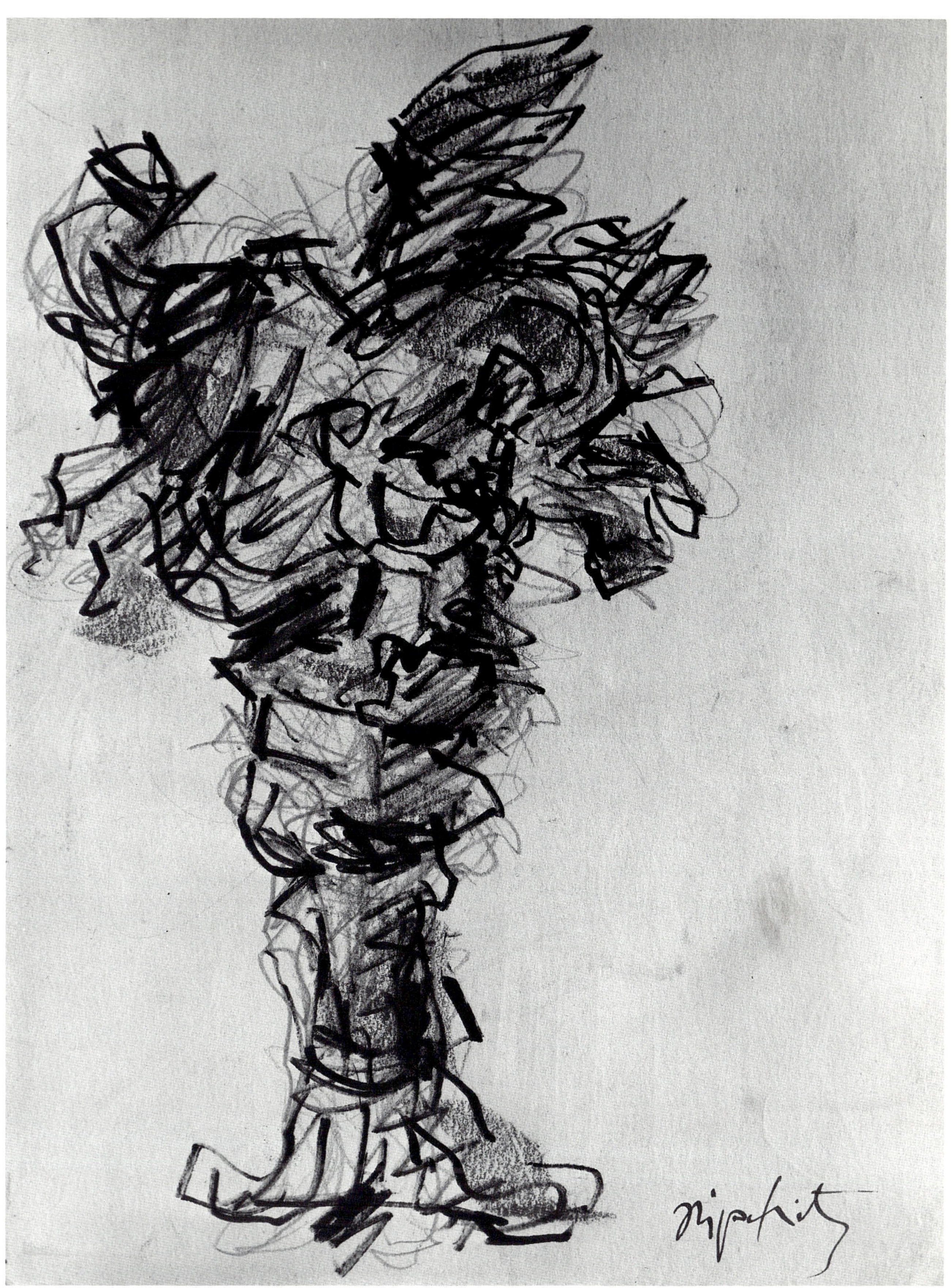

Notes

■

Notes to A Life in Sculpture

1. Clement Greenberg, *Art and Culture: Critical Essays* (Boston: Beacon Press, 1961): 105.
2. *A New Spirit in Painting* (London: Royal Academy of Arts, 1981): 14.
3. Ladislas Segy, *The Meaning of Jacques Lipchitz's Sculptures* (unpublished manuscript): 58–59.
4. Jacques Lipchitz and H. H. Arnason, *My Life in Sculpture* (New York: The Viking Press, 1972): 3.
5. Ibid., 3.
6. Ibid., 7.
7. Deborah A. Stott, *Jacques Lipchitz and Cubism* (New York and London: Garland Publishing, 1978): 10.
8. *My Life*, 8.
9. Arts Council of Great Britain, *Picasso: Sculpture, Ceramics, Graphic Work*, an exhibition held at the Tate Gallery, London, June 9 – August 13, 1967: 10.
10. Ibid., 10.
11. *My Life*, 18.
12. *My Life*: 18–19.
13. Ibid., 24.
14. Ibid., 26.
15. Ibid.
16. John Golding, *Cubism: A History and an Analysis 1907–1914* (London: Faber and Faber Limited, 1968): 87.
17. *My Life*, 32.
18. Ibid., 33.
19. Ibid., 37.
20. Ibid., 33.
21. Ibid., 42.
22. Ibid., 39.
23. Ibid., 41–42.
24. Stott, 48.
25. Ibid., 48–49.
26. Ibid., 49.
27. *My Life*, 50.
28. Ibid., 51.
29. Ibid., 52.
30. Ibid., 59.
31. Ibid., 57.
32. Ibid., 59.
33. Ibid., 67.
34. Ibid.
35. Ibid.
36. Ibid., 78.
37. Ibid., 95.
38. Ibid., 74.
39. Christopher Green, *Cubism and Its Enemies: Modern Movements and Reaction in French Art, 1916–1928* (New Haven and London: Yale University Press, 1987): 23.
40. Ibid., 24.
41. Ibid., 35.
42. *My Life*, 81.
43. Ibid.
44. Ibid.
45. Ibid., 85.
46. Ibid.
47. Ibid., 95.
48. Ibid.
49. Ibid., 93.
50. Greenberg, *Art and Culture*, 107.
51. *My Life*, 85.
52. Greenberg, *Art and Culture*, 107.
53. *My Life*, 85.
54. Ibid., 201.
55. Ibid., 82.
56. Ibid., 90.
57. Ibid.
58. Ibid., 96.
59. Ibid.
60. Ibid., 99.
61. Ibid., 115.
62. Ibid., 109.
63. Ibid.
64. Ibid., 119.
65. Ibid.
66. Ibid., 139.
67. Ibid., 119.
68. Ibid., 132.
69. Ibid.
70. Ibid., 136.
71. David Fraser Jenkins and Derek Pullen, *The Lipchitz Gift: Models for Sculpture* (London: Tate Gallery, 1986): 70.
72. *My Life*, 139.
73. Ibid.
74. Ibid., 60.
75. Ibid., 63.
76. Ibid.
77. Ibid., 140.
78. Ibid., 144.
79. Ibid., 147.
80. Ibid., 143.
81. Ibid., 140.
82. Ibid., 151.
83. John O'Brian, Ed., *Clement Greenberg: The Collected Essays and Criticism.* vol. 2, *Arrogant Prose*, 1945–1949 (Chicago and London: The University of Chicago Press, 1986): 17.
84. *My Life*, 151.
85. Ibid., 148.
86. Ibid., 159.
87. Ibid., 160, 163.
88. Ibid., 164.
89. Ibid., 175.
90. Ibid., 171.
91. Ibid.
92. Ibid.
93. Ibid., 167.
94. Ibid., 179–180.
95. Ibid., 183.
96. Ibid.
97. Ibid., 188.
98. Ibid.
99. Ibid., 188–189.
100. Ibid., 193–194.
101. Ibid., 201.
102. Ibid., 202.
103. Ibid.
104. James Johnson Sweeney, "An Interview with Jacques Lipchitz," *Partisan Review*, New York, vol. 12, no. 1 (Winter 1945): 89.
105. *My Life*, 177.

106. Ibid., 209.
107. Edward F. Fry, "Lipchitz's 'Images of Italy,'" in *Images of Italy: Lipchitz* (New York: Marlborough-Gerson Gallery, 1966): 2.
108. *My Life*, 208.
109. Ibid., 221.
110. Stott, 182.
111. Greenberg, *Art and Culture*, 110.
112. *The Selected Letters of John Keats*, selected and with an introduction by Lionel Trilling (Garden City, NY: Doubleday & Company Inc., 1956): 142.

Notes to Catalogue of the Exhibition

1. Deborah A. Stott, *Jacques Lipchitz and Cubism* (New York and London: Garland Pubishing, 1978): 98–99.
2. Jacques Lipchitz and H. H. Arnason, *My Life in Sculpture* (New York: The Viking Press, 1972): 11.
3. Ibid., 11.
4. Stott, 100.
5. *My Life*, 11.
6. Ibid.
7. Stott, 107.
8. See Stott, 12.
9. *My Life*, 16.
10. Stott, 109.
11. Alan G. Wilkinson, *Gauguin to Moore: Primitivism in Modern Sculpture* (Toronto: Art Gallery of Ontario, 1981): 212, illus. fig. 68.
12. *My Life*, 18–19.
13. Ibid., 19.
14. Ibid., 18–19.
15. Stott, 111.
16. *My Life*, 18.
17. Ibid.
18. Ibid., 19.
19. Stott, 112.
20. *My Life*, 24–25.
21. George Heard Hamilton, *Painting and Sculpture in Europe 1880–1940* (Harmondsworth, Middlesex: Penguin Books Ltd., 1967): 176.
22. Margit Rowell, *The Planar Dimension* (New York: Solomon R. Guggenheim Museum, 1979): 49.
23. See Stott, 114–115.
24. *My Life*, 25.
25. William Rubin, ed., *"Primitivism" in 20th Century Art: Affinity of the Tribal and the Modern* (New York: Museum of Modern Art, 1984), vol. 2, 427, illus., 426.
26. *My Life*, 26.
27. Ibid., 29.
28. Ibid., 32, 33.
29. Ibid., 33.
30. Stott, 18.
31. *My Life*, 33.
32. Ibid., 34.
33. The author is grateful to Barbara and Murray Frum for pointing out the close similarities between Lipchitz's *Head* and Bakota helmet masks.
34. David Fraser Jenkins and Derek Pullen, *The Lipchitz Gift: Models for Sculpture* (London: The Tate Gallery, 1986), 30.
35. *My Life*, 33.
36. Ibid., 34.
37. Ibid., 37.
38. Ibid.
39. See Stott, 237.
40. See Stott, 238.
41. *My Life*, 43, fig. 30.
42. Ibid., 44, fig. 32.
43. Ibid., 46.
44. Stott, 48–49.
45. *My Life*, 46–49.
46. Ibid., 49.
47. Ibid., 50.
48. Ibid., 51.
49. Ibid.
50. Ibid., 55, fig. 38.
51. Ibid., 51.
52. Ibid., 52.
53. Christopher Green, *Cubism and Its Enemies: Modern Movements and Reaction in French Art, 1916–1928* (New Haven and London: Yale University Press, 1987): 32.
54. John Golding, *Cubism: A History and an Analysis 1907–1914* (London: Faber and Faber Limited, 1968): 87.
55. *My Life*, 54.
56. Ibid., 58.
57. Douglas Cooper, *The Cubist Epoch* (London: Phaidon Press, in association with The Los Angeles County Museum of Art, Los Angeles, California, and the Metropolitan Museum of Art, New York, 1971): 259, plate 322.
58. Ibid., 255, plate 314.
59. *My Life*, 58–59.
60. Ibid., 59.
61. Gertrude Stein, *The Autobiography of Alice B. Toklas* (Harmondsworth, Middlesex: Penguin Books, 1966): 219.
62. *My Life*, 60, 63.
63. Ibid., 60.
64. Ibid., 67.
65. Stott, 158.
66. Christopher Green, *Cubism and Its Enemies: Modern Movements and Reaction in French Art, 1916–1928* (New Haven and London: Yale University Press, 1987): 23.
67. *My Life*, 68.
68. Ibid., 67.
69. Ibid., 70.
70. Stott, 160.
71. Rubin, ed., *"Primitivism" in 20th Century Art*, vol. I, 50–51.
72. *My Life*, 70.
73. Howard Greenfeld, *The Devil and Dr. Barnes: Portrait of an American Art Collector* (New York: Viking, 1987): 81.
74. *My Life*, 73.
75. Ibid.

76. Nicole Barbier, *Lipchitz: oeuvres de Jacques Lipchitz (1891–1973)* (Paris: Musée National d'Art Moderne, Centre Georges Pompidou, 1978): 62, illus.
77. Jenkins and Pullen, *The Lipchitz Gift*, 43, illus.
78. A. M. Hammacher, *Lipchitz in Otterlo* (Otterlo, Nederland: Rijksmuseum Kröller-Müller, 1977), illus., n.p.
79. *My Life*, 73.
80. Douglas Cooper and Gary Tinterow, *The Essential Cubism: Braque, Picasso and Their Friends 1907–1920* (London: Tate Gallery, 1983): 395, illus.
81. See also *Guitar, Glass and Water-Bottle*, December 1917, in Douglas Cooper, *Juan Gris: Catalogue raisonné de l'oeuvre peinte établi avec la collaboration de Margaret Potter* (Paris: Berggruen, 1977): plate 243.
82. *My Life*, 74.
83. Ibid., 81.
84. Ibid., 76, fig. 62.
85. Ibid., 81.
86. Ibid.
87. Ibid., 82.
88. Stott, 169.
89. *My Life*, 85.
90. Steven A. Nash and Jörn Merkert, eds., *Naum Gabo: Sixty Years of Constructivism* (Including Catalogue Raisonné of the Constructions and Sculptures) (Munich: Prestel-Verlag, 1985): 200, no. 3.1.
91. Stott, 84.
92. *My Life*, 89–90.
93. Ibid., 90.
94. Ibid.
95. Rubin, ed., *"Primitivism" in 20th Century Art*, vol. 1, 20, illus.
96. Ibid., vol. 2, 427, illus.
97. Stott, 181.
98. *My Life*, 95.
99. Stott, 182.
100. *My Life*, 103.
101. Ibid., 99.
102. Barbier, *Lipchitz*, 73, illus.
103. *My Life*, 100.
104. Ibid., 107.
105. Ibid., 106, fig. 89.
106. Ibid., 107–108.
107. Ezra Pound, *Gaudier-Brzeska: A Memoir* (London: John Lane, The Bodley Head, 1916): 9.
108. *My Life*, 115.
109. Werner Spies, *Picasso Sculpture with a Complete Catalogue* (London: Thames and Hudson, 1972), cat. no. 72, p. 81, illus.
110. Ibid., cat. no. 84, p. 88, illus.
111. *My Life*, 119.
112. Ibid., 109.
113. Ibid.
114. Ziva Amishai-Maisels, "Lipchitz and Picasso: Thematic Interpretations," *Journal of Jewish Art*, vol. 1 (1974): 86.
115. *My Life*, 105, fig. 85.
116. Ibid., 115.
117. Ibid., 111, fig. 94.
118. Ibid., 110.
119. Ibid.
120. Ibid., 120.
121. Ibid., 127.
122. Ibid.
123. Ibid., 128.
124. Martin Weyl, *Jacques Lipchitz Bronze Sketches: The Reuven Lipchitz Collection donated in memory of Abraham and Rachel Lipchitz* (Jerusalem: Israel Museum, 1971), no. 49, illus., n.p.
125. Ibid., no. 48, illus., n.p. (the maquette) and *My Life*, 133, fig. 118 (larger version).
126. *My Life*, 129, fig. 113.
127. Ibid., 127.
128. Ibid., 132.
129. Martin Weyl, *Jacques Lipchitz Bronze Sketches*, nos. 93–96, illus.
130. *My Life*, 132.
131. Ibid., 128.
132. Ibid., 136.
133. Ibid.
134. Ibid., 139.
135. Martin Weyl, *Jacques Lipchitz Bronze Sketches*, no. 117, illus., n.p.
136. *My Life*, 60.
137. Ibid., 63.
138. Ibid., 140.
139. Ibid., 142, fig. 130.
140. Ibid., 143.
141. Ibid., 142, fig. 131a.
142. Ibid., 151.
143. Ibid., 143.
144. Ibid., 148, 151. For a fuller discussion of Lipchitz's *Mother and Child II*, see Michael Parke-Taylor, *Jacques Lipchitz: Mother and Child*, an exhibition organized by The Norman Mackenzie Art Gallery, University of Regina, Regina, Saskatchewan, 1983.
145. *My Life*, 140.
146. Ibid., 159.
147. Ibid., 151.
148. Ibid., 151–152.
149. Ibid., 161, fig. 145.
150. Ibid., 160.
151. Ibid., 160, 163.
152. Ibid., 164.
153. Ibid.
154. Ibid., 168.
155. Jenkins and Pullen, *The Lipchitz Gift*, 77, illus.
156. *My Life*, 167.
157. John Rewald, *Degas Sculpture: The Complete Works* (London: Thames and Hudson, 1957): LXXI, plate 83.
158. *My Life*, 179.
159. Ibid., 179–180.
160. Ibid., 183.
161. Ibid., 184.
162. Jenkins and Pullen, *The Lipchitz Gift*, 80–82, illus.
163. *My Life*, 183.
164. Ibid., 180.
165. Ibid.
166. Ibid.
167. Ibid., 183.
168. Ibid., 188.
169. Ibid., 189.
170. Ibid.
171. Ibid., 171.
172. Ibid., 172.
173. Ibid., 170, fig. 155.
174. Ibid., 175.
175. Ibid., 187.
176. Jenkins and Pullen, *The Lipchitz Gift*, 86.
177. Albert E. Elsen, *Origins of Modern Sculpture: Pioneers and Premises* (New York: George Braziller, 1974): 3.

178. *My Life*, 187.

179. Ibid., 193.

180. William S. Rubin, *Dada, Surrealism, and Their Heritage* (New York: Museum of Modern Art, 1968): 64.

181. *My Life*, 194.

182. Ibid., 196.

183. In conversation with the author.

184. *My Life*, 197.

185. Ibid., 197–198.

186. Ibid., 174, figs. 158, 159.

187. Ibid., 197.

188. Ibid., 209.

189. Ibid., 192, fig. 175.

190. Ibid., 209.

191. Ibid.

192. Ibid., 210.

193. Spies, *Picasso Sculpture*, no. 463, 215, illus.

194. *My Life*, 210.

195. Ibid.

196. Ibid., 213.

197. Ibid.

198. Ibid., 214.

199. Ibid., 214, 217.

200. Ibid., 217.

201. Ibid., 215, fig. 195a–195d, and Jenkins and Pullen, *The Lipchitz Gift*, 92, illus.

202. *My Life*, 221.

203. Ibid.

204. Ibid.

205. Ibid., 174, fig. 160.

206. Ibid., 222.

207. Jenkins and Pullen, *The Lipchitz Gift*, 95.

208. *My Life*, 222.

209. Ibid.

210. Ibid.

211. Arthur Quiller-Couch, ed., *The Oxford Book of English Verse 1250–1900* (Oxford: Clarendon Press, 1921): 391.

212. *My Life*, 198.

213. Ibid., 199, fig. 181.

214. Jenkins and Pullen, *The Lipchitz Gift*, 88–89.

215. *A Tribute to Jacques Lipchitz: Lipchitz in America: 1941–1973* (New York: Marlborough Gallery Inc., 1973): 63.

216. Malcolm N. Carter, "The Lipchitz Imbroglio," *ARTNews*, vol. 78, no. 4 (April 1979): 50.

217. Ibid., 50–51.

218. The author is grateful to Michael Parke-Taylor and the Right Reverend G. H. Parke-Taylor for their help with the interpretation of *Our Tree of Life*.

219. *My Life*, 225.

List of Lenders

■

The Estate of Jacques Lipchitz represented by
Marlborough International Fine Art AG

The Baltimore Museum of Art, Baltimore

Albright-Knox Art Gallery, Buffalo

The Cleveland Museum of Art, Cleveland

The Detroit Institute of Arts, Detroit

The Nelson-Atkins Museum of Art, Kansas City, MO

Tate Gallery, London

The Minneapolis Institute of Arts, Minneapolis

The Montreal Museum of Fine Arts, Montreal

Solomon R. Guggenheim Museum, New York

The Jewish Museum, New York

National Gallery of Canada, Ottawa

Philadelphia Museum of Art, Philadelphia

Virginia Museum of Fine Arts, Richmond, VA

San Francisco Museum of Modern Art, San Francisco

Art Gallery of Ontario, Toronto

Hirshhorn Museum and Sculpture Garden,
Smithsonian Institution, Washington, DC

National Gallery of Art, Washington, DC

Kunsthaus, Zürich

Mrs. Andrea Bollt, New York

Walter Carsen, Toronto

Mr. and Mrs. Alejandro Freites, New York

Yulla Lipchitz, New York

Patsy R. and Raymond D. Nasher Collection, Dallas

Joey and Toby Tanenbaum, Toronto

Chronology

■

1891 Chaim Jacob Lipchitz born on August 22, at Druskieniki, Lithuania.

1902–06 Draws and models in clay. Attends commercial school in Bialystok.

1909 With his mother's help, he leaves for Paris, arriving in October.

1909–10 Studies at the École des beaux-arts, attends sculpture classes at the Académie Julian and drawing classes at the Académie Colarossi. Begins collecting tribal sculpture and the art of other cultures.

1912–13 Recalled to Russia for military service. Receives medical discharge. Returns to Paris and moves to Montparnasse, next door to Brancusi. Exhibits *Woman and Gazelles* at the Salon d'Automne. Meets Cubist painters through Diego Rivera; friendships with Max Jacob, Modigliani, Soutine and Picasso.

1913–14 Creates his first proto-Cubist sculptures.

1914 Visits Spain and island of Majorca with Rivera. Creates *Sailor with Guitar* and *Woman with Braid.* Visits the Prado in Madrid, where he admires the paintings of El Greco, Tintoretto and Goya. Returns to Paris in December.

1915 Meets and lives with poet Berthe Kitrosser. Creates first mature Cubist works: *Head* and wood detachable figures.

1916 Modigliani paints portrait of Lipchitz and his wife Berthe, now in the Art Institute of Chicago. Signs contract with dealer Léonce Rosenberg. Becomes close friend of Juan Gris.

1918 Leaves Paris with Berthe when the city is threatened by German bombing. Stays with Gris at Beaulieu-lès-Loches. Creates painted reliefs. Returns to Paris in the autumn.

1920 Executes portraits of Cocteau, Radiguet and Gertrude Stein. First one-man exhibition at Léonce Rosenberg's galerie de l'Effort Moderne, Paris. Subsequently breaks contract with Rosenberg to pursue more independent style. Critic Maurice Raynal publishes monograph on Lipchitz.

1921 Executes portrait of Coco Chanel.

1922 Dr. Albert C. Barnes visits Lipchitz in Paris, commissions him to create five stone reliefs to be installed at his mansion in Merion, Pennsylvania (now the Barnes Foundation) and purchases other sculptures.

1924 Becomes a French citizen.

1925 Moves to Boulogne-sur-Seine into a house designed for him by Le Corbusier. Creates *Pierrot*, the first of the series of "transparent" sculptures, which later impress Picasso and González.

1926–30 Works on the first of many large-scale sculptures, *Figure. La Joie de Vivre* commissioned for the garden of Viscomte Charles de Noailles at Hyères, near Toulon.

1928–29 His father and sister die. Creates *The Cry (The Couple).*

1930 Exhibits 100 works at Jeanne Bucher's galerie de la Renaissance, Paris.

1930–32 Begins to explore Biblical themes: *Return of the Prodigal Son*, *Jacob Struggling with the Angel.*

1935 First important exhibition, in the United States, held at the Brummer Gallery, New York.

1936–37 Creates *Prometheus Strangling the Vulture* for the entrance of the Science Pavilion at the Paris World Fair, where Picasso also shows *Guernica* at the Spanish Pavilion. He is awarded the Gold Medal. Opening of the Lipchitz Room at "Les Maîtres d'aujourd'hui," Petit Palais, Paris.

1940 German occupation of Paris. Lipchitz and his wife flee to Toulouse.

1941 Emigrates to New York.

1942 Begins to exhibit regularly at the Buchholz Gallery.

1946–47 Visits Paris, where he is made Chevalier de la Légion d'Honneur. Exhibits at Galerie Maeght. Père Couturier commissions *Nôtre-Dame de Liesse* for the church of Nôtre-Dame-de-Toute-Grâce at Assy, Haute-Savoie. Berthe remains in France, and they are divorced. Returns alone to New York and moves his home to Hastings-on-Hudson.

1948 Marries Yulla Halberstadt, a sculptor. His first child, Lolya Rachel, is born. Creates *Miracle II* and *Hagar I.*

1952 On January 5, fire in his Manhattan studio on 23rd Street destroys many works. Receives the George D. Widener Memorial Gold Medal from the Pennsylvania Academy of Arts, Philadelphia, for *Prometheus Strangling the Vulture.*

1953 Moves his studio to Hastings-on-Hudson after the fire.

1954 Retrospective exhibition at The Museum of Modern Art, New York; Walker Art Center, Minneapolis; The Cleveland Museum of Art.

1955 *Nôtre-Dame de Liesse* completed.

1958 Receives honorary doctorate from Brandeis University. Designs ornamental gates for Philip Johnson's Roofless Church in New Harmony, Indiana, which houses a second cast of *Nôtre-Dame de Liesse.* Large travelling exhibition in Europe at the Stedelijk Museum, Amsterdam, Rijksmuseum Kröller-Müller, Otterlo; Kunsthalle, Basel; Museum am Ostwall, Dortmund; Musée d'Art Moderne, Paris; Palais des beaux-arts, Brussels; Tate Gallery, London. Becomes a citizen of the United States. Serious illness interrupts work for several months. Creates series of bronzes from small objects for the exhibition *À la limite du possible (To the Limit of the Possible)* at the Fine Arts Associates, New York.

1961–62 Represented by the Otto Gerson Gallery, New York (later Marlborough-Gerson and presently Marlborough Gallery, Inc.). Receives commission for the Duluth monument. Visits Italy and begins working at Tommasi Foundry, Pietrasanta, near Carrara.

1963	First visit to Israel. Los Angeles County Music Center commissions monumental sculpture. Large travelling retrospective in the US at the University of California at Los Angeles; San Francisco Museum of Art; Denver Art Museum, Fort Worth Art Center; Walker Art Center; Des Moines Art Center; Philadelphia Museum of Art.
1963–65	*157 Bronze Sketchings 1912–1962* exhibition at the Marlborough-Gerson Gallery, New York, and subsequently at the Currier Gallery; Albright-Knox Art Gallery; Atlanta Art Association; Joslyn Art Museum; Tweed Gallery of the University of Minnesota; Arts Club of Chicago; Detroit Institute of the Arts; also circulated internationally at Buenos Aires; Santiago; Caracas; Lima; Melbourne; Auckland; Washington, DC.
1964	Exhibition of Cubist sculpture and reliefs at the Phillips Collection, Washington, DC.
1965	Receives award for cultural achievement from Boston University, where he has a one-day exhibition. Installation of his sculpture of John F. Kennedy in London and Newark.
1966	*Images of Italy* exhibition at Marlborough-Gerson Gallery, New York. Receives Gold Medal from Academy of Arts and Letters, New York.
1968	*Lipchitz: The Cubist Period (1913–1930)* exhibition at Marlborough-Gerson Gallery, New York.
1968–69	Casts major sculptures at Pietrasanta, Italy, and also at the Modern Art Foundry and the Avnet & Shaw Foundry, New York.
1969	On May 5, *Peace on Earth* (45 ft./13.7 m high) is dedicated at the Los Angeles County Music Center.
1970–72	Retrospective exhibition organized by the Neuer Berliner Kunstverein, Berlin, at the Nationalgalerie, Berlin; Wilhelm-Lehmbruck-Museum, Duisburg; Staatliche Kunsthalle, Baden-Baden; Museum des 20, Jahrhunderts, Vienna. Other retrospectives at the Tel Aviv Museum and Israel Museum, Jerusalem. Extensive work on monumental sculpture commissions for Columbia Law School (*Bellerophon Taming Pegasus*) and Municipal Plaza, Philadelphia (*Government of the People*) and Mount Scopus, Jerusalem (*Our Tree of Life*).
1972	Major exhibition at the Metropolitan Museum of Art, New York, and publication of autobiography, both entitled *My Life in Sculpture*.
1973	Died on May 26 on the island of Capri. Buried in Jerusalem. *A Tribute to Jacques Lipchitz: Lipchitz in America 1941–1973*, held at the Marlborough Gallery, New York, in November.

Bibliography

■

Compiled by
Larry Pfaff and Randall Speller

This bibliography is a survey of recent literature on Jacques Lipchitz. It does not include citations listed in "Lipchitz: A Documentary Review," by Bernard Karpel, in *My Life in Sculpture* by Jacques Lipchitz with H. H. Arnason (New York: Viking, 1972) and the bibliography in *Jacques Lipchitz* by A. M. Hammacher (New York: Abrams, 1975).

Articles

Amishai-Maisels, Z. "Lipchitz and Picasso: thematic interpretations." *Journal of Jewish Art* I (1974): 80–92.

Benezra, N. "A study in irony: Modigliani's *Jacques and Berthe Lipchitz*." *Museum Studies*, 12:2 (1985/1986): 188–99.

Buckley, C. E. "Three 20th century European acquisitions." *St. Louis Art Museum Bulletin*, 10;3 (May/June 1974): 42–6.

Carter, Malcolm N. "The Lipchitz imbroglio." *Art News*, 78:4 (April 1979): 50–54.

__________. "The Lipchitz *Tree of Life* controversy, continued." *Art News*, 78:7 (September 1979): 105–06.

Donohoe, Victoria. "Philadelphia: Clothespin and sculptural oratory." *Art News*, 75:7 (September 1976): 88–89.

Dorival, B. "Les omissions d'Archipenko et de Lipchitz." *Bulletin de la Société de l'Histoire de l'Art Français* (1974): 201–20.

Edwards, Ellen. "Miami: the Lipchitz legacy." *Art News*, 76:6 (Summer 1977): 166–68.

Elsen, Albert E. "Duets of line and shadow." *Art News*, 77:3 (March 1978): 64–6.

Hammacher, Abraham Marie. *Jacques Lipchitz* (New York: Abrams, 1975). Reviewed by Katherine Janszky Michaelsen, in *Art Bulletin*, 60:2 (June 1978): 383–384.

Hunisak, John M. "Transformations in the figurative tradition in twentieth century sculpture." *Honolulu Academy of Arts Journal* 3 (1978): 56–85.

Trier, E. "Ikonographische Traditionen im Werk von Jacques Lipchitz." *Munster*, 25:5–6 (1972): 381–388.

Weyl, M. "Jacques Lipchitz in Jerusalem." *Ariel*, No. 41 (1976): 53–59.

Books

Cooper, Douglas. *The Cubist Epoch*. (New York and Los Angeles: Phaidon and Los Angeles County Museum of Art, 1971)

Elsen, Albert Edward. *Origins of Modern Sculpture: Pioneers and Premises*. (New York: George Braziller, c.1974)

New York. Marlborough Gallery. *Jacques Lipchitz: Selected Sculpture in Large Scale 1927–1971*. Exhibition November 1981–February 1982. New York, 1981.

New York. Marlborough Gallery. *Jacques Lipchitz (1891–1973): Sculptures and Drawings from the Cubist Epoch*. Exhibition February 12–March 3, 1977. New York, 1977.

New York. Marlborough Gallery. *Jacques Lipchitz: Small Sculptures, Maquettes and Drawings 1915–1972*. Exhibition 1979. New York, 1979.

New York. Marlborough Gallery. *Jacques Lipchitz: The Cubist Period (1913–1930)*. Introduction by Alan G. Wilkinson. Exhibition 1987. New York, 1987.

New York. Museum of Modern Art. *"Primitivism" in 20th Century Art: Affinity of the Tribal and the Modern*. Edited by William Rubin. Exhibition September 27, 1984–January 5, 1985 (and circulating). New York, Little, Brown, 1984.

New York. Solomon R. Guggenheim Museum. *The Planar Dimension: Europe 1912–1932*, by Margit Rowell. Exhibition March 9–May 6, 1979. New York, 1979.

Regina. Norman Mackenzie Art Gallery. *Jacques Lipchitz: Mother and Child*, by Michael Parke-Taylor. Exhibition October 7–November 13, 1983. Regina, 1983.

Rochester, Michigan. Oakland University. Meadow Brook Gallery. *Art in Architecture*. Exhibition January 23–March 13, 1977. Rochester, 1977.

Saint-Paul-de-Vence. Fondation Maeght. *Sculpture du XXe Siècle, 1900–1945: tradition et ruptures*. Exhibition July 4–October 4, 1981. Saint-Paul, 1981.

Toronto. Dunkelman Gallery. *"Images of Italy" by Jacques Lipchitz*. Exhibition April–May 1967. Toronto, 1967.

Toronto. Art Gallery of Ontario. *Gauguin to Moore: Primitivism in Modern Sculpture*, by Alan G. Wilkinson. Exhibition November 7, 1981–January 3, 1982. Toronto, 1981.

Washington, DC. Hirshhorn Museum and Sculpture Garden. *The Golden Door: Artist-Immigrants of America, 1876–1976.* Text by Cynthia Jaffee McCabe. Exhibition May 20 - October 20, 1976. Washington, DC, Smithsonian Institution Press, 1976.

Winnipeg. Art Gallery. *Jacques Lipchitz.* Circulating exhibition 1958–1959. Winnipeg, 1958.

Green, Christopher. *Cubism and Its Enemies: Modern Movements and Reaction in French Art, 1916–1928* (New Haven and London: Yale University Press, 1987).

Otterlo. Rijksmuseum Kröller-Müller. *Lipchitz in Otterlo*, by A. M. Hammacher. Otterlo, 1977.

Paris. Musée national d'art moderne. *Lipchitz: Oeuvres de Jacques Lipchitz (1891–1973)*... par Nicole Barbier. Paris, 1978.

Stott, Deborah. *Jacques Lipchitz and Cubism.* Ph.D. dissertation. New York : Columbia University, 1975. (New York: Garland, 1978)

Strachan, Walter John. *Towards Sculpture: Maquettes and Sketches from Rodin to Oldenburg.* London : Thames and Hudson, 1976.

University of Arizona. Museum of Art. *Jacques Lipchitz, Sketches and Models in the Collection of the University of Arizona Museum of Art.* Tucson, 1982.

Exhibition Catalogues

Assisi. San Francesco. Cloister. *I grandi contemporanei dell'arte: Manzu, Moore, Lipchitz, Greco.* Exhibition, 1974.

Athens, Ohio. University. Trisolini Gallery. *Selected Master Drawings of Jacques Lipchitz: 1910–1958.* Exhibition November 7–25, 1974 (also at Marlborough Godard, Toronto, June 1975). Athens, 1974.

Brooklyn Museum. *An Exhibition of Paintings, Watercolours, Sculpture and Drawings from the Collection of Mr. and Mrs. Henry Pearlman and Henry and Rose Pearlman Foundation.* Exhibition May 22 - September 29, 1974. New York, 1974.

Buffalo. Albright-Knox Art Gallery. *Modern European Sculpture 1918–1945: Unknown Beings and Other Realities*, by Albert E. Elsen. Exhibition May 12 - June 24, 1979. Buffalo, 1979.

Cambridge. Massachusetts Institute of Technology. List Visual Arts Center. *Jacques Lipchitz: sculptor and collector.* Exhibition March 1 - June 9, 1985. Cambridge, 1985.

London. Marlborough Fine Art Limited. *Jacques Lipchitz: Sculpture and Drawings from the cubist epoch.* Exhibition October - November 1978. London, 1978.

London. Tate Gallery. *The Essential Cubism 1907–1920: Braque, Picasso and Their Friends*, by Douglas Cooper and Gary Tinterow. Exhibition April 27 - July 10, 1983. London, 1983.

London. Tate Gallery. *The Lipchitz Gift: Models for Sculpture*, by David Fraser Jenkins and Derek Pullen. Exhibition November 12, 1986 - February 15, 1987. London, 1986.

New York. Jewish Museum. *Circle of Montparnasse.* Exhibition 1986. New York, 1986.

Graphic Design:
Marilyn Bouma-Pyper

Typesetting:
Archetype

Colour Film Preparation:
Prolith Inc.

Printing:
Friesen Printers

Typography:
Heads in H.B. Univers 49
Text in Caslon 74

Paper Stock:
100 lb. Warrens Cameo Dull

Photo Credits

All photography by Carlo Catenazzi, Photographic Services, Art Gallery of Ontario, with the following exceptions: Albright-Knox Art Gallery, Buffalo, New York, no. 9, fig. 30; The Baltimore Museum of Art, no. 32; Lee Boltin, Croton, New York, no. 12 (front cover); The Institute of Chicago, fig. 1; The Cleveland Museum of Art, no. 64, fig. 39; Lee Clockman, Dallas, fig. 32; The Detroit Institute of Arts, no. 5; Solomon R. Guggenheim Museum, New York, Photo: Robert E. Mates, no. 20, fig. 34, Photo: David Heald, fig. 29; Hirshhorn Museum and Sculpture Garden, Smithsonian Institution, nos. 10, 53; The Israel Museum, Jerusalem, fig. 19, Photo: R. M. Kneller, fig. 2; The Jewish Museum, New York, Photo: Geoffrey Clements, no. 99; R. M. Kneller, fig. 21; Kunsthaus, Zürich, no. 52; F. K. Lloyd, fig. 3; Herbert Michel Fotograf, Zürich, nos. 33, 79, 131, 134 (back cover); The Minneapolis Institute of Arts, no. 7; The Montreal Museum of Fine Arts, no. 31; The Museum of Modern Art, New York, figs. 4, 6, 8, 16, 36, 38; Patsy R. and Raymond R. Nasher Collection, Dallas, Texas, no. 21; National Gallery of Canada, Ottawa, no. 22, fig. 35; The Nelson-Atkins Museum of Art, Kansas City, MO, nos. 24, 66; Kent Fine Art, New York, no. 25; National Gallery of Art, Washington, DC, no. 26; Öffentliche Kunstsammlung Basel, Kunstmuseum, figs. 11, 12, 37; Perls Galleries, New York, figs. 9, 33; Philadelphia Museum of Art, nos. 8, 88, fig. 10; San Francisco Museum of Modern Art, Photo: Don Myer, no. 30; Tate Gallery, London, no. 19, fig. 7; Virginia Museum of Fine Arts, Richmond, VA, no. 37; Marlborough Gallery Inc., New York, nos. 95, 116, 145, 147, 157, 162, 164, 165, figs. 17, 18, Photos: Robert E. Mates, nos. 50, 59, 83, 132, 135, 138, 140, 142, 144, 149, 150, 152, 153, 158, 161, Photos: Robert E. Mates and Paul Katz, nos. 136, 137, 139, 140, 143, 146, 148, 151, 154, 155, 156, fig. 14, Photo: George Moffett-Lensgroup, New York, fig. 23, Photos: O. E. Nelson, New York, nos. 160, 163; Marlborough Fine Art (London) Ltd., Photo: Prudence Cuming Assoc. Ltd., London, fig. 13; James K. Mellow, St. Louis, MO, figs. 25, 26; Alan G. Wilkinson, figs. 27, 40

Printed in Canada